GW00859489

WHY DID JESUS SAY THAT ONLY FIVE OUT OF EVERY TEN CHRISTIANS WILL BE RAPTURED?

Jesus Came Back for Virgins But Only Half Of Them Made It! Why?

Russell and Margie McDaniel

Copyright © 2013 by Russell and Margie McDaniel
Manifested Vision Outreach Ministries
P. O. Box 13567
Durham, N.C. 27709

WHY DID JESUS SAY THAT ONLY FIVE OUT OF
EVERY TEN CHRISTIANS WILL BE RAPTURED?
Jesus Came Back for Virgins But Only Half Of Them Made It! Why?
by Russell and Margie McDaniel

Printed in the United States of America

ISBN 9781625097217

www.xulonpress.com

Contents

Last Judgment and the Wise and Foolish Virgins (1450s) by unknown Flemish artist.

Introduction

The Parable of the Ten Virgins has been a question in the back of the minds of many Christians for hundreds of years. Many artists have painted portraits depicting this event as you will see throughout this book. But the answer to the question why five out of ten were left and why the ones that were left also had no oil in their lamps has not been fully understood. Jesus said that if we understand the parable of seed time and harvest time we would understand all parables.

Everything created was placed here for a purpose; everything living starts out as a seed and has to reach maturity. Once it reaches maturity, it has to perform a specific function that was pre-ordained by God from the foundation of the earth. Jesus uses as an analogy to the Body of Christ a fig tree that looked from a distance like it was full of figs. But when Jesus reached it there were no figs. The leaves and figs develop at the same time so when you see the leaves you will also find figs on the tree. Jesus cursed the fig tree because it was not doing what it was placed in the earth to do. The fruit from that tree was to provide food and to fulfill a need that hunger creates. The Body of Christ has the same responsibility. The fruit that the Body of Christ is commanded to bear are the fruit of the Spirit, love, joy, peace, faith, longsuffering, gentleness, meekness, kindness, and righteousness. Like corn can be used for many functions from food to fuel. The fruit of the Spirit have many functions in the Kingdom of God.

The fruit, their function, and how to cultivate them lies at the heart of God. It also explains why Jesus commanded us to seek the Kingdom first so we can understand how God thinks and how the Kingdom of Heaven operates. The important part that each of us has in causing God's will to be done on earth will also be revealed when we follow the instruction of "seek first the kingdom of God."

The barren fig tree that had leaves was like the foolish virgins who were not doing what they were created to do. They look like the wise virgins until you look closer and see that they were not bearing fruit and did not have any oil in their lamps.

Matthew 25: [31]When the Son of man shall come in his glory, and all the holy angels with him, then shall he sit upon the throne of his glory: [32]And before him shall be gathered all nations: and he shall separate them one from another, as a shepherd divideth his sheep from the goats: [33]And he shall set the sheep on his right hand, but the goats on the left. [34]Then shall the King say unto them on his right hand, Come, ye blessed of my Father, inherit the kingdom prepared for you from the foundation of the world: [35]For I was an hungred, and ye gave me meat: I was thirsty, and ye gave me drink: I was a stranger, and ye took me in: [36]Naked, and ye clothed me: I was sick, and ye visited me: I was in prison, and ye came unto me. [37]Then shall the righteous answer him, saying,

Lord, when saw we thee an hungred, and fed thee? or thirsty, and gave thee drink? [38]When saw we thee a stranger, and took thee in? or naked, and clothed thee? [39]Or when saw we thee sick, or in prison, and came unto thee? [40]And the King shall answer and say unto them, Verily I say unto you, Inasmuch as ye have done it unto one of the least of these my brethren, ye have done it unto me. [41] Then shall he say also unto them on the left hand, Depart from me, ye cursed, into everlasting fire, prepared for the devil and his angels.

This book with the help of God will hopefully bring clarity to these and other parables.

2 Corinthians (KJV) 11: [2]For I am jealous over you with godly jealousy: for I have espoused you to one husband, that I may present you as a chaste virgin to Christ. [3]But I fear, lest by any means, as the serpent beguiled Eve through his subtilty, so your minds should be corrupted from the simplicity that is in Christ.

As you will see, there are many portraits of God that depict Him as an old, gray-headed man, sometimes they have him appearing to be bald-headed. I don't agree. God is the source of all life; there is nothing old or aging about Him. Aging shows the effect of time, God created time in Genesis for us. He lives outside of time. He is the Alpha and Omega; He is the same yesterday, today, and forever. I still loved every one of them because they are so stunning and one picture is worth a thousand words; I hope you will love them too. They are very important because they help bring the Word of God to life.

The pictures of the fruit are very important to the entire book because God relates and compares the Body of Christ to fruit trees from Genesis to Revelation. God does not have any problems with His creations following instructions. It is when He gets to the children that He has birthed is when He has problems with getting them to obey.

CHAPTER 1

Why Jesus said Only Five out of Ten Virgins Will Be Raptured Part 1

To understand this statement we have to understand the Kingdom of Heaven, and seed time to harvest time. Everything in the Kingdom was created to perform a function. And by the same token every seed that God created and planted from the beginning of the creation of the earth already had its purpose and function embedded in its DNA. If it is not fulfilling its purpose there will be problems with its Creator.

Figure 1.1 Common culinary fruits by Bill Ebbesen.

The reason God wants us to Bear Fruit

Bearing fruit is mandatory for every living creature. When you plant an apple seed you do not have to tell it to sprout roots and begin the growing process. It is already programmed to do that once all the conditions are met for it to grow. The right soil, the right amount of water and sunlight, with time that seed will produce bushels of apples for years to come.

God is expecting the same from His children. He tells us what fruit we are to bear which are the fruit of the Spirit: love, joy, peace, longsuffering, gentleness, kindness, meekness, righteousness, and faith. The fruit of the Spirit performs three main functions. They operate as some of the keys to the Kingdom of God. They make up the armor of God. And they are the life forces that flow out of God the Father, God the Son, and God the Holy Spirit. Because we are born again of the incorruptible seed of the Word of God, these attributes, characteristics, are inside of us and they should be flowing out of us too.

The entire Kingdom of Heaven functions according to seed time and harvest time principles. To put it simply, harvest time is the end product of the seed, or the fruit that it produces. When the seed matures into an apple or a fig it is ready to be picked and is ready to be eaten. The purpose of the apple or fig is to fulfill a need. It is to feed someone who is hungry, in the natural realm, without food and water we will die. It works the same way in the spiritual realm. When we as Christians mature, part of our purpose and destiny is to help meet the needs of others. God has equipped us with the fruit of the Spirit to meet the needs of the less fortunate, and they perform many other functions. More on this later.

Romans 8: [15] For ye have not received the spirit of bondage again to fear; but ye have received the Spirit of adoption, whereby we cry, Abba, Father.[16] The Spirit itself beareth witness with our spirit, that we are the children of God: [17] And if children, then heirs; heirs of God, and joint-heirs with Christ; if so be that we suffer with him, that we may be also glorified together. [18] For I reckon that the sufferings of this present time are not worthy to be compared with the glory which shall be revealed in us. [19] For the earnest expectation of the creature waiteth for the manifestation of the sons of God. [20] For the creature was made subject to vanity, not willingly, but by reason of him who hath subjected the same in hope,[21] Because the creature itself also shall be delivered from the bondage of corruption into the glorious liberty of the children of God. [22] For we know that the whole creation groaneth and travaileth in pain together until now. [23] And not only they, but ourselves also, which have the firstfruits of the Spirit, even we ourselves groan within ourselves, waiting for the adoption, to wit, the redemption of our body. [24] For we are saved by hope: but hope that is seen is not hope: for what a man seeth, why doth he yet hope for? [25] But if we hope for that we see not, then do we with patience wait for it. [26] Likewise the Spirit also helpeth our infirmities: for we know not what we should pray for as we ought: but the Spirit itself maketh intercession for us with groanings which cannot be uttered. [27] And he that searcheth the hearts knoweth what is the mind of the Spirit, because he maketh intercession for the saints according to the will of God. *[28] And we know that all things work together for good to them that love God, to them who are the called according to his purpose. [29] For whom he did foreknow, he also did predestinate to be conformed to the image of his Son, that he might be the firstborn among many brethren. [30] Moreover whom he did predestinate, them he also called: and whom he called, them he also justified: and whom he justified, them he also glorified.*

John 15: [7]If ye abide in me, and my words abide in you, ye shall ask what ye will, and it shall be done unto you. [8]Herein is my Father glorified, that ye bear much fruit; so shall ye be my disciples. [9]As the Father hath loved me, so have I loved you: continue ye in my love.

Figure 1.2 Concord Grapes.

Bearing fruit means you are doing what God created you to do. At the end of the world that is what the angels will be looking for from the children of God.

Mark 13: *And as he went out of the Temple, one of his disciples saith unto him, Master, see what manner of stones and what buildings are here!* [2] *And Jesus answering said unto him, Seest thou these great buildings? there shall not be left one stone upon another, that shall not be thrown down.*

Figure 1.3 An etching by Jan Luyken
illustrating Mark 13:2 in the Bowyer Bible, Bolton, England.

Mark 13: *³ And as he sat upon the mount of Olives over against the Temple, Peter and James and John and Andrew asked him privately, ⁴ Tell us, when shall these things be? and what shall be the sign when all these things shall be fulfilled? ⁵ And Jesus answering them began to say, Take heed lest any man deceive you:⁶ For many shall come in my name, saying, I am Christ; and shall deceive many. ⁷ And when ye shall hear of wars and rumours of wars, be ye not troubled: for such things must needs be; but the end shall not be yet. ⁸ For nation shall rise against nation, and kingdom against kingdom: and there shall be earthquakes in divers places, and there shall be famines and troubles: these are the beginnings of sorrows. ⁹ But take heed to yourselves: for they shall deliver you up to councils; and in the synagogues ye shall be beaten: and ye shall be brought before rulers and kings for my sake, for a testimony against them. ¹⁰ And the gospel (of the Kingdom) must first be published among all nations.¹¹ But when they shall lead you, and deliver you up, take no thought beforehand what ye shall speak, neither do ye premeditate: but whatsoever shall he given you in that hour, that speak ye: for it is not ye that speak, but the Holy Ghost. ¹² Now the brother shall betray the brother to death, and the father the son; and children shall rise up against their parents, and shall cause them to be put to death. ¹³ And ye shall be hated of all men for my name's sake: but he that shall endure unto the end, the same shall be saved.¹⁴ But when ye shall see the abomination of desolation, spoken of by Daniel the prophet, standing where it ought not, (let him that readeth understand,) then let them that be in Judaea flee to the mountains: ¹⁵ And let him that is on the housetop not go down into the house, neither enter therein, to take anything out of his house:¹⁶ And* *let him that is in the field not turn back again for to take up his garment.*[17] *But woe to them that are with child, and to them that give suck in those days!* [18] *And pray ye that your flight be not in the winter.* [19]*For in those days shall be affliction, such as was not from the beginning of the creation which God created unto this time, neither shall be.* [20]*And except that the Lord had shortened those days, no flesh should be saved: but for the elect's sake, whom he hath chosen, he hath shortened the days.* [21]*And then if any man shall say to you, Lo, here is Christ; or, lo, he is there; believe him not:* [22]*For false Christs and false prophets shall rise, and shall shew signs and wonders, to seduce, if it were possible, even the elect.*

From verses 1 through 22 in this chapter Jesus explains to the disciples the condition the world would be in just before His return. He talks about what to look out for in the church with false prophets' signs and wonders so that we would not be ensnared by the devices of Satan. These are difficult times and his goal is to make sure that you miss God anyway he can. This is why we must draw closer to God for ourselves. God does not want any of us to be lost. This is another reason Jesus prayed, it is His heart's desire that we become one with the Trinity, and the reason He is living inside of us now.

God is ordered and structured in everything that He sets in motion from the beginning to the end. Read the next five verses carefully; Jesus gives us the order of events that will affect every person on the planet. Starting with verse 23 He is telling us to pay attention, because in the "Day of the Lord" all of creation is going to change, even the sun, the moon, and the stars will be affected, and if you have not gotten your spiritual walk with God right at that time it will be too late. Either you are ready or you are not, because the next event that we will see is "Jesus coming in the clouds with great glory." Then Jesus takes us line by line and tells us what He is expecting from all of us. All we have to do is obey. The angels are purely obedient; they will do only what they are commanded to do. They are going to be just like harvester working in a vineyard, picking only the ripen fruit out of the world. They will be sent out, looking for the "elect" from the four corners of the world and the "elect" will be the wise virgins: the virgins who have put their hope and trust in the return of Jesus and have purified themselves and were found doing the will of the Father.

Mark 13: [23] *But take ye heed: behold, I have foretold you all things.* [24]*But in those days, after that tribulation, the sun shall be darkened, and the moon shall not give her light,* [25]*And the stars of heaven shall fall, and the powers that are in heaven shall be shaken.* [26]*And then shall they see the Son of man coming in the clouds with great power and glory.* [27]*And then shall he send his angels, and shall gather together his elect from the four winds, from the uttermost part of the earth to the uttermost part of heaven.*

We are different from an apple, or any other creature on the planet. God places on us as Christians a greater responsibility because we have been given dominion in the earth and authority over all the power of the enemy. The apple seed fulfills its purpose by reproducing itself over and over again. Our responsibilities are greater than the apple seed. We fulfill our purpose by subduing the works of the devil, by the power of Holy Spirit, the name of Jesus, and His Blood.

We are to help feed and clothe the poor and see to it that this Gospel of the Kingdom of God is taught throughout the world. And we are to reproduce ourselves by leading others to Christ. There are many ministries within the Kingdom of God; we have pastors, teachers, evangelists, and so forth, and there is a specific assignment for each of us. Not everyone is called to preach, teach, or do miracles, but God does have a plan for each us. We are called to work out our salvation; God has a reason for us being in the earth.

One weekend I was cleaning out my garage and I threw away a lot of items that I had no use for. I saved the items that I knew that I was going to use sooner or later. Just like I saved those items to be used at a later time, God is doing the same thing with us. God saves us because He has a preordained purpose for us. He wants us to know what our purpose is.

In Matthew chapter 24-25, Jesus instructs us through the parables how God gives us responsibilities and then comes back to see if we are doing what He said or if we are just ignoring Him. He comes to see if He can trust us to follow instructions, and that we understand the importance of what we are doing and how it is directly related to the fulfillment of the Kingdom of God's main purpose to raise the quality of life for all people on Earth. That is the Lord's Prayer in a nutshell: "For God's will to be done on earth as it is in Heaven." There is no poverty, sickness, disease, or lack of any kind in Heaven, and He wants the same in the earth. (More on this in the chapter on **The Parable of the Ten Virgins: Five Were Wise and Five Were Foolish.**)

Philippians 2:[11] And that every tongue should confess that Jesus Christ is Lord, to the glory of God the Father. [12] **Wherefore, my beloved, as ye have always obeyed, not as in my presence only, but now much more in my absence, work out your own salvation with fear and trembling.** [13] **For it is God which worketh in you both to will and to do of his good pleasure.**

Part of bearing fruit in the earth is giving to meet the needs of the poor; there isn't any poverty in Heaven and God's will is for there to be none in the earth. He wants to funnel the resources needed through our hands and for us to pass it on to those who need it the most because that is where God's heart lies.

Part of our purpose is to meet the needs of the less fortunate; like the fig tree provides food, we are also responsible for teaching them how the Kingdom of God operates and the part each of us plays in fulfilling the ultimate will of the Lord. God's desire is for everyone to be saved and come to the knowledge of the truth concerning the Word of God.

Fig. 1.4 A Very Old Sycamore Tree

Mark 13: *²⁸Now learn a parable of the fig Tree and putteth forth leaves, ye know that summer is near:*

Figure 1.5 Bud of *Ficus carica* by Etienne.

Mark 13: *²⁹So ye in like manner, when ye shall see these things come to pass, know that it is nigh, even at the doors.*

The key to the fig tree parable are the leaves; the leaves mean the tree is bearing fruit and whenever the fruit matures and becomes ripe the harvest is next. Seed time and harvest time have come full circle, and this is what the Kingdom is all about and how it functions. This is why God tells the angels at the end of the world to bring in the "harvest."

Figure 1.6 Leaves and immature fruit of common fig tree.

Mark 13: [30]Verily I say unto you, that this generation shall not pass, till all these things are done. [31]Heaven and earth shall pass away: but my words shall not pass away. [32]But of that day and that hour knoweth no man, no, not the angels which are in heaven, neither the Son, but the Father. [33]Take ye heed, watch and pray: for ye know not when the time is. [34]For the Son of Man is as a man taking a far journey, who left his house, and gave authority to his servants, and to every man his work, and commanded the porter to watch. 35 Watch ye therefore: for ye know not when the master of the house cometh, at even, or at midnight, or at the cockcrowing, or in the morning: 36 Lest coming suddenly he find you sleeping. 37 And what I say unto you I say unto all, Watch.

From verses 30 to 37 Jesus says don't even try to figure out when that hour will come and that even He does not know, but only the Father knows when that time will come. Neither you nor I or anybody else will be able to figure out when the "hour will come when Jesus is going to return." We will just be wasting our time trying to figure when this event will occur. Then Jesus goes on to tell us what to do. The Son of Man is like a man who has a house or business and he has left instructions for everyone in the house. Most people in my generation understand this analogy from when we were growing up and our parents left us at home alone. Each of us had chores which had to be completed before our parents returned. If they were not completed we would be in trouble. It will be the same with the second coming of Jesus. He tells us what to do through the parable of the fig tree.

Luke 3: ²Annas and Caiaphas being the high priests, the word of God came unto John the son of Zacharias in the wilderness. ³And he came into all the country about Jordan, preaching the baptism of repentance for the remission of sins; ⁴As it is written in the book of the words of Esaias the prophet, saying, The voice of one crying in the wilderness, Prepare ye the way of the Lord, make his paths straight. ⁵Every valley shall be filled, and every mountain and hill shall be brought low; and the crooked shall be made straight, and the rough ways shall be made smooth; ⁶And all flesh shall see the salvation of God.⁷Then said he to the multitude that came forth to be baptized of him, O generation of vipers, who hath warned you to flee from the wrath to come? *⁸Bring forth therefore fruits worthy of repentance, and begin not to say within yourselves, we have Abraham to our father: for I say unto you, That God is able of these stones to raise up children unto Abraham. ⁹ "And now also the axe is laid unto the root of the trees: every tree therefore which bringeth not forth good fruit is hewn down, and cast into the fire. ¹⁰And the people asked him, saying, What shall we do then? ¹¹ He answereth and saith unto them, He that hath two coats, let him impart to him that hath none; and he that hath meat, let him do likewise."*

Figure 1.7 The Vine and the Branches

Jesus explains clearly what would happen to a tree that was not producing fruit; its destiny would be to be cast into the fire to be destroyed. He used a fig tree that had no figs as the example, and He spoke to the tree and it was dead the next morning because it was not fulfilling its destiny.

In This Next Parable, I Believe Jesus is Speaking Directly to the Church Today

Luke (AMP) 13: ⁶And He told them this parable: A certain man had a fig tree, planted in his vineyard, and he came looking for fruit on it, but did not find [any]. ⁷So he said to the vinedresser, See here! For these three years I have come looking for fruit on this fig tree and I find none. Cut it down! Why should it <u>continue</u> also to use up the ground [to deplete the soil, intercept the sun, and take up room]? ⁸But he replied to him, Leave it alone, sir, [just] this one more year, till I dig around it and put manure [on the soil]. ⁹Then perhaps it will bear fruit after this; but if not, you can cut it down *and* out.

In this example of a vineyard (and we are the vineyard; we are called God's garden) the owner of the vineyard (God) who had a nonproducing fruit tree. The other trees were producing or doing what they were created to do or fulfilling their destiny or, in other words, providing for the needs of others. The owner's first command was to have the gardener (Jesus) to cut the tree down and cast it into the fire. But the gardener (Jesus) intervened and said give me time let Me dig around it, let Me fertilize it; let Me give the tree (the individuals that are not bearing fruit) the Word of God in more detail and clarity and encourage them and urge them to be productive and bear fruit. If after that, they do not produce, the gardener (Jesus) will fulfill the owner of the vineyard's (God's) request of cutting the worthless nonbearing fruit tree down and casting it into the fire (hell).

Jesus and John the Baptist are saying the same thing. John warns the people that the ax is laid at the root of every tree. When I was little my mother would send me out to pull weeds out of her flowerbeds. To do it right you have to grab the weed by the roots so that it is completely separated from the life-giving resources that it gets from the soil, minerals, and the water and then it will die. John is saying the same thing about those of us that are not fulfilling God's purpose. Jesus, God, and the Holy Spirit are the source of our life (or we are partakers of His divine nature when we are fulfilling His purpose for our existence). If we are not allowing that flow of life to continue to be extended to others or fulfilling our destiny, we will be cut off too.

Then the people asked John the Baptist what must we do? John tells them:

Luke 3: ¹¹He answereth and saith unto them, He that hath two coats, let him impart to him that hath none; and he that hath meat, let him do likewise."

Part of bearing fruit in the earth is giving to meet the needs of the poor, praying for the sick, visiting those who are in prison, and teaching and preaching the Gospel of the Kingdom of God. There is no poverty or sickness in Heaven, and God's will is for there to be none of that in the earth. Even with the poorest of the poor, God has a purpose for them being on the planet and for seed time and harvest time to be manifested in their life. God wants to funnel the money through us and into the hands of others to meet their needs. The object of most importance is to teach them the Gospel of the Kingdom of God. When I read this scripture in the past it seemed not to be so important giving to the Poor. I would think to myself, "Okay, so what, I will give a little something to the poor. And maybe I will give a whole lot whenever my ship comes in, so to speak." This is what was going on in the back of my mind. But when you understand seed time and harvest time principles which we discussed earlier, the figs' purpose was to provide food. God is not just planting fruit trees in the earth just because they look good. God planted them to provide food not only for people but also for animals. That is why Jesus said the birds and the flowers were richer than Solomon, and He wanted to make us richer than the lilies of the field. Jesus found a nonproducing fruit tree, and He cursed it. The fig tree died the next day. Jesus was hungry and He wanted something to eat. The tree was deceitful; its looks were deceiving in the case of that tree. And at the return of Jesus each one of us will be judged just like the barren fig tree. At the return of Jesus each of us will be judged accordingly. Will you be found barren, not doing anything for anyone else except for yourself and maybe for your family members? Will you be found not knowing or doing what the will of the Lord is?

Knowing what the will of the Lord is and performing it are two totally different issues. It is a daily process of judging and weighing our actions, thoughts, deeds and motives against the Word of God because we want to prove to God that we love Him and we are willing to obey Him. We have to judge ourselves and make sure that our lives are paralleling His Word.. Do I need another pair of shoes or another watch, or should I use the extra money to help the needy in my community, or to help buy a well or provide food for a community or village overseas? Or can I visit the sick and join in agreement in prayer for them to be made whole? Or can I visit and encourage and pray for those who are in prison?

Sometimes I succeed, but a lot of the time I have to repent. God wants us to have wealth but in the right order, we are going to have to prove to Him that we are serious about seeking the Kingdom, and not just through lip service, like the rich young ruler who asked Jesus what he had to do to obtain "eternal life."

The Kingdom of God is about improving the quality of life for everyone on earth until it is equal to the quality of life in Heaven, which translates into God's Will in Heaven being performed in the earth.

God loves a cheerful "philanthropist" We all have seen in the news and other media where people from all walks of life give to meet the needs of someone hurting. This may be hard to understand or hard to believe but this is what the Lord's Prayer is all about and all things are possible with God. Jesus fed thousands with only a few fish and a couple of loaves of bread. This should be a global quest for the Body of Christ that can only be done by the power of the Holy Spirit. This is about setting your affections on things above where Christ sits at the right hand of the Father. His desire must become our divine purpose.

Luke 7: [18] And the disciples of John shewed him of all these things. [19] And John calling unto him two of his disciples sent them to Jesus, saying, Art thou he that should come? or look we for another? [20] When the men were come unto him, they said, John Baptist hath sent us unto thee, saying, Art thou he that should come? or look we for another? [21] And in that same hour he cured many of their infirmities and plagues, and of evil spirits; and unto many that were blind he gave sight. [22] *Then Jesus answering said unto them, Go your way, and tell John what things ye have seen and heard; how that the blind see, the lame walk, the lepers are cleansed, the deaf hear, the dead are raised, to the poor the gospel is preached.* [23] *And blessed is he, whosoever shall not be offended in me.*

The Rich Young Ruler asked Jesus this all important question which is what everyone should want to know the answer to. Today we do not hear a lot about inheriting eternal life. Today you have to be a giver of life in order to inherit life.

Mark 10: [17] And when he was gone forth into the way, there came one running, and kneeled to him, and asked him, Good Master, what shall I do that I may inherit eternal life? [18] And Jesus said unto him, Why callest thou me good? there is none good but one, that is, God. [19] Thou knowest the commandments, Do not commit adultery, Do not kill, Do not steal, Do not bear false witness, Defraud not, Honour thy father and mother. [20] And he answered and said unto him, Master, all these have I observed from my youth. [21] Then Jesus beholding him loved him, and said unto him, One thing thou lackest: go thy way, sell whatsoever thou hast, and give to the poor, and thou shalt have treasure in heaven: and come, take up the cross, and follow me. [22] And he was sad at that saying, and went away grieved: for he had great possessions.

Good Master, what shall I do that I may inherit eternal life?

Figure 1.8 The Rich Young Ruler by Joseph Jacques Tissot.

In order to inherit eternal life you have to be a giver of life by sowing into the lives of the needy, being born again is just the beginning of eternal life.

The Works of Mercy

apud: phillip medhurst   WORKS OF MERCY: VISITING THE SICK. MATTHEW 25:36. JAN LUYKEN   excudit: harry kossuth

**Figure 1.9 Visiting the Sick, An etching by Jan Luyken
illustrating Matthew 25:36 in the Bowyer Bible, Bolton, England.**

Figure 1.10 Clothing the Naked, An etching by Jan Luyken illustrating Matthew 25:36 in the Bowyer Bible, Bolton, England.

apud: phillip medhurst WORKS OF MERCY: SATISFYING THE THIRSTY. MATTHEW 25:35. JAN LUYKEN excudit: harry kossuth

Figure 1.11 Satisfying the Thirsty, An etching by Jan Luyken illustrating Matthew 25:35 in the Bowyer Bible, Bolton, England.

**Figure 1.12 Feeding the Hungry, An etching by Jan Luyken
illustrating Luke 10:33-34 in the Bowyer Bible, Bolton, England.**

**Figure 1.13 Visiting the Prisoner, An etching by Jan Luyken
illustrating Matthew 25:36 in the Bowyer Bible, Bolton, England.**

The rich young ruler who kept the commandments was not really keeping them; he had a problem with greed. He had a problem with pride, and he was selfish. You can be poor and still have those same problems. The widow with two mites caught on and she gave all that she had, Jesus said she gave more than the people who were wealthy.

Mark 12: [38] And he said unto them in his doctrine, Beware of the scribes, which love to go in long clothing, and love salutations in the marketplaces, [39] And the chief seats in the synagogues, and the uppermost rooms at feasts: [40] Which devour widows' houses, and for a pretence make long prayers: these shall receive greater damnation. [41] And Jesus sat over against the treasury, and beheld how the people cast money into the treasury: and many that were rich cast in much. [42] And there came a certain poor widow, and she threw in two mites, which make a farthing. [43] And he called unto him his disciples, and saith unto them, Verily I say unto you, That this poor widow hath cast more in, than all they which have cast into the treasury: [44] For all they did cast in of their abundance; but she of her want did cast in all that she had, even all her living.

Figure 1.14 The Widow's Mite by Rembrandt

Mark 10: [23] And Jesus looked round about, and saith unto his disciples, How hardly shall they that have riches enter into the kingdom of God! [24] And the disciples were astonished at his words. But Jesus answereth again, and saith unto them, Children, how hard is it for them that trust in riches to enter into the kingdom of God!

Figure 1.15 The Money Changers (1627) by Rembrandt.

Mark 10: [25] It is easier for a camel to go through the eye of a needle, than for a rich man to enter into the kingdom of God. [26] And they were astonished out of measure, saying among themselves, Who then can be saved? [27] And Jesus looking upon them saith, With men it is impossible, but not with God: for with God all things are possible. [28] Then Peter began to say unto him, Lo, we have left all, and have followed thee. [29] And Jesus answered and said, Verily I say unto you, There is no man that hath left house, or brethren, or sisters, or father, or mother, or wife, or children, or lands, for my sake, and the gospel's, [30] But he shall receive an hundredfold now in this time, houses, and brethren, and sisters, and mothers, and children, and lands, with persecutions; and in the world to come eternal life. [31] But many that are first shall be last; and the last first. [32] And they were in the way going up to Jerusalem; and Jesus went before them: and they were amazed; and as they followed, they were afraid. And he took again the twelve, and began to tell them what things should happen unto him,

Luke 12: [12] For the Holy Ghost shall teach you in the same hour what ye ought to say. [13] And one of the company said unto him, Master, speak to my brother, that he divide the inheritance with me. [14] And he said unto him, Man, who made me a judge or a divider over you? [15] And he said unto them, Take heed, and beware of covetousness: for a man's life consisteth not in the abundance of the things which he possesseth. [16] And he spake a parable unto them, saying, The ground of a certain rich man brought forth plentifully: [17] And he thought within himself, saying, What shall I do, because I have no room where to bestow my fruits? [18] And he said, This will I do: I will pull down my barns, and build greater; and there will I bestow all my fruits and my goods.

Figure 1.16 Parable of the Rich Man, an etching by Jan Luyken illustrating Luke 12:12-21 in the Bowyer Bible.

Luke 12: [19] And I will say to my soul, Soul, thou hast much goods laid up for many years; take thine ease, eat, drink, and be merry. [20] But God said unto him, Thou fool, this night thy soul shall be required of thee: then whose shall those things be, which thou hast provided? [21] So is he that layeth up treasure for himself, and is not rich toward God. [22] And he said unto his disciples, Therefore I say unto you, Take no thought for your life, what ye shall eat; neither for the body, what ye shall put on. [23] The life is more than meat, and the body is more than raiment. [24] Consider the ravens: for they neither sow nor reap; which neither have storehouse nor barn; and God feedeth them: how much more are ye better than the fowls? [25] And which of you with taking thought can add to his stature one cubit? [26] If ye then be not able to do that thing which is least, why take ye thought for the rest?

"Consider the lilies of the field, how they grow; they toil not . . ."

Figure 1.17 The Lilies of the Field by Andrew Massyn.

Luke 12:²⁷ *Consider the lilies how they grow: they toil not, they spin not; and yet I say unto you, that Solomon in all his glory was not arrayed like one of these.* ²⁸ *If then God so clothe the grass, which is today in the field, and tomorrow is cast into the oven; how much more will he clothe you, O ye of little faith?* ²⁹ *And seek not ye what ye shall eat, or what ye shall drink, neither be ye of doubtful mind.* ³⁰ *For all these things do the nations of the world seek after: and your Father knoweth that ye have need of these things.* ³¹ *But rather seek ye the kingdom of God; and all these things shall be added unto you.* ³² *Fear not, little flock; for it is your Father's good pleasure to give you the kingdom.* ³³ *Sell that ye have, and give alms; provide yourselves bags which wax not old, a treasure in the heavens that faileth not, where no thief approacheth, neither moth corrupteth.* ³⁴ *For where your treasure is, there will your heart be also.* ³⁵ *Let your loins be girded about, and your lights burning;* ³⁶ *And ye yourselves like unto men that wait for their lord, when he will return from the wedding; that when he cometh and knocketh, they may open unto him immediately.*

Figure 1.18 The Foolish Virgins Were Left by Tintoretto.

Mark 10: *[37] Blessed are those servants, whom the lord when he cometh shall find watching: verily I say unto you, that he shall gird himself, and make them to sit down to meat, and will come forth and serve them. [38] And if he shall come in the second watch, or come in the third watch, and find them so, blessed are those servants. [39] And this know, that if the goodman of the house had known what hour the thief would come, he would have watched, and not have suffered his house to be broken through. [40] Be ye therefore ready also: for the Son of man cometh at an hour when ye think not. [41] Then Peter said unto him, Lord, speakest thou this parable unto us, or even to all? [42] And the Lord said, Who then is that faithful and wise steward, whom his lord shall make ruler over his household, to give them their portion of meat in due season? [43] Blessed is that servant, whom his lord when he cometh shall find so doing. [44] Of a truth I say unto you, that he will make him ruler over all that he hath. [45] But and if that servant say in his heart, My lord delayeth his coming; and shall begin to beat the menservants and maidens, and to eat and drink, and to be drunken; [46] The lord of that servant will come in a day when he looketh not for him, and at an hour when he is not aware, and will cut him in sunder, and will appoint him his portion with the unbelievers. [47] And that servant, which knew his lord's will, and prepared not himself, neither did according to his will, shall be beaten with many stripes. [48] But he that knew not, and did commit things worthy of stripes, shall be beaten with few stripes. For unto whomsoever much is given, of him shall be much required: and to whom men have committed much, of him they will ask the more. [49] I am come to send fire on the earth; and what will I, if it be already kindled? [50] But I have a baptism to be baptized with; and how am I straitened till it be accomplished! [51] Suppose ye that I am come to give peace on earth?*

I tell you, Nay; but rather division: [52] For from henceforth there shall be five in one house divided, three against two, and two against three. [53] The father shall be divided against the son, and the son against the father; the mother against the daughter, and the daughter against the mother; the mother in law against her daughter in law, and the daughter in law against her mother in law. [54] And he said also to the people, When ye see a cloud rise out of the west, straightway ye say, There cometh a shower; and so it is. [55] And when ye see the south wind blow, ye say, There will be heat; and it cometh to pass. [56] Ye hypocrites, ye can discern the face of the sky and of the earth; but how is it that ye do not discern this time? [57] Yea, and why even of yourselves judge ye not what is right? [58] When thou goest with thine adversary to the magistrate, as thou art in the way, give diligence that thou mayest be delivered from him; lest he hale thee to the judge, and the judge deliver thee to the officer, and the officer cast thee into prison. [59] I tell thee, thou shalt not depart thence, till thou hast paid the very last mite.

Luke 16: [19] There was a certain rich man, which was clothed in purple and fine linen, and fared sumptuously every day:

Figure 1.19 Kitchen interior with the parable of the rich man and poor Lazarus (c. 1610).

Luke 16: [20] And there was a certain beggar named Lazarus, which was laid at his gate, full of sores, [21] And desiring to be fed with the crumbs which fell from the rich man's table: moreover the dogs came and licked his sores.

Figure 1.20 Beggar named Lazazus

**Figure 1.21 The Parable of the Rich Man and Lazarus (c. 1620–1630)
by Bartholomeus van Bassen.**

Luke 16: ²² And it came to pass, that the beggar died, and was carried by the angels into Abraham's bosom: the rich man also died, and was buried; ²³ And in hell he lift up his eyes, being in torments, and seeth Abraham afar off, and Lazarus in his bosom.

Figure 1.22 The Rich Man in Hell by Artist James Tissot (1836-1902)

Luke 16: [24] And he cried and said, Father Abraham, have mercy on me, and send Lazarus, that he may dip the tip of his finger in water, and cool my tongue; for I am tormented in this flame. [25] But Abraham said, Son, remember that thou in thy lifetime receivedst thy good things, and likewise Lazarus evil things: but now he is comforted, and thou art tormented. [26] And beside all this, between us and you there is a great gulf fixed: so that they which would pass from hence to you cannot; neither can they pass to us, that would come from thence. [27] Then he said, I pray thee therefore, father, that thou wouldest send him to my father's house: [28] For I have five brethren; that he may testify unto them, lest they also come into this place of torment. [29] Abraham saith unto him, They have Moses and the prophets; let them hear them. [30] And he said, Nay, father Abraham: but if one went unto them from the dead, they will repent. [31] And he said unto him, If they hear not Moses and the prophets, neither will they be persuaded, though one rose from the dead.

The rich man could have been like the Good Samaritan. He could have taken Lazarus in, fed him, and taken care of him until he was better. He could have given him a job and a place to stay, which would have been the right (or righteous) thing to do.

The Righteousness of God

Providing for the needs of others and seedtime and harvest and bearing fruit lies at the center of the Kingdom of the God. The fruit of the Spirit come from our Heavenly Father, and like all fruit, they have to be cultivated and developed by applying them to our daily walk with God and by reaching out and ministering to the people that we come in contact with daily. We have been made the righteousness of God, the joy of the Lord is our strength, the love of God is shed abroad in our hearts by the Holy Spirit which has been given to us, and we have been given the faith of God, gentleness, longsuffering, and so on.

If we have given our hearts to Christ and we have been filled with the Holy Spirit, our will still has to be broken to agree with God and His Word. With each one of these fruit you can do just the opposite of them. We can become unrighteous, we can hate, we can worry, we can be depressed, and sad, frustrated, impatient, mean-spirited, evil, and so forth.. We all know we have a choice to do good or we can do evil; we can chose to hate or we choose to walk in love. Even Jesus had to make a decision in the Garden of Gethsemane He did not have to go to hell and He did not have to go to the cross. He said:

Matthew 26: [38] Then saith he unto them, My soul is exceeding sorrowful, even unto death: tarry ye here, and watch with me. [39] And he went a little farther, and fell on his face, and prayed, saying, O my Father, if it be possible, let this cup pass from me: nevertheless not as I will, but as thou wilt.

I know Jesus knew His main purpose was to die for our sins. He gave His life so we could have eternal life. He knew He was going to be crucified and tormented, but in my own opinion I think He was grieving because He was going to have to be separated from the Holy Spirit (just before Jesus died on the cross the scripture says that He gave up the Ghost or the Holy Spirit) while He went into hell for three days and nights. But Jesus said not my will, but the will of My Father.

We are faced with the same decisions that Paul fought with daily, the fight against sin:

Romans 7: [7] What shall we say then? Is the law sin? God forbid. Nay, I had not known sin, but by the law: for I had not known lust, except the law had said, Thou shalt not covet.[8] But sin, taking occasion by the commandment, wrought in me all manner of concupiscence. For without the law sin was dead.[9] For I was alive without the law once: but when the commandment came, sin revived, and I died.[10] And the commandment, which was ordained to life, I found to be unto death.[11] For sin, taking occasion by the commandment, deceived me, and by it slew me.[12] Wherefore the law is holy, and the commandment holy, and just, and good. [13] Was then that which is good made death unto me? God forbid. But sin, that it might appear sin, working death in me by that which is good; that sin by the commandment might become exceeding sinful.[14] For we know that the law is spiritual: but I am carnal, sold under sin.[15] For that which I do I allow not: for what I would, that do I not; but what I hate, that do I. [16] If then I do that which I would not, I consent unto the law that it is good. [17] Now then it is no more I that do it, but sin that dwelleth in me.[18] For I know that in me (that is, in my flesh,) dwelleth no good thing: for to will is present with me; but how to perform that which is good I find not. [19] For the good that I would I do not: but the evil which I would not, that I do. [20] Now if I do that I would not, it is no more I that do it, but sin that dwelleth in me. [21] I find then a law, that, when I would do good, evil is present with me. [22] For I delight in the law of God after the inward man: [23] But I see another law in my members, warring against the law of my mind, and bringing me into captivity to the law of sin which is in my members. [24] O wretched man that I am! who shall deliver me from the body of this death? [25] I thank God through Jesus Christ our Lord. So then with the mind I myself serve the law of God; but with the flesh the law of sin.

Walking in the Spirit

Galatians shows us that the fruit of the Spirit also represent the character of God and when we nurture them they also help us to overcome the sin that is in our life.

Galatians 5: Stand fast therefore in the liberty wherewith Christ hath made us free, and be not entangled again with the yoke of bondage. [2] Behold, I Paul say unto you, that if ye be circumcised, Christ shall profit you nothing. [3] For I testify again to every man that is circumcised, that he is a debtor to do the whole law. [4] Christ is become of no effect unto you, whosoever of you are justified by the law; ye are fallen from grace. [5] For we through the Spirit wait for the hope of righteousness by faith. [6] For in Jesus Christ neither circumcision availeth anything, nor uncircumcision; but faith which worketh by love. [7] Ye did run well; who did hinder you that ye should not obey the truth? [8] This persuasion cometh not of him that calleth you. [9] A little leaven leaveneth the whole lump. [10] I have confidence in you through the Lord, that ye will be none otherwise minded: but he that troubleth you shall bear his judgment, whosoever he be. [11] And I, brethren, if I yet preach circumcision, why do I yet suffer persecution? then is the offence of the cross ceased. [12] I would they were even cut off which trouble you. *[13] For, brethren, ye have been called unto liberty; only use not liberty for an occasion to the flesh, but by love serve one another. [14] For all the law is fulfilled in one word, even in this; Thou shalt love thy neighbour as ` thyself. [15] But if ye bite and devour one another, take heed that ye be not consumed one of another. [16] This I say then, Walk in the Spirit, and ye shall not fulfil the lust of the flesh. [17] For the flesh lusteth against the Spirit, and the Spirit against the flesh: and these are contrary the one to the other: so that ye cannot do the things that ye would. [18] But if ye be led of the Spirit, ye are not under the law. [19] Now the works of the flesh are manifest, which are these; Adultery, fornication, uncleanness, lasciviousness, [20] Idolatry, witchcraft, hatred, variance, emulations, wrath, strife, seditions, heresies, [21] Envyings, murders, drunkenness, revellings, and such like: of the which I tell you before, as I have also told you in time past, that they which do such things shall not inherit the kingdom of God.(the Fruit of the Spirit allow access into the Kingdom of God) [22] But the fruit of the Spirit is love, joy, peace, longsuffering, gentleness, goodness, faith, [23] Meekness, temperance: against such there is no law. [24] And they that are Christ's have crucified the flesh with the affections and lusts. [25] If we live in the Spirit, let us also walk in the Spirit. [26] Let us not be desirous of vain glory, provoking one another, envying one another.*

The fruit of the Spirit also becomes the armor of God that He has given to us to protect our spirits, souls, and bodies.

Figure 1.23 The Whole Armor of God,

Royal Military College of Canada memorial window to Ian Sutherland Brown.

Ephesians 6: Children, obey your parents in the Lord: for this is right. ² Honour thy father and mother; which is the first commandment with promise;³ That it may be well with thee, and thou mayest live long on the earth.⁴ And, ye fathers, provoke not your children to wrath: but bring them up in the nurture and admonition of the Lord. ⁵ Servants, be obedient to them that are your masters according to the flesh, with fear and trembling, in singleness of your heart, as unto Christ;⁶ Not with eyeservice, as menpleasers; but as the servants of Christ, doing the will of God from the heart; ⁷ With good will doing service, as to the Lord, and not to men: ⁸ Knowing that whatsoever good thing any man doeth, the same shall he receive of the Lord, whether he be bond or free. ⁹ And, ye masters, do the same things unto them, forbearing threatening: knowing that your Master also is in heaven; neither is there respect of persons with him. *¹⁰ Finally, my brethren, be strong in the*

Lord, and in the power of his might.[11] Put on the whole armor of God, that ye may be able to stand against the wiles of the devil.[12] For we wrestle not against flesh and blood, but against principalities, against powers, against the rulers of the darkness of this world, against spiritual wickedness in high places. [13] Wherefore take unto you the whole armor of God, that ye may be able to withstand in the evil day, and having done all, to stand. [14] Stand therefore, having your loins girt about with truth, and having on the breastplate of righteousness; [15] And your feet shod with the preparation of the gospel of peace; [16] Above all, taking the shield of faith, wherewith ye shall be able to quench all fiery darts of the wicked. [17] And take the helmet of salvation, and the sword of the Spirit, which is the word of God: [18] Praying always with all prayer and supplication in the Spirit, and watching thereunto with all perseverance and supplication for all saints; [19] And for me, that utterance may be given unto me, that I may open my mouth boldly, to make known the mystery of the gospel, [20] For which I am an ambassador in bonds: that therein I may speak boldly, as I ought to speak.

God wants us to know that the armor of God has been given to us because we are in the midst of a war. And the warfare is over our soul, and over the control of the earth in the spirit realm. Again, the fruit of the Spirit, love, joy, peace, longsuffering, gentleness, kindness, meekness, faith, and righteousness, are to be used to quench everything that Satan can use against us. If we are sick God has given us the shield of faith which is the Word of God, we have been given the Blood of Jesus. The power of life and death is in our tongue so when our heart is filled with the Word of God, when we pray in faith, the Word becomes a living thing and it will prosper whereever it is sent.

Mark (KJV) 11: [22] And Jesus answering saith unto them, Have faith in God. [23] For verily I say unto you, That whosoever shall say unto this mountain, Be thou removed, and be thou cast into the sea; and shall not doubt in his heart, but shall believe that those things which he saith shall come to pass; he shall have whatsoever he saith. [24] Therefore I say unto you, What things soever ye desire, when ye pray, believe that ye receive them, and ye shall have them. [25] And when ye stand praying, forgive, if ye have ought against any: that your Father also which is in heaven may forgive you your trespasses. [26] But if ye do not forgive, neither will your Father which is in heaven forgive your trespasses.

When we are attacked with depression, oppression, worry, failure, and defeat, we can use the joy of the Lord which is our strength; we can use the love of God because love never fails. And if we know God's love for us, we do not have to let fear consume our heart and mind because we know that God has given us everything that we need to overcome and be victorious over the kingdom of darkness.

1 Thessalonians 5: But of the times and the seasons, brethren, ye have no need that I write unto you. [2] For yourselves know perfectly that the day of the Lord so cometh as a thief in the night. [3] For when they shall say, Peace and safety; then sudden destruction cometh upon them, as travail upon a woman with child; and they shall not escape. [4] But ye, brethren, are not in darkness, that that day should overtake you as a thief. [5] Ye are all the children of light, and the children of the day: we are not of the night, nor of darkness. [6] Therefore let us not sleep, as do others; but let us watch and be sober. [7] For they that sleep sleep in the night; and they that be drunken are drunken in the night. [8] But let us, who are of the day, be sober, putting on the breastplate of faith and love; and for an helmet, the hope of salvation. [9] For God hath not appointed us to wrath, but to obtain salvation by our Lord Jesus Christ, [10] Who died for us, that, whether we wake or sleep, we should live together with him. [11] Wherefore comfort yourselves together, and edify one another, even as also ye do. [12] And we beseech you, brethren, to know them which labour among you, and are over you in the Lord, and admonish you; [13] And to esteem them very highly in love for their work's sake. And be at peace among yourselves. [14] Now we exhort you, brethren, warn them that are unruly, comfort the feebleminded, support the weak, be patient toward all men. [15] See that none render evil for evil unto any man; but ever follow that which is good, both among yourselves, and to all men. [16] Rejoice evermore. [17] Pray without ceasing. [18] In everything give thanks: for this is the will of God in Christ Jesus concerning you. [19] Quench not the Spirit. [20] Despise not prophesyings. [21] Prove all things; hold fast that which is good. [22] Abstain from all appearance of evil. [23] And the very God of peace sanctify you wholly; and I pray God your whole spirit and soul and body be preserved blameless unto the coming of our Lord Jesus Christ. [24] Faithful is he that calleth you, who also will do it.

The time that we are living in now is a copy of Ezekiel 22 and God was looking for an intercessor to stand in the gap for the lost. Our warfare is the same, and it is a major part of our purpose for being in the earth.

Ezekiel (AMP) 22: Moreover, the word of the Lord came to me, saying, [2] And you son of man [Ezekiel], will you judge, will you judge the blood shedding city? Then cause her to know all her abominations, [3] And say, Thus says the Lord God: A city that sheds blood in the midst of her so that her time [of doom] will come, and makes idols [over those who worship them] to defile her! [4] In your blood which you have shed you have become guilty, and you are defiled by the idols which you have made, and you have caused your time [of judgment and punishment] to draw near and have arrived at the full measure of your years. Therefore have I made you a reproach to the [heathen] nations and a mocking to all countries. [5] Those who are near and those who are far from you will mock you, you infamous one, full of tumult. [6] Behold, the princes of Israel in you, every one according to his power, have been intending to shed blood. [7] In you have they treated father and mother lightly; in the midst of you they have dealt unjustly *and* by oppression in relation to the stranger; in you they have wronged the fatherless and the widow. [8] You have despised *and* scorned My sacred things and have profaned My Sabbaths. [9] In you are slanderous men who arouse suspicions to shed blood, and in you are they who have eaten [food offered to idols] upon the mountains; in the midst of you they have committed lewdness. [10] In you men have uncovered their fathers' nakedness [the nakedness of mother or stepmother]; in you they have humbled women who are [ceremonially] unclean [during their periods or because of childbirth]. [11] And one has committed abomination with his neighbor's wife, another has lewdly defiled his daughter-in-law, and another in you has humbled his sister, his father's daughter. [12] In you they have accepted bribes to shed blood; you have taken [forbidden] interest and [percentage of] increase, and you have greedily gained from your neighbors by oppression *and* extortion and have forgotten Me, says the Lord God. [13] Behold therefore, I have struck My hands together at your dishonest gain which you have made and at the blood which has been in the midst of you. [14] Can your heart *and* courage endure or can your hands be strong in the days that I shall deal with you? I the Lord have spoken it, and I will do it. [15] And I will scatter you among the nations and disperse you through the countries, and I will consume your filthiness out of you. [16] And you shall be dishonored *and* profane yourself in the sight of the nations, and you shall know (understand and realize) that I am the Lord. [17] And the word of the Lord came to me, saying, [18] Son of man, the house of Israel has become to Me scum *and* waste matter. All of them are bronze and tin and iron and lead in the midst of the furnace; they are the dross of silver. ¹⁹ Therefore thus says the Lord God: Because you have all become scum *and* waste matter, behold therefore, I will gather you [O Israel] into the midst of Jerusalem. ²⁰ *As they gather silver and bronze and iron and lead and tin into the midst of the furnace, to blow the fire upon it in order to melt it, so will I gather you in My anger and in My wrath, and I will put you in and melt you. ²¹ Yes, I will gather you and blow upon you with the fire of My wrath, and you shall be melted in the midst of it. ²² As silver is melted in the midst of the furnace, so shall you be melted in the midst of it, and you shall know, understand, and realize that I the Lord have poured out My wrath upon you [O Israel]. ²³ And the word of the Lord came to me, saying, ²⁴ Son of man, say to her, You are a land that is not cleansed nor rained upon in the day of indignation. ²⁵ There is a conspiracy of [Israel's false] prophets in the midst of her, like a roaring lion tearing the prey; they have devoured human lives; they have taken [in their greed] treasure and precious things; they have made many widows in the midst of her. ²⁶ Her priests have done violence to My law and have profaned My holy things. They have made no distinction between the sacred and the secular, neither have they taught people the difference between the unclean and the clean and have hid their eyes from My Sabbaths, and I am profaned among them. ²⁷ Her princes in the midst of her are like wolves rending and devouring the prey, shedding blood and destroying lives to get dishonest gain. ²⁸ And her prophets have daubed them over with whitewash, seeing false visions and divining lies to them, saying, Thus says the Lord God—when the Lord has not spoken. ²⁹ The people of the land have used oppression and extortion and have committed robbery; yes, they have wronged and vexed the poor and needy; yes, they have oppressed the stranger and temporary resident wrongfully. ³⁰ And I sought a man among them who should build up the wall and stand in the gap before Me for the land, that I should not destroy it, but I found none. ³¹ Therefore have I poured out My indignation upon them; I have consumed them with the fire of My wrath; their own way have I repaid [by bringing it] upon their own heads, says the Lord God.*

2 Corinthians 10: ³ For though we walk in the flesh, we do not war after the flesh: ⁴ (For the weapons of our warfare are not carnal, but mighty through God to the pulling down of strong holds;) ⁵ Casting down imaginations, and every high thing that exalteth itself against the knowledge of God, and bringing into captivity every thought to the obedience of Christ;

Another purpose for our being in the earth is to intercede for all nations. God placed us in the earth not only just to feed the hungry, clothe the naked, to give water to the thirsty, and to visit the sick, and those who are in prison. God has placed us here to intercede for all the lost. They are part of our inheritance.

Psalm (KJV) 2: ⁵ Then shall he speak unto them in his wrath, and vex them in his sore displeasure. ⁶ Yet have I set my king upon my holy hill of Zion. ⁷ I will declare the decree: the LORD hath said unto me, Thou art my Son; this day have I begotten thee. ⁸ Ask of me, and I shall give thee the heathen for thine inheritance, and the uttermost parts of the earth for thy possession. ⁹ Thou shalt break them with a rod of iron; thou shalt dash them in pieces like a potter's vessel. ¹⁰ Be wise now therefore, O ye kings: be instructed, ye judges of the earth.

1 Timothy 1: ¹⁵ This is a faithful saying, and worthy of all acceptation, that Christ Jesus came into the world to save sinners; of whom I am chief. ¹⁶ Howbeit for this cause I obtained mercy, that in me first Jesus Christ might shew forth all longsuffering, for a pattern to them which should here-after believe on him to life everlasting. [17] Now unto the King eternal, immortal, invisible, the only wise God, be honour and glory for ever and ever. Amen. [18] This charge I commit unto thee, son Timothy, according to the prophecies which went before on thee, that thou by them mightest war a good warfare; [19] Holding faith, and a good conscience; which some having put away concerning faith have made shipwreck:

Matthew 11: [11] Verily I say unto you, Among them that are born of women there hath not risen a greater than John the Baptist: notwithstanding he that is least in the kingdom of heaven is greater than he. [12] And from the days of John the Baptist until now the kingdom of heaven suffereth vio-lence, and the violent take it by force. [13] For all the prophets and the law prophesied until John.

This is why Jesus asked us to pray that God's Kingdom would come and God's will would be done on Earth as it is in Heaven.

1 John 5:[3] For this is the love of God, that we keep his commandments: and his commandments are not grievous. [4] For whatsoever is born of God overcometh the world: and this is the victory that overcometh the world, even our faith. [5] Who is he that overcometh the world, but he that believeth that Jesus is the Son of God? (There will be more on the armor of God later.)

The Definition of Biblical Fruit

The Fruit of the Spirit are love, joy, peace, longsuffering, gentleness, kindness, meekness, faith, and righteousness.

First of all, every fruit starts out as a seed then it has to mature into Fruit before it can be useful or beneficial to others (more on this later).

2 Corinthians (KJV) 9: *[10] Now he that ministereth seed to the sower both minister bread for your food, and multiply your seed sown, and increase the fruits of your righteousness;*

Fruit in the natural is a source of food that provides substance and fulfills the need that hunger creates. In the spiritual realm, fruit means the same thing, but on a broader spectrum and that is why everything that is created has a purpose and a divine connection. Fruit is a sustainer of life.

To simply put it, in the Kingdom of God fruit is anything that provides or fulfills a necessity in the life of an individual or a group of people. It could be food, clothing, shelter, money, and so forth. It could be emotional, spiritual, or physical.

We all need a liberator, a redeemer, or rescuer of some type at some point in our lifetime. God raised up Moses to deliver the Jews out of bondage from Pharaoh. Moses asked God, who shall I say sent me? God told him to say, "I am that I am" sent you. That meant God became whatever the children of Israel needed to obtain their freedom. That is why God has so many different names. He was and still is "Jehovah I am That" (Jireh, Shammah, Shalom, etc.). God called Moses and worked through him by demonstrating His power and providing everything needed to deliver His children out of bondage from Pharaoh. God went from having Moses ask Pharaoh nicely to let His people go, to bringing the ten plagues that brought hardship and deprivation to the Egyptians, to the death of all the firstborn including Pharaoh's own son. Even that still did not convince Pharaoh that God was the only true and living God. Pharaoh probably did not realize who he was dealing with until he found himself drowning along with his army in the Red Sea. Pharaoh could have said the first day, "Okay, your people can go, and let me give your people a little spending money for all the hard work that they did for four hundred years. After all, I owe them something." God kept the promise that He made to Abraham over four hundred years earlier.

When we give of our time, energy, money, and resources into someone else's life, we are sowing seeds into their lives and giving them a portion of our life, all at the same time. We all work hard for our money so we can buy clothes, food, and shelter for ourselves. But when we turn around and freely give it to someone else, who for whatever reason is unable to do that for themselves, we are literally giving them a portion of our life. That is why God says He will multiply (30, 40, 60, and 100 fold) whatever we sow back to us so we can continue to give more and more to other people as we prove to God that He can trust us. This is what salvation is all about. Jesus gave the ultimate gift of life. He gave Himself to redeem, rescue, and deliver us from hell, so we can be given "eternal life" and continue that flow of life to the people around us. He is asking us to do the same except on a smaller scale. We are to bear fruit so we can sow seeds of life into people all around us. When we do it as unto the Lord and not to gain attention to our self, it will be God working through us, which is what He has been trying to do for over 2,000 years. The Bible teaches us how to produce the fruit of the Spirit.

Producing the Fruit of Righteousness

The fruit of righteousness starts with seeking His righteousness. It is about us agreeing with God and with what He says is right and separating ourselves from what He says is wrong. Seeking His righteousness is the beginning of our salvation, which is a free gift from God. It is the second request that Jesus asked us to do while we are "seeking the Kingdom of God." The first is to ask Him to come into your heart.

Hebrews 1: [8] But unto the Son he saith, Thy throne, O God, is forever and ever: a scepter of righteousness is the scepter of thy kingdom. **[9] Thou hast loved righteousness, and hated iniquity;** therefore God, even thy God, hath anointed thee with the oil of gladness above thy fellows. [10] And, Thou, Lord, in the beginning hast laid the foundation of the earth; and the heavens are the works of thine hands:

Romans 10: Brethren, my heart's desire and prayer to God for Israel is, that they might be saved.[2] For I bear them record that they have a zeal of God, but not according to knowledge.[3] For they being ignorant of God's righteousness, and going about to establish their own righteousness, have not submitted themselves unto *the righteousness of God.* [4] *For Christ is the end of the law for righteousness to everyone that believeth.* [5] *For Moses describeth the righteousness which is of the law, That the man which doeth those things shall live by them. But the righteousness which is of faith speaketh on this wise, Say not in thine heart, Who shall* [6] *ascend into heaven? (that is, to bring Christ down from above:)* [7] *Or, Who shall descend into the deep? (that is, to bring up Christ again from the dead.)* [8] *But what saith it? The word is nigh thee, even in thy mouth, and in thy heart: that is, the word of faith, which we preach;* [9] *That if thou shalt confess with thy mouth the Lord Jesus, and shalt believe in thine heart that God hath raised him from the dead, thou shalt be saved.*[10]

For with the heart man believeth unto righteousness; and with the mouth confession is made unto salvation. [11] For the scripture saith, Whosoever believeth on him shall not be ashamed. [12] For there is no difference between the Jew and the Greek: for the same Lord over all is rich unto all that call upon him. [13] For whosoever shall call upon the name of the Lord shall be saved. [14] How then shall they call on him in whom they have not believed? and how shall they believe in him of whom they have not heard? and how shall they hear without a preacher?[15] And how shall they preach, except they be sent? as it is written, How beautiful are the feet of them that preach the gospel of peace, and bring glad tidings of good things! [16] But they have not all obeyed the gospel. For Esaias saith, Lord, who hath believed our report? [17] So then faith cometh by hearing, and hearing by the word of God.[18] But I say, Have they not heard? Yes verily, their sound went into all the earth, and their words unto the ends of the world. [19] But I say, Did not Israel know? First Moses saith, I will provoke you to jealousy by them that are no people, and by a foolish nation I will anger you. [20] But Esaias is very bold, and saith, I was found of them that sought me not; I was made manifest unto them that asked not after me.[21] But to Israel he saith, All day long I have stretched forth my hands unto a disobedient and gainsaying people.

We were made the righteousness of God at the time of the new birth. But we have to maintain the gift of righteousness, because we all sin and fall short of the Glory of God. Again this is the reason God made us priests because as priests we are responsible for keeping ourselves holy at all times because we are the Temple of the Holy Spirit. When we do sin we have the Blood of Jesus to cleanse us after we ask for forgiveness.

1 John (KJV) 1: [6] If we say that we have fellowship with him, and walk in darkness, we lie, and do not the truth: [7] But if we walk in the light, as he is in the light, we have fellowship one with another, and the blood of Jesus Christ his Son cleanseth us from all sin. [8] If we say that we have no sin, we deceive ourselves, and the truth is not in us. [9] If we confess our sins, he is faithful and just to forgive us our sins, and to cleanse us from all unrighteousness. [10] If we say that we have not sinned, we make him a liar, and his word is not in us.

1 Corinthians1: [7] *So that ye come behind in no gift; waiting for the coming of our Lord Jesus Christ: [8] Who shall also confirm you unto the end, that ye may be blameless in the day of our Lord Jesus Christ. [9] God is faithful, by whom ye were called unto the fellowship of his Son Jesus Christ our Lord.*

Philippians 2: [14] *Do all things without murmurings and disputings: [15] That ye may be blameless and harmless, the sons of God, without rebuke, in the midst of a crooked and perverse nation, among whom ye shine as lights in the world; [16] Holding forth the word of life; that I may rejoice in the day of Christ, that I have not run in vain, neither laboured in vain.*

When you decide to open your heart to the Lord for correction, righteousness begins to take root. The Lord wants to reveal to us areas in our life that are hindering Him from blessing us, which will also prevent the power of God from flowing through us.

Hebrews 12: [5] And ye have forgotten the exhortation which speaketh unto you as unto children, My son, despise not thou the chastening of the Lord, nor faint when thou art rebuked of him: [6] For whom the Lord loveth he chasteneth, and scourgeth every son whom he receiveth.[7] If ye endure chastening, God dealeth with you as with sons; for what son is he whom the father chasteneth not? [8] But if ye be without chastisement, whereof all are partakers, then are ye bastards, and not sons. [9] Furthermore we have had fathers of our flesh which corrected us, and we gave them reverence: shall we not much rather be in subjection unto the Father of spirits, and live? [10] For they verily for a few days chastened us after their own pleasure; but he for our profit, that we might be partakers of his holiness. [11] Now no chastening for the present seemeth to be joyous, but grievous: nevertheless *afterward it yieldeth the peaceable fruit of righteousness unto them which are exercised thereby.*

James 3: [13] Who is a wise man and endued with knowledge among you? let him shew out of a good conversation his works with meekness of wisdom. [14] But if ye have bitter envying and strife in your hearts, glory not, and lie not against the truth. [15] This wisdom descendeth not from above, but is earthly, sensual, devilish.[16] For where envying and strife is, there is confusion and every evil work. *[17] But the wisdom that is from above is first pure, then peaceable, gentle, and easy to be intreated, full of mercy and good fruits, without partiality, and without hypocrisy. [18] And the fruit of righteousness is sown in peace of them that make peace.*

The fruit of righteousness has several sources—one is our giving. Our finances are important in the Kingdom of God because they lie at the heart of God when they are used properly. In the Old Testament the Jews were commanded to help the poor.

Leviticus 23:22 And when ye reap the harvest of your land, thou shalt not make clean riddance of the corners of thy field when thou reapest, neither shalt thou gather any gleaning of thy harvest: thou shalt leave them unto the poor, and to the stranger: I am the LORD your God.

So think twice about the people standing on the corner begging; they might be angels or it could be Jesus himself. Provision for the homeless and poor was started in the Old Testament, with God commanding that provision be left especially for them. This is confirmed in **Malachi 3:5** as you will see later.

Galatians 6: [4] But let every man prove his own work, and then shall he have rejoicing in himself alone, and not in another.[5] For every man shall bear his own burden. [6] Let him that is taught in the word communicate unto him that teacheth in all good things. [7] Be not deceived; God is not mocked: for whatsoever a man soweth, that shall he also reap. [8] For he that soweth to his flesh shall of the flesh reap corruption; but he that soweth to the Spirit shall of the Spirit reap life everlasting.[9] And let us not be weary in well doing: for in due season we shall reap, if we faint not. [10] As we have therefore opportunity, let us do good unto all men, especially unto them who are of the household of faith.

The Cheerful Giver

Our giving is linked to the seed-and-harvest-time principle of the Kingdom of God. God provides us with the seed (the seed can be finances, food, clothing, the Word of God, etc.), When we sow it into the life of a person that needs it, that seed provides life to that individual; that seed fulfills a need that was missing in that person's life. In some cases that individual gets another chance to live another day. The money becomes a seed, the seed sprouts then buds then blossoms, then the fruit of righteousness is reborn all over again. As you will learn a little later, righteousness is another word for charity.

2 Corinthians (NKJV) 9: [6] But this *I say:* He who sows sparingly will also reap sparingly, and he who sows bountifully will also reap bountifully. [7] *So let* each one *give* as he purposes in his heart, not grudgingly or of necessity; for God loves a cheerful giver. [8] And God *is* able to make all grace abound toward you, that you, always having all sufficiency in all *things,* may have an abundance for every good work. [9] As it is written:

> "He has dispersed abroad,
> He has given to the poor;
> His righteousness endures forever."

[10] Now may He who supplies seed to the sower, and bread for food, supply and multiply the seed you have sown and increase the fruits of your righteousness, [11] while you are enriched in everything for all liberality, which causes thanksgiving through us to God. [12] For the administration of this service not only supplies the needs of the saints, but also is abounding through many thanksgivings to God, [13] while, through the proof of this ministry, they glorify God for the obedience of your confession to the gospel of Christ, and for your liberal sharing with them and all men, [14] and by their prayer for you, who long for you because of the exceeding grace of God in you. [15] Thanks be to God for His indescribable gift.

Tithes and offerings will determine whether or not everything that we have been sowing will mature at harvest time.

Malachi Chapter 3 explains why tithing is so important to our covenant with God, because He promised to rebuke the devourer for our sake, and our harvest will not spoil at the very point in time when Jesus sends His angels to bring in the harvest at His second coming. So if you are not tithing, any seeds that you have sown will spoil or not mature into fruit at harvest time at the end of the world.

Matthew (KJV) 13: [39] The enemy that sowed them is the devil; the harvest is the end of the world; and the reapers are the angels.

Jesus' visitation will be personal. Will you be found holy and doing His will by bearing fruit?

Malachi 3: *[1] Behold, I will send my messenger, and he shall prepare the way before me: and the LORD, whom ye seek, shall suddenly come to his Temple, even the messenger of the covenant, whom ye delight in: behold, he shall come, saith the LORD of hosts.*

1.24 The Ark carried into the Temple from the early 15th.

Très Riches Heures du Duc de Berry

[2] But who may abide the day of his coming? and who shall stand when he appeareth? for he is like a refiner's fire, and like fullers' soap:[3] And he shall sit as a refiner and purifier that they may offer unto the LORD an offering in righteousness. [4] Then shall the offering of Judah and Jerusalem be pleasant unto the LORD, as in the days of old, and as in former years.[5] And I will come near to you to judgment; and I will be a swift witness against the sorcerers, and against the adulterers, and against false swearers, and against those that oppress the hireling in his wages, the widow, and the fatherless, and that turn aside the stranger from his right, and fear not me, saith the LORD of hosts.[6] For I am the LORD, I change not; therefore ye sons of Jacob are not consumed.[7] Even from the days of your fathers ye are gone away from mine ordinances, and have not kept them.

Not paying tithes and offerings is robbing God, and you really do not want to do that if you sincerely want to come back to God.

Return unto me, and I will return unto you, saith the LORD of hosts. But ye said, Wherein shall we return? [8] Will a man rob God? Yet ye have robbed me. But ye say, Wherein have we robbed thee? In tithes and offerings. [9] Ye are cursed with a curse: for ye have robbed me, even this whole nation.

When we are obedient and pay tithes and offerings, the curse is lifted and God's blessing will flow in our lives, but if not we will not bear any fruit (including the Fruit of the Spirit) to maturity because we are stealing from God.

[10] *Bring ye all the tithes into the storehouse, that there may be meat in mine house, and prove me now herewith, saith the LORD of hosts, if I will not open you the windows of heaven, and pour you out a blessing, that there shall not be room enough to receive it. [11] And I will rebuke the devourer for your sakes, and he shall not destroy the fruits of your ground;*

Figure 1.25 Fruit on display at La Boqueria market in Barcelona.

neither shall your vine cast her fruit before the time in the field, saith the LORD of hosts. [12] And all nations shall call you blessed: for ye shall be a delightsome land, saith the LORD of hosts. [13] Your words have been stout against me, saith the LORD. Yet ye say, What have we spoken so much against thee? [14] Ye have said, It is vain to serve God: and what profit is it that we have kept his ordinance, and that we have walked mournfully before the LORD of hosts? [15] And now we call the proud happy;

yea, they that work wickedness are set up; yea, they that tempt God are even delivered. [16] Then they that feared the LORD spake often one to another: and the LORD hearkened, and heard it, and a book of remembrance was written before him for them that feared the LORD, and that thought upon his name. [17] And they shall be mine, saith the LORD of hosts, in that day when I make up my jewels; and I will spare them, as a man spareth his own son that serveth him. [18] Then shall ye return, and discern between the righteous and the wicked, between him that serveth God and him that serveth him not.

Tithing is a must for all Christians. It establishes our covenant with God to protect us and bless us and make us a blessing. It will also determine the difference between the righteous and the wicked and those who are truly serving God and the ones that are not. You have to remember the angels will be sent to bring in the harvest at the end of the world.

Matthew (KJV) 13: *[38] The field is the world; the good seed are the children of the kingdom; but the tares are the children of the wicked one; [39] The enemy that sowed them is the devil; the harvest is the end of the world; and the reapers are the angels. [39] The enemy that sowed them is the devil; the harvest is the end of the world; and the reapers are the angels.*

God was very serious about the priest teaching the people the importance of tithing and if they did not their punishment was very harsh, read Malachi Chapter 1 and 2.

Proverbs (KJV) 11: [29] He that troubleth his own house shall inherit the wind: and the fool shall be servant to the wise of heart. [30] The fruit of the righteous is a tree of life; and he that winneth souls is wise. [31] Behold, the righteous shall be recompensed in the earth: much more the wicked and the sinner.

Proverbs 15: [3] The eyes of the LORD are in every place, beholding the evil and the good. [4] A wholesome tongue is a tree of life: but perverseness therein is a breach in the spirit.

Psalm 112: Praise ye the LORD. Blessed is the man that feareth the LORD, that delighteth greatly in his commandments. [2] His seed shall be mighty upon earth: the generation of the upright shall be blessed. [3] Wealth and riches shall be in his house: and his righteousness endureth forever. [8] Unto the upright there ariseth light in the darkness: he is gracious, and full of compassion, and righteous. [5] A good man sheweth favour, and lendeth: he will guide his affairs with discretion. [6] Surely he shall not be moved forever: the righteous shall be in everlasting remembrance. [7] He shall not be afraid of evil tidings: his heart is fixed, trusting in the LORD. [8] His heart is established, he shall not be afraid, until he see his desire upon his enemies. [9] He hath dispersed, he hath given to the poor; his righteousness endureth for ever; his horn shall be exalted with honour. [10] The wicked shall see it, and be grieved; he shall gnash with his teeth, and melt away: the desire of the wicked shall perish.

Matthew 5: And seeing the multitudes, he went up into a mountain: and when he was set, his disciples came unto him: [2] And he opened his mouth, and taught them, saying,

Figure 1.26 The Sermon on the Mount by Carl Heinrich Bloch.

³ Blessed are the poor in spirit: for theirs is the kingdom of heaven. ⁴ Blessed are they that mourn: for they shall be comforted. ⁵ Blessed are the meek: for they shall inherit the earth. ⁶ Blessed are they which do hunger and thirst after righteousness: for they shall be filled. ⁷ Blessed are the merciful: for they shall obtain mercy. ⁸ Blessed are the pure in heart: for they shall see God. ⁹ Blessed are the peacemakers: for they shall be called the children of God. ¹⁰ Blessed are they which are persecuted for righteousness' sake: for theirs is the kingdom of heaven. ¹¹ Blessed are ye, when men shall revile you, and persecute you, and shall say all manner of evil against you falsely, for my sake. ¹² Rejoice, and be exceeding glad: for great is your reward in heaven: for so persecuted they the prophets which were before you.

Matthew 5: ¹⁹ Whosoever therefore shall break one of these least commandments, and shall teach men so, he shall be called the least in the kingdom of heaven: but whosoever shall do and teach them, the same shall be called great in the kingdom of heaven. ²⁰ For I say unto you, That except your righteousness shall exceed the righteousness of the scribes and Pharisees, ye shall in no case enter into the kingdom of heaven. ²¹ Ye have heard that it was said of them of old time, Thou shalt not kill; and whosoever shall kill shall be in danger of the judgment:

James 1: ¹⁰ But the rich, in that he is made low: because as the flower of the grass he shall pass away. ¹¹ For the sun is no sooner risen with a burning heat, but it withereth the grass, and the flower thereof falleth, and the grace of the fashion of it perisheth: so also shall the rich man fade away in his ways. ¹² Blessed is the man that endureth temptation: for when he is tried, he shall receive the crown of life, which the Lord hath promised to them that love him. ¹³ Let no man say when he is tempted, I am tempted of God: for God cannot be tempted with evil, neither tempteth he any man: [14] But every man is tempted, when he is drawn away of his own lust, and enticed. [15] Then when lust hath conceived, it bringeth forth sin: and sin, when it is finished, bringeth forth death. [16] Do not err, my beloved brethren. [17] Every good gift and every perfect gift is from above, and cometh down from the Father of lights, with whom is no variableness, neither shadow of turning. [18] Of his own will begat he us with the word of truth, that we should be a kind of firstfruits of his creatures. [19] Wherefore, my beloved brethren, let every man be swift to hear, slow to speak, slow to wrath: [20] For the wrath of man worketh not the righteousness of God. [21] Wherefore lay apart all filthiness and superfluity of naughtiness, and receive with meekness the engrafted word, which is able to save your souls. [22] But be ye doers of the word, and not hearers only, deceiving your own selves. [23] For if any be a hearer of the word, and not a doer, he is like unto a man beholding his natural face in a glass: [24] For he beholdeth himself, and goeth his way, and straightway forgetteth what manner of man he was. [25] But whoso looketh into the perfect law of liberty, and continueth therein, he being not a forgetful hearer, but a doer of the work, this man shall be blessed in his deed. [26] *If any man among you seem to be religious, and bridleth not his tongue, but deceiveth his own heart, this man's religion is vain. [27] Pure religion and undefiled before God and the Father is this, To visit the fatherless and widows in their affliction, and to keep himself unspotted from the world.*

This is what is happening in our nation and around the world today. Remember Jesus said see to it that you are not troubled about it. The separation of the righteous and unrighteous is already happening. Those who are supposed to be upright are compromising the Word and they are teaching others to do so, and they are bringing about their own destruction. We have to make sure that we do not compromise God's Word and that our hearts are fixed, trusting in and standing on the Word of God. Even if other Christians around us are wavering and are agreeing with the world's view on morality, we must stay separated from sin.

While Moses was on top of Mount Sinai some of the Jews turned back to worshiping a golden calf, and they yielded to corruption again. God did not even give them the luxury of dying; because of their disobedience they received a one-way ticket to hell. The earth opened up and swallowed 3,000 rebellious Jews in an instant for everyone else to see as a warning.

**Figure 1.27 Destruction of Korah, Dathan, and Abiram,
illustration from the 1890 Holman Bible**

God promised to lead the rest of them to the land of milk and honey, but because of their murmuring, complaining and their rebellion, three million Jews, including Moses, never made it to the Promised Land. They died in the desert. They saw a pillar of fire by night that kept them warm at night, and a cloud covered them during the day. God protected and fed them for forty years. Only Joshua and Caleb and everyone who was twenty years old and younger made it to the Promised Land. God was merciful to Moses; God did let him see it from the mountaintop before he died.

**Figure 1.28 Moses Views the Land of Israel,
woodcut by Julius Schnorr von Carolsfeld from the 1860 *Bible in Pictures***

Jesus is saying the same thing that only five out of every ten Christians will be taken at the end. We should learn from what happened to the Jews. And we are in the same situation today. If He can leave Moses and three million Jews behind because of their disobedience, unbelief, and rebellion, then none of us can be exempt—or think that we can have a free ride just because we go to church, read the Bible, and say Hallelujah occasionally. Each one of us has an assignment from God.

Revelation (KJV) 3: [13] He that hath an ear, let him hear what the Spirit saith unto the churches. [14] And unto the angel of the church of the Laodiceans write; These things saith the Amen, the faithful and true witness, the beginning of the creation of God; [15] I know thy works, that thou art neither cold nor hot: I would thou wert cold or hot. [16] So then because thou art lukewarm, and neither cold nor hot, I will spue thee out of my mouth. [17] Because thou sayest, I am rich, and increased with goods, and have need of nothing; and knowest not that thou art wretched, and miserable, and poor, and blind, and naked: [18] I counsel thee to buy of me gold tried in the fire, that thou mayest be rich; and white raiment, that thou mayest be clothed, and that the shame of thy nakedness do not appear; and anoint thine eyes with eyesalve, that thou mayest see. [19] As many as I love, I rebuke and chasten: be zealous therefore, and repent.

The next fruit we want to look at is love.

Romans 5: [2] By whom also we have access by faith into this grace wherein we stand, and rejoice in hope of the glory of God. [3] And not only so, but we glory in tribulations also: knowing that tribulation worketh patience; [4] And patience, experience; and experience, hope: [5] And hope maketh not ashamed; because the love of God is shed abroad in our hearts by the Holy Ghost which is given unto us.

When we ask God to fill us with the Holy Spirit, He fills us with the love of God. God and love are the same. God has placed this love in our hearts, but we have to cultivate it. One of the signs of the end is the lack of love that will be in the earth; this is how we will know the end is near.

Matthew 24: *[11] And many false prophets shall rise, and shall deceive many. [12] And because iniquity shall abound, the love of many shall wax cold. [13] But he that shall endure unto the end, the same shall be saved.*

The first person that we are commanded to love is God and we are to love Him with all our heart, soul, mind, strength, and then to love our neighbor as we do ourselves. I think this is why we have so many problems with some of our next-door neighbors. Satan works overtime to keep strife and confusion going between neighbors, co-workers, church members, and so on. But we have to deal with them in the love of God. Sometimes we have to keep silent and make sure that our heart is right towards them. We cannot make them love us but we have to still love and pray for them. We cannot have any room in our hearts for hatred, revenge, animosity, resentment or anything else but the love of God for all people.

Proverbs 16: The preparation of the heart in man, and the answer of the tongue, is from the LORD. [2] All the ways of a man are clean in his own eyes; but the LORD weigheth the spirits. [3] Commit thy works unto the LORD, and thy thoughts shall be established. [4] The LORD hath made all things for himself: yea, even the wicked for the day of evil. [5] Every one that is proud in heart is an abomination to the LORD: though hand join in hand, he shall not be unpunished. [6] By mercy and truth iniquity is purged: and by the fear of the LORD men depart from evil. [7] When a man's ways please the LORD, he maketh even his enemies to be at peace with him. [8] Better is a little with righteousness than great revenues without right. [9] A man's heart deviseth his way: but the LORD directeth his steps.

You have to remember the love that Jesus had for the people who wanted Him to die on the cross. Through all the torment and beatings He said, "Father forgive them because they do not know what they are doing." We have been given the same capacity to love and forgive because it was rooted and grounded in our spirits by the Holy Spirit.

Ephesians 3: [16] That he would grant you, according to the riches of his glory, to be strengthened with might by his Spirit in the inner man; [17] That Christ may dwell in your hearts by faith; that ye, being rooted and grounded in love,

1 John 4 Beloved, believe not every spirit, but try the spirits whether they are of God: because many false prophets are gone out into the world. [2] Hereby know ye the Spirit of God: Every spirit that confesseth that Jesus Christ is come in the flesh is of God: [3] And every spirit that confesseth not that Jesus Christ is come in the flesh is not of God: and this is that spirit of antichrist, whereof ye have heard that it should come; and even now already is it in the world. [4] Ye are of God, little children, and have overcome them: because greater is he that is in you, than he that is in the world. [5] They are of the world: therefore speak they of the world, and the world heareth them. [6] We are of God: he that knoweth God heareth us; he that is not of God heareth not us. Hereby know we the spirit of truth, and the spirit of error. [7] Beloved, let us love one another: for love is of God; and every one that loveth is born of God, and knoweth God. [8] He that loveth not knoweth not God; for God is love. [9] In this was manifested the love of God toward us, because that God sent his only begotten Son into the world, that we might live through him. [10] Herein is love, not that we loved God, but that he loved us, and sent his Son to be the propitiation for our sins. [11] Beloved, if God so loved us, we ought also to love one another.[12] No man hath seen God at any time. If we love one another, God dwelleth in us, and his love is perfected in us. [13] Hereby know we that we dwell in him, and he in us, because he hath given us of his Spirit.[14] And we have seen and do testify that the Father sent the Son to be the Saviour of the world.[15] Whosoever shall confess that Jesus is the Son of God, God dwelleth in him, and he in God. [16] And we have known and believed the love that God hath to us. God is love; and he that dwelleth in love dwelleth in God, and God in him. *[17] Herein is our love made perfect, that we may have boldness in the Day of Judgment: because as he is, so are we in this world.* [18] There is no fear in love; but perfect love casteth out fear: because fear hath torment. He that feareth is not made perfect in love. [19] We love him, because he first loved us. [20] If a man say, I love God, and hateth his brother, he is a liar: for he that loveth not his brother whom he hath seen, how can he love God whom he hath not seen? -[21] And this commandment have we from him, That he who loveth God love his brother also.

The Definition of Love and Charity

Figure 1.29 Allegorical personification of Charity as a mother with three infants by Anthony van Dyck In Christian theology charity, or *love (agapē)*, means an unlimited loving-kindness toward all others.

From Wikipedia, the free encyclopedia

Charity may refer to: *Tzedakah*, a Hebrew concept, literally meaning righteousness (Genesis 18:19) but commonly used to signify charity, and giving to worthy causes or people in need.

- Charity (practice), the practice of benevolent giving and caring
- Charity (virtue), the Christian theological concept of unlimited love and kindness

Philanthropy etymologically means "the love of humanity"—love in the sense of caring for, nourishing, developing, or enhancing; humanity in the sense of "what it is to be human," or "human potential." In modern practical terms, it is "private initiatives for public good, focusing on quality of life"—balancing the social-scientific aspect emphasized in the twentieth century, with the long-traditional and original humanist core of the word's ancient coinage. This formulation distinguishes it from business (private initiatives for private good, focusing on material prosperity) and government (public initiatives for public good, focusing on law and order).[1]

God, love, charity, agape are one and the same, and we should be the same way. There are many facets to the love of God. Faith, which is another fruit, will not work without the power of love driving it.

1 Corinthians 13: Though I speak with the tongues of men and of angels, and have not charity (or love) I am become as sounding brass, or a tinkling cymbal. [2] And though I have the gift of prophecy, and understand all mysteries, and all knowledge; and though I have all faith, so that I could remove mountains, and have not charity (or love), I am nothing. [3] And though I bestow all my goods to feed the poor, and though I give my body to be burned, and have not charity (or Love), it profiteth me nothing.[4] Charity (or love) suffereth long, and is kind; charity (or love) envieth not; charity (or love) vaunteth not itself, is not puffed up,[5] Doth not behave itself unseemly, seeketh not her own, is not easily provoked, thinketh no evil;[6] Rejoiceth not in iniquity, but rejoiceth in the truth;[7] Beareth all things, believeth all things, hopeth all things, endureth all things. [8] Charity (or love) never faileth: but whether there be prophecies, they shall fail; whether there be tongues, they shall cease; whether there be knowledge, it shall vanish away. *[9] For we know in part, and we prophesy in part.[10] But when that which is perfect is come, then that which is in part shall be done away.[11] When I was a child, I spake as a child, I understood as a child, I thought as a child: but when I became a man, I put away childish things. [12] For now we see through a glass, darkly; but then face to face: now I know in part; but then shall I know even as also I am known.*

Figure 1.30 A Wall Mirror Reflecting a Vase.

The Bible used to be called many years ago the "Perfect Looking Glass"; the more you study it, it will transform you into the image of God inside and out.

1 John 3: Behold, what manner of love the Father hath bestowed upon us, that we should be called the sons of God: therefore the world knoweth us not, because it knew him not. *2 Beloved, now are we the sons of God, and it doth not yet appear what we shall be: but we know that, when he shall appear, we shall be like him; for we shall see him as he is. 3 And every man that hath this hope in him purifieth himself, even as he is pure.*

I Corinthians 13: [13] And now abideth faith, hope, charity (or Love), these three; but the greatest of these is charity (or Love). *[14]Follow peace with all men, and holiness, without which no man shall see the Lord: [15]Looking diligently lest any man fail of the grace of God; lest any root of bitterness springing up trouble you, and thereby many be defiled; [16]Lest there be any fornicator, or profane person, as Esau,*

Figure 1.31 Esau Sells His Birthright for Pottage of Lentils, as in Genesis 25:32-33, "And Esau said, Behold, I am at the point to die: and what profit shall this birthright do to me? And Jacob said, Swear to me this day; and he sware unto him: and he sold his birthright unto Jacob."; illustration from the 1728 *Figures de la Bible*; illustrated by Gerard Hoet (1648-1733) and others, and published by P. de Hondt in The Hague; image courtesy Bizzell Bible Collection, University of Oklahoma Libraries.

who for one morsel of meat sold his birthright. [17]For ye know how that afterward, when he would have inherited the blessing, he was rejected: for he found no place of repentance, though he sought it carefully with tears.

CHAPTER 2

Why Jesus said Only Five Out of Ten Virgins Will Be Raptured Part 2

Figure 2.1 "I am the <u>Good Shepherd</u>." Jesus is the personification of the fruit of love which is what we should become.

John (AMP) 21: [14] This was now the third time that Jesus revealed Himself (appeared, was manifest) to the disciples after He had risen from the dead. [15] When they had eaten, Jesus said to Simon Peter, Simon, son of John, do you love Me more than these [others do—with reasoning, intentional, spiritual devotion, as one loves the Father]? He said to Him, Yes, Lord, You know that I love you [that I have deep, instinctive, personal affection for You, as for a close friend]. He said to him, Feed My lambs.

When Jesus asked Peter to feed His sheep, He was asking him to provide the right spiritual food for the growth of His flock. What Jesus is saying is, if Peter really loves Him with all his heart, soul, and his strength, which is the agape kind of love (or the God kind of love that a parent should have toward their children which should be "unconditional love") then he would feed the flock of God properly. Jesus is expecting Peter and the other disciples to use that same diligence and effort to feed His sheep. Jesus is encouraging them to fulfill the Great Commission of preaching the Gospel of the Kingdom to every creature. The Gospel of the Kingdom is about teaching the children of God how to seek the Kingdom and learn how it functions and the part that each child of God has in the Kingdom of God.

The purpose of the fig tree that Jesus went to when He was looking for food was to satisfy a need. The outward appearance of leaves on the tree meant figs were guaranteed to be there to fulfill Jesus' need. The Kingdom of God is looking at us the same way; we call ourselves children of God, but are we really giving life to fulfill the needs of the people around us. Now the "Kingdom of God" and seed and harvest time are coming full circle. Just like in the natural the right food is needed for everything to grow and mature; the right spiritual food is vital for us to grow and mature spiritually. Jesus was concerned that the disciples continue His ministry; they were responsible for meeting the spiritual, and to a certain point physical, needs of His flock.

1 Peter (KJV) 2: Wherefore laying aside all malice, and all guile, and hypocrisies, and envies, and all evil speaking, [2] As newborn babes, desire the sincere milk of the word, that ye may grow thereby: [3] If so be ye have tasted that the Lord is gracious.

John (NKJV) 6: [32] Then Jesus said to them, "Most assuredly, I say to you, Moses did not give you the bread from heaven, but My Father gives you the true bread from heaven. [33] For the bread of God is He who comes down from heaven and gives life to the world." [34] Then they said to Him, "Lord, give us this bread always." [35] And Jesus said to them, "I am the bread of life. He who comes to Me shall never hunger, and he who believes in Me shall never thirst. [36] But I said to you that you have seen Me and yet do not believe. [37] All that the Father gives Me will come to Me, and the one who comes to Me I will by no means cast out. [38] For I have come down from heaven, not to do My own will, but the will of Him who sent Me.

John (AMP) 21: [13] Jesus came and took the bread and gave it to them, and so also [with] the fish. [14] This was now the third time that Jesus revealed Himself (appeared, was manifest) to the disciples after He had risen from the dead. [15] When they had eaten, Jesus said to Simon Peter, Simon, son of John, do you love Me more than these [others do—with reasoning, intentional, spiritual devotion, as one loves the Father]? He said to Him, Yes, Lord, You know that I love You [that I have deep, instinctive, personal affection for You, as for a close friend]. He said to him, Feed My lambs.

Figure 2.2 Christ's Charge to Peter (1515) by Raphael,

John (AMP) 21: [16] Again He said to him the second time, Simon, son of John, do you love Me [with reasoning, intentional, spiritual devotion, as one loves the Father]? He said to Him, Yes, Lord, You know that I love You [that I have a deep, instinctive, personal affection for You, as for a close friend]. He said to him, Shepherd (tend) My sheep. [17] He said to him the third time, Simon, son of John, do you love Me [with a deep, instinctive, personal affection for Me, as for a close friend]? Peter was grieved (was saddened and hurt) that He should ask him the third time, Do you love Me? And he said to Him, Lord, You know everything; You know that I love You [that I have a deep, instinctive, personal affection for You, as for a close friend]. Jesus said to him, Feed My Sheep.

Knowing God through Love

1 John (NKJV) 4: [7] Beloved, let us love one another, for love is of God; and everyone who loves is born of God and knows God. [8] He who does not love does not know God, for God is love. [9] In this the love of God was manifested toward us, that God has sent His only begotten Son into the world, that we might live through Him.

1 John 4: [15] whosoever confesses that Jesus is the Son of God, God abides in him, and he in God. [16] And we have known and believed the love that God has for us. God is love, and he who abides in love abides in God and God in him.

The Consummation of Love

[17] Love has been perfected among us in this: that we may have boldness in the day of judgment; because as He is, so are we in this world. [18] There is no fear in love; but perfect love casts out fear, because fear involves torment. But he who fears has not been made perfect in love. [19] We love Him because He first loved us.

Obedience by Faith

[20] If someone says, "I love God," and hates his brother, he is a liar; for he who does not love his brother whom he has seen, how can he love God whom he has not seen? [21] And this commandment we have from Him: that he who loves God must also love his brother also.

I want to go back to the Wikipedia free encyclopedia definition of charity, but this time I want to add something which will help you understand why Jesus questioned Peter concerning just how deep his love was toward Himself and for our Heavenly Father. This time I want to add to that definition the name of God. And if you understand it, you will see why Jesus told John in Revelation to tell the churches that have fallen away that they needed to return to their first love. I want to exchange the word charity for God.

Information taken from Wikipedia:

(God) Charity may refer to: *Tzedakah*, a Hebrew concept, literally meaning righteousness (Genesis 18:19) but commonly used to signify charity, and giving to worthy causes or people in need.
- (God) Charity (practice), the practice of benevolent giving and caring
- (God) Charity (virtue), the Christian theological concept of unlimited love and kindness

(God) is the ultimate philanthropist; this definition of philanthropist perfectly describes God. It also can be used for the definition of God's will being done on earth as it is in Heaven. This means "the love of humanity"—love in the sense of caring for, nourishing, developing, or enhancing; humanity in the sense of "what it is to be human" or "human potential." In modern practical terms, it is "private initiatives for public good, focusing on quality of life"—balancing the social-scientific aspect emphasized since the beginning of the world, with the long-traditional and original humanist core of the word's ancient coinage. This formulation distinguishes it from business (private initiatives for private good, focusing on material and spirit, soul, and physical, prosperity) and government (public initiatives for public good, focusing on law and order) and the Word of God.

This is why God is so concerned for the poor, and in the eyes of God we are all poor to some degree! But when we allow the Kingdom of God to be manifested in our life our poverty comes to an end! God wants the best for every person on earth. That is why Jesus told His disciples "this Gospel of the Kingdom of God shall be preached to all nations and then the end will come".

3 John (KJV) 1:[1] The elder unto the well beloved Gaius, whom I love in the truth. [2] Beloved, I wish above all things that thou mayest prosper and be in health, even as thy soul prospereth.[3] For I rejoiced greatly, when the brethren came and testified of the truth that is in thee, even as thou walkest in the truth. [4] I have no greater joy than to hear that my children walk in truth. [5] Beloved, thou doest faithfully whatsoever thou doest to the brethren, and to strangers; [6] Which have borne witness of thy charity before the church: whom if thou bring forward on their journey after a godly sort, thou shalt do well:

The Kingdom of God is all about raising the quality of life for all people on earth to be equal to that of Heaven. It is God's will that we all come to the knowledge of the truth into a perfect man unto the measure of the statue of Jesus Christ. God has sent us the Holy Spirit to lead and guide us into all truth about the Kingdom; if we are hungry for righteousness we will search for it. If you will draw near to God, He promises to meet you.

Matthew (KJV) 7: [6] Give not that which is holy unto the dogs, neither cast ye your pearls before swine, lest they trample them under their feet, and turn again and rend you. [7] Ask, and it shall be given you; seek, and ye shall find; knock, and it shall be opened unto you: [8] For everyone that asketh receiveth; and he that seeketh findeth; and to him that knocketh it shall be opened.

You have to be hungry enough to seek the Kingdom of God for yourself; God will only meet you halfway. If you draw nigh to Him, He will draw nigh to you.

2 Corinthians 4: Therefore seeing we have this ministry, as we have received mercy, we faint not; [2] But have renounced the hidden things of dishonesty, not walking in craftiness, nor handling the word of God deceitfully; but by manifestation of the truth commending ourselves to every man's conscience in the sight of God. [3] But if our gospel (of the Kingdom) be hid, it is hid to them that are lost: [4] In whom the god of this world hath blinded the minds of them which believe not, lest the light of the glorious gospel of Christ, who is the image of God, should shine unto them. [5] For we preach not ourselves, but Christ Jesus the Lord; and ourselves your servants for Jesus' sake. [6] For God, who commanded the light to shine out of darkness, hath shined in our hearts, to give the light of the knowledge of the glory of God in the face of Jesus Christ.

God wants to give us the knowledge, the understanding, and the wisdom of the glory of God that Jesus has because we have been given the mind of Christ. But we need the right knowledge to go into that mind and in this case we need "the light of the knowledge of the glory of God that is in the face of Jesus." Your mind will not fill by itself; you have to ask the Holy Spirit for wisdom by faith, then seek it.

A Proverb to the Foolish or One for the Wise

Proverbs (KJV) 1:1 The proverbs of Solomon the son of David, king of Israel; [2] To know wisdom and instruction; to perceive the words of understanding; [3] To receive the instruction of wisdom, justice, and judgment, and equity; [4] To give subtilty to the simple, to the young man knowledge and discretion. [5] A wise man will hear, and will increase learning; and a man of understanding shall attain unto wise counsels: [6] To understand a proverb, and the interpretation; the words of the wise, and their dark sayings. [7] The fear of the LORD is the beginning of knowledge: but fools despise wisdom and instruction. [8] My son, hear the instruction of thy father, and forsake not the law of thy mother: [9] For they shall be an ornament of grace unto thy head, and chains about thy neck. [10] My son, if sinners entice thee, consent thou not. [11] If they say, Come with us, let us lay wait for blood, let us lurk privily for the innocent without cause: [12] Let us swallow them up alive as the -grave; and whole, as those who go down into the pit: [13] We shall find all precious substance, we shall fill our houses with spoil: [14] Cast in thy lot among us; let us all have one purse: [15] My son, walk not thou in the way with them; refrain thy foot from their path: [16] For their feet run to evil, and make haste to shed blood. [17] Surely in vain the net is spread in the sight of any bird. [18] And they lay wait for their own blood; they lurk privily for their own lives. [19] So are the ways of everyone that is greedy of gain; which taketh away the life of the owners thereof. [20] Wisdom crieth without; she uttereth her voice in the streets: [21] She crieth in the chief place of concourse, in the openings of the gates: in the city she uttereth her words, saying, [22] How long, ye simple ones, will ye love simplicity? and the scorners delight in their scorning, and fools hate knowledge? [23] Turn you at my reproof: behold, I will pour out my spirit unto you, I will make known my words unto you. [24] Because I have called, and ye refused; I have stretched out my hand, and no man regarded; [25] But ye have set at nought all my counsel, and would none of my reproof: [26] I also will laugh at your calamity; I will mock when your fear cometh; [27] When your fear cometh as desolation, and your destruction cometh as a whirlwind; when distress and anguish cometh upon you. [28] Then shall they call upon me, but I will not answer; they shall seek me early, but they shall not find me: [29] For that they hated knowledge, and did not choose the fear of the Lord: [30] They would none of my counsel: they despised all my reproof. [31] Therefore shall they eat of the fruit of their own way, and be filled with their own devices. [32] For the turning away of the simple shall slay them, and the prosperity of fools shall destroy them. [33] But whoso hearkeneth unto me shall dwell safely, and shall be quiet from fear of evil.

[Like all parents we want to see our children grow up, be successful in life and be productive, and above all make a difference in the world. But to be successful we have to have knowledge; either it has to come from an institution or it is learned through life's experiences. That is why we see some people who are very successful and never have achieved any degrees from a university who are more successful than people who have their masters and doctorate degrees.

God wants us to overcome Satan in the spirit realm, but we have to be taught and we have to be willing and want to learn. This is why God sent the Holy Spirit, the same guide that Jesus had. We have to establish a personal relationship with God the Son, God the Father, and God the Holy Spirit. God is going to empower His children who are willing to obey His will. This is why Jesus said seek the Kingdom first. We have to spend more time with God beyond just going to church once or twice a week. Jesus came to give sight to the blind not only physical but spiritually. Christianity is a lifestyle change, and love, joy, peace, longsuffering, gentleness, goodness, faith, meekness, and temperance are the godly characteristics that we have to adopt because the just shall live by these fruit. The Bible tells us not to be conformed to the world but to be transformed by the renewing of our mind that we may prove what the good and perfect will of the Lord is.]

2 Corinthians 4: [7] But we have this treasure in earthen vessels, that the excellency of the power may be of God, and not of us. [8] We are troubled on every side, yet not distressed; we are perplexed, but not in despair; [9] Persecuted, but not forsaken; cast down, but not destroyed; [10] Always bearing about in the body the dying of the Lord Jesus, that the life also of Jesus might be made manifest in our body. [11] For we which live are always delivered unto death for Jesus' sake, that the life also of Jesus might be made manifest in our mortal flesh.

[After Jesus was raised from the dead, He appeared to His disciples to encourage them to feed His sheep. Feeding the people of God was Jesus' main concern from beginning to end. Feeding means providing everything needed to cause our spiritual growth to come to full maturity. Jesus began teaching on this through the parable about the nonbearing fig tree which was going to be given a second chance to bear fruit once it was fed and watered properly. When we become born-again we are like babies, and all babies have to be nourished properly. Jesus held the disciples responsible for feeding His flock. As you read their letters to the different churches they followed his instructions to the letter.

In the New Testament each epistle centers on understanding how the Kingdom of God works. Nearly every epistle teaches sowing into the lives of the less fortunate, keeping ourselves holy before the Lord, and teaching us that as the children of God we are expected to come up to the measure and statue of Christ. Nearly every book keeps reminding us that Jesus is coming back and for us to stay ready by doing the will of God by serving and providing for the needs of others. Not only natural food but spiritual food must be provided. We must walk in love and in faith we have to stay in unity with the Trinity because He said if we do not He will come at a time when we are not expecting Him. Jesus explains clearly what would happen to a tree that had no figs as an example, and He spoke to the tree. He told the tree, "no one shall eat from you again forever," and the next morning it had no choice—it was dead. It was not fulfilling its divine destiny.

The owner's first command was to have the gardener (Jesus) to cut the tree down and cast it into the fire. But the gardener (Jesus) intervened and said let Me dig around it, fertilize it; let Me give the tree (the individuals that are not bearing fruit) the Word of God in more detail and clarity and encourage them and urge them to be productive and bear fruit, because if they do not the gardener (Jesus) will fulfill the owner of the vineyard's (God's) request of cutting the worthless nonbearing fruit tree down and cast it into the fire (hell). Jesus said the same thing again if you are going to be connected to Him and we are members of His body, we have to be a provider to the less fortunate, whether it is physical food or spiritual. I know you think I am repeating myself a lot, but that is okay; Jesus and the disciples have been repeating these things for two thousand years, and we are just now getting it. Jesus is saying the same thing to all ministers who have been given charge over His sheep the same question. Do you really have the agape love from Him to feed and nourish His sheep? Are you a true shepherd, or are you just a hireling.]

Isaiah chapters 11, 65 and 66 are prophecies to our generation about the "End of Days." Please read them and examine your heart because it explains the importance of being nourished by the Holy Spirit.

Isaiah (AMP) 66: *Thus says the Lord: Heaven is My throne, and the earth is My footstool. What kind of house would you build for Me? And what kind can be My resting-place? ² For all these things My hand has made, and so all these things have come into being [by and for Me], says the Lord. But this is the man to whom I will look and have regard: he who is humble and of a broken or wounded spirit, and who trembles at My word and reveres My commands. ³ [The acts of the hypo-crite's worship are as abominable to God as if they were offered to idols.] He who kills an ox [then] will be as guilty as if he slew and sacrificed a man; he who sacrifices a lamb or a kid, as if he broke a dog's neck and sacrificed him; he who offers a cereal offering, as if he offered swine's blood; he who burns incense [to God], as if he blessed an idol. [Such people] have chosen their own ways, and they delight in their abominations; ⁴ So I also will choose their delusions and mockings, their* *calamities and afflictions, and I will bring their fears upon them—because when I called, no one answered; when I spoke, they did not listen or obey. But they did what was evil in My sight and chose that in which I did not delight. [5] Hear the word of the Lord, you who tremble at His word: Your brethren who hate you, who cast you out for My name's sake, have said, Let the Lord be glorified, that we may see your joy! But it is they who shall be put to shame. [6] [Hark!] An uproar from the city! A voice from the temple! The voice of the Lord, rendering recompense to His enemies! [7] Before [Zion] travailed, she gave birth; before her pain came upon her, she was delivered of a male child. [8] Who has heard of such a thing? Who has seen such things? Shall a land be born in one day? Or shall a nation be brought forth in a moment? For as soon as Zion was in labor, she brought forth her children. [9] Shall I bring to the [moment of] birth and not cause to bring forth? says the Lord. Shall I Who causes to bring forth shut the womb? says your God. [10] Rejoice with Jerusalem and be glad for her, all you who love her; rejoice for joy with her, all you who mourn over her, [11] That you may nurse and be satisfied from her consoling breasts, that you may drink deeply and be delighted with the abundance and brightness of her glory.*

Shaddai: meaning fertility

Hebrew *šad* meaning "breast," giving the meaning "the one of the Breast," as Asherah at Ugarit is "the one of the Womb."[9] A similar theory proposed by Albright is that the name Shaddai is connected to *shadayim*, the Hebrew word for "breasts."

Information taken from the Bible Encyclopedia

(Gen. 28:3). "I am God Almighty [El Shaddai]: be fruitful and increase in number" (Gen. 35:11). "By the Almighty [El Shaddai] who will bless you with blessings of heaven above, blessings of the deep that lies beneath, blessings of the breasts [shadayim] and of the womb [racham]" (Gen. 49:25).

In other words God is the source of all life, He provided for everything living when He created the earth. Right now we need spiritual life from God, which is another reason Jesus wanted us to become "one." When you become "one" with someone you think and act alike, you know how they think, what they are going to say, and what they are going to do, and you mimic them because you are in unity: spirit, soul, and body. You love what they love, and you will not betray them for any reason.

Proverbs (KJV) 10: [20] The tongue of the just is as choice silver: the heart of the wicked is little worth. [21] The lips of the righteous feed many: but fools die for want of wisdom. [22] The blessing of the LORD, it maketh rich, and he addeth no sorrow with it.

Proverbs (KJV) 15: [13] A merry heart maketh a cheerful countenance: but by sorrow of the heart the spirit is broken. [14] The heart of him that hath understanding seeketh knowledge: but the mouth of fools feedeth on foolishness.

Figure 2.3 Charity (1878) by William-Adolphe Bouguereau.

Notice the two babies sitting on the steps, and the one that is asleep is full or milked out; the other one is still feeding, and the last one is waiting its turn. But the mother, like God, is making sure all of His real children that come to Him are properly fed. That is why Jesus said we must become like children because such is the Kingdom of God. He is going to care for them just like this mother is caring for her children with "agape love." Jesus was telling Peter, "It is vital that you nourish My sheep, teach them everything that they need to know so they can flourish and fulfill their God-given purposes."

Isaiah (AMP) 66: *[12] For thus says the Lord: Behold, I will extend peace to her like a river, and the glory of the nations like an overflowing stream; then you will be nursed, you will be carried on her hip and trotted [lovingly bounced up and down] on her [God's maternal] knees. [13] As one whom his mother comforts, so will I comfort you; you shall be comforted in Jerusalem. [14] When you see this, your heart shall rejoice; your bones shall flourish like green and tender grass. And the [powerful] hand of the Lord shall be revealed and known to be with His servants,* but His indignation [shown] to be against His enemies. [15] For behold, the Lord will come in fire, and His chariots will be like the stormy wind, to render His anger with fierceness, and His rebuke with flames of fire.[16] For by fire and by His sword will the Lord execute judgment upon all flesh, and the slain of the

Lord will be many. [17] Those who [attempt to] sanctify themselves and cleanse themselves to enter [and sacrifice to idols] in the gardens, following after one in the midst, eating hog's flesh and the abomination [creeping things] and the [mouse—their works and their thoughts] shall come to an end together, says the Lord. [18] For I know their works and their thoughts. And the time is coming when I will gather all nations and tongues, and they will come and see My glory. [19] And I will set up a [miraculous] sign among them, and from them I will send survivors to the nations—to Tarshish, Pul (Put), and Lud, who draw the bow, to Tubal and Javan, to the isles *and* coastlands afar off that have not heard of My fame nor seen My glory. And they will declare *and* proclaim My glory among the nations. [20] And they shall bring all your brethren from all the nations as an offering to the Lord—upon horses and in chariots and in litters and upon mules and upon camels—to My holy mountain Jerusalem, says the Lord, just as the children of Israel bring their cereal offering in a clean vessel to the house of the Lord. [21] And I will also take some of them for priests and for Levites, says the Lord.

Figure 2.4 The New Jerusalem coming down (Tapestry of the Apocalypse).

When This Event Occurs Will You Be Looking Up or Down?

Isaiah (AMP) 66: [22] For as the new heavens and the new earth which I make shall remain before Me, says the Lord, so shall your offspring and your name remain. [23] And it shall be that from one New Moon to another New Moon and from one Sabbath to another Sabbath, all flesh shall come to worship before Me, says the Lord. [24] **And they shall go forth and gaze upon the dead bodies of the [rebellious] men who have stepped over against Me; for their worm shall not die, their fire shall not be quenched, and they shall be an abhorrence to all mankind.**

Even my wife, who reads through the Bible over and over again as many people do, said she did not notice what this verse says. After the New Heaven and New Earth are created, you will still be able to look down and see people in hell still suffering throughout eternity, as a reminder to all of us. It is God's will that everyone be saved, but God has given all of us a free will and we as individuals have to make a decision. God tells us we have two choices, and He strongly recommends that we should choose LIFE!

Deuteronomy (KJV)30: [18] I denounce unto you this day, that ye shall surely perish, and that ye shall not prolong your days upon the land, whither thou passest over Jordan to go to possess it. [19] I call heaven and earth to record this day against you, that I have set before you life and death, blessing and cursing: therefore choose life, that both thou and thy seed may live: [20] That thou mayest love the LORD thy God, and that thou mayest obey his voice, and that thou mayest cleave unto him: for he is thy life, and the length of thy days: that thou mayest dwell in the land which the LORD sware unto thy fathers, to Abraham, to Isaac, and to Jacob, to give them.

Remember Lazarus and the rich man: the rich man is still in hell today, and Lazarus is in Heaven. While we are in the land of the living we have to decide if we are going to live for God or live for ourselves and the devil.

The Lord Answers Isaiah's Prayer

Isaiah (AMP) 65: I was [ready to be] inquired of by those who asked not; I was [ready to be] found by those who sought Me not. I said, Here I am, here I am [says I AM] to a nation [Israel] that has not called on My name. [2] I have spread out My hands all the day long to a rebellious people, who walk in a way that is not good, after their own thoughts—[3] A people who provoke Me to My face continually, sacrificing [to idols] in gardens and burning incense upon bricks [instead of at God's prescribed altar];[4] Who sit among the graves [trying to talk with the dead] and lodge among the secret places [or caves where familiar spirits were thought to dwell]; who eat swine's flesh, and the broth of abominable *and* loathsome things is in their vessels; [5] Who say, Keep to yourself; do not come near me, for I am set apart from you [and lest I sanctify you]! These are smoke in My nostrils, a fire that burns all the day. [6] Behold, it is written before Me: I will not keep silence but will repay; yes, I will repay into their bosom [7] Both your own iniquities and the iniquities of your fathers, says the Lord. Because they too burned incense upon the mountains and reviled *and* blasphemed Me upon the hills, therefore will I measure *and* stretch out their former doings into their own bosom. [8] *Thus says the Lord: As the juice [of the grape] is found in the cluster, and one says, Do not destroy it, for there is a blessing in it, so will I do for My servants' sake, that I may not destroy them all. [9] And I will bring forth an offspring from Jacob, and from Judah an inheritor of My mountains; My chosen and elect will inherit it, and My servants will dwell there. [10] And [the plain of] Sharon shall be a pasture and fold for flocks, and the Valley of Achor a place for herds to lie down, for My people who seek Me, inquire of Me, and require Me [by right of their necessity and by right of My invitation].*[11] But you who forsake the Lord, who forget *and* ignore My holy Mount [Zion], who prepare a table for Gad [the Babylonian god of fortune] and who furnish mixed drinks for Meni [the god of destiny]—[12] I will destine you [says the Lord] for the sword, and you shall all bow down to the slaughter, because when I called, you did not answer; when I spoke, you did not listen *or* obey. But you did what was evil in My eyes, and you chose that in which I did not delight. [13] Therefore thus says the Lord God: Behold, My servants shall eat, but you shall be hungry; behold, My servants shall drink, but you shall be thirsty; behold, My servants shall rejoice, but you shall be put to shame. [14] Behold, My servants shall sin

Figure 2.5 The Last Judgment by Jean Cousin the Younger.

but you shall cry out for pain and sorrow of heart and shall wail and howl for anguish, vexation, and breaking of spirit. ¹⁵ And you will leave your name to My chosen [to those who will use it] for a curse; and the Lord God will slay you, but He will call His servants by another name [as much greater than the former name as the name Israel was greater than the name Jacob]. ¹⁶ So [it shall be] that he who invokes a blessing on himself in the land shall do so by saying, May the God of truth and fidelity [the Amen] bless me; and he who takes an oath in the land shall swear by the God of truth and faithfulness to His promises [the Amen], because the former troubles are forgotten and because they are hidden from My eyes.¹⁷ For behold, I create new heavens and a new earth. And the former things shall not be remembered or come into mind.¹⁸ But be glad and rejoice forever in that which I create; for behold, I create Jerusalem to be a rejoicing and her people a joy. ¹⁹ And I will rejoice in Jerusalem and be glad in My people; and the sound of weeping will no more be heard in it, nor the cry of distress. ²⁰ There shall no more be in it an infant who lives but a few days, or an old man who dies prematurely; for the child shall die a hundred years old, and the sinner who dies when only a hundred years old shall be [thought only a child, cut off because he is] accursed. ²¹ They shall build houses and inhabit them, and they shall plant vineyards and eat the fruit of them. ²² They shall not build and another in habit; they shall not plant and another eat [the fruit]. For as the days of a tree, so shall be the days of My people, and My chosen and elect shall long make use of and enjoy the work of their hands. ²³ They shall not labor in vain or bring forth [children] for sudden terror or calamity; for they shall be the descendants of the blessed of the Lord, and their offspring with them. ²⁴ And it shall be that before they call I will answer; and while they are yet speaking I will hear.²⁵ The wolf and the lamb shall feed together, and the lion *shall eat straw like the ox; and dust shall be the serpent's food. They shall not hurt or destroy in all My holy Mount [Zion], says the Lord.*

Figure 2.6 Image of an etching by artist William Strutt in 1896. Isaiah 11: 6, 7.

Isaiah (AMP) 11: *And there shall come forth a Shoot out of the stock of Jesse [David's father], and a Branch out of his roots shall grow and bear fruit. [2] And the Spirit of the Lord shall rest upon Him—the Spirit of wisdom and understanding, the Spirit of counsel and might, the Spirit of knowledge and of the reverential and obedient fear of the Lord—[3] And shall make Him of quick understanding, and His delight shall be in the reverential and obedient fear of the Lord. And He shall not judge by the sight of His eyes, neither decide by the hearing of His ears; [4] But with righteousness and justice shall He judge the poor and decide with fairness for the meek, the poor, and the downtrodden of the earth; and He shall smite the earth and the oppressor with the rod of His mouth, and with the breath of His lips He shall slay the wicked.[5] And righteousness shall be the girdle of His waist and faithfulness the girdle of His loins.[6] And the wolf shall dwell with the lamb, and the leopard shall lie down with the kid, and the calf and the young lion and the fatted domestic animal together; and a little child shall lead them.[7] And the cow and the bear shall feed side by side, their young shall lie down together, and the lion shall eat straw like the ox. [8] And the sucking child shall play over the hole of the asp, and the weaned child shall put his hand on the adder's den. [9] They shall not hurt or destroy in all My holy mountain, for the earth shall be full of the knowledge of the Lord as the waters cover the sea. [10] And it shall be in that day that the Root of Jesse shall stand as a signal for the peoples; of Him shall the nations inquire and seek knowledge, and His dwelling shall be glory [His rest glorious]! [11] And in that day the Lord shall again lift up His hand a second time to recover (acquire and deliver) the remnant of His people which is left, from Assyria, from Lower Egypt, from Pathros, from Ethiopia, from Elam [in Persia], from Shinar [Babylonia], from Hamath [in Upper Syria], and from the countries bordering on the [Mediterra-*

nean] Sea. [12] And He will raise up a signal for the nations and will assemble the outcasts of Israel and will gather together the dispersed of Judah from the four corners of the earth. [13] The envy and jealousy of Ephraim also shall depart, and they who vex and harass Judah from outside or inside shall be cut off; Ephraim shall not envy Judah, and Judah shall not vex and harass Ephraim. [14] But [with united forces Ephraim and Judah] will swoop down upon the shoulders of the Philistines' [land sloping] toward the west; together they will strip the people on the east [the Arabs]. They will lay their hands upon Edom and Moab, and the Ammonites will obey them. [15] And the Lord will utterly destroy (doom and dry up) the tongue of the Egyptian sea [the west fork of the Red Sea]; and with His [mighty] scorching wind He will wave His hand over the river [Nile] and will smite it into seven channels and will cause men to cross over dry-shod. [16] And there shall be a highway from Assyria for the remnant left of His people, as there was for Israel when they came up out of the land of Egypt.

1 Peter (KJV) 2: Wherefore laying aside all malice, and all guile, and hypocrisies, and envies, and all evil speakings, [2] As newborn babes, desire the sincere milk of the word, that ye may grow thereby: [3] If so be ye have tasted that the Lord is gracious. [4] To whom coming, as unto a living stone, disallowed indeed of men, but chosen of God, and precious, [5] Ye also, as lively stones, are built up a spiritual house, an holy priesthood, to offer up spiritual sacrifices, acceptable to God by Jesus Christ.

Hebrews 5: [8] Though he were a Son, yet learned he obedience by the things which he suffered; [9] And being made perfect, he became the author of eternal salvation unto all them that obey him; [10] Called of God an high priest after the order of Melchisedec. [11] Of whom we have many things to say, and hard to be uttered, seeing ye are dull of hearing. *[12] For when for the time ye ought to be teachers, ye have need that one teach you again which be the first principles of the oracles of God; and are become such as have need of milk, and not of strong meat. [13] For every one that useth milk is unskilful in the word of righteousness: for he is a babe. [14] But strong meat belongeth to them that are of full age, even those who by reason of use have their senses exercised to discern both good and evil.*

2 Thessalonians 3: [4] And we have confidence in the Lord touching you, that ye both do and will do the things which we command you. [5] And the Lord direct your hearts into the love of God, and into the patient waiting for Christ. [6] Now we command you, brethren, in the name of our Lord Jesus Christ, that ye withdraw yourselves from every brother that walketh disorderly, and not after the tradition which he received of us.

Jude 1: *[20] But ye, beloved, building up yourselves on your most holy faith, praying in the Holy Ghost, [21] Keep yourselves in the love of God, looking for the mercy of our Lord Jesus Christ unto eternal life. [22] And of some have compassion, making a difference: [23] And others save with fear, pulling them out of the fire; hating even the garment spotted by the flesh. [24] Now unto him that is able to keep you from falling, and to present you faultless before the presence of his glory with exceeding joy, [25] To the only wise God our Saviour, be glory and majesty, dominion and power, both now and ever. Amen.*

1 John 5: [2] By this we know that we love the children of God, when we love God, and keep his commandments. [3] For this is the love of God, that we keep his commandments: and his commandments are not grievous. [4] For whatsoever is born of God overcometh the world: and this is the victory that overcometh the world, even our faith.

As we established earlier, the fruit of the Spirit also function as the keys to the Kingdom. They form and make up the different parts of the armor of God as mentioned before. The seeds of each fruit (love, joy, peace, etc.) were sown in our hearts at the time of the new birth and when we were filled with the Holy Spirit.

In order for us to develop these fruits, we will be faced with opportunities to exercise the faith of God. We will be confronted with situations that will cause our faith to grow stronger. That is why Jesus said if we are bearing fruit we will be pruned so our faith will be forced to grow even more. The same goes for the other fruit because God wants us to cultivate all the fruit of the Spirit.

Galatians (KJV) 5: [21] Envyings, murders, drunkenness, revellings, and such like: of the which I tell you before, as I have also told you in time past, that they which do such things shall not inherit the kingdom of God. [22] But the fruit of the Spirit is love, joy, peace, longsuffering, gentleness, goodness, faith, [23] Meekness, temperance: against such there is no law.

2 Peter (KJV) 1:1 Simon Peter, a servant and an apostle of Jesus Christ, to them that have obtained like precious faith with us through the righteousness of God and our Saviour Jesus Christ: [2] Grace and peace be multiplied unto you through the knowledge of God, and of Jesus our Lord, [3] According as his divine power hath given unto us all things that pertain unto life and godliness, through the knowledge of him that hath called us to glory and virtue: [4] Whereby are given unto us exceeding great and precious promises: that by these ye might be partakers of the divine nature, having escaped the corruption that is in the world through lust. [5] And beside this, giving all diligence, add to your faith virtue; and to virtue knowledge; [6] And to knowledge temperance; and to temperance patience; and to patience godliness; [7] And to godliness brotherly kindness; and to brotherly kindness charity. [8] For if these things be in you, and abound, they make you that ye shall neither be barren nor unfruitful in the knowledge of our Lord Jesus Christ.

We have to love God enough with all our heart, soul, mind, and strength that we are willing to change because we want to escape the destruction that is coming on the earth. God wants His children to be with Him; He does not want His children to suffer with the wicked.

The definitions below were taken from Merriam-Webster.com.

Knowledge—the fact or condition of knowing something with familiarity gained through experience of knowing something with familiarity gained through experience or association: the body of truth, information, and principles acquired by humankind. The fact or condition of knowing something with familiarity gained through experience or association.

Understand—a mental grasp: COMPREHENSION the power of comprehending; *especially*: the capacity to apprehend general relations of particulars *b*: the power to make experience intelligible by applying concepts and categories

Wisdom—accumulated philosophic or scientific learning : KNOWLEDGE *b*: ability to discern inner qualities and relationships : INSIGHT *c*: good sense : JUDGMENT *d*: generally accepted belief <challenges what has become accepted *wisdom* among many historians — Robert Darnton> : a wise attitude, belief, or course of action: the teachings of the ancient wise men.

Biblical wisdom is when you take knowledge from the Bible and understand it through explanation and interpretation through pastors, teachers, and so forth, but it does not become wisdom until you apply it to your spiritual life.

Figure 2.7 The Blind Leading the Blind (c. 1561) by Pieter van der Heyden

2 Peter (KJV) 1: [9] But he that lacketh these things is blind, and cannot see afar off, and hath forgotten that he was purged from his old sins. [10] Wherefore the rather, brethren, give diligence to make your calling and election sure: for if ye do these things, ye shall never fall: [11] For so an entrance shall be ministered unto you abundantly into the everlasting kingdom of our Lord and Saviour Jesus Christ. [12] Wherefore I will not be negligent to put you always in remembrance of these things, though ye know them, and be established in the present truth. [13] Yea, I think it meet, as long as I am in this tabernacle, to stir you up by putting you in remembrance; [14] Knowing that shortly I must put off this my tabernacle, even as our Lord Jesus Christ hath shewed me.

Matthew (KJV) 5: [18] For verily I say unto you, Till heaven and earth pass, one jot or one tittle shall in no wise pass from the law, till all be fulfilled. [19] Whosoever therefore shall break one of these least commandments, and shall teach men so, he shall be called the least in the kingdom of heaven.

Matthew (KJV) 7: [20] Wherefore by their fruits ye shall know them. [21] Not every one that saith unto me, Lord, Lord, shall enter into the kingdom of heaven; but he that doeth the will of my Father which is in heaven. [22] *Many will say to me in that day, Lord, Lord, have we not prophesied in thy name? and in thy name have cast out devils? and in thy name done many wonderful works?* but whosoever shall do and teach them, the same shall be called great in the kingdom of heaven. [20] *For I say unto you, That except your righteousness shall exceed the righteousness of the scribes and Pharisees, ye shall in no case enter into the kingdom of heaven.*

Matthew (KJV) 8: [11] And I say unto you, That many shall come from the east and west, and shall sit down with Abraham, and Isaac, and Jacob, in the kingdom of heaven. [12] But the children of the kingdom (the Jews that refuse to believe that Jesus is the Savior) shall be cast out into outer darkness: there shall be weeping and gnashing of teeth.

Matthew (KJV) 13: [40] *As therefore the tares are gathered and burned in the fire; so shall it be in the end of this world.* [41] *The Son of man shall send forth his angels, and* they shall gather out of his kingdom all things that offend, and them which do iniquity; [42] And shall cast them into a furnace of fire: there shall be wailing and gnashing of teeth. [43] Then shall the righteous shine forth as the sun in the kingdom of their Father. Who hath ears to hear, let him hear.

Matthew (KJV) 16: [18] And I say also unto thee, *That thou art Peter, and upon this rock I will build my church; and the gates of hell shall not prevail against it.* [19] *And I will give unto thee the keys of the kingdom of heaven: and whatsoever thou shalt bind on earth shall be bound in Heaven: and whatsoever thou shalt loose on earth shall be loosed in heaven.*

Matthew (KJV)18: [2] And Jesus called a little child unto him, and set him in the midst of them, [3] *And said, Verily I say unto you, Except ye be converted, and become as little children, ye shall not enter into the kingdom of heaven. [4] Whosoever therefore shall humble himself as this little child, the same is greatest in the kingdom of heaven.*

Matthew 19: [13] Then were there brought unto him little children, that he should put his hands on them, and pray: and the disciples rebuked them. [14] But Jesus said, Suffer little children, and forbid them not, to come unto me: for of such is the kingdom of heaven. [15] And he laid his hands on them, and departed thence. Wherefore the rather, brethren, give diligence to make your calling and election sure: for if ye do these things, ye shall never fall: For so an entrance shall be ministered unto you abundantly into the everlasting kingdom of our Lord and Saviour Jesus Christ.

Hebrews (KJV) 11: Now faith is the substance of things hoped for, the evidence of things not seen.

Romans (KJV) 10: [16] But have not all obeyed the gospel. For Esaias saith, Lord, who hath believed our report? [17] So then faith cometh by hearing, and hearing by the word of God. [18] But I say, have they not heard? Yes verily, their sound went into all the earth, and their words unto the ends of the world.

Mark 11: [20] And in the morning, as they passed by, they saw the fig tree dried up from the roots. [21] And Peter calling to remembrance saith unto him, Master, behold, the fig tree which thou cursedst is withered away. [22] And Jesus answering saith unto them, Have faith in God. [23] For verily I say unto you, That whosoever shall say unto this mountain, Be thou removed, and be thou cast into the sea; and shall not doubt in his heart, but shall believe that those things which he saith shall come to pass; he shall have whatsoever he saith. [24] Therefore I say unto you, What things soever ye desire, when ye pray, believe that ye receive them, and ye shall have them. [25] And when ye stand praying, forgive, if ye have ought against any: that your Father also which is in heaven may forgive you your trespasses. [26] But if ye do not forgive, neither will your Father which is in heaven forgive your trespasses. [27] And they come again to Jerusalem: and as he was walking in the temple, there come to him the chief priests, and the scribes, and the elders, [28] And say unto him, By what authority doest thou these things? and who gave thee this authority to do these things? [29] And Jesus answered and said unto them, I will also ask of you one question, and answer me, and I will tell you by what authority I do these things. [30] The baptism of John, was it from heaven, or of men? answer me. [31] And they reasoned with themselves, saying, If we shall say, From heaven; he will say, Why then did ye not believe him? [32] But if we shall say, Of men; they feared the people: for all men counted John, that he was a prophet indeed. [33] And they answered and said unto Jesus, We cannot tell. And Jesus answering saith unto them, Neither do I tell you by what authority I do these things.

I Peter 1 tells us how to begin nourishing and cultivating the fruit of the Spirit.

Your faith is a key fruit that we must develop to bring us into the Lord's presence at the time of His appearing. I know that we are all dealing with issues in our lives now: whether it is health, finances, job situations, and so on, it all comes with the process of developing our faith and taking it to a higher level. We must remember that we have been justified by faith, and we must live by our faith which is a lifestyle, or how we should live on day-to-day basis. The same holds true for all the other Fruit of the Spirit, we will be faced with situations that cause us to develop and use the love of God and drive out hatred, lust, violence and so forth.

Notice how many times that your faith is required and what it is used for.

1 Peter (KJV)1: I, Peter, an apostle of Jesus Christ, to the strangers scattered throughout Pontus, Galatia, Cappadocia, Asia, and Bithynia, [2] Elect according to the foreknowledge of God the Father, through sanctification of the Spirit, unto obedience and sprinkling of the blood of Jesus Christ: Grace unto you, and peace, be multiplied. [3] Blessed be the God and Father of our Lord Jesus Christ, which according to his abundant mercy hath begotten us again unto a lively hope by the resurrection of Jesus Christ from the dead, [4] To an inheritance incorruptible, and undefiled, and that fadeth not away, reserved in heaven for you, *[5] Who are kept by the power of God through faith unto salvation ready to be revealed in the last time. [6] Wherein ye greatly rejoice, though now for a season, if need be, ye are in heaviness through manifold temptations: [7] That the trial of your faith, being much more precious than of gold that perisheth, though it be tried with fire, might be found unto praise and honour and glory at the appearing of Jesus Christ: [8] Whom having not seen, ye love; in* *whom, though now ye see him not, yet believing, ye rejoice with joy unspeakable and full of glory: ⁹ Receiving the end of your faith, even the salvation of your souls. ¹⁰ Of which salvation the prophets have enquired and searched diligently, who prophesied of the grace that should come unto you: ¹¹ Searching what, or what manner of time the Spirit of Christ which was in them did signify, when it testified beforehand the sufferings of Christ, and the glory that should follow.¹² Unto whom it was revealed, that not unto themselves, but unto us they did minister the things, which are now reported unto you by them that have preached the gospel unto you with the Holy Ghost sent down from heaven; which things the angels desire to look into. ¹³ Wherefore gird up the loins of your mind, be sober, and hope to the end for the grace that is to be brought unto you at the revelation of Jesus Christ; ¹⁴ As obedient children, not fashioning yourselves according to the former lusts in your ignorance: ¹⁵ But as he which hath called you is holy, so be ye holy in all manner of conversation; ¹⁶ Because it is written, Be ye holy; for I am holy. ¹⁷ And if ye call on the Father, who without respect of persons judgeth according to every man's work, pass the time of your sojourning here in fear: ¹⁸ Forasmuch as ye know that ye were not redeemed with corruptible things, as silver and gold, from your vain conversation received by tradition from your fathers; ¹⁹ But with the precious blood of Christ, as of a lamb without blemish and without spot: ²⁰ Who verily was foreordained before the foundation of the world, but was manifest in these last times for you,²¹ Who by him do believe in God, that raised him up from the dead, and gave him glory; that your faith and hope might be in God. ²² Seeing ye have purified your souls in obeying the truth through the Spirit unto unfeigned love of the brethren, see that ye love one another with a pure heart fervently: ²³ Being born again, not of corruptible seed, but of incorruptible, by the word of God, which liveth and abideth forever. ²⁴ For all flesh is as grass, and all the glory of man as the flower of grass. The grass withereth, and the flower thereof falleth away: ²⁵ But the word of the Lord endureth forever. And this is the word which by the gospel is preached unto you.*

Matthew 17: ¹³ Then the disciples understood that he spake unto them of John the Baptist. ¹⁴ And when they were come to the multitude, there came to him a certain man, kneeling down to him, and saying, ¹⁵ Lord, have mercy on my son: for he is lunatick, and sore vexed: for ofttimes he falleth into the fire, and oft into the water. ¹⁶ And I brought him to thy disciples, and they could not cure him. ¹⁷ Then Jesus answered and said, O faithless and perverse generation, how long shall I be with you? how long shall I suffer you? bring him hither to me. ¹⁸ And Jesus rebuked the devil; and he departed out of him: and the child was cured from that very hour.

Figure 2.8 Transfiguration by Raphael.

Matthew 17: ¹⁹ Then came the disciples to Jesus apart, and said, Why could not we cast him out? ²⁰ And Jesus said unto them, Because of your unbelief: for verily I say unto you If ye have faith as a grain of mustard seed, ye shall say unto this mountain, Remove hence to yonder place; and it shall remove; and nothing shall be impossible unto you. ²¹ Howbeit this kind goeth not out but by prayer and fasting.

John 20: *²⁴ But Thomas, one of the twelve, called Didymus, was not with them when Jesus came. ²⁵ The other disciples therefore said unto him, We have seen the L*ORD*. But he said unto them, Except I shall see in his hands the print of the nails, and put my finger into the print of the nails, and thrust my hand into his side, I will not believe. ²⁶ And after eight days again his disciples were within, and Thomas with them: then came Jesus, the doors being shut, and stood in the midst, and said, Peace be unto you. ²⁷ Then saith he to Thomas, Reach hither thy finger, and behold my hands; and reach hither thy hand, and thrust it into my side: and be not faithless, but believing. ²⁸ And Thomas answered and said unto him, My L*ORD *and my God.*

Figure 2.9 The Incredulity of <u>Saint Thomas</u> by <u>Caravaggio</u>.

John 20: [29] Jesus saith unto him, Thomas, because thou hast seen me, thou hast believed: blessed are they that have not seen, and yet have believed. [30] And many other signs truly did Jesus in the presence of his disciples, which are not written in this book: [31] But these are written, that ye might believe that Jesus is the Christ, the Son of God; and that believing ye might have life through his name.

Luke 18: And he spake a parable unto them to this end, that men ought always to pray, and not to faint; [2] Saying, There was in a city a judge, which feared not God, neither regarded man: [3] And there was a widow in that city; and she came unto him, saying, Avenge me of mine adversary.

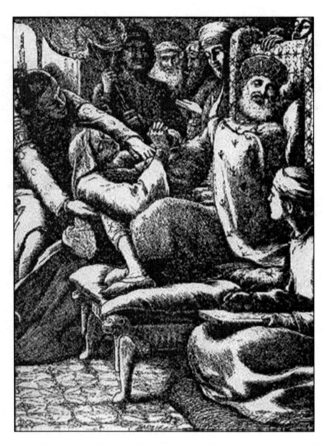

Figure 2.10 Illustration of the Parable of the Unjust Judge from the New Testament Gospel of Luke (Luke 18:1-9) by John Everett Millais for *The Parables of Our Lord* (1863).

Luke 18: ⁴And he would not for a while: but afterward he said within himself, Though I fear not God, nor regard man; ⁵Yet because this widow troubleth me, I will avenge her, lest by her continual coming she weary me. ⁶And the Lord said, Hear what the unjust judge saith. ⁷*And shall not God avenge his own elect, which cry day and night unto him, though he bear long with them? ⁸I tell you that he will avenge them speedily. Nevertheless when the Son of man cometh, shall he find faith on the earth? ⁹And he spake this parable unto certain which trusted in themselves that they were righteous, and despised others:*

We must stay in the Word through studying, meditating, praying, examining our thoughts, actions and true motives to make sure that they match and mimic what we hear in our spirits from being *one* with God, and walk in the fruits of the Spirit and we must put on the whole armor of God. We must establish a personal relationship with the Holy Spirit. Always ask God to give you a deeper understanding of the Word of God, especially about the things that you currently do not understand and any other questions that you may have in your heart about the Word of God. But remember when you are asking for wisdom from the Holy Spirit about the Bible, always ask in faith. That means you are expecting an answer from God, it also means you are doing your daily Bible study and praying. The Holy Spirit will lead you to the answers that you are seeking; this is a promise from God. But if you never ask for wisdom He will not lead or guide you into the truth. He will not say one word. If we draw near to God and He will draw near to us.

Colossians (KJV) 3: [15] And let the peace of God rule in your hearts, to the which also ye are called in one body; and be ye thankful. *[16] Let the word of Christ dwell in you richly in all wisdom; teaching and admonishing one another in psalms and hymns and spiritual songs, singing with grace in your hearts to the Lord. [17] And whatsoever ye do in word or deed, do all in the name of the Lord Jesus, giving thanks to God and the Father by him.*

John (KJV) 16: [12] I have yet many things to say unto you, but ye cannot bear them now. [13] Howbeit when he, the Spirit of truth, is come, he will guide you into all truth: for he shall not speak of himself; but whatsoever he shall hear, that shall he speak *and he will shew you things to come*. [14] He shall glorify me: for he shall receive of mine, and shall shew it unto you.

This is the purpose for which Jesus sent the Holy Spirit—it is for our benefit. It is really sad for a born-again Christian to never take advantage of the next greatest gift that has been given to mankind. We must daily put on the armor of God because our warfare is against the kingdom of darkness. Satan wants to stop our spiritual growth any way he can because he wants to keep us in bondage.

Ephesians 4: [17] This I say therefore, and testify in the Lord, that ye henceforth walk not as other *Gentiles walk, in the vanity of their mind, [18] Having the understanding darkened, being alienated from the life of God through the ignorance that is in them, because of the blindness of their heart: [19] Who being past feeling have given themselves over unto lasciviousness, to work all uncleanness with greediness.* [20] But ye have not so learned Christ; [21] If so be that ye have heard him, and have been taught by him, as the truth is in Jesus: [22] That ye put off concerning the former conversation the old man, which is corrupt according to the deceitful lusts; 23And be renewed in the spirit of your mind; [24] And that ye put on the new man, which after God is created in righteousness and true holiness. [25] Wherefore putting away lying, speak every man truth with his neighbour: for we are members one of another. [26] Be ye angry, and sin not: let not the sun go down upon your wrath: [27] Neither give place to the devil. [28] Let him that stole steal no more: but rather let him labour, working with his hands the thing which is good, that he may have to give to him that needeth. (This is bearing Fruit providing for the needs of others.) [29] Let no corrupt communication proceed out of your mouth, *but that which is good to the use of edifying, that it may minister grace unto the hearers. [30] And grieve not the Holy Spirit of God, whereby ye are sealed unto the day of redemption.*

James (KJV) 3: [6] And the tongue is a fire, a world of iniquity: so is the tongue among our members, that it defileth the whole body, and setteth on fire the course of nature; and it is set on fire of hell. [7] For every kind of beasts, and of birds, and of serpents, and of things in the sea, is tamed, and hath been tamed of mankind: [8] But the tongue can no man tame; it is an unruly evil, full of deadly poison. [9] Therewith bless we God, even the Father; and therewith curse we men, which are made after the similitude of God. [10] Out of the same mouth proceedeth blessing and cursing. My brethren, these things ought not so to be. and bitter? [12] Can the fig tree, my brethren, bear olive berries? either a vine, figs? so can no fountain both yield salt water and fresh. [13] Who is a wise man and endued with knowledge among you? let him shew out of a good conversation his works with meekness of wisdom. [14] But if ye have bitter envying and strife in your hearts, glory not, and lie not against the truth.[15] This wisdom descendeth not from above, but is earthly, sensual, devilish. [16] For where envying and strife is, there is confusion and every evil work. *[17] But the wisdom that is from above* *is first pure, then peaceable, gentle, and easy to be intreated, full of mercy and good fruits, without partiality, and without hypocrisy.* [18] *And the fruit of righteousness is sown in peace of them that make peace.*

James 5: Go to now, ye rich men, weep and howl for your miseries that shall come upon you. [2] Your riches are corrupted, and your garments are moth eaten. [3] Your gold and silver is cankered; and the rust of them shall be a witness against you, and shall eat your flesh as it were fire. Ye have heaped treasure together for the last days. [4] Behold, the hire of the labourers who have reaped down your fields, which is of you kept back by fraud, crieth: and the cries of them which have reaped are entered into the ears of the Lord of sabaoth. [5] Ye have lived in pleasure on the earth, and been wanton; ye have nourished your hearts, as in a day of slaughter. [6] Ye have condemned and killed the just; and he doth not resist you. [7] *Be patient therefore, brethren, unto the coming of the Lord. Behold, the husbandman waiteth for the precious fruit of the earth, and hath long patience for it, until he receive the early and latter rain.*

The return of the Lord is linked to our bearing Fruit.

Notice in James 5:7 how the coming of the Lord is linked to the "precious fruit of the Earth," and God is waiting for us to bear fruit—or in other words, He is waiting for us to start *living the Word*. Now is the time for us to fulfill our God-given destinies by reaching out to help meet the needs of others. What we do to help others will determine whether or not Jesus knows us or not. Are you doing your best to feed the hungry, clothe the naked, visit the sick and those who are in prison? Remember the widow's mite? She gave more than all the people who had great wealth. Jesus is looking at what you are holding back, like Ananias with Sapphira. They promised to give a certain amount but they did not and lied to the Holy Spirit and died instantly. God is revealing to us what He is expecting of us so we will have time to prepare ourselves for His return, so we can do what we have been pre-ordained to accomplish.

Mark 13: [28]*Now learn a parable of the fig tree; When her branch is yet tender, and putteth forth leaves, ye know that summer is near:* [29] *So ye in like manner, when ye shall see these things come to pass, know that it is nigh, even at the doors.*[30] *Verily I say unto you, that this generation shall not pass, till all these things be done.* [31] *Heaven and earth shall pass away: but my words shall not pass away.*[32] *But of that day and that hour knoweth no man, no, not the angels which are in heaven, neither the Son, but the Father.* [33] *Take ye heed, watch and pray: for ye know not when the time is.*

James 5: [7] *Be patient therefore, brethren, unto the coming of the Lord. Behold, the /husbandman waiteth for the precious fruit of the earth, and hath long patience for it, until he receive the early and latter rain.* [8] *Be ye also patient; establish your hearts: for the coming of the Lord draweth nigh.*

I want to review Psalm 112 again because it describes how to establish your heart.

Psalm (KJV) 112 Praise ye the LORD. Blessed is the man that feareth the LORD, that delighteth greatly in his commandments. [2] His seed shall be mighty upon earth: the generation of the upright shall be blessed. [3] Wealth and riches shall be in his house: and his righteousness endureth forever. [4] Unto the upright there ariseth light in the darkness: he is gracious, and full of compassion, and righteous. [5] A good man sheweth favour, and lendeth: he will guide his affairs with discretion. [6] Surely he shall not be moved forever: the righteous shall be in everlasting remembrance. [7] He shall not be afraid of evil tidings: his heart is fixed, trusting in the LORD. [8] *His heart is established,* he shall not be afraid, until he see his desire upon his enemies. [9] He hath dispersed, he hath given to the poor; his righteousness endureth for ever; his horn shall be exalted with honour. [10] The wicked shall see it, and be grieved; he shall gnash with his teeth, and melt away: the desire of the wicked shall perish.

James 5: *[9] Grudge not one against another, brethren, lest ye be condemned: behold, the judge standeth before the door. [10] Take, my brethren, the prophets, who have spoken in the name of the Lord, for an example of suffering affliction, and of patience. [11] Behold, we count them happy which endure. Ye have heard of the patience of Job, and have seen the end of the Lord; that the Lord is very pitiful, and of tender mercy. [12] But above all things, my brethren, swear not, neither by heaven, neither by the earth, neither by any other oath: but let your yea be yea; and your nay, nay; lest ye fall into condemnation.*

Ephesians 5: *[5] For this ye know, that no whoremonger, nor unclean person, nor covetous man, who is an idolater, hath any inheritance in the kingdom of Christ and of God. [6] Let no man deceive you with vain words: for because of these things cometh the wrath of God upon the children of disobedience. [7] Be not ye therefore partakers with them. [8] For ye were sometimes darkness, but now are ye light in the Lord: walk as children of light: [9] (For the fruit of the Spirit is in all goodness and righteousness and truth;) [10] Proving what is acceptable unto the Lord. [11] And have no fellowship with the unfruitful works of darkness, but rather reprove them. [12] For it is a shame even to speak of those things which are done of them in secret. [13] But all things that are reproved are made manifest by the light: for whatsoever doth make manifest is light.*

2 Corinthians 6: *[1] We then, as workers together with him, beseech you also that ye receive not the grace of God in vain. [2] (For he saith, I have heard thee in a time accepted, and in the day of salvation have I succoured thee: behold, now is the accepted time; behold, now is the day of salvation.) [3] Giving no offence in anything, that the ministry be not blamed:* [4] But in all things approving ourselves as the ministers of God, in much patience, in afflictions, in necessities, in distresses, [5] In stripes, in imprisonments, in tumults, in labours, in watchings, in fastings; [6] By pureness, by knowledge, by long suffering, by kindness, by the Holy Ghost, by love unfeigned, [7] By the word of truth, by the power of God, by the armour of righteousness on the right hand and on the left, [8] By honour and dishonour, by evil report and good report: as deceivers, and yet true; [9] As unknown, and yet well known; as dying, and, behold, we live; as chastened, and not killed; [10] As sorrowful, yet alway rejoicing; as poor, yet making many rich; as having nothing, and yet possessing all things.

Colossians 3: *[1] If ye then be risen with Christ, seek those things which are above, where Christ sitteth on the right hand of God. [2] Set your affection on things above, not on things on the earth. [3] For ye are dead, and your life is hid with Christ in God. [4] When Christ, who is our life, shall appear, then shall ye also appear with him in glory. [5] Mortify therefore your members which are upon the earth; fornication, uncleanness, inordinate affection, evil concupiscence, and covetousness, which is idolatry: [6] For which things' sake the wrath of God cometh on the children of disobedience: [7] In the which ye also walked some time, when ye lived in them. [8] But now ye also put off all these;*

anger, wrath, malice, blasphemy, filthy communication out of your mouth. ⁹Lie not one to another, seeing that ye have put off the old man with his deeds; ¹⁰And have put on the new man, which is renewed in knowledge after the image of him that created him: ¹¹Where there is neither Greek nor Jew, circumcision nor uncircumcision, Barbarian, Scythian, bond nor free: but Christ is all, and in all. ¹²Put on therefore, as the elect of God, holy and beloved, bowels of mercies, kindness, humbleness of mind, meekness, longsuffering; ¹³Forbearing one another, and forgiving one another, if any man have a quarrel against any: even as Christ forgave you, so also do ye. ¹⁴And above all these things put on charity, which is the bond of perfectness. ¹⁵And let the peace of God rule in your hearts, to the which also ye are called in one body; and be ye thankful. ¹⁶Let the word of Christ dwell in you richly in all wisdom; teaching and admonishing one another in psalms and hymns and spiritual songs, singing with grace in your hearts to the Lord. ¹⁷And whatsoever ye do in word or deed, do all in the name of the Lord Jesus, giving thanks to God and the Father by him.

Romans (KJ) 11: ¹I say then, Hath God cast away his people? God forbid. For I also am an Israelite, of the seed of Abraham, of the tribe of Benjamin. ²God hath not cast away his people which he foreknew. Wot ye not what the scripture saith of Elias? how he maketh intercession to God against Israel saying, ³Lord, they have killed thy prophets, and digged down thine altars; and I am left alone, and they seek my life. ⁴But what saith the answer of God unto him? I have reserved to myself seven thousand men, who have not bowed the knee to the image of Baal. ⁵Even so then at this present time also there is a remnant according to the election of grace. ⁶And if by grace, then is it no more of works: otherwise grace is no more grace, But if it be of works, then it is no more grace: otherwise work is no more work. ⁷What then? Israel hath not obtained that which he seeketh for; but the election hath obtained it, and the rest were blinded. ⁸(According as it is written, God hath given them the spirit of slumber, eyes that they should not see, and ears that they should not hear;) unto this day. ⁹And David saith, Let their table be made a snare, and a trap, and a stumblingblock, and a recompence unto them: ¹⁰Let their eyes be darkened, that they may not see, and bow down their back alway. ¹¹I say then, Have they stumbled that they should fall? God forbid: but rather through their fall salvation is come unto the Gentiles, for to provoke them to jealousy. ¹²Now if the fall of them be the riches of the world, and the diminishing of them the riches of the Gentiles; how much more their fulness? ¹³For I speak to you Gentiles, inasmuch as I am the apostle of the Gentiles, I magnify mine office: ¹⁴If by any means I may provoke to emulation them which are my flesh, and might save some of them. ¹⁵For if the casting away of them be the reconciling of the world, what shall the receiving of them be, but life from the dead? ¹⁶For if the firstfruit be holy, the lump is also holy: and if the root be holy, so are the branches. ¹⁷And if some of the branches be broken off, and thou, being a wild olive tree, wert grafted in among them, and with them partakest of the root and fatness of the olive tree; ¹⁸Boast not against the branches. But if thou boast, thou bearest not the root, but the root thee. ¹⁹Thou wilt say then, The branches were broken off, that I might be grafted in. ²⁰Well; because of unbelief they were broken off, and thou standest by faith. Be not highminded, but fear: ²¹For if God spared not the natural branches, take heed lest he also spare not thee. *²²Behold therefore the goodness and severity of God: on them which fell, severity; but toward thee, goodness, if thou continue in his goodness: otherwise thou also shalt be cut off. ²³ And they also, if they abide not still in unbelief, shall be grafted in: for God is able to graft them in again. ²⁴For if thou wert cut out of the olive tree which is wild by nature, and wert grafted contrary to nature into a good olive tree: how much more shall these, which be the natural branches, be grafted into their own olive tree? ²⁵For I would not, brethren, that ye should be ignorant of this* *mystery , lest ye should be wise in your own conceits; that blindness in part is happened to Israel, until the fulness of the Gentiles be come in. [26]And so all Israel shall be saved: as it is written, There shall come out of Sion the Deliverer, and shall turn away ungodliness from Jacob: [27]For this is my covenant unto them, when I shall take away their sins. [28]As concerning the gospel, they are enemies for your sakes: but as touching the election, they are beloved for the father's sakes. [29]For the gifts and calling of God are without repentance. [30]For as ye in times past have not believed God, yet have now obtained mercy through their unbelief: [31]Even so have these also now not believed, that through your mercy they also may obtain mercy. [32]For God hath concluded them all in unbelief, that he might have mercy upon all. [33]O the depth of the riches both of the wisdom and knowledge of God! how unsearchable are his judgments, and his ways past finding out! [34]For who hath known the mind of the Lord? or who hath been his counsellor? [35]Or who hath first given to him, and it shall be recompensed unto him again? [36]For of him, and through him, and to him, are all things: to whom be glory forever. Amen.*

John 15: [7]If ye abide in me, and my words abide in you, ye shall ask what ye will, and it shall be done unto you. [8]Herein is my Father glorified, that ye bear much fruit; so shall ye be my disciples. [9]As the Father hath loved me, so have I loved you: continue ye in my love.

The New Testament constantly reminds us not to make the same mistakes of our predecessors.

2 Peter 2: But there were false prophets also among the people, even as there shall be false teachers among you, who privily shall bring in damnable heresies, even denying the Lord that bought them, and bring upon themselves swift destruction. [2]And many shall follow their pernicious ways; by reason of whom the way of truth shall be evil spoken of. [3]And through covetousness shall they with feigned words make merchandise of you: whose judgment now of a long time lingereth not, and their damnation slumbereth not. [4]For if God spared not the angels that sinned

Figure 2.11 Saint Michael and the fall of angels by Johann Georg

but cast them down to hell,

Figure 2.12 1776 representation of the Archangel Michael in the battle against Lucifer by Matthaus Gunther and delivered them into chains of darkness, to be reserved unto judgment;

[5] And spared not the old world, but saved Noah the eighth person, a preacher of righteousness,

Figure 2.13 Noah's Ark (c. 1675) by Französischer Meister.

bringing in the flood upon the world of the ungodly;

Figure 2.14 The Flood by Nicolas Poussin (1594–1665)

2 Peter 2: [6] And turning the cities of Sodom and Gomorrah into ashes condemned them with an overthrow, taking them an ensample unto those who after should live ungodly; [7] And delivered just Lot,

**Figure 2.15 Landscape with the destruction of Sodom and Gomorrah
By Joachim Patinir**

2 Peter 2: [8] (For that righteous man dwelling among them, in seeing and hearing, vexed his righteous soul from day to day with their unlawful deeds;) [9] The Lord knoweth how to deliver the godly out of temptations, and to reserve the unjust unto the day of judgment to be punished: [10] But chiefly them that walk after the flesh in the lust of uncleanness, and despise government. Presumptuous are they, self willed, they are not afraid to speak evil of dignities. [11] Whereas angels, which are greater in power and might, bring not railing accusation against them before the Lord. [12] But these, as natural brute beasts, made to be taken and destroyed, speak evil of the things that they understand not; and shall utterly perish in their own corruption; [13] And shall receive the reward of unrighteousness, as they that count it pleasure to riot in the day time. Spots they are and blemishes, sporting themselves with their own deceivings while they feast with you; [14] Having eyes full of adultery, and that cannot cease from sin; beguiling unstable souls: an heart they have exercised with covetous practices; cursed children: [15] Which have forsaken the right way, and are gone astray, following the way of Balaam the son of Bosor, who loved the wages of unrighteousness;

Figure 2.16 Balaam and His Ass (1626) by Rembrandt

2 Peter 2: [16] But was rebuked for his iniquity: the dumb ass speaking with man's voice forbad the madness of the prophet. [17] These are wells without water, clouds that are carried with a tempest; to whom the mist of darkness is reserved forever. [18] For when they speak great swelling words of vanity, they allure through the lusts of the flesh, through much wantonness, those who were clean escaped from them who live in error. [9] While they promise them liberty, they themselves are the servants of corruption: for of whom a man is overcome, of the same is he brought in bondage. [20] For if after they have escaped the pollutions of the world through the knowledge of the Lord and Saviour Jesus Christ, they are again entangled therein, and overcome, the latter end is worse with them than the beginning. [21] For it had been better for them not to have known the way of righteousness, than, after they have known it, to turn from the holy commandment delivered unto them. [22] But it is happened unto them according to the true proverb, The dog is turned to his own vomit again; and the sow that was washed to her wallowing in the mire.

2 Peter 3: *This second epistle, beloved, I now write unto you; in both which I stir up your pure minds by way of remembrance: ² That ye may be mindful of the words which were spoken before by the holy prophets, and of the commandment of us the apostles of the Lord and Saviour: ³ Knowing this first, that there shall come in the last days scoffers, walking after their own lusts, ⁴ And saying, Where is the promise of his coming? for since the fathers fell asleep, all things continue as they were from the beginning of the creation. ⁵ For this they willingly are ignorant of, that by the word of God the heavens were of old, and the earth standing out of the water and in the water: ⁶ Whereby the world that then was, being overflowed with water, perished:*

Figure 2.17 The Deluge by Léon Comerre.

2 Peter 3: *⁷ But the heavens and the earth, which are now, by the same word are kept in store, reserved unto fire against the day of judgment and perdition of ungodly men.*

Figure 2.18 The End of the World also known as The Great Day of His Wrath (1853) by John Martin.

[8] But, beloved, be not ignorant of this one thing, that one day is with the Lord as a thousand years, and a thousand years as one day. [9] The Lord is not slack concerning his promise, as some men count slackness; but is longsuffering to us-ward, not willing that any should perish, but that all should come to repentance. *[10] But the day of the Lord will come as a thief in the night; in the which the heavens shall pass away with a great noise, and the elements shall melt with fervent heat, the earth also and the works that are therein shall be burned up.*

Figure 2.19 Image of what Earth may look like 5-7 billion years from now, when the sun swells and becomes a red giant by Fsgregs.

2 Peter 3: [11] *Seeing then that all these things shall be dissolved, what manner of persons ought ye to be in all holy conversation and godliness,* [12] *Looking for and hasting unto the coming of the day of God, wherein the heavens being on fire shall be dissolved, and the elements shall melt with fervent heat?* [13] *Nevertheless we, according to his promise, look for new heavens and a new earth, wherein dwelleth righteousness.*

Figure 2.20 The Last Judgement (1853) by John Martin.

Remember: Isaiah (AMP) 66: [22] For as the new heavens and the new earth which I make shall remain before Me, says the Lord, so shall your offspring and your name remain. [23] And it shall be that from one New Moon to another New Moon and from one Sabbath to another Sabbath, all flesh shall come to worship before Me, says the Lord. [24] *And they shall go forth and gaze upon the dead bodies of the [rebellious] men who have stepped over against Me; for their worm shall not die, their fire shall not be quenched, and they shall be an abhorrence to all mankind.*

There is something that I noticed that keeps coming up over and over, again and again, that is so important because some of us have children and we have other relatives with whose salvation we are concerned about. We all want to see all of our relatives saved and filled with the Holy Spirit and on their way to Heaven. I kept seeing a finely woven piece of thread that God keeps sewing from the end of one dispensation to the next.

If you go back to Abraham and Lot, before God brought destruction on Sodom and Gomorrah, He went to Abraham because of his cousin Lot and his family. God sent angels to deliver Lot's family but his wife looked back and turned into a pillar of salt. But Lot and his daughters were saved. Noah and his family were delivered from the deluge that destroyed everyone else. Noah was a preacher of righteousness for 100 years. He told of the impending destruction but the people chose to ignore it, and suffered the consequences.

I believe that God will save our family members if we continue to pray and intercede for them because of how He saved Lot and his family on account of Abraham's intercession for them.

Remember: Isaiah (AMP) 66: [22] *For as the new heavens and the new earth which I make shall remain before Me, says the Lord, so shall your offspring and your name remain.*

After lifting up our three sons for many years, they are all saved—praise God—and we continue to pray for them daily. There was a period of time when they were not saved as all of us were at one time or another. But we are praising God that they are working out their salvation as we all are. Keep praying for your loved ones, stop worrying about every negative situation that comes up concerning them. Always roll your cares over onto God and leave them at His feet and do not take them back by worrying about them again. Worrying is faithlessness and sin; we have done it so long we do not even recognize it as sin. It has become so comfortable for us to worry that we sit up at night just so we can lose sleep over it. We think it is sin not to worry; that has to change. When Jesus returns, He will be looking for *faith*. Learn the difference, make the change and grow up.

2 Peter 3: [14] Wherefore, beloved, seeing that ye look for such things, be diligent that ye `may be found of him in peace, without spot, and blameless. [15] And account that the longsuffering of our Lord is salvation; even as our beloved brother Paul also according to the wisdom given unto him hath written unto you; **[16] As also in all his epistles, speaking in them of these things; in which are some things hard to be understood, which they that are unlearned and unstable wrest, as they do also the other scriptures, unto their own destruction.** [17] Ye therefore, beloved, seeing ye know these things before, beware lest ye also, being led away with the error of the wicked, fall from your own stedfastness. [18] But grow in grace, and in the knowledge of our Lord and Saviour Jesus Christ. To him be glory both now and forever. Amen.

Romans 1: [16] For I am not ashamed of the gospel of Christ: for it is the power of God unto salvation to everyone that believeth; to the Jew first, and also to the Greek. [17] *For therein is the righteousness of God revealed from faith to faith: as it is written, The just shall live by faith.* [18] *For the wrath of God is revealed from heaven against all ungodliness and unrighteousness of men, who hold the truth in unrighteousness;*

Galatians 3: [10] For as many as are of the works of the law are under the curse: for it is written, Cursed is every one that continueth not in all things which are *written in the book of the law to do them.* [11] *But that no man is justified by the law in the sight of God, it is evident: for, The just shall live by faith.* [12] *And the law is not of faith: but, The man that doeth them shall live in them.*

Hebrews 10: [37] *For yet a little while, and he that shall come will come, and will not tarry.* [38] *Now the just shall live by faith:* [39] *But we are not of them who draw back unto perdition; but of them that believe to the saving of the soul.*

"I came back for virgins but half had turned into whores."

One Saturday morning, I think it was about 4:00 a.m., I was meditating on these scriptures and the Lord spoke to my heart. I heard Him say, "I came back for virgins but half of them had turned into whores," Immediately I set straight up in bed. That phrase put a Godly fear in my heart, which I still feel to this day. I did not sleep for days. I have heard how people who had near death experiences had their whole life flash before them. As soon as I heard that phrase, that same thing happened to me, but it was my spiritual life that was flashing before me, everything that was out of line with the Word of God came up before me. I had to correct wrong attitudes, emotions, wrong motives, actions, and deeds that are somewhat lacking when I compare them to the Word, and I am still working on them now.

**Figure 2.21 The Last Judgment and the Wise and Foolish Virgins (1450s)
by unknown Flemish master.**

John 6: [64] But there are some of you that believe not. For Jesus knew from the beginning who they were that believed not, and who should betray him.

Make sure that is not you!

CHAPTER 3

The Fruit of Faith Part I

The First Step into the Kingdom of God

Hebrews 6: [1]Therefore leaving the principles of the doctrine of Christ, let us go on unto perfection; not laying again the foundation of repentance from dead works, and of faith toward God, [2]Of the doctrine of baptisms, and of laying on of hands, and of resurrection of the dead, and of eternal judgment. [3]And this will we do, if God permit.

Figure 3.1 Resurrection of the Widow's son from Nain, altar panel by Lucas Cranach the Younger, c. 1569, in the Stadtkirche Wittenberg.

Luke 7: [11]And it came to pass the day after, that he went into a city called Nain; and many of his disciples went with him, and much people. [12]Now when he came nigh to the gate of the city, behold, there was a dead man carried out, the only son of his mother, and she was a widow: and much people of the city was with her. [13]And when the Lord saw her, he had compassion on her, and said unto her, Weep not. [14]And he came and touched the bier: and they that bare him stood still. And he said, Young man, I say unto thee, Arise.

Figure 3.2 Resurrection at Nain. Picture of the altar in the chapel at Nain, Israel

[15]And he that was dead sat up, and began to speak. And he delivered him to his mother. [16]And there came a fear on all: and they glorified God, saying, That a great prophet is risen up among us; and, That God hath visited his people. [17]And this rumour of him went forth throughout all Judaea, and throughout all the region round about.

Figure 3.3 Christ cleansing a leper (1864) by Jean-Marie Melchior Doze.

Jesus never restored sight to the blind, healed the sick, cleansed the leper, opened deaf ears, or raised the dead. When He came to earth, He emptied Himself of all His deity as the Son of God when He was in Heaven. He explains in detail who was really doing all the miracles. But while He emptied Himself, He became filled with the Spirit of God, and it was Jesus' faith in His Father who answered every one of His prayer requests as He stood in agreement with a family member or someone else's intercession for a friend.

John 5: [18]Therefore the Jews sought the more to kill him, because he not only had broken the sabbath, but said also that God was his Father, making himself equal with God. [19]Then answered Jesus and said unto them, Verily, verily, I say unto you, The Son can do nothing of himself, but what he seeth the Father do: for what things soever he doeth, these also doeth the Son likewise. [20]For the Father loveth the Son, and sheweth him all things that himself doeth: and he will shew him greater works than these, that ye may marvel. [21]For as the Father raiseth up the dead, and quickeneth them; even so the Son quickeneth whom he will. (the word *quickeneth* means to make super alive)

The definition of the Kingdom of God is all about you becoming "one" with God the Father, God the Son, and God the Holy Spirit. The Kingdom of God is righteousness, which means you have to live a righteous lifestyle. Righteous means you are in agreement with God that you will separate yourself from sin in order to stay connected to God. Sin cannot stand in the presence of God, and when we do sin we place ourselves outside of the Kingdom of God.

Peace is when we keep our mind stayed on Jesus regardless of the situation that we are confronted with, from the worst of situations, to the best of times. You are part of the only Kingdom that will be left standing when God recreates the new Heaven and new earth where only righteousness will dwell, where we will not worry, have doubt, or unbelief, and failure will not consume our thinking.

Worry is a sin; it forms the bases of doubt and unbelief, and it places a stranglehold on your faith. God calls unbelief evil because it says that God may not help or He will not help us this time. Jesus went to His own hometown and could not do any mighty works because of the people's unbelief.

Hebrews 3:[12]Take heed, brethren, lest there be in any of you an evil heart of unbelief, in departing from the living God.

Twenty-four hours a day, Satan constantly tries to capture your mind to fill it with fear of what might or what could happen. Now if you will, think for a moment about all the situations in your past that kept you up nights crying and worrying about finances or other problems and God stepped in and did a miracle. As you look back to all the time you spent in sin, worrying because you did not understand the Kingdom of God principles concerning peace! Worrying, which is a sin of unrighteousness, has kept us out of the Kingdom because we did not keep our minds stayed on Jesus. I know, I use to be a professional worrier at one time, and it is still a warfare at times that has become easier to win once I understood the meaning of peace and learning how to guard against every negative thought that tries to consume my thinking. When I realized that it was taking me out of the Kingdom of God, I started learning how to overcome worry.

The next definition of the Kingdom of God is joy in the Holy Spirit. The only way to have true joy is being in His presence, and in His presence is fullness of joy. If you remember from the Old Testament only the priest could go beyond the veil into the Holy of Holies into the presence of the Lord where the ark of the covenant and the mercy seat were. Another reason why God made us priests is because only they could stand in the presence of God. To make things a little easier on us He made our bodies His temple. God cannot change and become corrupt; we have to change and come into agreement with God to be holy as He is. God wants us to experience the Kingdom of God on earth in our lifetime. God knew what He was doing when He made our bodies His temple.

1 Peter 1: *[1]Peter, an apostle of Jesus Christ, to the strangers scattered throughout Pontus, Galatia, Cappadocia, Asia, and Bithynia, [2]Elect according to the foreknowledge of God the Father, through sanctification of the Spirit, unto obedience and sprinkling of the blood of Jesus Christ: Grace unto you, and peace, be multiplied. [3]Blessed be the God and Father of our Lord Jesus Christ, which according to his abundant mercy hath begotten us again unto a lively hope by the resurrection of Jesus Christ from the dead, [4]To an inheritance incorruptible, and undefiled, and that fadeth not away, reserved in heaven for you, [5]Who are kept by the power of God through faith unto salvation ready to be revealed in the last time. [6]Wherein ye greatly rejoice, though now for a season,* *if need be, ye are in heaviness through manifold temptations:⁷That the trial of your faith, being much more precious than of gold that perisheth, though it be tried with fire, might be found unto praise and honour and glory at the appearing of Jesus Christ: ⁸Whom having not seen, ye love; in whom, though now ye see him not, yet believing, ye rejoice with joy unspeakable and full of glory: ⁹Receiving the end of your faith, even the salvation of your souls.¹⁰Of which salvation the prophets have enquired and searched diligently, who prophesied of the grace that should come unto you: ¹¹Searching what, or what manner of time the Spirit of Christ which was in them did signify, when it testified beforehand the sufferings of Christ, and the glory that should follow. ¹²Unto whom it was revealed, that not unto themselves, but unto us they did minister the things, which are now reported unto you by them that have preached the gospel unto you with the Holy Ghost sent down from heaven; which things the angels desire to look into. ¹³Wherefore gird up the loins of your mind, be sober, and hope to the end for the grace that is to be brought unto you at the revelation of Jesus Christ; ¹⁴As obedient children, not fashioning yourselves according to the former lusts in your ignorance: ¹⁵But as he which hath called you is holy, so be ye holy in all manner of conversation; ¹⁶Because it is written, Be ye holy; for I am holy.¹⁷And if ye call on the Father, who without respect of persons judgeth according to every man's work, pass the time of your sojourning here in fear: ¹⁸Forasmuch as ye know that ye were not redeemed with corruptible things, as silver and gold, from your vain conversation received by tradition from your fathers;¹⁹But with the precious blood of Christ, as of a lamb without blemish and without spot: ²⁰Who verily was foreordained before the foundation of the world, but was manifest in these last times for you,*

The Lamb That Was Slain before the Foundation of the Earth Was Laid

**Figure 3.4 Adoration of the Mystic Lamb, with gushing blood, Ghent Altarpiece
by Jan van Eyck.**

²¹Who by him do believe in God, that raised him up from the dead, and gave him glory; that your faith and hope might be in God. ²²Seeing ye have purified your souls in obeying the truth through the Spirit unto unfeigned love of the brethren, see that ye love one another with a pure heart fervently: ²³Being born again, not of corruptible seed,

Figure 3.5 Fresh figs cut open showing the flesh and seeds inside by Eric Hunt.

but of incorruptible, by the word of God, which liveth and abideth forever. ⁴For all flesh is as grass, and all the glory of man as the flower of grass. The grass withereth, and the flower thereof falleth away: ²⁵But the word of the Lord endureth forever. And this is the word which by the gospel is preached unto you.

[The first tabernacle is no longer standing, because Jesus became the temple of the Holy Spirit. The priest had to sanctify himself with the blood of a lamb or young bull that was spotless and without blemish. If the blood was from a lamb that was blind or had some type of defect the priest would die instantly, because the lamb was not pure and the blood from it would be corrupt. The sacrifice would not be accepted. The sins of the priest would not be cleansed and the priest would die once he entered the presence of God.

Inside of the tabernacle, a veil separated the inner court from the Holy of Holies; the High Priest had to cleanse and purify himself before he could go beyond the veil into the presence of the Holy Spirit. The priest would sprinkle the blood on himself, then on the veil then he would be able to go through the veil into the presence of The Lord.]

Figure 3.6 The Sacrifice of the Old Covenant (1626) by Peter Paul Rubens.

Numbers 7: [88]And all the oxen for the sacrifice of the peace offerings were twenty and four bullocks, the rams sixty, the he goats sixty, the lambs of the first year sixty. This was the dedication of the altar, after that it was anointed. [89]And when Moses was gone into the tabernacle of the congregation to speak with him, then he heard the voice of one speaking unto him from off the mercy seat that was upon the ark of testimony, from between the two cherubims: and he spake unto him.

Holy of Holies.

Figure 3.7

The Holy of Holies, illustration in The History of the Church of God from the Creation to the Present Day Part I - Bible History, by Rev. B. J. Spalding (1883).

Shekinah

From Wikipedia, the free encyclopedia

Shekinah (alternative transliterations **Shekinah, Shechinah, Shekina, Shechina, Schechinah,** שׁכינה) is the English spelling of a grammatically feminine Hebrew word that means the *dwelling* or *settling,* and is used to denote the dwelling or settling divine presence of God, especially in the Temple in Jerusalem.

2 Corinthians 6: [15]And what concord hath Christ with Belial? Or what part hath he that believeth with an infidel? [16]And what agreement hath the Temple of God with idols? *For ye are the Temple of the living God; as God hath said, I will dwell in them, and walk in them; and I will be their God, and they shall be my people.* [17]*Wherefore come out from among them, and be ye separate, saith the Lord, and touch not the unclean thing; and I will receive you.*

To understand how God could raise the dead through *faith in* Jesus you have to know what is inside of the ark of the covenant in the Old Testament. Everything in the Old Testament tabernacle is repeated in the New Testament temple (which is us):

First there was a jar of manna.

Figure 3.8 The Gathering of the Manna (c. 1460-1470).

John 6: [47]Verily, verily, I say unto you, He that believeth on me hath everlasting life. [48]I am that bread of life. [49]Your fathers did eat manna in the wilderness, and are dead. [50]This is the bread which cometh down from heaven, that a man may eat thereof, and not die. [51]I am the living bread which came down from heaven: if any man eat of this bread, he shall live forever: and the bread that I will give is my flesh, which I will give for the life of the world.

The second item was the Torah, which are the first five books of the Bible, written by Moses.

Figure 3.9 Sefer Torah at old Glockengasse Synagogue (reconstruction), Cologne by photographer Willy Horsch.

Our body is the temple of the Holy Spirit. Inside the ark of the covenant in the Old Testament was the Torah (the first five books of the Old Testament). The Word of God should dwell in your heart and mind, because to be spiritually minded is life but to be carnally minded is death. Just your thoughts alone can separate you from the life of the Father, the Son, and the Holy Spirit.

Romans 8: [8]So then they that are in the flesh cannot please God. *[9]But ye are not in the flesh, but in the Spirit, if so be that the Spirit of God dwell in you.* Now if any man have not the Spirit of Christ, he is none of his. [10]And if Christ be in you, the body is dead because of sin; but the Spirit is life because of righteousness. [11]But if the Spirit of him that raised up Jesus from the dead dwell in you, he that raised up Christ from the dead shall also quicken your mortal bodies by his Spirit that dwelleth in you. [12]Therefore, brethren, we are debtors, not to the flesh, to live after the flesh.

Colossians 3: [15]And let the peace of God rule in your hearts, to the which also ye are called in one body; and be ye thankful. *[16]Let the word of Christ dwell in you richly in all wisdom; teaching and admonishing one another in psalms and hymns and spiritual songs, singing with grace in your hearts to the Lord. [7]And whatsoever ye do in word or deed, do all in the name of the Lord Jesus, giving thanks to God and the Father by him.*

The third item inside the ark of the covenant, were the two tablets of stone with the Ten Commandments written on them.

Hebrews 8: [9]Not according to the covenant that I made with their fathers in the day when I took them by the hand to lead them out of the land of Egypt; because they continued not in my covenant, and I regarded them not, saith the Lord. *¹⁰For this is the covenant that I will make with the house of Israel after those days, saith the Lord; I will put my laws into their mind, and write them in their hearts: and I will be to them a God, and they shall be to me a people:* ¹¹And they shall not teach every man his neighbor, and every man his brother, for all shall know me, from the least to the greatest. ¹² For I will be merciful to their unrighteousness, and their sins and their iniquities will I remember no more. ¹³ In that he saith, A new covenant, he hath made the first old. Now that which decayeth and waxeth old is ready to vanish away.

Figure 3.10 Moses and the Ten Commandments (1638) by José de Ribera.

Figure 3.11 Aaron's Rod Budding (1728).

The fourth item was Aaron's rod that budded and bore fruit.

Aaron's rod, which was budding, is at the center of the power of God and why the dead were raised, the sick were healed, blind eyes were opened, and the crippled walked. The Word of God is like a sharp, two-edged sword. One side heals, restores, and makes whole and well. The other side brings sudden death in the presence of sin and corruption. One side is judgment and justice with the power to enforce both swiftly. God is merciful, gracious, full of compassion, longsuffering, and always willing to communicate. He wants to talk to us every day. He wants to lead us and guide us into His perfect will for our lives. That is why He made our body a temple and He is living inside of us. If we draw nigh to Him, He will draw nigh to us. He made us priests as a reminder to keep our walk before Him holy. So when we do sin, we can ask for forgiveness and stay in fellowship with Him and in oneness with the Trinity.

Isaiah (KJV) 55: [11] So shall my word be that goeth forth out of my mouth: it shall not return unto me void, but it shall accomplish that which I please, and it shall prosper in the thing whereto I sent it.

Revelation 1: [15] And his feet like unto fine brass, as if they burned in a furnace; and his voice as the sound of many waters. *[16] And he had in his right hand seven stars: and out of his mouth went a sharp two edged sword: and his countenance was as the sun shinneth in his strength.*

John 14: *[1] Let not your heart be troubled: ye believe in God, believe also in me. [2] In my Father's house are many mansions: if it were not so, I would have told you. I go to prepare a place for you. [3] And if I go and prepare a place for you, I will come again, and receive you unto myself; that where I am, there ye may be also.* [4] And whither I go ye know, and the way ye know. [5] Thomas saith unto him, Lord, we know not whither thou goest; and how can we know the way? [6] Jesus saith unto him, I am the way, the truth, and the life: no man cometh unto the Father, but by me. [7] If ye had known me, ye should have known my Father also: and from henceforth ye know him, and have seen him. [8] Philip saith unto him, Lord, show us the Father, and it sufficeth us. [9] Jesus saith unto him, Have I been so long time with you, and yet hast thou not known me, Philip? he that hath seen me hath seen the Father; and how sayest thou then, Show us the Father? [10] Believest thou not that I am in the Father, and the Father in me? the words that I speak unto you I speak not of myself: but the Father that dwelleth in me, he doeth the works. [11] Believe me that I am in the Father, and the Father in me: or else believe me for the very works' sake.

Again, notice because the Father, the Son, and the Holy Spirit dwell together as "One," Jesus goes on to tell us that every miracle was done by His Father who is dwelling inside of Him.

John 6: [62] What and if ye shall see the Son of man ascend up where he was before? *[63] It is the spirit that quickeneth; the flesh profiteth nothing: the words that I speak unto you, they are spirit, and they are life.*

Mark 11: [20] And in the morning, as they passed by, they saw the fig tree dried up from the roots. [21] And Peter calling to remembrance saith unto him, Master, behold, the fig tree which thou cursedst is withered away. *[22] And Jesus answering saith unto them, Have faith in God. [23] For verily I say unto you, That whosoever shall say unto this mountain, Be thou removed, and be thou cast into the sea; and shall not doubt in his heart, but shall believe that those things which he saith shall come to pass; he shall have whatsoever he saith. [24] Therefore I say unto you, What things soever ye desire, when ye pray, believe that ye receive them, and ye shall have them. [25] And when ye stand praying, forgive, if ye have ought against any: that your Father also which is in heaven may forgive you your trespasses. [26] But if ye do not forgive, neither will your Father which is in heaven forgive your trespasses.*

Proverbs 18:21 Death and life are in the power of the tongue: and they that love it shall eat the fruit thereof.

Jesus explains why God did miracles through Him, and He set the example.

John 14: [12]Verily, verily, I say unto you, He that believeth on me, the works that I do shall he do also; and greater works than these shall he do; because I go unto my Father. [13]And whatsoever ye shall ask in my name, that will I do, that the Father may be glorified in the Son. [14]If ye shall ask anything in my name, I will do it. [15]If ye love me, keep my commandments. [16]And I will pray the Father, and he shall give you another Comforter, that he may abide with you forever; [17]Even the Spirit of truth; whom the world cannot receive, because it seeth him not, neither knoweth him: but ye know him; for he dwelleth with you, and shall be in you. [18]I will not leave you comfortless: I will come to you. *[19]Yet a little while, and the world seeth me no more; but ye see me: because I live, ye shall live also. [20]At that day ye shall know that I am in my Father, and ye in me, and I in you.* [21]He that hath my commandments, and keepeth them, he it is that loveth me: and he that loveth me shall be loved of my Father, and I will love him, and will manifest myself to him. [22]Judas saith unto him, not Iscariot, Lord, how is it that thou wilt manifest thyself unto us, and not unto the world? [23]Jesus answered and said unto him, If a man love me, he will keep my words: and my Father will love him, and we will come unto him, and make our abode with him. [24] He that loveth me not keepeth not my sayings: and the word which ye hear is not mine, but the Father's which sent me. [25]These things have I spoken unto you, being yet present with you. [26]But the Comforter, which is the Holy Ghost, whom the Father will send in my name, he shall teach you all things, and bring all things to your remembrance, whatsoever I have said unto you. [27]Peace I leave with you, my peace I give unto you: not as the world giveth, give I unto you. Let not your heart be troubled, neither let it be afraid. [28]Ye have heard how I said unto you, I go away, and come again unto you. If ye loved me, ye would rejoice, because I said, I go unto the Father: for my Father is greater than I. [29]And now I have told you before it come to pass, that, when it is come to pass, ye might believe. [30]Hereafter I will not talk much with you: for the prince of this world cometh, and hath nothing in me. [31] But that the world may know that I love the Father; and as the Father gave me commandment, even so I do. Arise, let us go hence.

Figure 3.12 The Agony in the Garden (c. 1590) by El Greco.

John 17: ¹These words spake Jesus, and lifted up his eyes to heaven, and said, Father, the hour is come; glorify thy Son, that thy Son also may glorify thee: ²As thou hast given him power over all flesh, that he should give eternal life to as many as thou hast given him. ³And this is life eternal, that they might know thee the only true God, and Jesus Christ, whom thou hast sent. ⁴I have glorified thee on the earth: I have finished the work which thou gavest me to do. ⁵And now, O Father, glorify thou me with thine own self with the glory which I had with thee before the world was. ⁶I have manifested thy name unto the men which thou gavest me out of the world: thine they were, and thou gavest them me; and they have kept thy word. ⁷Now they have known that all things whatsoever thou hast given me are of thee. ⁸For I have given unto them the words which thou gavest me; and they have received them, and have known surely that I came out from thee, and they have believed that thou didst send me. ⁹I pray for them: I pray not for the world, but for them which thou hast given me; for they are thine. ¹⁰And all mine are thine, and thine are mine; and I am glorified in them. ¹¹And now I am no more in the world, but these are in the world, and I come to thee. Holy Father, keep through thine own name those whom thou hast given me, may be one, as we are. ¹²While I was with them in the world, I kept them in thy name: those who thou gavest me I have kept, and none of them is lost, but the son of perdition; that the scripture might be fulfilled. ¹³And now come I to thee; and these things I speak in the world, that they might have my joy fulfilled in themselves. ¹⁴I have given them thy word; and the world hath hated them, because they are not of the world, even as I am not of the world. [15]I pray not that thou shouldest take them out of the world, but that thou shouldest keep them from the evil. [16]They are not of the world, even as I am not of the world. [17]Sanctify them through thy truth: thy word is truth. [18]As thou hast sent me into the world, even so have I also sent them into the world. [19]And for their sakes I sanctify myself, that they also might be sanctified through the truth. [20]Neither pray I for these alone, but for them also which shall believe on me through their word; [21]That they all may be one; as thou, Father, art in me, and I in thee, that they also may be one in us: that the world may believe that thou hast sent me. [22]And the glory which thou gavest me I have given them; that they may be one, even as we are one: [23]I in them, and thou in me, that they may be made perfect in one; and that the world may know that thou hast sent me, and hast loved them, as thou hast loved me. [24]Father, I will that they also, whom thou hast given me, be with me where I am; that they may behold my glory, which thou hast given me: for thou lovedst me before the foundation of the world. [25]O righteous Father, the world hath not known thee: but I have known thee, and these have known that thou hast sent me. [26]And I have declared unto them thy name, and will declare it: that the love wherewith thou hast loved me may be in them, and I in them.

The Kingdom of God is about you becoming *one* with the Trinity, and it started in Deuteronomy with keeping the commandments.

Deuteronomy 6: [1]Now these are the commandments, the statutes, and the judgments, which the LORD your God commanded to teach you, that ye might do them in the land whither ye go to possess it: [2]That thou mightest fear the LORD thy God, to keep all his statutes and his commandments, which I command thee, thou, and thy son, and thy son's son, all the days of thy life; and that thy days may be prolonged. [3]Hear therefore, O Israel, and observe to do it; that it may be well with thee, and that ye may increase mightily, as the LORD God of thy fathers hath promised thee, in the land that floweth with milk and honey. *[4]Hear, O Israel: The LORD our God is one LORD: [5]And thou shalt love the LORD thy God with all thine heart, and with all thy soul, and with all thy might. [6]And these words, which I command thee this day, shall be in thine heart:* [7]And thou shalt teach them diligently unto thy children, and shalt talk of them when thou sittest in thine house, and when thou walkest by the way, and when thou liest down, and when thou risest up. [8]And thou shalt bind them for a sign upon thine hand, and they shall be as frontlets between thine eyes. [9]And thou shalt write them upon the posts of thy house, and on thy gates. [10]And it shall be, when the LORD thy God shall have brought thee into the land which he sware unto thy fathers, to Abraham, to Isaac, and to Jacob, to give thee great and goodly cities, which thou buildedst not, [11]And houses full of all good things, which thou filledst not, and wells digged, which thou diggedst not, vineyards and olive trees, which thou plantedst not; when thou shalt have eaten and be full; [12]Then beware lest thou forget the LORD, which brought thee forth out of the land of Egypt, from the house of bondage. [13]Thou shalt fear the LORD thy God, and serve him, and shalt swear by his name. [14]Ye shall not go after other gods, of the gods of the people which are round about you; [15](For the LORD thy God is a jealous God among you) lest the anger of the LORD thy God be kindled against thee, and destroy thee from off the face of the earth. [16]Ye shall not tempt the LORD your God, as ye tempted him in Massah. [17]Ye shall diligently keep the commandments of the LORD your God, and his testimonies, and his statutes, which he hath commanded thee. [18]And thou shalt do that which is right and good in the sight of the LORD: that it may be well with thee, and that thou mayest go in and possess the good land which the LORD sware unto thy fathers. [19]To cast out all thine enemies from before thee, as the LORD hath spoken. ²⁰And when thy son asketh thee in time to come, saying, What mean the testimonies, and the statutes, and the judgments, which the LORD our God hath commanded you? ²¹Then thou shalt say unto thy son, We were Pharaoh's bondmen in Egypt; and the LORD brought us out of Egypt with a mighty hand: ²²And the LORD shewed signs and wonders, great and sore, upon Egypt, upon Pharaoh, and upon all his household, before our eyes: ²³And he brought us out from thence, that he might bring us in, to give us the land which he sware unto our fathers. ²⁴And the LORD commanded us to do all these statutes, to fear the LORD our God, for our good always, that he might preserve us alive, as it is at this day. ²⁵And it shall be our righteousness, if we observe to do all these commandments before the LORD our God, as he hath commanded us.

John 14: ²²Judas saith unto him, not Iscariot, Lord, how is it that thou wilt manifest thyself unto us, and not unto the world? ²³Jesus answered and said unto him, *If a man love me, he will keep my words: and my Father will love him, and we will come unto him, and make our abode with him.* ²⁴He that loveth me not keepeth not my sayings: and the word which ye hear is not mine, but the Father's which sent me.

God truly has chosen to dwell in us and to make His abode within us.

Figure 3.13 The Ark carried into the Temple (c. early 15th century)
Très Riches Heures du Duc de Berry.

Next, the ark of the covenant was carried inside the temple. Now God has made our body the temple of the Holy Spirit and when we asked Jesus to come into our heart, He came with the Holy Spirit, and with His Father. Again this has been God's desire from the beginning when He delivered the children of Israel out of Egypt. God wanted to make them all a kingdom of priests; He wanted to have a *one-on-one* relationship with all His people.

Exodus 19: [4]Ye have seen what I did unto the Egyptians, and how I bare you on eagles' wings, and brought you unto myself. [5]Now therefore, if ye will obey my voice indeed, and keep my covenant, then ye shall be a peculiar treasure unto me above all people: for all the earth is mine: [6]And ye shall be unto me a kingdom of priests, and an holy nation. These are the words which thou shalt speak unto the children of Israel. [7]And Moses came and called for the elders of the people, and laid before their faces all these words which the LORD commanded him. [8]And all the people answered together, and said, All that the LORD hath spoken we will do. And Moses returned the words of the people unto the LORD. [9]And the LORD said unto Moses, Lo, I come unto thee in a thick cloud, that the people may hear when I speak with thee, and believe thee forever. And Moses told the words of the people unto the LORD. [10]And the LORD said unto Moses, Go unto the people, and sanctify them today and tomorrow, and let them wash their clothes... ...[18]And all the people saw the thunderings, and the lightnings, and the noise of the trumpet, and the mountain smoking: and when the people saw it, they removed, and stood afar off. . .

Exodus 20: [19]And they said unto Moses, Speak thou with us, and we will hear: but let not God speak with us, lest we die. [20]And Moses said unto the people, Fear not: for God is come to prove you, and that his fear may be before your faces, that ye sin not. [21]And the people stood afar off, and Moses drew near unto the thick darkness where God was. [22]And the LORD said unto Moses, Thus thou shalt say unto the children of Israel, Ye have seen that I have talked with you from heaven.

But they did not want any part of it because they were afraid that God would kill them. That was ignorance on their part; why would God tell them to come forth then change His mind just so He could kill them?

In the New Testament, God made us kings and priests, and our bodies His temple. We did not get a chance to choose because God knew what He was doing, and we need to understand His reasons for doing things His way. His way was to make us His children because the man that He created failed to fulfill His purpose. We are born of God; we are different from the man that God created in the Garden of Eden. Adam could never pray the Lord's Prayer, he could not pray, "Our Father," Adam could not cry out, "Abba Father." Adam was a creature that God formed out of the dust of the ground and breathed the breath of life into him, and then he became a living soul. But Adam was not born of God. There is a big difference between being born again and being created. It is an honor and a privilege to be a child of God; it is far better than being one of His creations.

Jesus prayed that we would be united as one with the Trinity and one with each other as members of the Body of Christ for the purpose of God living and dwelling inside of us so that God could do the same miracles that He did through Jesus, and that was to destroy the works of the devil and to make the kingdoms of this world the Kingdom of our God. Jesus is expecting us to do even greater miracles then He did, because He left us with the Holy Spirit. One of the last prayers Jesus prayed was that we would take the next step after being born again and being filled with the Holy

Spirit. God wants us to become one with the Trinity, one with all the members of the Body Christ and understand our purpose and part in the Kingdom of Heaven.

Colossians 3: ¹If ye then be risen with Christ, seek those things which are above, where Christ sitteth on the right hand of God. *²Set your affection on things above, not on things on the earth. ³For ye are dead, and your life is hid with Christ in God.*

Everything in the Kingdom of Heaven revolves around Seed Time and Harvest.

Ephesians (KJV) 4:¹⁷This I say therefore, and testify in the Lord, that ye henceforth walk not as other Gentiles walk, in the vanity of their mind, ¹⁸Having the understanding darkened, being alienated from *the life of God* through the ignorance that is in them, because of the blindness of their heart: ¹⁹Who being past feeling have given themselves over unto lasciviousness, to work all uncleanness with greediness. *²⁰But ye have not so learned Christ; ²¹If so be that ye have heard him, and have been taught by him, as the truth is in Jesus: ²²That ye put off concerning the former conversation the old man, which is corrupt according to the deceitful lusts; ²³And be renewed in the spirit of your mind; ²⁴And that ye put on the new man, which after God is created in righteousness and true holiness.*

The reason that God raised the dead and did other miracles is because of His presence dwelling inside of His Son. God is the source of all life. The Bible says that we are separated from the life of God because we do not discern, or understand, what or who we have living in the midst of us. He sets before us daily life and death, blessings and curses; we have to choose, and the decision could be devastating if we do not make the right choices. The Word of God is a lamp unto our feet and a light unto our paths. To be carnally minded is death, but to be spiritually minded is life and peace. If we sow to the Spirit we will reap life, but if we sow to the flesh, death will be our reward.

1 John (KJV) 3: ¹Behold, what manner of love the Father hath bestowed upon us, that we should be called the sons of God: therefore the world knoweth us not, because it knew him not. *²Beloved, now are we the sons of God, and it doth not yet appear what we shall be: but we know that, when he shall appear, we shall be like him; for we shall see him as he is. ³And every man that hath this hope in him purifieth himself, even as he is pure.* ⁴Whosoever committeth sin transgresseth also the law: for sin is the transgression of the law. ⁵And ye know that he was manifested to take away our sins; and in him is no sin. ⁶Whosoever abideth in him sinneth not: whosoever sinneth hath not seen him, neither known him. ⁷Little children, let no man deceive you: he that doeth righteousness is righteous, even as he is righteous. ⁸He that committeth sin is of the devil; for the devil sinneth from the beginning. *⁹Whosoever is born of God doth not commit sin; for his seed remaineth in him: and he cannot sin, because he is born of God. ¹⁰In this the children of God are manifest, and the children of the devil: whosoever doeth not righteousness is not of God, neither he that loveth not his brother. ¹¹For this is the message that ye heard from the beginning, that we should love one another.* ¹²Not as Cain, who was of that wicked one, and slew his brother. And wherefore slew he him? Because his own works were evil, and his brother's righteous. ¹³Marvel not, my brethren, if the world hate you. ¹⁴We know that we have passed from death unto life, because we love the brethren. He that loveth not his brother abideth in death. ¹⁵Whosoever hateth his brother is a murderer: and ye know that no murderer hath eternal life abiding in him. *¹⁶Hereby perceive we the love of God, because* *he laid down his life for us: and we ought to lay down our lives for the brethren.* ¹⁷*But whoso hath this world's good, and seeth his brother have need, and shutteth up his bowels of compassion from him, how dwelleth the love of God in him?* ¹⁸*My little children, let us not love in word, neither in tongue; but indeed and in truth.*¹⁹*And hereby we know that we are of the truth, and shall assure our hearts before him.* ²⁰For if our heart condemn us, God is greater than our heart, and knoweth all things. ²¹Beloved, if our heart condemn us not, then have we confidence toward God. ²²And whatsoever we ask, we receive of him, because we keep his commandments, and do those things that are pleasing in his sight. ²³And this is his commandment, That we should believe on the name of his Son Jesus Christ, and love one another, as he gave us commandment. ²⁴And he that keepeth his commandments dwelleth in him, and he in him. And hereby we know that he abideth in us, by the Spirit which he hath given us.

The Last Enemy "Death"

The purpose and the divine destiny of the Kingdom of God is to destroy the works of the devil. The works of the devil are the kingdoms of this world that Satan offered to give to Jesus the power and control over if He would bow down and worship him. The work of the devil is all the corruption (murder, lying, sexual perversion, etc.) that is still in the earth today and appears to be escalating. But it will be reversed as we come together in unity and in prayer.

Matthew 6: ¹Take heed that ye do not your alms before men, to be seen of them: otherwise ye have no reward of your Father which is in heaven. ²Therefore when thou doest thine alms, do not sound a trumpet before thee, as the hypocrites do in the synagogues and in the streets, that they may have glory of men. Verily I say unto you, They have their reward. ³But when thou doest alms, let not thy left hand know what thy right hand doeth: ⁴That thine alms may be in secret: and thy Father which seeth in secret himself shall reward thee openly. ⁵And when thou prayest, thou shalt not be as the hypocrites are: for they love to pray standing in the synagogues and in the corners of the streets, that they may be seen of men. Verily I say unto you, They have their reward. ⁶But thou, when thou prayest, enter into thy closet, and when thou hast shut thy door, pray to thy Father which is in secret; and thy Father which seeth in secret shall reward thee openly. ⁷But when ye pray, use not vain repetitions, as the heathen do: for they think that they shall be heard for their much speaking. ⁸Be not ye therefore like unto them: *for your Father knoweth what things ye have need of, before ye ask him.* ⁹*After this manner therefore pray ye: Our Father which art in heaven, Hallowed be thy name.* ¹⁰*Thy kingdom come, Thy will be done in earth, as it is in heaven.* ¹¹*Give us this day our daily bread.* ¹²*And forgive us our debts, as we forgive our debtors.* ¹³*And lead us not into temptation, but deliver us from evil: For thine is the kingdom, and the power, and the glory, forever. Amen.* ¹⁴*For if ye forgive men their trespasses, your heavenly Father will also forgive you:* ¹⁵*But if ye forgive not men their trespasses, neither will your Father forgive your trespasses.*

2 Corinthians 10: ³ For though we walk in the flesh, we do not war after the flesh: ⁴ (For the weapons of our warfare are not carnal, but mighty through God to the pulling down of strong holds;)

The strongholds that we are to pull down are the ungodly systems that Satan has established in the earth.

Figure 3.14 The Temptation of Christ (1854) by Ary Scheffer.

Matthew (KJV) 4: [6] And saith unto him, If thou be the Son of God, cast thyself down: for it is written, He shall give his angels charge concerning thee: and in their hands they shall bear thee up, lest at any time thou dash thy foot against a stone. [7] Jesus said unto him, It is written again, Thou shalt not tempt the Lord thy God. [8] Again, the devil taketh him up into an exceeding high mountain, and sheweth him all the kingdoms of the world, and the glory of them; [9] And saith unto him, All these things will I give thee, if thou wilt fall down and worship me. [10] Then saith Jesus unto him, Get thee hence, Satan: for it is written, Thou shalt worship the Lord thy God, and him only shalt thou serve.

1 Corinthians 15: [25]For he must reign, till he hath put all enemies under his feet. [26]The last enemy that shall be destroyed is death. [27]For he hath put all things under his feet. But when he saith all things are put under him, it is manifest that he is excepted, which did put all things under him.

1 Corinthians 12: *[12]For as the body is one, and hath many members, and all the members of that one body, being many, are one body: so also is Christ. [13]For by one Spirit are we all baptized into one body, whether we be Jews or Gentiles, whether we be bond or free; and have been all made to drink into one Spirit. [14]For the body is not one member, but many. [15]If the foot shall say, Because I am not the hand, I am not of the body; is it therefore not of the body? [16]And if the ear shall say, Because I am not the eye, I am not of the body; is it therefore not of the body? [17]If the whole body were an eye, where were the hearing? If the whole were hearing, where were the smelling? [18]But now hath God set the members every one of them in the body, as it hath pleased him. [19]And if they were all one member, where were the body? [20]But now are they many members, yet but one body. [21]And the eye cannot say unto the hand, I have no need of thee: nor again the head to the feet, I have no need of you. [22]Nay, much more those members of the body, which seem to be more feeble, are necessary: [23]And those members of the body, which we think to be less honourable, upon these we bestow more abundant honour; and our uncomely parts have more abundant comeliness. [24]For our comely parts have no need: but God hath tempered the body together, having given more abundant honour to that part which lacked. [25]That there should be no schism in the body; but that the members should have the same care one for another. [26]And whether one member suffer, all the members suffer with it; or one member be honoured, all the members rejoice with it.* **[27]Now ye are the body of Christ, and members in particular.**

As we learned earlier, the Kingdom of God is about us becoming one with the Trinity, and we are also individual members of Jesus' body. In order for His body to function properly, each body part has to know what its purpose is, just like your hands, fingers, feet, eyes, stomach, heart, and brain do. In order for you to make a decision to get up and go to work in the morning, your brain makes decisions and controls the body to wake up, get up, take a bath, put on clothes, prepare breakfast, eat it, wash the dishes, get in a car, drive to work, park, walk into a building, and go to work. Imagine for a moment if you were paralyzed and half your body could not obey your head. The Kingdom of God works the same way. Jesus is the head of the church. His instructions are:

Mark 16: [14]Afterward he appeared unto the eleven as they sat at meat, and upbraided them with their unbelief and hardness of heart, because they believed not them which had seen him after he was Risen.

Figure 3.15 Supper at Emmaus (1601) by Caravaggio.

Jesus had been telling them for three and a half years that He was going to be crucified but after three days He would be raised from the dead. The disciples should have had a three day revival in front of Jesus's tomb. Then, perhaps, more Jews would believe today.

Mark 16: [15]And he said unto them, Go ye into all the world, and preach the gospel to every creature. [16]He that believeth and is baptized shall be saved; but he that believeth not shall be damned. [17]And these signs shall follow them that believe; In my name shall they cast out devils; they shall speak with new tongues; [18]They shall take up serpents; and if they drink any deadly thing, it shall not hurt them; they shall lay hands on the sick, and they shall recover. [19]So then after the Lord had spoken unto them, he was received up into heaven, and sat on the right hand of God. [20]And they went forth, and preached everywhere, the Lord working with them, and confirming the word with signs following. Amen.

Matthew 24: [14]*And this gospel of the kingdom shall be preached in all the world for a witness unto all nations; and then shall the end come.*

Death is swallowed up in victory.

1 Corinthians 15:55 O death, where is thy sting? O grave, where is thy victory? The sting of death is sin, and the strength of sin is the law.

John 11: ¹Now a certain man was sick, named Lazarus, of Bethany, the town of Mary and her sister Martha. ²(It was that Mary which anointed the Lord with ointment, and wiped his feet with her hair, whose brother Lazarus was sick.) ³Therefore his sisters sent unto him, saying, Lord, behold, he whom thou lovest is sick. *⁴When Jesus heard that, he said, This sickness is not unto death, but for the glory of God, that the Son of God might be glorified thereby.* ⁵Now Jesus loved Martha, and her sister, and Lazarus. ⁶When he had heard therefore that he was sick, he abode two days still in the same place where he was. ⁷Then after that saith he to his disciples, Let us go into Judaea again. ⁸His disciples say unto him, Master, the Jews of late sought to stone thee; and goest thou thither again? ⁹Jesus answered, Are there not twelve hours in the day? If any man walk in the day, he stumbleth not, because he seeth the light of this world. ¹⁰But if a man walk in the night, he stumbleth, because there is no light in him. ¹¹These things said he: and after that he saith unto them, Our friend Lazarus sleepeth; but I go, that I may awake him out of sleep. ¹²Then said his disciples, Lord, if he sleep, he shall do well. ¹³Howbeit Jesus spake of his death: but they thought that he had spoken of taking of rest in sleep. ¹⁴Then said Jesus unto them plainly, *Lazarus is dead*. ¹⁵And I am glad for your sakes that I was not there, to the intent ye may believe; nevertheless let us go unto him. ¹⁶Then said Thomas, which is called Didymus, unto his fellow disciples, Let us also go, that we may die with him. ¹⁷Then when Jesus came, he found that he had lain in the grave four days already. ¹⁸Now Bethany was nigh unto Jerusalem, about fifteen furlongs off: ¹⁹And many of the Jews came to Martha and Mary, to comfort them concerning their brother. ²⁰Then Martha, as soon as she heard that Jesus was coming, went and met him: but Mary sat still in the house. ²¹Then said Martha unto Jesus, Lord, if thou hadst been here, my brother had not died. ²²But I know, that even now, whatsoever thou wilt ask of God, God will give it thee. ²³Jesus saith unto her, Thy brother shall rise again. ²⁴Martha saith unto him, I know that he shall rise again in the resurrection at the last day. *²⁵Jesus said unto her,* **I am** *the resurrection, and the life: he that believeth in me, though he were dead, yet shall he live:* ²⁶And whosoever liveth and believeth in me shall never die. Believest thou this? ²⁷She saith unto him, Yea, Lord: I believe that thou art the Christ, the Son of God, which should come into the world. ²⁸And when she had so said, she went her way, and called Mary her sister secretly, saying, The Master is come, and calleth for thee. ²⁹As soon as she heard that, she arose quickly, and came unto him. ³⁰Now Jesus was not yet come into the town, but was in that place where Martha met him. ³¹The Jews then which were with her in the house, and comforted her, when they saw Mary, that she rose up hastily and went out, followed her, saying, She goeth unto the grave to weep there. ³²Then when Mary was come where Jesus was, and saw him, she fell down at his feet, saying unto him, Lord, if thou hadst been here, my brother had not died. ³³When Jesus therefore saw her weeping, and the Jews also weeping which came with her, he groaned in the spirit, and was troubled. ³⁴And said, Where have ye laid him? They said unto him, Lord, come and see. ³⁵Jesus wept. ³⁶Then said the Jews, Behold how he loved him! ³⁷And some of them said, Could not this man, which opened the eyes of the blind, have caused that even this man should not have died? ³⁸Jesus therefore again groaning in himself cometh to the grave. It was a cave, and a stone lay upon it. ³⁹Jesus said, Take ye away the stone. Martha, the sister of him that was dead, saith unto him, Lord, by this time he stinketh: for he hath been dead four days. *⁴⁰Jesus saith unto her, Said I not unto thee, that, if thou wouldest believe, thou shouldest see the glory of God?*

⁴¹Then they took away the stone from the place where the dead was laid. And Jesus lifted up his eyes, and said, Father, I thank thee that thou hast heard me. ⁴²And I knew that thou hearest me always: but because of the people which stand by I said it, that they may believe that thou hast sent me. ⁴³And when he thus had spoken, he cried with a loud voice, Lazarus, come forth.

Figure 3.16 The Raising of Lazarus by Alessandro Magnasco (1667–1749).

⁴⁴And he that was dead came forth, bound hand and foot with grave clothes: and his face was bound about with a napkin. Jesus saith unto them, Loose him, and let him go. ⁴⁵Then many of the Jews which came to Mary, and had seen the things which Jesus did, believed on him.

[When Jesus prayed in faith to God, God answered His prayer and Lazarus was raised from the dead by faith. God is the source and center of all life. Seed time and harvest time are at the center of the Kingdom of Heaven. The purpose of every seed is already embedded in its DNA by God. An apple seed has to produce an apple tree, and the tree must produce apples. You can tell what type of tree that Aaron's rod came from by the fruit it bore. We know that Aaron's rod bore almonds because once the creation is placed in the presence of the Creator, whatever is broken gets fixed, whatever is missing gets replaced. Whatever is dead has to come back to life, if certain conditions exist. The branch or rod, even though it is separated from the tree trunk where all the life giving resources are, came back to life because it was placed in the presence of God who is the original source of all "life".

One of Aaron's rods was placed inside the Holy of Holies, which is symbolic of Jesus Christ. Jesus was crucified on the cross, He died and was buried, then He came back to life just as Aaron's rod that budded and bore fruit. Jesus continues to bear fruit through His body (us).

God raised Jesus from the dead just like Aaron's rods came back to life after three days of being in the presence of God in the Holy of Holies. Three days after the crucifixion Jesus was raised from the dead. In the Old Testament, Jesus is sometimes called the Wild Olive Branch. . In the New Testament, He refers to Himself as the True Vine, and we are the branches and we must bear fruit or we will be cut off. The foolish virgins never understood seed-time and harvest-time principles, and they never sought the Kingdom of God. They never bore any fruit; the saddest thing is that they never knew that they were supposed to be doing anything else except being good church-goers. They are like the fig tree that Jesus found that had leaves on it. The tree looked like a fig tree from a distance. But all Jews know when a fig tree has leaves, figs will be present. But when Jesus examined the tree a little closer he saw something was missing; there was no fruit present. It was not doing what it was created to do. It was not being productive. It was the same thing with the foolish virgins who in the end were cast into outer darkness.]

John 15: ⁴Abide in me, and I in you. As the branch cannot bear fruit of itself, except it abide in the vine; no more can ye, except ye abide in me. ⁵I am the vine, ye are the branches: He that abideth in me, and I in him, the same bringeth forth much fruit: for without me ye can do nothing. ⁶If a man abide not in me, he is cast forth as a branch, and is withered; and men gather them, and cast them into the fire, and they are burned.

Figure 3.17 Jesus as the True Vine (sixteenth century)

This example of Jesus cursing a fig tree is a warning for all Christians. If we are not producing fruit there is a disconnection between us and Jesus. Most Christians have not been taught how to bear fruit. And if we do not get this down inside of our innermost being we will be like the foolish virgins. They looked like the other virgins, but they were not doing what they were created to do or, in other words they were not bearing fruit. They were not productive on behalf of the Kingdom of God. The chapter on "**The Garden of Whatever Your Name Is**" will cover this in more detail.

A COMMENTARY BY PHILLIP MEDHURST ON THE GOSPEL OF MARK

H1. BOWYER BIBLE PRINT 4911. THE BARREN FIG TREE. FRENCH SCHOOL

Figure 3.18 The Barren Fig Tree by Philip De Vere.

Matthew 7: [13]Enter ye in at the strait gate: for wide is the gate, and broad is the way, that leadeth to destruction, and many there be which go in thereat: [14]Because strait is the gate, and narrow is the way, which leadeth unto life, and few there be that find it. (The wise virgins Found the strait gate). [15]Beware of false prophets, which come to you in sheep's clothing, but inwardly they are ravening wolves. [16]Ye shall know them by their fruits. Do men gather grapes of thorns, or figs of thistles? [17]Even so every good tree bringeth forth good fruit; but a corrupt tree bringeth forth evil fruit. [18]A good tree cannot bring forth evil fruit, neither can a corrupt tree bring forth good fruit. [19]Every tree that bringeth not forth good fruit is hewn down, and cast into the fire. [20]Wherefore by their fruits ye shall know them. **[21]Not every one that saith unto me, Lord, Lord, shall enter into the kingdom of heaven; but he that doeth the will of my Father which is in heaven.**

The reason that God could raise the dead through Jesus and do other miracles is because of His presence dwelling inside of His Son. Jesus was *one* with the Trinity and the power of God to heal, restore, and make whole could flow freely to a certain point. We know that unbelief in our heart would prevent the flow of the power of God to heal. In Hebrews 3, if you remember, the Jews that never made it to the Promised Land had an "evil heart of unbelief." A heart is called "evil" because it says you have no faith in God and you do not trust Him.

The Spirit of God cannot dwell in an unclean temple. Jesus never committed any sin. We know that Jesus said on many occasions that His body is the temple of the Holy Spirit. The book of Hebrews gives us more insight into the fact that Jesus' flesh is also the veil, and in the Old Testament the veil separated the Inner Court from the Holy of Holies. The Holy of Holies was where the ark of the covenant, and the mercy seat which had two statues of angels which were facing each other, was placed.

Figure 3.19 The erection of the Tabernacle and the Sacred vessels, as in Exodus 40:17-19, "And it came to pass in the first month in the second year, on the first day of the month, that the tabernacle was reared up. And Moses reared up the tabernacle, and fastened his sockets, and set up the boards thereof, and put in the bars thereof, and reared up his pillars. And he spread abroad the tent over the tabernacle, and put the covering of the tent above upon it; as the Lord commanded Moses."; illustration from the 1728 *Figures de la Bible*; illustrated by Gerard Hoet (1648–1733) and others, and published by P. de Hondt in The Hague; image courtesy Bizzell Bible Collection, University of Oklahoma Libraries.

Luke (KJV) 11:[11] If a son shall ask bread of any of you that is a father, will he give him a stone? or if he ask a fish, will he for a fish give him a serpent? [12] Or if he shall ask an egg, will he offer him a scorpion? [13] *If ye then, being evil, know how to give good gifts unto your children: how much more shall your heavenly Father give the Holy Spirit to them that ask him?*

Jesus' body is the temple of the Holy Spirit but He has also become the Holy of Holies. His flesh is the veil, and inside Him dwells God the Father and God the Holy Spirit, who are living inside of us now. They came when we asked Jesus to come into our hearts. When we ask God to fill us with the Holy Spirit in faith, the Holy Spirit honors our request and we become the temple of the Holy Spirit. Now we must understand why Jesus prayed that we would become *one* with the Trinity. We will discuss this further in the chapter on "The Power and Force of One."

Hebrews (KJV) 6:[18] That by two immutable things, in which it was impossible for God to lie, we might have a strong consolation, who have fled for refuge to lay hold upon the hope set before us: **[19] Which hope we have as an anchor of the soul, both sure and stedfast, and which entereth into that within the veil; [20] Whither the forerunner is for us entered, even Jesus, made an high priest for ever after the order of Melchisedec.**

Hebrews (KJV) 10: [19] Having therefore, brethren, boldness to enter into the holiest by the blood of Jesus, [20] By a new and living way, which he hath consecrated for us, through the veil, that is to say, his flesh; [21] And having an high priest over the house of God; [22] Let us draw near with a true heart in full assurance of faith, having our hearts sprinkled from an evil conscience, and our bodies washed with pure water.

Figure 3.20 Aaron's rod that budded (illustration from the 1890 Holman Bible)

Once Aaron's rods were placed inside the Holy of Holies, they budded after three days. . Those rods were actually from a branch from an almond tree. If you take a limb from any tree and cut it off, that limb will die. The leaves will wither and the fruit will die because it has been separated from the base of the tree or its source of life. But when that limb or that rod is placed in the presence of God who is the creator of the universe even though the rod is dead, it will come back to life and start producing fruit again because of the *absolute life of God* that is flowing through it again from being in the **presence of God** . When we start doing what God created and predestined for us to do, God's anointing will rest on us and empower us to fulfill our destiny. This explains why Jesus said when we are separated from Him, we cannot do anything.

Acts 4: [9] If we this day be examined of the good deed done to the impotent man, by what means he is made whole; [10] Be it known unto you all, and to all the people of Israel, that by the name of Jesus Christ of Nazareth, whom ye crucified, whom God raised from the dead, even by him doth this man stand here before you whole. [11] This is the stone which was set at nought of you builders, which is become the head of the corner. [12]Neither is there salvation in any other: for there is none other name under heaven given among men, whereby we must be saved.

Figure 3.21 Budding of Aaron's Staff by Julius Schnorr von Carolsfeld (1794–1872).

Numbers 17: [6]And Moses spake unto the children of Israel, and every one of their princes gave him a rod apiece, for each prince one, according to their fathers' houses, even twelve rods: and the rod of Aaron was among their rods. [7]And Moses laid up the rods before the LORD in the tabernacle of witness. [8]And it came to pass, that on the morrow Moses went into the tabernacle of witness; and, behold, the rod of Aaron for the house of Levi was budded, and brought forth buds, and bloomed blossoms, and yielded almonds.

[God is the source of all life. The Bible says that we are separated from the life of God because we have not discerned, or understood, what we have living in the midst of us. He sets before us daily life and death; we have to choose between the two. The decision will be devastating if we do not make the right choice. The Word of God is a lamp unto our feet and a light onto our paths.

To be carnally minded is death; to be spiritually minded is life and peace. If we sow to the spirit we will reap life, but if we sow to the flesh then death will be our reward. If you sow the Word of God into your spirit and meditate on it daily, allowing it to govern your daily walk with God, you will reap life.]

Colossians 3: ¹⁰And have put on the new man, which is renewed in knowledge after the image of him that created him: ¹¹Where there is neither Greek nor Jew, circumcision nor uncircumcision, Barbarian, Scythian, bond nor free: but Christ is all, and in all.

The fruit that all Christians should be bearing are the fruit of the Spirit. Some of them are listed in the next verse. There are many other ways to produce fruit; they will be discussed in the next chapter.

Colossians 3: ¹²Put on therefore, as the elect of God, holy and beloved, bowels of mercies, kindness, humbleness of mind, meekness, longsuffering; ¹³Forbearing one another, and forgiving one another, if any man have a quarrel against any: even as Christ forgave you, so also do ye. ¹⁴And above all these things put on charity, which is the bond of perfectness. ¹⁵And let the peace of God rule in your hearts, to the which also ye are called in one body; and be ye thankful. ¹⁶Let the word of Christ dwell in you richly in all wisdom; teaching and admonishing one another in psalms and hymns and spiritual songs, singing with grace in your hearts to the Lord. ¹⁷And whatsoever ye do in word or deed, do all in the name of the Lord Jesus, giving thanks to God and the Father by him.

Ephesians 4: ¹⁷This I say therefore, and testify in the Lord, that ye henceforth walk not as other Gentiles walk, in the vanity of their mind, ¹⁸Having the understanding darkened, being alienated from the life of God through the ignorance that is in them, because of the blindness of their heart:

1 Corinthians 15: ¹Moreover, brethren, I declare unto you the gospel which I preached unto you, which also ye have received, and wherein ye stand; ²By which also ye are saved, if ye keep in memory what I preached unto you, unless ye have believed in vain. ³For I delivered unto you first of all that which I also received, how that Christ died for our sins according to the scriptures; ⁴And that he was buried, and that he rose again the third day according to the scriptures: ⁵And that he was seen of Cephas, then of the twelve: ⁶After that, he was seen of above five hundred brethren at once; of whom the greater part remain unto this present, but some are fallen asleep. ⁷After that, he was seen of James; then of all the apostles. ⁸And last of all he was seen of me also, as of one born out of due time. ⁹For I am the least of the apostles, that am not meet to be called an apostle, because I persecuted the church of God. ¹⁰But by the grace of God I am what I am: and his grace which was bestowed upon me was not in vain; but I laboured more abundantly than they all: yet not I, but the grace of God which was with me. ¹¹Therefore whether it were I or they, so we preach, and so ye believed. ¹²Now if Christ be preached that he rose from the dead, how say some among you that there is no resurrection of the dead? ¹³But if there be no resurrection of the dead, then is Christ not risen: ¹⁴And if Christ be not risen, then is our preaching vain, and your faith is also vain. ¹⁵Yea, and we are found false witnesses of God; because we have testified of God that he raised up Christ: whom he raised not up, if so be that the dead rise not. ¹⁶For if the dead rise not, then is not Christ raised: ¹⁷And if Christ be not raised, your faith is vain; ye are yet in your sins. ¹⁸Then they also which are fallen asleep in Christ are perished. *¹⁹If in this life only we have hope in Christ, we are of all men most miserable. ²⁰But `now is Christ risen from the dead, and become the first fruits of them that slept. ²¹For since by man came death, by man came also the resurrection of the dead. ²²For as in Adam all die, even so in Christ shall all be made alive ²³But every man in his own order: Christ the first fruits; afterward they that are Christ's at his coming. ²⁴Then cometh the end, when he shall have delivered up the kingdom to God, even the Father; when he shall have put down all rule and all authority and power. ²⁵For he must reign, till he hath put all enemies under* his feet. ²⁶The last enemy that shall be destroyed is death. ²⁷For he hath put all things under his feet. But when he saith all things are put under him, it is manifest that he is excepted, which did put all things under him. ²⁸And when all things shall be subdued unto him, then shall the Son also himself be subject unto him that put all things under him, that God may be all in all. ²⁹Else what shall they do which are baptized for the dead, if the dead rise not at all? why are they then baptized for the dead? ³⁰And why stand we in jeopardy every hour? ³¹I protest by your rejoicing which I have in Christ Jesus our Lord, I die daily. ³²If after the manner of men I have fought with beasts at Ephesus, what advantageth it me, if the dead rise not? let us eat and drink; for tomorrow we die. ³³Be not deceived: evil communications corrupt good manners. ³⁴Awake to righteousness, and sin not; for some have not the knowledge of God: I speak this to your shame.

Remember from II Corinthians 4: ⁶For God, who commanded the light to shine out of darkness, hath shined in our hearts, to give the light of the knowledge of the glory of God in the face of Jesus Christ. ⁷But we have this treasure in earthen vessels, that the excellency of the power may be of God, and not of us.

God has been trying to give us this knowledge since the resurrection of Jesus. God wants us to grow up spiritually and to take dominion over the kingdom of darkness because that is where all of the corruption in the earth comes from. Our warfare truly is not against flesh and blood but it is against the kingdom of darkness. God has placed us in the earth to bring about the end of the reign of Satan's kingdom in the earth. When Jesus was crucified He switched places with us. Our sins were placed on Him and He was crucified in our place; the foundation of this started in Leviticus.

(Notice what happened to Aaron's two sons who did not respect the office of the priesthood, which is what every Christian is faced with today because we are now the priests and the temple.)

Figure 3.22 Aaron's Sons, Nadab and Abihu, Destroyed by Fire (c. 1625–30), engraving by Matthäus Merian.

Leviticus 16*:* [1]And the LORD spake unto Moses after the death of the two sons of Aaron, when they offered before the LORD, and died; [2]And the LORD said unto Moses, Speak unto Aaron thy brother, that he come not at all times into the holy place within the vail before the mercy seat, which is upon the ark; that he die not: for I will appear in the cloud upon the mercy seat. [3]Thus shall Aaron come into the holy place: with a young bullock for a sin offering, and a ram for a burnt offering. [4]He shall put on the holy linen coat, and he shall have the linen breeches upon his flesh, and shall be girded with a linen girdle, and with the linen mitre shall he be attired: these are holy garments; therefore shall he wash his flesh in water, and so put them on. *[5]And he shall take of the congregation of the children of Israel two kids of the goats for a sin offering, and one ram for a burnt offering.* [6]And Aaron shall offer his bullock of the sin offering, which is for himself, and make an atonement for himself, and for his house. *[7]And he shall take the two goats, and present them before the LORD at the door of the tabernacle of the congregation. [8]And Aaron shall cast lots upon the two goats; lot for the LORD, and the other lot for the scapegoat. [9]And Aaron shall bring the goat upon which the LORD's lot fell, and offer him for a sin offering. [10]But the goat, on which the lot fell to be the scapegoat, shall be presented alive before the LORD, to make an atonement with him, and to let him go for a scapegoat into the wilderness.* [11]And Aaron shall bring the bullock of the sin offering, which is for himself, and shall make an atonement for himself, and for his house, and shall kill the bullock of the sin offering which is for himself: [12]And he shall take a censer full of burning coals of fire from off the altar before the LORD, and his hands full of sweet incense beaten small, and bring it within the vail: [13]And he shall put the incense upon the fire before the LORD, that the cloud of the incense may cover the mercy seat that is upon the testimony, that he die not: *[14]And he shall take of the blood of the bullock, and sprinkle it with his finger upon the mercy seat eastward; and before the mercy seat shall he sprinkle of the blood with his finger seven times. [15]Then shall he kill the goat of the sin offering, that is for the people, and bring his blood within the vail, and do with that blood as he did with the blood of the bullock, and sprinkle it upon the mercy seat, and before the mercy seat: [16]And he shall make an atonement for the holy place, because of the uncleanness of the children of Israel, and because of their transgressions in all their sins: and so shall he do for the tabernacle of the congregation, that remaineth among them in the midst of their uncleanness. [17]And there shall be no man in the tabernacle of the congregation when he goeth in to make an atonement in the holy place, until he come out, and have made an atonement for himself, and for his household, and for all the congregation of Israel. [18]And he shall go out unto the altar that is before the LORD, and make an atonement for it; and shall take of the blood of the bullock, and of the blood of the goat, and put it upon the horns of the altar round about. [19]And he shall sprinkle of the blood upon it with his finger seven times, and cleanse it, and hallow it from the uncleanness of the children of Israel.*

Figure 3.23 The Scapegoat (1854–1855) by William Holman Hunt.

Jesus became our Scapegoat.

Isaiah (KJV) 53: Who hath believed our report? and to whom is the arm of the LORD revealed? 2 For he shall grow up before him as a tender plant, and as a root out of a dry ground: he hath no form nor comeliness; and when we shall see him, there is no beauty that we should desire him.

Figure 3.24 The Taking of Christ (c. 1602) by Caravaggio.

[3] He is despised and rejected of men; a man of sorrows, and acquainted with grief: and we hid as it were our faces from him; he was despised, and we esteemed him not.

Figure 3.25 Taking of Christ with the Malchus Episode (c. 1620) by Gerard Douffet.

[4] Surely he hath borne our griefs, and carried our sorrows:

Figure 3.26 The Taking of Christ (c. 1616–1617) by Dirck van Baburen.

yet we did esteem him stricken, smitten of God, and afflicted.
[5] But he was wounded for our transgressions

Figure 3.27 Christ in front of Pilate (1881) by Mihály Munkácsy (1844-1900).

Figure 3.28 The Flagellation of Christ (c. 1780) by Anton Raphael Mengs.

Isaiah 53: [5] he was bruised for our iniquities:

Figure 3.29 Artist: Peter Paul Rubens, Flagellation of Christ by Peter Paul Rubens.

the chastisement of our peace was upon him; and with his stripes we are healed.

Figure 3.30 Flagellate Jesus (seventeenth century) artist unknown.

[6]All we like sheep have gone astray; we have turned everyone to his own way; and the LORD hath laid on him the iniquity of us all.

The Crown of Thorns

Figure 3.31 The Crown of Thorns by Caravaggio.

[7]He was oppressed, and he was afflicted, yet he opened not his mouth: he is brought as a lamb to the slaughter, and as a sheep before her shearers is dumb, so he openeth not his mouth.

Figure 3.32 Christ leaving the courtroom by Gustave Doré (1832–1883).

[8]He was taken from prison and from judgment: and who shall declare his generation?

Figure 3.33 Christ Carrying the Cross (c. 1565) by Titian (1490–1576).

**Figure 3.34 Christ on the Cross between the Two Thieves (1619–1620)
by Peter Paul Rubens.**

Figure 3.35 Deposition of Christ by Rogier van der Weyden (1399/1400–1464).

for he was cut off out of the land of the living: for the transgression of my people was he stricken.

Figure 3.36 The Burial of Christ (1559) by Titian.

[9]And he made his grave with the wicked, and with the rich in his death; because he had done no violence, neither was any deceit in his mouth.

Figure 3.37 Christ's Descent into Hell (1568) by Tintoretto.

Isaiah 53: ¹⁰Yet it pleased the LORD to bruise him; he hath put him to grief: when thou shalt make his soul an offering for sin, he shall see his seed, he shall prolong his days, and the pleasure of the LORD shall prosper in his hand. ¹¹He shall see of the travail of his soul, and shall be satisfied: by his knowledge shall my righteous servant justify many; for he shall bear their iniquities. ¹²Therefore will I divide him a portion with the great, and he shall divide the spoil with the strong; because he hath poured out his soul unto death: and he was numbered with the transgressors; and he bare the sin of many, and made intercession for the transgressors.

I Corinthians 2: ¹And I, brethren, when I came to you, came not with excellency of speech or of wisdom, declaring unto you the testimony of God. ²For I determined not to know anything among you, save Jesus Christ, and him crucified. ³And I was with you in weakness, and in fear, and in much trembling. ⁴And my speech and my preaching was not with enticing words of man's wisdom, but in demonstration of the Spirit and of power: ⁵That your faith should not stand in the wisdom of men, but in the power of God. ⁶Howbeit we speak wisdom among them that are perfect: yet not the wisdom of this world, nor of the princes of this world, that come to nought: *⁷But we speak the wisdom of God in a mystery, even the hidden wisdom, which God ordained before the world unto our glory: ⁸Which none of the princes of this world knew: for had they known it, they would not have crucified the Lord of glory.* ⁹But as it is written, Eye hath not seen, nor ear heard, neither have entered into the heart of man, the things which God hath prepared for them that love him. ¹⁰But God hath revealed them unto us by his Spirit: for the Spirit searcheth all things, yea, the deep things of God. ¹¹For what man knoweth the things of a man, save the spirit of man which is in him? even so the things of God knoweth no man, but the Spirit of God. ¹²Now we have received, not the spirit of the world, but the spirit which is of God; that we might know the things that are freely given to us of God. ¹³Which things also we speak, not in the words which man's wisdom teacheth, but which the Holy Ghost teacheth; comparing spiritual things with spiritual. ¹⁴But the natural man receiveth not the things of the Spirit of God: for they are foolishness unto him: neither can he know them, because they are spiritually discerned. ¹⁵But he that is spiritual judgeth all things, yet he himself is judged of no man. ¹⁶For who hath known the mind of the Lord, that he may instruct him? but we have the mind of Christ.

Genesis 3: ¹⁵ And the LORD God said unto the woman, What is this that thou hast done? And the woman said, The serpent beguiled me, and I did eat. ¹⁵ And the LORD God said unto the serpent, Because thou hast done this, thou art cursed above all cattle, and above every beast of the field; upon thy belly shalt thou go, and dust shalt thou eat all the days of thy life: ¹⁵And I will put enmity between thee and the woman, and between thy seed and her seed; it shall bruise thy head, and thou shalt bruise his heel.

God promised Satan, alias Lucifer, alias the devil, which is *lived* spelled backwards, a beating in Genesis and if God promises to give you something, you will get it. Satan is still rubbing his head today.

Figure 3.38 Lucifer, on the Back of the Chair by Guillaume Geefs. Photographer: Vassil.

God promised Satan that there was one coming who would stomp his head so hard it would not only leave a bruise on Satan's head, it would bruise that individual's (that person was Jesus) heel. It happened over two thousand years ago when God raised Jesus from the dead and fulfilled the promise.

Revelation (KJV) 1: [18] I am he that liveth, and was dead; and, behold, I am alive for evermore, Amen; and have the keys of hell and of death.

Figure 3.39 The Ascension (1636) by Rembrandt (1606–1669).

Adam lost his God-given authority over the earth when he obeyed Satan instead of God and sin entered the world, separating God from His creation, man. But God had a plan to redeem man back and it started in Leviticus with the priest.

Leviticus 16: [15]Then shall he kill the goat of the sin offering, that is for the people, and bring his blood within the vail, and do with that blood as he did with the blood of the bullock, and sprinkle it upon the mercy seat, and before the mercy seat: [16]And he shall make an atonement for the holy place, because of the uncleanness of the children of Israel, and because of their transgressions in all their sins: and so shall he do for the tabernacle of the congregation, that remaineth among them in the midst of their uncleanness. [17]And there shall be no man in the tabernacle of the congregation when he goeth in to make an atonement in the holy place, until he come out, and have made an atonement for himself, and for his household, and for all the congregation of Israel. [18]And he shall go out unto the altar that is before the LORD, and make an atonement for it; and shall take of the blood of the bullock, and of the blood of the goat, and put it upon the horns of the altar round about. [19]And he shall sprinkle of the blood upon it with his finger seven times, and cleanse it, and hallow it from the uncleanness of the children of Israel. *²⁰And when he hath made an end of reconciling the holy place, and the tabernacle of the congregation, and the altar, he shall bring the live goat: ²¹And Aaron shall lay both his hands upon the head of the live goat, and confess over him all the iniquities of the children of Israel, and all their transgressions in all their sins, putting them upon the head of the goat, and shall send him away by the hand of a fit man into the wilderness: ²²And the goat shall bear upon him all their iniquities unto a land not inhabited: and he shall let go the goat in the wilderness.*

Colossians (KJV) 2: ⁸ Beware lest any man spoil you through philosophy and vain deceit, after the tradition of men, after the rudiments of the world, and not after Christ. ⁹ For in him dwelleth all the fulness of the Godhead bodily. *¹⁰And ye are complete in him, which is the head of all principality and power: ¹¹ In whom also ye are circumcised with the circumcision made without hands, in putting off the body of the sins of the flesh by the circumcision of Christ: ¹² Buried with him in baptism, wherein also ye are risen with him through the faith of the operation of God, who hath raised him from the dead. ¹³ And you, being dead in your sins and the uncircumcision of your flesh, hath he quickened together with him, having forgiven you all trespasses; ¹⁴ Blotting out the handwriting of ordinances that was against us, which was contrary to us, and took it out of the way, nailing it to his cross; ¹⁵ And having spoiled principalities and powers, he made a shew of them openly, triumphing over them in it.*

We became the goat that got away.

Figure 3.40 The Scapegoat (1854) by William Holman Hunt (1827-1910).

Jesus went through all this for us. If you have not asked Jesus to forgive you of your sins and to cleanse you from all unrighteousness, ask Him to come into your heart now. You may not get another chance; tomorrow is not promised to any of us.

Romans (KJV) 10: ⁶ But the righteousness which is of faith speaketh on this wise, Say not in thine heart, Who shall ascend into heaven? (that is, to bring Christ down from above:) ⁷ Or, Who shall descend into the deep? (that is, to bring up Christ again from the dead.) **⁸ But what saith it? The word is nigh thee, even in thy mouth, and in thy heart: that is, the word of faith, which we preach;**

The first step of the fruit of faith starts with the seed of salvation.

Visions of the Rapture

"I was in the Spirit on the Lord's Day "

John (AMP) 3: Now there was a certain man among the Pharisees named Nicodemus, a ruler (a leader, an authority) among the Jews, ² Who came to Jesus at night and said to Him, Rabbi, we know *and* are certain that You have come from God [as] a Teacher; for no one can do these signs (these wonderworks, these miracles—and produce the proofs) that You do unless God is with him. ³ Jesus answered him, I assure you, most solemnly I tell you, that unless a person is born again (anew, from above), he cannot ever surprised, astonished] at My telling you, You must all be born anew (from above). **⁸ The wind blows (breathes) where it wills; and though you hear its sound, yet you neither know where it comes from nor where it is going. So it is with everyone who is born of the Spirit. ⁹ Nicodemus answered by asking, how can all this be possible? 10 Jesus replied, Are you the teacher of Israel, and yet do not know nor understand these things? [Are they strange to you?]** see (know, be acquainted with, and experience) the kingdom of God.⁴ Nicodemus said to Him, How can a man be born when he is old? Can he enter his mother's womb again and be born? ⁵ Jesus answered, I assure you, most solemnly I tell you, unless a man is born of water and [even] the Spirit, he cannot [ever] enter the kingdom of God. ⁶ What is born of [from] the flesh is flesh [of the physical is physical]; and what is born of the Spirit is spirit. ⁷ Marvel not [do not be surprised, astonished] at My telling you, You must all be born anew (from above). 8 The wind blows (breathes) where it wills; and though you hear its sound, yet you neither know where it comes from nor where it is going. So it is with everyone who is born of the Spirit. 9 Nicodemus answered by asking, How can all this be possible?

Nicodemus one of the leaders among Jews came to Jesus to compliment Him and to let Him know that he believed that He was sent by God and that the miracles were done because of God working through Him. Then Jesus began to explain to him the process by which a person can enter the Kingdom of God and that it starts with the process of being Born Again. You have to have Royalty in your blood-line in order for someone to say that they are members of a Royal Family. Jesus told Nicodemus that he had to be Born of God and everyone Born of God is just like the wind. Jesus questioned Nicodemus because he was supposed to be a teacher among the Jews but he did not understand that the first principal of entering the Kingdom of God came by birth right. And that everyone born of God, Jesus says has the capability to come and go like the wind. One minute they are standing right in front of you then the next minute they are gone (Remember Enoch). Then in John 6 Jesus give's His disciples a demonstration.

Jesus Walks on Water

John (ESV) 6: [16] When evening came, his disciples went down to the sea, [17] got into a boat, and started across the sea to Capernaum. It was now dark, and Jesus had not yet come to them. [18] The sea became rough because a strong wind was blowing. [19] When they had rowed about three or four miles they saw Jesus walking on the sea and coming near the boat, and they were frightened. [20] But he said to them, "It is I; do not be afraid." **[21] Then they were glad to take him into the boat, and immediately the boat was at the land to which they were going.**

One minute the Disciples were watching what appeared to be a ghost until Jesus spoke up then as soon as Jesus foot touched the boat they went from being 3 or 4 miles off the coast of Tiberias to the boat loaded with disciples and Jesus being found resting on the dock of the Bay at Capernaum. The people on the dock did not know where the boat came from. This was done by the power of God for the purpose of ministering the Gospel of the Kingdom (There is no time or distance in the realm of the Spirit so walk in the Spirit).

Do you remember Philip and the Ethiopian?

Act 8: [26] And the angel of the Lord spake unto Philip, saying, Arise, and go toward the south unto the way that goeth down from Jerusalem unto Gaza, which is desert. [27] And he arose and went: and, behold, a man of Ethiopia, an eunuch of great authority under Candace queen of the Ethiopians, who had the charge of all her treasure, and had come to Jerusalem for to worship, [28] Was returning, and sitting in his chariot read Esaias the prophet. [29] Then the Spirit said unto Philip, Go near, and join thyself to this chariot. [30] And Philip ran thither to him, and heard him read the prophet Esaias, and said, Understandest thou what thou readest? [31] And he said, How can I, except some man should guide me? And he desired Philip that he would come up and sit with him. [32] The place of the scripture which he read was this, He was led as a sheep to the slaughter; and like a lamb dumb before his shearer, so opened he not his mouth: [33] In his humiliation his judgment was taken away: and who shall declare his generation? for his life is taken from the earth. [34] And the eunuch answered Philip, and said, I pray thee, of whom speaketh the prophet this? of himself, or of some other man? [35] Then Philip opened his mouth, and began at the same scripture, and preached unto him Jesus. [36] And as they went on their way, they came unto a certain water: and the eunuch said, See, here is water; what doth hinder me to be baptized? [37] And Philip said, If thou believest with all thine heart, thou mayest. And he answered and said, I believe that Jesus Christ is the Son of God. [38] And he commanded the chariot to stand still: and they went down both into the water, both Philip and the eunuch; and he baptized him. **[39] And when they were come up out of the water, the Spirit of the Lord caught away Philip, that the eunuch saw him no more: and he went on his way rejoicing. [40] But Philip was found at Azotus: and passing through he preached in all the cities, till he came to Caesarea.**

One minute Phillip is ministering to the eunuch the next minute God translates him to Azotus where he continues preaching the Gospel of the Kingdom throughout all the cities in that region. Again God uses this method of supernatural transportation for the purpose of distributing the message of the Kingdom of Heaven. It is not so we can get to work on time or rob a bank and no one ever knew where the money went.

Do You Remember St. John and Revelations

John the Apostle

From Wikipedia, the free encyclopedia

Roman Catholic tradition states that after the Assumption, John went to Ephesus **and from there wrote the three epistles traditionally attributed to him. John was allegedly banished by the Roman authorities to the** Greek **island of** Patmos**, where some believe that he wrote the** Book of Revelation. **According to** Tertullian **(in** *The Prescription of Heretics***) John was banished (presumably to Patmos) after being plunged into boiling oil in Rome and suffering nothing from it. It is said that all in the entire** Coliseum **audience were converted to Christianity upon witnessing this miracle. This event would have occurred during the reign of** Domitian**, a Roman emperor who was known for his persecution of Christians in the late 1st century.**

Revelation (KJV) 4: After this I looked, and, behold, a door was opened in heaven: and the first voice which I heard was as it were of a trumpet talking with me; which said, Come up hither, and I will shew thee things which must be hereafter.[2] **And immediately I was in the spirit: and, behold, a throne was set in heaven, and one sat on the throne.[3] And he that sat was to look upon like a jasper and a sardine stone: and there was a rainbow round about the throne, in sight like unto an emerald.**

One minute John was on the Island of Patmos the next he minute he is in Heaven receiving the Book of Revelation.

CHAPTER 4

The Fruit of Faith Part 2

Romans (KJV) 10: [9] That if thou shalt confess with thy mouth the Lord Jesus, and shalt believe in thine heart that God hath raised him from the dead, thou shalt be saved. [10] For with the heart man believeth unto righteousness; and with the mouth confession is made unto salvation. [11] For the scripture saith, Whosoever believeth on him shall not be ashamed. [12] For there is no difference between the Jew and the Greek: for the same Lord over all is rich unto all that call upon him.[13] For whosoever shall call upon the name of the Lord shall be saved. **[14] How then shall they call on him in whom they have not believed? and how shall they believe in him of whom they have not heard? and how shall they hear without a preacher? [15] And how shall they preach, except they be sent? as it is written, How beautiful are the feet of them that preach the gospel of peace, and bring glad tidings of good things! [16] But they have not all obeyed the gospel. For Esaias saith, Lord, who hath believed our report? [17] So then faith cometh by hearing, and hearing by the word of God**

Jesus went into hell to take back authority over the earth and to give dominion back to the children of God because by birthright it is their inheritance. The earth and the universe belong to God. When God raised Jesus from the dead He told Jesus to "sit here, while I make your enemies your footstool." God is going to do it by working through His children.

**Figure 4.1 God Inviting Christ to sit on the Throne at His Right Hand (1645)
by Pieter de Grebber.**

Hebrews 2: Therefore we ought to give the more earnest heed to the things which we have heard, lest at any time we should let them slip. [2] For if the word spoken by angels was stedfast, and every transgression and disobedience received a just recompence of reward; [3] How shall we escape, if we neglect so great salvation; which at the first began to be spoken by the Lord, and was confirmed unto us by them that heard him; [4] God also bearing them witness, both with signs and wonders, and with divers miracles, and gifts of the Holy Ghost, according to his own will? [5] For unto the angels hath he not put in subjection the world to come, whereof we speak. [6] But one in a certain place testified, saying, What is man, that thou art mindful of him? or the son of man that thou visitest him? [7] Thou madest him a little lower than the angels; thou crownedst him with glory and honour, and didst set him over the works of thy hands: [8] Thou hast put all things in subjection under his feet. For in that he put all in subjection under him, he left nothing that is not put under him. But now we see not yet all things put under him. *[9] But we see Jesus, who was made a little lower than the angels for the suffering of death, crowned with glory and honour; that he by the grace of God should taste death for every man. [10] For it became him, for whom are all things, and by whom are all things, in bringing many sons unto glory, to make the captain of their salvation perfect through sufferings. [11] For both he that sanctifieth and they who are sanctified are all of one: for which cause he is not ashamed to call them brethren, [12] Saying, I will declare thy name unto my brethren, in the midst of* *the church will I sing praise unto thee. [13]And again, I will put my trust in him. And again, Behold I and the children which God hath given me. [14]Forasmuch then as the children are partakers of flesh and blood, he also himself likewise took part of the same;*

Figure 4.2 Satan Presiding at the Infernal Council (1824) by John Martin (1789–1854).

That through death he might destroy him that had the power of death, that is, the devil; [15]And deliver them who through fear of death were all their lifetime subject to bondage. [16]For verily he took not on him the nature of angels; but he took on him the seed of Abraham. [17]Wherefore in all things it behoved him to be made like unto his brethren, that he might be a merciful and faithful high priest in things pertaining to God, to make reconciliation for the sins of the people. [18]For in that he himself hath suffered being tempted, he is able to succour them that are tempted.

1 Corinthians 15: *[35]But some man will say, How are the dead raised up? and with what body do they come? [36]Thou fool, that which thou sowest is not quickened, except it die:* [37]And that which thou sowest, thou sowest not that body that shall be, but bare grain, it may chance of wheat, or of some other grain: [38]But God giveth it a body as it hath pleased him, and to every seed his own body. [39]All flesh is not the same flesh: but there is one kind of flesh of men, another flesh of beasts, another of fishes, and another of birds. [40]There are also celestial bodies, and bodies terrestrial: but the glory of the celestial is one, and the glory of the terrestrial is another. [41]There is one glory of the sun, and another glory of the moon, and another glory of the stars: for one star differeth from another star in glory. [42]So also is the resurrection of the dead. It is sown in corruption; it is raised in incorruption:

Figure 4.3 The Death of Christ (eighteenth century) by unknown painter.

1 Corinthians 15: [43]It is sown in dishonour; it is raised in glory: it is sown in weakness; it is raised in power: [44]It is sown a natural body; it is raised a spiritual body. There is a natural body, and there is a spiritual body. [45]And so it is written, The first man Adam was made a living soul; the last Adam was made a quickening spirit. [46]Howbeit that was not first which is spiritual, but that which is natural; and afterward that which is spiritual. [47]The first man is of the earth, earthy; the second man is the Lord from heaven. [48]As is the earthy, such are they also that are earthy: and as is the heavenly, such are they also that are heavenly. [49]And as we have borne the image of the earthy, we shall also bear the image of the heavenly. [50]Now this I say, brethren, that flesh and blood cannot inherit the kingdom of God; neither doth corruption inherit incorruption. [51]Behold, I shew you a mystery; We shall not all sleep, but we shall all be changed, [52]In a moment, in the twinkling of an eye, at the last trump: for the trumpet shall sound, and the dead shall be raised incorruptible, and we shall be changed.

Figure 4.4 Last Judgment (1904) by Viktor Vasnetsov.

[53]*For this corruptible must put on incorruption, and this mortal must put on immortality.*[54]*So when this corruptible shall have put on incorruption, and this mortal shall have put on immortality, then shall be brought to pass the saying that is written, Death is swallowed up in victory.* [55]*O death, where is thy sting? O grave, where is thy victory?* [56]*The sting of death is sin; and the strength of sin is the law.* [57]*But thanks be to God, which giveth us the victory through our Lord Jesus Christ.* [58]*Therefore, my beloved brethren, be ye stedfast, unmoveable, always abounding in the work of the Lord, forasmuch as ye know that your labour is not in vain in the Lord.*

God can raise the dead and heal the sick through Jesus to a certain extent; unbelief will stop the flow of God's power to heal.

Matthew 13:[52]Then said he unto them, Therefore every scribe which is instructed unto the kingdom of heaven is like unto a man that is an householder, which bringeth forth out of his treasure things new and old. [53]And it came to pass, that when Jesus had finished these parables, he departed thence. [54]And when he was come into his own country, he taught them in their synagogue, insomuch that they were astonished, and said, Whence hath this man this wisdom, and these mighty works? [55]Is not this the carpenter's son? is not his mother called Mary? and his brethren, James, and Joses, and Simon, and Judas? [56]And his sisters, are they not all with us? Whence then hath this man all these things? [57]And they were offended in him. But Jesus said unto them, A prophet is not without honour, save in his own country, and in his own house. *He did not many mighty works there because of their unbelief.*

Can you imagine Jesus in His hometown could not do any great miracles because the people only knew Him as a child that they saw growing up in their midst? Their own unbelief prevented them from receiving their healing.

Ephesians 3: [19]And to know the love of Christ, which passed knowledge, that ye might be filled with all the fulness of God. *[20]Now unto him that is able to do exceeding abundantly above all that we ask or think, according to the power that worketh in us, [21]Unto him be glory in the church by Christ Jesus throughout all ages, world without end. Amen.*

John 15:[7]If ye abide in me, and my words abide in you, ye shall ask what ye will, and it shall be done unto you. *[8]Herein is my Father glorified, that ye bear much fruit; so shall ye be my disciples. [9]As the Father hath loved me, so have I loved you: continue ye in my love.*

The Hall of Fame of Faith

Hebrews 11: [1]Now faith is the substance of things hoped for, the evidence of things not seen. [2]For by it the elders obtained a good report. [3]Through faith we understand that the worlds were framed by the word of God, so that things which are seen were not made of things which do appear.

Figure 4.5 God as Architect/Builder/Geometer/Craftsman (mid-thirteenth century).

[*Science*, and particularly *geometry* and *astronomy/astrology*, was linked directly to the divine for most medieval scholars. The compass in this 13th century manuscript is a symbol of God's act of *creation*. God has created the universe after geometric and harmonic principles, to seek these principles was therefore to seek and worship God.

- Title: God as Architect/Builder/Geometer/Craftsman
- From: The Frontispiece of Bible Moralisee
- Style: Gothic
- Date: mid-13th C.
- Location: France
- Famously used as the first color illustration to Benoit B. Mandelbrot's The Fractal Geometry of Nature.Codex Vindobonensis 2554 (French, ca. 1250), in the Österreichische Nationalbibliothek.

[4]*By faith* Abel offered unto God a more excellent sacrifice than Cain, by which he obtained witness that he was righteous, God testifying of his gifts: and by it he being dead yet speaketh.

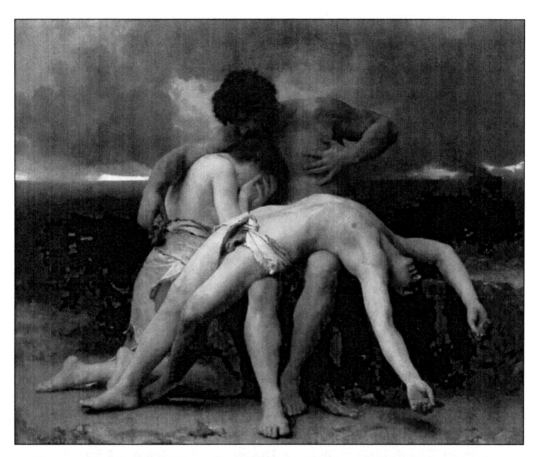

Figure 4.6 The First Mourning (1888) by William-Adolphe Bouguereau.

[5]By faith Enoch was translated that he should not see death;

Figure 4.7 God took Enoch, as in Genesis 5:24: "And Enoch walked with God: and he was not; for God took him." (KJV) illustration from the 1728 *Figures de la Bible*; illustrated by Gerard Hoet (1648–1733) and others, and published by P. de Hondt in The Hague; image courtesy Bizzell Bible Collection, University of Oklahoma Libraries.

and was not found, because God had translated him: for before his translation he had this testimony, that he pleased God. [6]But without faith it is impossible to please him: for he that cometh to God must believe that he is, and that he is a rewarder of them that diligently seek him. [7]By faith Noah, being warned of God of things not seen as yet,

Figure 4.8 The Earth was corrupt before God and filled with violence (right plate); as in Genesis 6:5: "And God saw that the wickedness of man was great in the earth, and that every imagination of the thoughts of his heart was only evil continually."; illustration from the 1728 *Figures de la Bible*; illustrated by Gerard Hoet (1648–1733) and others, and published by P. de Hondt in The Hague; image courtesy Bizzell Bible Collection, University of Oklahoma Libraries.

moved with fear, prepared an ark to the saving of his house; by the which he condemned the world, and became heir of the righteousness which is by faith.

[8]*By faith* Abraham, when he was called to go out into a place which he should after receive for an inheritance, obeyed; and he went out, not knowing whither he went.

Figure 4.9 Abraham's Journey from Ur to Canaan (1850) by József Molnár

[9]*By faith* he sojourned in the land of promise, as in a strange country, dwelling in tabernacles with Isaac and Jacob, the heirs with him of the same promise: [10]For he looked for a city which hath foundations, whose builder and maker is God. [11]*Through faith* also Sara herself received strength to conceive seed, and was delivered of a child when she was past age, *because she judged him faithful who had promised.* [12]Therefore sprang there even of one, and him as good as dead, so many as the stars of the sky in multitude, and as the sand which is by the sea shore innumerable. [13]*These all died in faith,* not having received the promises, but having seen them afar off, and were persuaded of them, and embraced them, and confessed that they were strangers and pilgrims on the earth. [14]For they that say such things declare plainly that they seek a country. [15]And truly, if they had been mindful of that country from whence they came out, they might have had opportunity to have returned. [16]But now they desire a better country, that is, an heavenly: wherefore God is not ashamed to be called their God: for he hath prepared for them a city.

[17]By faith Abraham, when he was tried, offered up Isaac:

Figure 4.10 Sacrifice of Isaac (1635) by Rembrandt.

and he that had received the promises offered up his only begotten son, [18]Of whom it was said, That in Isaac shall thy seed be called: [19]Accounting that God was able to raise him up, even from the dead; from whence also he received him in a figure. [20]*By faith* Isaac blessed Jacob and Esau concerning things to come. [21]*By faith* Jacob, when he was a dying, blessed both the sons of Joseph; and worshipped, leaning upon the top of his staff.

Figure 4.11 Isaac blesses his son Jacob (Rebekah looking on, and Esau in the background), as in Genesis 27:22-29, "And Jacob went near unto Isaac his father; and he felt him, and said, The voice is Jacob's voice, but the hands are the hands of Esau. And he discerned him not, because his hands were hairy, as his brother Esau's hands: so he blessed him. And he said, Art thou my very son Esau? And he said, I am. And he said, Bring it near to me, and I will eat of my son's venison, that my soul may bless thee. And he brought it near to him, and he did eat: And he brought him wine, and he drank. And his father Isaac said unto him, Come near now, and kiss me, my son. And he came near, and kissed him: and he smelled the smell of his raiment, and blessed him, and said, See, the smell of my son is as the smell of a field which the Lord hath blessed: Therefore God give thee of the dew of heaven, and the fatness of the earth, and plenty of corn and wine: Let people serve thee, and nations bow down to thee: be lord over thy brethren, and let thy mother's sons bow down to thee: cursed be every one that curseth thee, and blessed be he that blesseth thee."; illustration from the 1728 *Figures de la Bible*; illustrated by Gerard Hoet (1648-1733) and others, and published by P. de Hondt in The Hague; image courtesy Bizzell Bible Collection, University of Oklahoma Libraries.

[22]*By faith* Joseph, when he died, made mention of the departing of the children of Israel; and gave commandment concerning his bones. [23]*By faith* Moses, when he was born, was hid three months of his parents, because they saw he was a proper child; and they were not afraid of the king's commandment.

Figure 4.12 The Finding of Moses (1904) by Lawrence Alma-Tadema.

Figure 4.13 Moses Trampling on Pharaoh's Crown (1846) by Enrico Tempestini.

[24]*By faith* Moses, when he was come to years, refused to be called the son of Pharaoh's daughter; [25]Choosing rather to suffer affliction with the people of God, than to enjoy the pleasures of sin for a season; [26]Esteeming the reproach of Christ greater riches than the treasures in Egypt: for he had respect unto the recompence of the reward. [27]*By faith* he forsook Egypt, not fearing the wrath of the king: for he endured, as seeing him who is invisible.

[28]*Through faith* he kept the passover, and the sprinkling of blood, lest he that destroyed the first-born should touch them.

The Death of the Firstborn

Figure 4.14 "This is the house of an Egyptian. How different it is from the house of the Israelites. The angel has been here. But when he saw there were no marks of blood on the door he did not pass over it. The angel went into all the houses of the Egyptians and caused their oldest sons to die. God sent him to do this so Pharaoh would let the Israelites go away from Egypt." Illustration from the 1897 Bible Pictures and What They Teach Us: Containing 400 Illustrations from the Old and New Testaments: With brief descriptions by Charles Foster.

[29]*By faith* they passed through the Red sea as by dry land: which the Egyptians assaying to do were drowned.

Figure 4.15 Pharaoh's Army Engulfed by the Red Sea (1900)
by Frederick Arthur Bridgman

[30]*By faith* the walls of Jericho fell down, after they were compassed about seven days. [31]*By faith* The harlot Rahab perished not with them that believed not, when she had received the spies with peace. [32]And what shall I more say? for the time would fail me to tell of Gideon,

Figure 4.16 Gideon (c. 1550) by Martin van Heemskerck.
and of Barak, and of Samson,

**Figure 4.17 Title English: Samson Captured by the Philistines,
Artist Guercino (1591–1666)and of Jephthae; of David**

**Figure 4.18 David Thanking God after the Death of Goliath
by Artist Italian Anonymous Date 1700 - 1750**

also, and Samuel, and of the prophets: [33]*Who through faith subdued kingdoms, wrought righteousness,* obtained promises, stopped the mouths of lions.

Figure 4.19 Daniel's Answer to the King (1890) by Domenico Fetti (1588–1623).

[34]Quenched the violence of fire,

Figure 4.20 Shadrach, Meshach, and Abednego (1863) by Gustave Doré

escaped the edge of the sword, out of weakness were made strong, waxed valiant in fight, turned to flight the armies of the aliens.

Figure 4.21 Joshua Commanding the Sun to Stand Still upon Gibeon (1816).

[35]Women received their dead raised to life again:

Figure 4.22 Elijah Resuscitating the Son of the Widow of Zarephath by Louis Hersent.

and others were tortured, not accepting deliverance; that they might obtain a better resurrection: [36]And others had trial of cruel mockings and scourgings, yea, moreover of bonds and imprisonment: [37]They were stoned,

Figure 4.23 Nero's Torches (Christian Candlesticks) (1876) by Henryk Siemiradzki.

Notice the Christians at the top of the poles on the right side being burned at the stake.

How faithful would we be today if we were faced with this situation?

they were sawn asunder, were tempted, were slain with the sword: they wandered about in sheep-skins and goatskins; being destitute, afflicted, tormented;

**Figure 4.24 The Christian Martyrs' Last Prayer (1883)
by Jean-Léon Gérôme (1824–1904).**

[38](Of whom the world was not worthy:) they wandered in deserts, and in mountains, and in dens and caves of the earth.

Figure 4.25 Belsazar's Feast by Rembrandt (1606–1669).

National Gallery Notes According to Daniel 5:1-31, King Belshazzar of Babylon takes sacred golden and silver vessels from the Jewish Temple in Jerusalem by his predecessor Nebuchadnezzar. Using these holy items, the King and his court praise 'the gods of gold and silver, bronze, iron, wood, and stone'. Immediately, the disembodied fingers of a human hand appear and write on the wall of the royal palace the words "MENE," "MENE," "TEKEL," "UPHARSIN" References RKD images, Art-work number 48717. Source/Photographer National Gallery London

Daniel 5: [26]This is the interpretation of the thing: MENE; God hath numbered thy kingdom, and finished it. [27]TEKEL; Thou art weighed in the balances, and art found wanting. [28]PERES; Thy kingdom is divided, and given to the Medes and Persians. [29]Then commanded Belshazzar, and they clothed Daniel with scarlet, and put a chain of gold about his neck, and made a proclamation concerning him, that he should be the third ruler in the kingdom. [30]**In that night was Belshazzar the king of the Chaldeans slain.** [31]**And Darius the Median took the kingdom, being about threescore and two years old.**

When we are weighed will we be found wanting in the end.

Hebrews 11: ³⁹And these all, having obtained a good report through faith, received not the promise: ⁴⁰God having provided some better thing for us, that they without us should not be made perfect.

Hebrews 12: ¹Wherefore seeing we also are compassed about with so great a cloud of witnesses, let us lay aside every weight, and the sin which doth so easily beset us, and let us run with patience the race that is set before us, ²Looking unto Jesus the author and finisher of our faith; who for the joy that was set before him endured the cross, despising the shame, and is set down at the right hand of the throne of God. ³For consider him that endured such contradiction of sinners against himself, lest ye be wearied and faint in your minds. ⁴Ye have not yet resisted unto blood, striving against sin. ⁵And ye have forgotten the exhortation which speaketh unto you as unto children, My son, despise not thou the chastening of the Lord, nor faint when thou art rebuked of him: ⁶For whom the Lord loveth he chasteneth, and scourgeth every son whom he receiveth. ⁷If ye endure chastening, God dealeth with you as with sons; for what son is he whom the father chasteneth not? ⁸But if ye be without chastisement, whereof all are partakers, then are ye bastards, and not sons. ⁹Furthermore we have had fathers of our flesh which corrected us, and we gave them reverence: shall we not much rather be in subjection unto the Father of spirits, and live? ¹⁰For they verily for a few days chastened us after their own pleasure; but he for our profit, that we might be partakers of his holiness. ¹¹Now no chastening for the present seemeth to be joyous, but grievous: nevertheless afterward it yieldeth the peaceable fruit of righteousness unto them which are exercised thereby. ¹²Wherefore lift up the hands which hang down, and the feeble knees; ¹³And make straight paths for your feet, lest that which is lame be turned out of the way; but let it rather be healed. *¹⁴Follow peace with all men, and holiness, without which no man shall see the Lord: ¹⁵Looking diligently lest any man fail of the grace of God; lest any root of bitterness springing up trouble you, and thereby many be defiled; ¹⁶Lest there be any fornicator, or profane person, as Esau, who for one morsel of meat sold his birthright. ¹⁷For ye know how that afterward, when he would have inherited the blessing, he was rejected: for he found no place of repentance, though he sought it carefully with tears.* ¹⁸For ye are not come unto the mount that might be touched, and that burned with fire, nor unto blackness, and darkness, and tempest, ¹⁹And the sound of a trumpet, and the voice of words; which voice they that heard intreated that the word should not be spoken to them any more: ²⁰(For they could not endure that which was commanded, And if so much as a beast touch the mountain, it shall be stoned, or thrust through with a dart: ²¹And so terrible was the sight, that Moses said, I exceedingly fear and quake:) *²²But ye are come unto mount Sion, and unto the city of the living God, the heavenly Jerusalem, and to an innumerable company of angels, ²³To the general assembly and church of the firstborn, which are written in heaven, and to God the Judge of all, and to the spirits of just men made perfect, ²⁴And to Jesus the mediator of the new covenant, and to the blood of sprinkling, that speaketh better things than that of Abel. ²⁵See that ye refuse not him that speaketh. For if they escaped not who refused him that spake on earth, much more shall not we escape, if we turn away from him that speaketh from heaven: ²⁶Whose voice then shook the earth: but now he hath promised, saying, Yet once more I shake not the earth only, but also heaven. ²⁷And this word, Yet once more, signifieth the removing of those things that are shaken, as of things that are made, that those things which cannot be shaken may remain. ²⁸Wherefore we receiving a kingdom which cannot be moved, let us have grace, whereby we may serve God acceptably with reverence and godly fear: ²⁹For our God is a consuming fire.*

Faith is empowered by the love of God. These are all parts of the fruit of the Spirit, and they work together as one powerful weapon against Satan. As we learned earlier the fruit of the Spirit are also the keys to the Kingdom of God. When these forces come together they will bring down every stronghold of the kingdom of darkness through prayer. We have been given the power of the Holy Spirit, the Blood of the Lamb and the word of our testimony. The power of God is inside of us to do miracles, but He is looking for agreement in faith between the believers and them walking in holiness before the Lord. Then we can see God do miracles even among the unbelievers. In every situation where Jesus was praying, he had to keep encouraging the people to not lose faith.

Matthew 18: [19]Again I say unto you, That if two of you shall agree on earth as touching anything that they shall ask, it shall be done for them of my Father which is in heaven. [20]For where two or three are gathered together in my name, there am I in the midst of them.

Mark 9: [17]And one of the multitude answered and said, Master, I have brought unto thee my son, which hath a dumb spirit; [18]And wheresoever he taketh him, he teareth him: and he foameth, and gnasheth with his teeth, and pineth away: and I spake to thy disciples that they should cast him out; and they could not. [19]He answereth him, and saith, O faithless generation, how long shall I be with you? how long shall I suffer you? bring him unto me. [20]And they brought him unto him: and when he saw him, straightway the spirit tare him; and he fell on the ground, and wallowed foaming. [21]And he asked his father, How long is it ago since this came unto him? And he said, Of a child. [22]And ofttimes it hath cast him into the fire, and into the waters, to destroy him: but if thou canst do anything, have compassion on us, and help us.

Figure 4.26 Exorcising a boy possessed by a demon from
Très Riches Heures du Duc de Berry, **15th century.**

23Jesus said unto him, If thou canst believe, all things are possible to him that believeth. 24And straightway the father of the child cried out, and said with tears, Lord, I believe; help thou mine unbelief. 25When Jesus saw that the people came running together, he rebuked the foul spirit, saying unto him, Thou dumb and deaf spirit, I charge thee, come out of him, and enter no more into him. 26And the spirit cried, and rent him sore, and came out of him: and he lifted him up; and he arose. 28And when he was come into the house, his disciples asked him privately, Why could not we cast him out? 29And he said unto them, This kind can come forth by nothing, but by prayer and fasting.

Matthew 8: 23And when he was entered into a ship, his disciples followed him. 24And, behold, there arose a great tempest in the sea, insomuch that the ship was covered with the waves: but he was asleep. 25And his disciples came to him, and awoke him, saying, Lord, save us: we perish. *26And he saith unto them, Why are ye fearful, O ye of little faith? Then he arose, and rebuked the* *winds and the sea; and there was a great calm.* [27]But the men marvelled, saying, What manner of man is this, that even the winds and the sea obey him!

Figure 4.27 Christ in the storm on the Sea of Galilee by Rembrandt (1606–1669)

Luke 22: [30]That ye may eat and drink at my table in my kingdom, and sit on thrones judging the twelve tribes of Israel. [31]And the Lord said, Simon, Simon, behold, Satan hath desired to have you, that he may sift you as wheat: *[32]But I have prayed for thee, that thy faith fail not: and when thou art converted, strengthen thy brethren.*

Fear is the biggest enemy of our faith, and it stands between victory and failure. It has caused many deaths and many other disasters because we have not learned to overcome fear. If Jesus had not been in the boat the disciples would have died that day. When failure does come, it is not God's fault. Jesus told Peter that He would pray a specific prayer for him, and that was that Peter's faith would not fail him. Jesus is praying that same prayer for each one of us: that our faith does not fail us.

1 John 4: [14]And we have seen and do testify that the Father sent the Son to be the Saviour of the world. [15]Whosoever shall confess that Jesus is the Son of God, God dwelleth in him, and he in God. [16]And we have known and believed the love that God hath to us. God is love; and he that dwelleth in love dwelleth in God, and God in him. *[17]Herein is our love made perfect, that we may have boldness in the day of judgment: because as he is, so are we in this world. [18]There is no fear in love; but perfect love casteth out fear: because fear hath torment. He that feareth is not made perfect in love. [19]We love him, because he first loved us. [20]If a man say, I love God, and hateth his brother, he is a liar: for he that loveth not his brother whom he hath seen, how can he love God whom he hath not seen? [21]And this commandment have we from him, That he who loveth God love his brother also.*

Matthew 15: [22]And, behold, a woman of Canaan came out of the same coasts, and cried unto him, saying, Have mercy on me, O Lord, thou son of David; my daughter is grievously vexed with a devil. [23]But he answered her not a word. And his disciples came and besought him, saying, Send her away; for she crieth after us. [24]But he answered and said, I am not sent but unto the lost sheep of the house of Israel.

**Figure 4.28 Jesus Exorcising the Canaanite Woman's Daughter
from Très Riches Heures du Duc de Berry, 15th century.**

[25]Then came she and worshipped him, saying, Lord, help me. [26]But he answered and said, It is not meet to take the children's bread, and to cast it to dogs. [27]And she said, Truth, Lord: yet the dogs eat of the crumbs which fall from their masters' table. [28]Then Jesus answered and said unto her, O woman, great is thy faith: be it unto thee even as thou wilt. And her daughter was made whole from that very hour. [29]And Jesus departed from thence, and came nigh unto the sea of Galilee; and went up into a mountain, and sat down there.

Begging for God to answer a prayer will work for a little while, when you are young in the Lord, but as you grow in Christ, begging and pleading are emotions that do not generate faith. They should never be involved in your prayer life. Trying to make God feel sorry for us does not move God. What God wants is our faith to grow; even faith the size of a mustard seed can move mountains. God wants us to cultivate that seed because He made us more than a conqueror. Jesus is the author and finisher of our faith, so you have to have a personal relationship that goes beyond a Sunday morning and a midweek service relationship.

The people in Hebrews 11 were strong in faith, which brought glory to God. God did great miracles on their behalf and not because they were begging. Our faith is not activated when we have a begging attitude towards God. Dogs beg; we do not have to beg for anything that already belongs to us from His promises. Healing is already ours; Jesus has already bled and died for us to have healing freely because the stripes on His back are healed now. The Bible says it will be done according to the power or the level of our faith. Even the disciples did not want to have anything to do with the woman of Canaan. When Jesus called her a dog for begging, she realized what she was doing, and she as much said "I'll be a dog and you can call me Fido and I'll eat the crumbs, but you are going heal my daughter." Her begging turned into faith. Then Jesus received her faith and He said her daughter was made whole instantly.

Mark 5: [35]While he yet spake, there came from the ruler of the synagogue's house certain which said, Thy daughter is dead: why troublest thou the Master any further? [36]As soon as Jesus heard the word that was spoken, he saith unto the ruler of the synagogue, *Be not afraid, only believe. [37]And he suffered no man to follow him, save Peter, and James, and John the brother of James. [38]And he cometh to the house of the ruler of the synagogue, and seeth the tumult, and them that wept and wailed greatly. [39]And when he was come in, he saith unto them, Why make ye this ado, and weep? the damsel is not dead, but sleepeth. [40]And they laughed him to scorn. But when he had put them all out, he taketh the father and the mother of the damsel, and them that were with him, and entereth in where the damsel was lying.*

The presence of unbelief can choke, and prevent the power of God from working. Jesus put the unbelievers out of the home because of the effect it could have on the people who were trusting God for a miracle. We all know this is important when we have loved ones who are bedridden or hospitalized.

Figure 4.29 Raising of the Daughter of Jairus by Paolo Veronese (1528–1588)

Mark 5: ⁴¹And he took the damsel by the hand, and said unto her, Talitha cumi; which is, being interpreted, Damsel, I say unto thee, arise. ⁴²And straightway the damsel arose, and walked; for she was of the age of twelve years. And they were astonished with a great astonishment. ⁴³And he charged them straitly that no man should know it; and commanded that something should be given her to eat.

The rarely used and mostly unknown Covenant of Rest

Hebrews 3: ⁷Wherefore (as the Holy Ghost saith, Today if ye will hear his voice, ⁸Harden not your hearts, as in the provocation, in the day of temptation in the wilderness: ⁹When your fathers tempted me, proved me, and saw my works forty years. ¹⁰Wherefore I was grieved with that generation, and said, *They do alway err in their heart; and they have not known my ways.* ¹¹*So I sware in my wrath, They shall not enter into my rest.*) ¹²*Take heed, brethren, lest there be in any of you an evil heart of unbelief, in departing from the living God.* ¹³But exhort one another daily, while it is called Today; lest any of you be hardened through the deceitfulness of sin. [14] For we are made partakers of Christ, if we hold the beginning of our confidence steadfast unto the end; [15] While it is said, Today if ye will hear his voice, harden not your hearts, as in the provocation. [16] For some, when they had heard, did provoke: howbeit not all that came out of Egypt by Moses. [17] But with whom was he grieved forty years? was it not with them that had sinned, whose carcases fell in the wilderness? [18] And to whom sware he that they should not enter into his rest, but to them that believed not? [19] So we see that they could not enter in because of unbelief.

Hebrews (KJ) 4: Let us therefore fear, lest, a promise being left us of entering into his rest, any of you should seem to come short of it. [2] For unto us was the gospel preached, as well as unto them: but the word preached did not profit them, not being mixed with faith in them that heard it. *[3] For we which have believed do enter into rest, as he said, As I have sworn in my wrath, if they shall enter into my rest: although the works were finished from the foundation of the world .*[4] For he spake in a certain place of the seventh day on this wise, And God did rest the seventh day from all his works. [5] And in this place again, If they shall enter into my rest. [6] Seeing therefore it remaineth that some must enter therein, and they to whom it was first preached entered not in because of unbelief.

In the eyes of God, a person with doubt, failure, unbelief, and worry is a person whose heart is evil because it is full of fear. Fear is the basis of doubt, unbelief, and so forth. Fear prevents faith that is the size of a mustard seed from maturing into the "faith of God." Lastly, unbelief prevents us from entering into the covenant of rest which God refused to let the Israelites to have. They died in the desert and never entered the Promise Land.

1 John 4: [17] Herein is our love made perfect, *that we may have boldness in the day of judgment: because as he is, so are we in this world.* [18] There is no fear in love; but perfect love casteth out fear: because fear hath torment. He that feareth is not made perfect in love. [19] We love him, because he first loved us.

**Figure 4.30 The Woman with the Issue of Blood by Artist (1570)
by Paolo Veronese (1528–1588).**

Mark 5: [24] And Jesus went with him; and much people followed him, and thronged him.[25] And a certain woman, which had an issue of blood twelve years, [26] And had suffered many things of many physicians, and had spent all that she had, and was nothing bettered, but rather grew worse,[27] When she had heard of Jesus, came in the press behind, and touched his garment. [28] For she said, If I may touch but his clothes, I shall be whole. [29] And straightway the fountain of her blood was dried up; and she felt in her body that she was healed of that plague.[30] And Jesus, immediately knowing in himself that virtue had gone out of him, turned him about in the press, and said, Who touched my clothes? [31] And his disciples said unto him, Thou seest the multitude thronging thee, and sayest thou, Who touched me? [32] And he looked round about to see her that had done this thing.[33] But the woman fearing and trembling, knowing what was done in her, came and fell down before him, and told him all the truth.[34] And he said unto her, Daughter, thy FAITH hath made thee whole; go in peace, and be whole of thy plague.

This lady did not ask Jesus to heal her. She did not go to the disciples and ask them to pray for her. All Jesus knew was that He literally felt the power of God flow out of Him to heal someone, and He had no idea where or to who it went into. He questioned His disciples who did not know anymore then He did; they said "everybody is touching you." Finally the lady came forth and confessed to the whole matter. Jesus said it was her faith that made her whole. This is proof that the power to heal, to restore, and to raise the dead totally is controlled by God and the faith of the individual or individuals involved. Jesus' body was the earthen vessel that housed the treasure of the Holy Spirit. Now He has given us this treasure II Corinthians 4:7.

Figure 4.31 Christ Heals a Man Paralyzed by the Gout (1780) Engraving by Bernhard Rode.

Paralytic lowered through the roof'

Luke 5: [7]And it came to pass on a certain day, as he was teaching, that there were Pharisees and doctors of the law sitting by, which were come out of every town of Galilee, and Judaea, and Jerusalem: and the power of the Lord was present to heal them. [18]And, behold, men brought in a bed a man which was taken with a palsy: and they sought means to bring him in, and to lay him before him. [19]And when they could not find by what way they might bring him in because of the multitude, they went upon the housetop, and let him down through the tiling with his couch into the midst before Jesus. [20]*And when he saw their faith, he said unto him, Man, thy sins are forgiven thee.* [21]*And the scribes and the Pharisees began to reason, saying, Who is this which speaketh blasphemies? Who can forgive sins, but God alone?* [22]*But when Jesus perceived their thoughts, he answering said unto them, What reason ye in your hearts?* [23]*Whether is easier, to say, Thy sins be forgiven thee; or to say, Rise up and walk?* [24]*But that ye may know that the Son of man hath power*

189

upon earth to forgive sins, (he said unto the sick of the palsy,) I say unto thee, Arise, and take up thy couch, and go into thine house. ²⁵And immediately he rose up before them, and took up that whereon he lay, and departed to his own house, glorifying God. ²⁶And they were all amazed, and they glorified God, and were filled with fear, saying, We have seen strange things today.

When God looks at your heart does He see faith or an evil heart of unbelief?

Jesus Walking on the Sea

Matthew 14: ²⁵And in the fourth watch of the night Jesus went unto them, walking on the sea. ²⁶And when the disciples saw him walking on the sea, they were troubled, saying, *It is a spirit; and they cried out for fear.*

Figure 4.32 Saint Peter Attempting to Walk on Water by François Boucher (1703–1770)

Matthew 14: [27]But straightway Jesus spake unto them, saying, Be of good cheer; it is I; be not afraid. [28]And Peter answered him and said, Lord, if it be thou, bid me come unto thee on the water. [29]And he said, Come. And when Peter was come down out of the ship, he walked on the water, to go to Jesus. [30]But when he saw the wind boisterous, he was afraid; and beginning to sink, he cried, saying, Lord, save me. [31]And immediately Jesus stretched forth his hand, and caught him, and said unto him, O thou of little faith, wherefore didst thou doubt? [32]And when they were come into the ship, the wind ceased. [33]Then they that were in the ship came and worshipped him, saying, Of a truth thou art the Son of God.

**Figure 4.33 Christ Healing the Sick at the Pool of Bethesda
by Carl Heinrich Bloch (1834–1890).**

John 5: [5] After this there was a feast of the Jews; and Jesus went up to Jerusalem.[2] Now there is at Jerusalem by the sheep market a pool, which is called in the Hebrew tongue Bethesda, having five porches.[3] In these lay a great multitude of impotent folk, of blind, halt, withered, waiting for the moving of the water. [4] For an angel went down at a certain season into the pool, and troubled the water: whosoever then first after the troubling of the water stepped in was made whole of whatsoever disease he had. *[5] And a certain man was there, which had an infirmity thirty and eight years.[6] When Jesus saw him lie, and knew that he had been now a long time in that case, he saith unto him, Wilt thou be made whole? [7] The impotent man answered him, Sir, I have no man, when the water is troubled, to put me into the pool: but while I am coming, another steppeth down before me.[8] Jesus saith unto him, Rise, take up thy bed, and walk. [9] And immediately the man was made whole, and* *took up his bed, and walked: and on the same day was the sabbath. [10] The Jews therefore said unto him that was cured, It is the sabbath day: it is not lawful for thee to carry thy bed.[11] He answered them, He that made me whole, the same said unto me, Take up thy bed, and walk.*

A Well of Water Springing Up into Everlasting Life

When I was very young I used to hear a lot about the Fountain of Youth, and if you found it and drank from it you would live forever. That fountain never existed. God has provided something better than the fountain of youth and it is real!

John 4: [3]He left Judaea, and departed again into Galilee. [4]And he must needs go through Samaria. [5]Then cometh he to a city of Samaria, which is called Sychar, near to the parcel of ground that Jacob gave to his son Joseph. [6]Now Jacob's well was there. Jesus therefore, being wearied with his journey, sat thus on the well: and it was about the sixth hour. [7]There cometh a woman of Samaria to draw water: Jesus saith unto her, Give me to drink. [8](For his disciples were gone away unto the city to buy meat.) [9]Then saith the woman of Samaria unto him, How is it that thou, being a Jew, askest drink of me, which am a woman of Samaria? for the Jews have no dealings with the Samaritans. *[10]Jesus answered and said unto her, If thou knewest the gift of God, and who it is that saith to thee, Give me to drink; thou wouldest have asked of him, and he would have given thee living water. [11]The woman saith unto him, Sir, thou hast nothing to draw with, and the well is deep: from whence then hast thou that living water?*

**Figure 4.34 Jesus with the Samaritan Woman at the Well
by Angelica Kauffman (1741–1807)**

John 4: [12]Art thou greater than our father Jacob, which gave us the well, and drank thereof himself, and his children, and his cattle? [13]Jesus answered and said unto her, Whosoever drinketh of this water shall thirst again: [14]*But whosoever drinketh of the water that I shall give him shall never thirst; but the water that I shall give him shall be in him a well of water springing up into everlasting life.*

The "Word of God" Takes Many Forms

In order for any seed to grow it has to be watered. Like the fruit of the Spirit have many functions, the Word of God also has many functions. One of its major functions is that it becomes water that washes us spiritually as we read it, and it shows us our faults. When we make the corrections, the Word cleanses and His Blood purifies us. When Jesus died on the cross His Blood and water was left in the earth for that purpose. They both are a source of life and the Word gives us direction.

Figure 4.35 Jesus' Side is pierced with a Spear by Fra. Angelico.

John 19: ³⁰When Jesus therefore had received the vinegar, he said, It is finished: and he bowed his head, and gave up the ghost. ³¹The Jews therefore, because it was the preparation, that the bodies should not remain upon the cross on the sabbath day, (for that sabbath day was an high day,) besought Pilate that their legs might be broken, and that they might be taken away. *³²Then came the soldiers, and brake the legs of the first, and of the other which was crucified with him. ³³But when they came to Jesus, and saw that he was dead already, they brake not his legs: ³⁴But one of the soldiers with a spear pierced his side, and forthwith came there out blood and water. ³⁵And he that saw it bare record, and his record is true: and he knoweth that he saith true, that ye might believe. ³⁶For these things were done, that the scripture should be fulfilled, A bone of him shall not be broken. ³⁷And again another scripture saith, They shall look on him whom they pierced.*

The "Word" was Transformed into Flesh

1 John (KJV) 1: *1That which was from the beginning, which we have heard, which we have seen with our eyes, which we have looked upon, and our hands have handled, of the Word of life;*

2(For the life was manifested, and we have seen it, and bear witness, and shew unto you that eternal life, which was with the Father, and was manifested unto us;) 3That which we have seen and heard declare we unto you, that ye also may have fellowship with us: and truly our fellowship is with the Father, and with his Son Jesus Christ. 4 And these things write we unto you, that your joy may be full. 5 This then is the message which we have heard of him, and declare unto you, that God is light, and in him is no darkness at all. *6 This is he that came by water and blood, even Jesus Christ; not by water only, but by water and blood. And it is the Spirit that beareth witness, because the Spirit is truth. 7 For there are three that bear record in heaven, the Father, the Word, and the Holy Ghost: and these three are one. 8 And there are three that bear witness in earth, the Spirit, and the water, and the blood: and these three agree in one. 9 If we receive the witness of men, the witness of God is greater: for this is the witness of God which he hath testified of his Son. 10 He that believeth on the Son of God hath the witness in himself: he that believeth not God hath made him a liar; because he believeth not the record that God gave of his Son.11And this is the record that God hath given to us eternal life, and this life is in his Son. 12He that hath the Son hath life; and he that hath not the Son of God hath not life. 13These things have I written unto you that believe on the name of the Son of God; that ye may know that ye have eternal life, and that ye may believe on the name of the Son of God.*

The "Word" was made Flesh and we have been joined to that Flesh

Ephesians 5: *25 Husbands, love your wives, even as Christ also loved the church, and gave himself for it; 26That he might sanctify and cleanse it with the washing of water by the word, 27That he might present it to himself a glorious church, not having spot, or wrinkle, or any such thing; but that it should be holy and without blemish. 28So ought men to love their wives as their own bodies. He that loveth his wife loveth himself. 29For no man ever yet hated his own flesh; but nourisheth and cherisheth it, even as the Lord the church:*

The Spirit of *oneness* flows from the Kingdom of God to us, to being *one* with Jesus and being *one* with each other as members in particular of the Body of Christ. Everything in the Kingdom functions in unity. Jesus is representative of a husband taking care of His wife, by giving her what she needs so she can mature. We need the Word more than ever because it is what causes us to mature in Christ.

Ephesians 5: 30For we are members of his body, of his flesh, and of his bones. 31For this cause shall a man leave his father and mother, and shall be joined unto his wife, and they two shall be one flesh. 32This is a great mystery: but I speak concerning Christ and the church. 33Nevertheless let every one of you in particular so love his wife even as himself; and the wife see that she reverence her husband.

[In John chapter 6; The children of Israel saw the miracles that Jesus did and how He fed thousands with just a few fish. They were seeking Christ because of the miracle supply of food that they were given and they wanted more. But Jesus said they were looking for things, and this is the problem with some churches today. They are looking for things, more money, a bigger house, more clothes, the biggest car, and so forth. Jesus told them that is not what the Kingdom of Heaven is all about. That is what the Gentiles do, and if that is your goal for getting saved, going to church, paying tithes and if that is all that you are praying for then you are missing God. You have become like the five foolish virgins. God had already cut them off, and they had no idea that they were cut off. They were not on fire for God; they were lukewarm. Jesus tells the people this in so many words and they caught on quickly. They said OK, tell us what shall we do to do the works or the will of God, or fulfill God's will on the earth. He was trying to get them to understand that they have to become partaker's of His Flesh and Blood because Everlasting Life is found in them.]

John 6: ²³(Howbeit there came other boats from Tiberias nigh unto the place where they did eat bread, after that the Lord had given thanks:) ²⁴When the people therefore saw that Jesus was not there, neither his disciples, they also took shipping, and came to Capernaum, seeking for Jesus. ²⁵And when they had found him on the other side of the sea, they said unto him, Rabbi, when camest thou hither? ²⁶Jesus answered them and said, Verily, verily, I say unto you, Ye seek me, not because ye saw the miracles, but because ye did eat of the loaves, and were filled. ²⁷Labour not for the meat which perisheth, but for that meat which endureth unto everlasting life, which the Son of man shall give unto you: for him hath God the Father sealed.²⁸*Then said they unto him, What shall we do, that we might work the works of God? ²⁹Jesus answered and said unto them, This is the work of God, that ye believe on him whom he hath sent. ³⁰They said therefore unto him, What sign shewest thou then, that we may see, and believe thee? what dost thou work? ³¹Our fathers did eat manna in the desert; as it is written, He gave them bread from heaven to eat. ³²Then Jesus said unto them, Verily, verily, I say unto you, Moses gave you not that bread from heaven; but my Father giveth you the true bread from heaven. ³³For the bread of God is he which cometh down from heaven, and giveth life unto the world. ³⁴Then said they unto him, Lord, evermore give us this bread. ³⁵And Jesus said unto them, I am the bread of life: he that cometh to me shall never hunger; and he that believeth on me shall never thirst. ³⁶But I said unto you, That ye also have seen me, and believe not. ³⁷All that the Father giveth me shall come to me; and him that cometh to me I will in no wise cast out. ³⁸For I came down from heaven, not to do mine own will, but the will of him that sent me. ³⁹And this is the Father's will which hath sent me, that of all which he hath given me I should lose nothing, but should raise it up again at the last day. ⁴⁰And this is the will of him that sent me, that everyone which seeth the Son, and believeth on him, may have everlasting life: and I will raise him up at the last day. ⁴¹The Jews then murmured at him, because he said, I am the bread which came down from heaven. ⁴²And they said, Is not this Jesus, the son of Joseph, whose father and mother we know? how is it then that he saith, I came down from heaven? ⁴³Jesus therefore answered and said unto them, Murmur not among yourselves. ⁴⁴No man can come to me, except the Father which hath sent me draw him: and I will raise him up at the last day. ⁴⁵It is written in the prophets, And they shall be all taught of God. Every man therefore that hath heard, and hath learned of the Father, cometh unto me. ⁴⁶Not that any man hath seen the Father, save he which is of God, he hath seen the Father. ⁴⁷Verily, verily, I say unto you, He that believeth on me hath everlasting life. ⁴⁸I am that bread of life. ⁴⁹Your fathers did eat manna in the wilderness, and are dead. ⁵⁰This is the bread which cometh down from heaven, that a man may eat thereof, and not die. ⁵¹I am the living bread which came down from heaven: if any man eat of this bread, he shall live forever: and the bread that I will give is my flesh, which I will give for the life of the world.*

[52]*The Jews therefore strove among themselves, saying, How can this man give us his flesh to eat?* [53]*Then Jesus said unto them, Verily, verily, I say unto you, Except ye eat the flesh of the Son of man, and drink his blood, ye have no life in you.* [54]*Whoso eateth my flesh, and drinketh my blood, hath eternal life; and I will raise him up at the last day.* [55]*For my flesh is meat indeed, and my blood is drink indeed.* [56]*He that eateth my flesh, and drinketh my blood, dwelleth in me, and I in him.* [57]*As the living Father hath sent me, and I live by the Father: so he that eateth me, even he shall live by me.* [58]*This is that bread which came down from heaven: not as your fathers did eat manna, and are dead: he that eateth of this bread shall live forever.*[59]*These things said he in the synagogue, as he taught in Capernaum.* [60]*Many therefore of his disciples, when they had heard this, said, This is an hard saying; who can hear it?* [61]*When Jesus knew in himself that his disciples murmured at it, he said unto them, Doth this offend you?* [62]*What and if ye shall see the Son of man ascend up where he was before?* [63]*It is the spirit that quickeneth; the flesh profiteth nothing: the words that I speak unto you, they are spirit, and they are life.*[64]*But there are some of you that believe not. For Jesus knew from the beginning who they were that believed not, and who should betray him.* [65]*And he said, Therefore said I unto you, that no man can come unto me, except it were given unto him of my Father.*[66]**From that time many of his disciples went back, and walked no more with him.**

Figure 4.36 Seventy Apostles by Ikonopisatelj

John 6: ⁶⁷Then said Jesus unto the twelve, Will ye also go away? *⁶⁸Then Simon Peter answered him, Lord, to whom shall we go? thou hast the words of eternal life.* ⁶⁹And we believe and are sure that thou art that Christ, the Son of the living God. ⁷⁰Jesus answered them, Have not I chosen you twelve, and one of you is a devil? ⁷¹He spake of Judas Iscariot the son of Simon: for he it was that should betray him, being one of the twelve.

**Figure 4.37 Jesus with the <u>Eucharist</u> (detail),
by <u>Joan de Juanes</u>, mid–late sixteenth century.**

At the beginning of Jesus' ministry, seventy of the disciples could not accept what Jesus was saying about eating His flesh and drinking His Blood. They could not understand the concept but we understand it today. What Jesus was saying is that the wine represented His Blood and the bread represented His flesh. They should have known this because this was part of their Jewish heritage. Jesus was fulfilling Old Testament promises so that Old Testament was going to be done away with, and so the New Testament and its promises could be established. The New Testament did away with sacrificing animals to get forgiveness for our sins because the blood of animals did not get rid of sins; it just covered it. But the Blood of Jesus completely erased it and opened the door for us to become a child that was birth by God, with Jesus being our oldest brother.

The last plague that God brought on the Egyptians was that all their firstborn would die.

Exodus 12: And the Lord spake unto Moses and Aaron in the land of Egypt saying, [2] This month shall be unto you the beginning of months: it shall be the first month of the year to you.[3] Speak ye unto all the congregation of Israel, saying, In the tenth day of this month they shall take to them every man a lamb, according to the house of their fathers, a lamb for an house: [4] And if the household be too little for the lamb, let him and his neighbour next unto his house take it according to the number of the souls; every man according to his eating shall make your count for the lamb. [5] Your lamb shall be without blemish, a male of the first year: ye shall take it out from the sheep, or from the goats: [6] And ye shall keep it up until the fourteenth day of the same month: and the whole assembly of the congregation of Israel shall kill it in the evening. [7] And they shall take of the blood, and strike it on the two side posts and on the upper door post of the houses, wherein they shall eat it. [8] And they shall eat the flesh in that night, roast with fire, and unleavened bread; and with bitter herbs they shall eat it. [9] Eat not of it raw, nor sodden at all with water, but roast with fire; his head with his legs, and with the purtenance thereof. [10] And ye shall let nothing of it remain until the morning; and that which remaineth of it until the morning ye shall burn with fire.[11] And thus shall ye eat it; with your loins girded, your shoes on your feet, and your staff in your hand; and ye shall eat it in haste: it is the Lord's passover.

Figure 4.38 The Angel of Death and the First Passover,
Illustrators of the 1897 *Bible Pictures and What They Teach Us* by Charles Foster.

The Angel of Death and the First Passover. Caption: "The angel is going through King Pharaoh's land. He is going through it in the night. The angel will go into King Pharaoh's house and make his son to die. He will go into all the people's houses and make their sons to die because they have been so cruel to the Israelites. But the angel will not go into the houses where the Israelites live, to make their sons die. God told the Israelites that the angel was coming, and he told them to kill a lamb, and take its blood and sprinkle it over the doors of the houses. And when the angel saw the blood, God said, he would not come into the house to hurt them. In the picture we see the blood sprinkled over the door and at each side of it. The angel sees the blood. He will pass over this house and not harm any one in it. We can see the family inside. They are eating the Feast of the Passover." Illustration from the 1897 *Bible Pictures and What They Teach Us: Containing 400 Illustrations from the Old and New Testaments: With brief descriptions by Charles Foster*

Exodus12: [12] For I will pass through the land of Egypt this night, and will smite all the firstborn in the land of Egypt, both man and beast; and against all the gods of Egypt I will execute judgment: I am the LORD. [13] And the blood shall be to you for a token upon the houses where ye are: and when I see the blood, I will pass over you, and the plague shall not be upon you to destroy you, when I smite the land of Egypt. [14] And this day shall be unto you for a memorial; and ye shall keep it a feast to the LORD throughout your generations; ye shall keep it a feast by an ordinance forever.

"After the death of the first born in Egypt came the Departure of the Israelites"

Figure 4.39 The Israelites Leaving Egypt (1830) by David Roberts.

The children of Israel were to take a lamb without blemish and sacrifice it. They were to cook the flesh, and the families were commanded to eat the lamb. They were to take the blood from the lamb and spread it over the doorpost of their home. So that when the death angel came, he would pass over every Jewish home where the blood of that lamb was spread over the doorpost and the two side posts. Their firstborn would be spared.

Now Jesus is our Passover lamb. He is the lamb that was slain before the foundation of the earth was laid. Jesus fulfilled this prophecy when He was crucified. Satan made the second worst mistake that he could ever make by crucifying Jesus because He was sinless and allowing Jesus' Blood to be left in the earth. The first mistake was when he tried to take God's throne. The Blood that Satan allowed to be spilled was his downfall. Satan forgot about the lamb sacrifices of the Old Testament. It was a trap that was set by the Father, the Son, and Holy Spirit. Satan fell for it.

The Kingdom of God is going to bring about the destruction to the kingdom of darkness. Revelation lets us know that the spotless, blameless Blood of Jesus will be used to overcome the power of the kingdom of darkness.

John 6: [28]Then said they unto him, What shall we do, that we might work the works of God? [29]Jesus answered and said unto them, This is the work of God, that ye believe on him whom he hath sent.

Jesus tells them if you want to see God do the same miracles and even greater miracles they would have to "drink My Blood and eat My flesh." He is talking about the reason for communion.

Now we understand why Jesus said there is power in the Blood because it is His life and its source comes from the presence of God living, dwelling, and flowing through Him. God is the source of all life. When Jesus allowed our sins to be placed on Him, He agreed to be the lamb that was slain before the foundation of the Earth was laid. It was prophesied in the Old Testament:

Psalm (KJV) 40: [6]Sacrifice and offering thou didst not desire; mine ears hast thou opened: burnt offering and sin offering hast thou not required. [7]**Then said I, Lo, I come: in the volume of the book it is written of me,** [8]**I delight to do thy will, O my God: yea, thy law is within my heart.**

Now we understand why Jesus said; "not My will but Thy will" and it was fulfilled in the New Testament:

Hebrews (KJV) 10: [6]In burnt offerings and sacrifices for sin thou hast had no pleasure. [7]**Then said I, Lo, I come (in the volume of the book it is written of me,) to do thy will, O God.** [8]Above when he said, Sacrifice and offering and burnt offerings and offering for sin thou wouldest not, neither hadst pleasure therein; which are offered by the law;

Figure 4.40 Adoration of the Lamb, "Ghent Altarpiece," (1432) by Jan van Eyck.

John (KJV) 1: [28] These things were done in Bethabara beyond Jordan, where John was baptizing. [29] The next day John seeth Jesus coming unto him, and saith, Behold the Lamb of God, which taketh away the sin of the world. [30] This is he of whom I said, After me cometh a man which is preferred before me: for he was before me. [31] And I knew him not: but that he should be made manifest to Israel, therefore am I come baptizing with water. [32] And John bare record, saying, I saw the Spirit descending from heaven like a dove, and it abode upon him. [33] And I knew him not: but he that sent me to baptize with water, the same said unto me, Upon whom thou shalt see the Spirit descending, and remaining on him, the same is he which baptizeth with the Holy Ghost. [34] And I saw, and bare record that this is the Son of God.

**Figure 4.41 The Baptism of Christ in the Jordan River Artist
Follower of Jan van Scorel (1495–1552)**

Leviticus (KJV) 17: [11] For the life of the flesh is in the blood: and I have given it to you upon the altar to make an atonement for your souls: for it is the blood that maketh an atonement for the soul.

John 6: [47]Verily, verily, I say unto you, He that believeth on me hath everlasting life. [48]I am that bread of life. [49]Your fathers did eat manna in the wilderness, and are dead. [50]This is the bread which cometh down from heaven, that a man may eat thereof, and not die. [51]I am the living bread which came down from heaven: if any maneat of this bread, he shall live forever: and the bread that I will give is my flesh, which I will give for the life of the world. [52]The Jews therefore strove among themselves, saying, How can this man give us his flesh to eat? [53]Then Jesus said unto them, Verily, verily, I say unto you, Except ye eat the flesh of the Son of man, and drink his blood, ye have no life in you. [54]Whoso eateth my flesh, and drinketh my blood, hath eternal life; and I will raise him up at the last day. [55]For my flesh is meat indeed, and my blood is drink indeed. [56]He that eateth my flesh, and drinketh my blood, dwelleth in me, and I in him. [57]As the living Father hath sent me, and I live by the Father: so he that eateth me, even he shall live by me. *[58]This is that bread which came down from heaven: not as your fathers did eat manna, and are dead: he that eateth of this bread shall live forever.[59]These things said he in the synagogue, as he taught in Capernaum.*

Mark 6: [31] And he said unto them, Come ye yourselves apart into a desert place, and rest a while: for there were many coming and going, and they had no leisure so much as to eat. [32] And they departed into a desert place by ship privately.[33] And the people saw them departing, and many knew him, and ran afoot thither out of all cities, and outwent them, and came together unto him.[34] And Jesus, when he came out, saw much people, and was moved with compassion toward them, because they were as sheep not having a shepherd: and he began to teach them many things. [35] And when the day was now far spent, his disciples came unto him, and said, This is a desert place, and now the time is far passed: [36] Send them away, that they may go into the country round about, and into the villages, and buy themselves bread: for they have nothing to at. [37] He answered and said unto them, Give ye them to eat. And they say unto him, Shall we go and buy two hundred pennyworth of bread, and give them to eat? [38] He saith unto them, How many loaves have ye? go and see. And when they knew, they say, Five, and two fishes.[39] And he commanded them to make all sit down by companies upon the green grass.[40] And they sat down in ranks, by hundreds, and by fifties. *[41] And when he had taken the five loaves and the two fishes, he looked up to heaven, and blessed, and brake the loaves, and gave them to his disciples to set before them; and the two fishes divided he among them all.*

**Figure 4.42 Jesus Feeding a Crowd with Five Loaves of Bread and Two Fish
by Bernardo Strozzi.**

[42] And they did all eat, and were filled. [43] And they took up twelve baskets full of the fragments, and of the fishes. [44] And they that did eat of the loaves were about five thousand men.

[45] And straightway he constrained his disciples to get into the ship, and to go to the other side before unto Bethsaida, while he sent away the people. [46] And when he had sent them away, he departed into a mountain to pray. [47] And when even was come, the ship was in the midst of the sea, and he alone on the land. [48] And he saw them toiling in rowing; for the wind was contrary unto them: and about the fourth watch of the night he cometh unto them, walking upon the sea, and would have passed by them.

**Figure 4.43 Title Christ in the Storm on the Sea of Galilee, (1695)
by Artist Ludolf Bakhuizen (1631–1708)**

Mark 6: [49] But when they saw him walking upon the sea, they supposed it had been a spirit, and cried out: [50] For they all saw him, and were troubled. And immediately he talked with them, and saith unto them, Be of good cheer: it is I; be not afraid. [51] And he went up unto them into the ship; and the wind ceased: and they were sore amazed in themselves beyond measure, and wondered. [52] For they considered not the miracle of the loaves: for their heart was hardened. [53] And when they had passed over, they came into the land of Gennesaret, and drew to the shore.

Figure 4.44 Jesus Healing the Sick by Gustave Doré.

Mark 6: [54] And when they were come out of the ship, straightway they knew him, [55] And ran through that whole region round about, and began to carry about in beds those who were sick, where they heard he was.[56] And whithersoever he entered, into villages, or cities, or country, they laid the sick in the streets, and besought him that they might touch if it were but the border of his garment: and as many as touched him were made whole.

Summary

The power to heal the sick and do other miracles, as Jesus stated many times, is all in the hands of God. Jesus said that He could not do any miracles out of His own strength. Jesus had to keep Himself holy before God. He had to be obedient to the Word and His Father. Jesus knew that in order for miracles to be manifested, agreement had to be present in faith between Himself and the individual being prayed for. The agreement could be indirectly from family members or a friend, but the key is that faith had to be present for miracles to be manifested.

Even Jesus with the Holy Spirit could not do great miracles in His own hometown because of the people's unbelief.

Matthew (KJV) 17: [18]And Jesus rebuked the devil; and he departed out of him: and the child was cured from that very hour. [19]Then came the disciples to Jesus apart, and said, Why could not we cast him out? [20]*And Jesus said unto them, Because of your unbelief: for verily I say unto you, If ye have faith as a grain of mustard seed, ye shall say unto this mountain, Remove hence to yonder place; and it shall remove; and nothing shall be impossible unto you.*

Mark (KJV) 11: [22]And Jesus answering saith unto them, *Have faith in God.* [23]For verily I say unto you, That whosoever shall say unto this mountain, Be thou removed, and be thou cast into the sea; and shall not doubt in his heart, but shall believe that those things which he saith shall come to pass; he shall have whatsoever he saith. [24]*Therefore I say unto you, What things soever ye desire, when ye pray, believe that ye receive them, and ye shall have them.* [25]*And when ye stand praying, forgive, if ye have ought against any: that your Father also which is in heaven may forgive you your trespasses.* [26]*But if ye do not forgive, neither will your Father which is in heaven forgive your trespasses.*

Hebrews (KJV) 12: [2]Looking unto Jesus the author and finisher of our faith;

Colossians 1: [8]Who also declared unto us your love in the Spirit. [9]For this cause we also, since the day we heard it, do not cease to pray for you, and to desire that ye might be filled with the knowledge of his will in all wisdom and spiritual understanding; [10]That ye might walk worthy of the Lord unto all pleasing, fruitful in every good work, and increasing in the knowledge of God; [11]Strengthened with all might, according to his glorious power, unto all patience and longsuffering with joyfulness; [12]*Giving thanks unto the Father, which hath made us meet to be partakers of the inheritance of the saints in light:*[13]*Who hath delivered us from the power of darkness, and hath translated us into the kingdom of his dear Son:* [14]*In whom we have redemption through his blood, even the forgiveness of sins:* [15]*Who is the image of the invisible God, the firstborn of every creature:* [16]*For by him were all things created, that are in heaven, and that are in earth, visible and invisible, whether they be thrones, or dominions, or principalities, or powers: all things were created by him, and for him:* [17]*And he is before all things, and by him all things consist.* [18]*And he is the head of the body, the church: who is the beginning, the firstborn from the dead; that in all things he might have the preeminence.* [19]*For it pleased the Father that in him should all fulness dwell;* [20]*And, having made peace through the blood of his cross, by him to reconcile all things unto himself; by him, I say, whether they be things in earth, or things in heaven.* [21]*And you, that were sometime alienated and enemies in your mind by wicked works, yet now hath he reconciled* [22]*In the body of his flesh through death, to present you holy and unblameable and unreproveable in his sight:* [23]*If ye continue in the faith grounded and settled, and be not moved away from the hope of the gospel, which ye have heard, and which was preached to every creature which is under heaven; whereof I Paul am made a minister;* [24]*Who now rejoice in my sufferings for you, and fill up that which is behind of the afflictions of Christ in my flesh for his body's sake, which is the church:* [25]*Whereof I am made a minister, according to the dispensation of God which is given to me for you, to fulfil the word of God;* [26]*Even the mystery which hath been hid from ages and from generations, but now is made manifest to his saints:* [27]*To whom God would make known what is the riches of the glory* *of this mystery among the Gentiles; which is Christ in you, the hope of glory:* [28]*Whom we preach, warning every man, and teaching every man in all wisdom;* **that we may present every man perfect in Christ Jesus:** [29]Whereunto I also labour, striving according to his working, which worketh in me mightily.

Revelation (KJV) 1:[17] And when I saw him, I fell at his feet as dead. And he laid his right hand upon me, saying unto me, Fear not; I am the first and the last: [18] I am he that liveth, and was dead; and, behold, I am alive for evermore, Amen; and have the keys of hell and of death.

CHAPTER 5

THE KEYS TO THE KINGDOM OF HEAVEN

Matthew (KJV) 16: [18] And I say also unto thee, That thou art Peter, and upon this rock I will build my church; and the gates of hell shall not prevail against it. [19] And I will give unto thee the keys of the kingdom of heaven: and whatsoever thou shalt bind on earth shall be bound in heaven: and whatsoever thou shalt loose on earth shall be loosed in heaven.

Figure 5:1 Saint Peter by Peter Paul Rubens (1577–1640)

The Wise Virgins sought the wisdom of God first.

Stop seeking wealth; there are more important things God warns us.
Proverbs (KJV) 8

Doth not wisdom cry? and understanding put forth her voice? [2] She standeth in the top of high places, by the way in the places of the paths. [3] She crieth at the gates, at the entry of the city, at the coming in at the doors. [4] Unto you, O men, I call; and my voice is to the sons of man. [5] O ye simple, understand wisdom: and, ye fools, be ye of an understanding heart. [6] Hear; for I will speak of excellent things; and the opening of my lips shall be right things. [7] For my mouth shall speak truth; and wickedness is an abomination to my lips. [8] All the words of my mouth are in righteousness; there is nothing froward or perverse in them. [9] They are all plain to him that understandeth, and right to them that find knowledge. [10] Receive my instruction, and not silver; and knowledge rather than choice gold. [11] For wisdom is better than rubies; and all the things that may be desired are not to be compared to it. [12] I wisdom dwell with prudence, and find out knowledge of witty inventions. [13] The fear of the LORD is to hate evil: pride, and arrogancy, and the evil way, and the froward mouth, do I hate. [14] Counsel is mine, and sound wisdom: I am understanding; I have strength. [15] By me kings reign, and princes decree justice. [16] By me princes rule, and nobles, even all the judges of the earth. [17] I love them that love me; and those who seek me early shall find me. [18] Riches and honour are with me; yea, durable riches and righteousness. [19] My fruit is better than gold, yea, than fine gold; and my revenue than choice silver. [20] I lead in the way of righteousness, in the midst of the paths of judgment: [21] That I may cause those who love me to inherit substance; and I will fill their treasures. [22] The LORD possessed me in the beginning of his way, before his works of old. [23] I was set up from everlasting, from the beginning, or ever the earth was. [24] When there were no depths, I was brought forth; when there were no fountains abounding with water. [25] Before the mountains were settled, before the hills was I brought forth: [26] While as yet he had not made the earth, nor the fields, nor the highest part of the dust of the world. [27] When he prepared the heavens, I was there: when he set a compass upon the face of the depth: [28] When he established the clouds above: when he strengthened the fountains of the deep: [29] When he gave to the sea his decree, that the waters should not pass his commandment: when he appointed the foundations of the earth: [30] Then I was by him, as one brought up with him: and I was daily his delight, rejoicing always before him; [31] Rejoicing in the habitable part of his earth; and my delights were with the sons of men. [32] Now therefore hearken unto me, O ye children: for blessed are they that keep my ways. [33] Hear instruction, and be wise, and refuse it not. [34] Blessed is the man that heareth me, watching daily at my gates, waiting at the posts of my doors. [35] For whoso findeth me findeth life, and shall obtain favour of the LORD. [36] But he that sinneth against me wrongeth his own soul: all they that hate me love death.

Begin your Search for the Kingdom Daily

When I was a child one of the first games I learned to play was "hide and seek." Most kids today probably have never heard of it. The object of the game was for one person (the seeker) to choose a base, usually a tree; then they would cover their eyes and count to 100 while the rest of the kids would run and hide. Once the seeker reached 100, his job was to go out and find one of the other kids. They had to call their name out, and they both had to race back to the home base. Whoever the loser was had to become the seeker and they had to start the game all over again. It was a game that everyone enjoyed. There was no real reward, only the excitement of playing together as children. The rewards of seeking the Kingdom of God are unfathomable; you really cannot imagine the wealth, health, and power over the devil that God has in store for those that love Him and "are called according to His purpose."

1 Corinthians 2: *⁴And my speech and my preaching was not with enticing words of man's wisdom, but in demonstration of the Spirit and of power: ⁵That your faith should not stand in the wisdom of men, but in the power of God. ⁶Howbeit we speak wisdom among them that are perfect: yet not the wisdom of this world, nor of the princes of this world, that come to nought:⁷But we speak the wisdom of God in a mystery, even the hidden wisdom, which God ordained before the world unto our glory: ⁸Which none of the princes of this world knew: for had they known it, they would not have crucified the Lord of glory. ⁹But as it is written, Eye hath not seen, nor ear heard, neither have entered into the heart of man, the things which God hath prepared for them that love him. ¹⁰ But God hath revealed them unto us by his Spirit: for the Spirit searcheth all things, yea, the deep things of God. ¹¹ For what man knoweth the things of a man, save the spirit of man which is in him? even so the things of God knoweth no man, but the Spirit of God. ¹² Now we have received, not the spirit of the world, but the spirit which is of God; that we might know the things that are freely given to us of God.*

The Kingdom is not all about wealth, but the destruction of the kingdom of darkness. God wants to make us wealthy; as a matter of fact He wants to make us wealthier than Solomon, but seeking the Kingdom of Heaven has to come first.

Seeking to understand how God's Kingdom works and fulfilling God's destiny for our lives is imperative because each one of us has a separate assignment. We cannot fulfill our destiny without the power of the Holy Spirit. Jesus prayed, "That we would become one with the Father, Son, and Holy Spirit." God's desire is for no one to be lost but that we all come to the knowledge of the truth. Most of us have read Matthew 6:25-33 that teaches us divine order on how and what to seek after first.

Matthew 6: ²⁵Therefore I say unto you, Take no thought for your life, what ye shall eat, or what ye shall drink; nor yet for your body, what ye shall put on. Is not the life more than meat, and the body than raiment? ²⁶Behold the fowls of the air: for they sow not, neither do they reap, nor gather into barns; yet your heavenly Father feedeth them. Are ye not much better than they? ²⁷Which of you by taking thought can add one cubit unto his stature? ²⁸And why take ye thought for raiment? Consider the lilies of the field, how they grow; they toil not, neither do they spin: ²⁹And yet I say unto you, That even Solomon in all his glory was not arrayed like one of these. ³⁰Wherefore, if God so clothe the grass of the field, which today is, and tomorrow is cast into the oven, shall he not much more clothe you, O ye of little faith? ³¹Therefore take no thought, saying, What shall we eat? or, What shall we drink? or, Wherewithal shall we be clothed? ³²(For after all these things do the Gentiles seek:) for your heavenly Father knoweth that ye have need of all these things. ³³ But seek first the kingdom of God and His righteousness, and all these things shall be added to you.

If you have read these verses carefully you will see the order that God wants us to follow. He wants us to be wealthier than Solomon. He wants us not to worry about anything because He already knows what our needs are and He will take care of them. Worrying about these things is what the Gentiles (or heathens do). We are to concentrate on seeking the Kingdom of God. If you do that everything else will fall into place. For the most part we have done it backwards, we pray for God to bless us with millions of dollars and at the beginning of every year, we hear it is always going to happen this year, and if not it will be next year, just wait your turn. The truth is the wealth will be added after we follow His instructions.

But just like when I was a child playing hide and seek, it is the same with the Kingdom of God, it is hidden; we have to seek it. Our Heavenly Father has given us favor and He tells us where to hunt for it.

Matthew 13: [44]Again, the kingdom of heaven is like unto treasure hid in a field; the which when a man hath found, he hideth, and for joy thereof goeth and selleth all that he hath, and buyeth that field.

We have to place that same value on our love for God; to want to search out the wisdom of God which is more valuable than all the wealth in the world. The foolish virgins became misguided, lost their focus and ended up missing God and missing Heaven in the end.

The destruction of the kingdom of darkness is the number one goal of the Kingdom of Heaven. Jesus came to earth for one purpose, to redeem everything back to God that Adam lost by disobeying Him and obeying Satan by eating the forbidden fruit. Whoever you obey becomes your God. Jesus paid the price to set us free but He did not use money, but He gave His life and God raised Him from the dead. All of the problems that are in the world come from one source and that is Satan. The weapons that we are to use is our intercessory prayer life, which is able to pull down every stronghold that Satan has established in the earth, and re-establish the true ownership of the Earth which belongs to God and is part of the Kingdom of Heaven. We have been given the Blood of the Lamb, the word of our testimony, the name of Jesus, all the angels of heaven, and the power of the Holy Spirit to accomplish this task. God has already given us the victory. Seek God for a deeper understanding for yourself because it is going to be all about you and your personal relationship with God. You have to place a higher value on your search for the Kingdom of God.

Figure 5.2 The Pearl of Great Price, by <u>Domenico Fetti</u>, seventeenth century.

[45]Again, the kingdom of heaven is like unto a merchant man, seeking goodly pearls: [46]Who, when he had found one pearl of great price, went and sold all that he had, and bought it.

2 Corinthians (KJV) 4: [3]But if our gospel be hid, it is hid to them that are lost: [4]In whom the god of this world hath blinded the minds of them which believe not, lest the light of the glorious gospel of Christ, who is the image of God, should shine unto them. [5]For we preach not ourselves, but Christ Jesus the Lord; and ourselves your servants for Jesus' sake. [6]For God, who commanded the light to shine out of darkness, hath shined in our hearts, to give the light of the knowledge of the glory of God in the face of Jesus Christ. [7]But we have this treasure in earthen vessels, that the excellency of the power may be of God, and not of us.

The Kingdom of God is hidden, but Jesus tells us exactly where it is. The Kingdom of God is the most valuable possession that we can ever own. We really take the Kingdom of Heaven for granted because we do not fully understand all the benefits that have been made available to us. We have not learned how to tap into that source. We can get involved with so many distractions around us that we do not realize what is really important. And most of all, what is important to

God must become important to us! We must set our affections on God's desire for us to fulfill His purpose for us being here in the first place. "No eye has seen no ears have heard what God has in store for those who love Him."

1 Corinthians (KJV) 2: [8] Which none of the princes of this world knew: for had they known it, they would not have crucified the Lord of glory. [9] But as it is written, Eye hath not seen, nor ear heard, neither have entered into the heart of man, the things which God hath prepared for them that love him. *[10] But God hath revealed them unto us by his Spirit: for the Spirit searcheth all things, yea, the deep things of God.*

Luke 17: (KJV) [20]And when he was demanded of the Pharisees, when the kingdom of God should come, he answered them and said, The kingdom of God cometh not with observation: [21]Neither shall they say, Lo here! or, lo there! for, behold, the kingdom of God is within you. [22]And he said unto the disciples, The days will come, when ye shall desire to see one of the days of the Son of man, and ye shall not see it.

Jesus tells us where to look for the Kingdom. The moment we asked Him to come into our heart we became born again and Jesus stepped inside our spirit man.

2 Corinthians 6: [16]And what agreement hath the temple of God with idols? *for ye are the temple of the living God; as God hath said, I will dwell in them, and walk in them; and I will be their God, and they shall be my people.*

Isaiah (KJV) 9: [6]For unto us a child is born, unto us a son is given: and the government shall be upon his shoulder: and his name shall be called Wonderful, Counselor, The mighty God, The everlasting Father, The Prince of Peace. [7]Of the increase of his government and peace there shall be no end, upon the throne of David, and upon his kingdom, to order it, and to establish it with judgment and with justice from henceforth even forever. The zeal of the LORD of hosts will perform this.

This is why Jesus said that the Kingdom of God is in all of us if we have asked Him to come into our hearts. He came with His Father and the Holy Spirit, as Isaiah 9:6 says, "the government of Heaven was upon His shoulders." That is why He said whatever we bind on earth, is bound in Heaven and whatever we loose on earth is loosed in Heaven. The authority has been given to us, but we have to learn how to and what it takes to walk in that authority.

The number one priority for all Christians is to understand how the Kingdom of God functions, and understand why God birth us as His very own children. The foolish virgins did not seek the Kingdom with their whole hearts. Jesus tells us where the Kingdom is, but there is another problem. The Kingdom of God must have a number of different kinds of locks on it, because Jesus told Peter He has given Him the keys. That means there are more than one key required to gain entrance into the Kingdom of God, so that not just anybody can get in.

**Figure 5.3 I Give Unto Thee The Keys of the Kingdom of God,
by Pietro Perugino (1448-1523)**

Keys work in the natural realm the same way that they do in the spiritual realm. Locks perform several functions: they can be used to keep people out of a home or a car, and so forth, while the person with the correct key has free access to come and go as they will. Jesus said that there are keys, meaning it will take more than one to gain access to the Kingdom of God. In order for us to gain access to the Kingdom of God we have to have the right keys and then we have to know how to use them.

Figure 5.4 Saint Peter, Painted by Grão Vasco (1506)
The Key of Righteousness

The first three keys come from the definition of the Kingdom of God, like in Hebrews 11, where the Bible gives us the definition of faith.

Hebrews 11: Now faith is the substance of things hoped for, the evidence of things not seen.

The Bible does the same thing about the Kingdom of God; it gives us the definition of it.
The definition of the "Kingdom of God" is not meat and drink (it is not about things); but righteousness, peace, and joy in the Holy Spirit, and they are also the first three keys that allow us into the Kingdom of God.
I will not make a lot of comments because the Word will speak for itself. The keys have always been there; we just did not realize it. Just knowing what the keys are will not unlock the Kingdom of God for you. You have to apply them in your day-to-day walk with God.

1 Corinthians 6: ⁸Nay, ye do wrong, and defraud, and that your brethren. *⁹Know ye not that the unrighteous shall not inherit the kingdom of God?*

Be not deceived: neither fornicators, nor idolaters, nor adulterers, nor effeminate, nor abusers of themselves with mankind, [10]Nor thieves, nor covetous, nor drunkards, nor revilers, nor extortioners, *shall inherit the kingdom of God.*

Romans 6: [12]Let not sin therefore reign in your mortal body, that ye should obey it in the lusts thereof. [13]Neither yield ye your members as instruments of *unrighteousness* unto sin: but yield yourselves unto God, as those who are alive from the dead, and your members as instruments of *righteousness* unto God. [14]For sin shall not have dominion over you: for ye are not under the law, but under grace.

Romans 1:[17]For therein is *the righteousness* of God revealed from faith to faith: as it is written, The just shall live by faith. [18]For the wrath of God is revealed from heaven against all *ungodliness* and *unrighteousness* of men, who hold the truth in *unrighteousness*; [19]Because that which may be known of God is manifest in them; for God hath shewed it unto them. [20]For the invisible things of him from the creation of the world are clearly seen, being understood by the things that are made, even his eternal power and Godhead; so that they are without excuse: [21]Because that, when they knew God, they glorified him not as God, neither were thankful; but became vain in their imaginations, and their foolish heart was darkened. [22]Professing themselves to be wise, they became fools, [23]And changed the glory of the *un-corruptible God* into an image made like to corruptible man, and to birds, and four footed beasts, and creeping things. [24]Wherefore God also gave them up to uncleanness through the lusts of their own hearts, to dishonour their own bodies between themselves: [25]Who changed the truth of God into a lie, and worshipped and served the creature more than the Creator, who is blessed forever. Amen. [26]For this cause God gave them up unto vile affections: for even their women did change the natural use into that which is against nature: [27]And likewise also the men, leaving the natural use of the woman, burned in their lust one toward another; men with men working that which is unseemly, and receiving in themselves that recompence of their error which was meet. [28]And even as they did not like to retain God in their knowledge, God gave them over to a reprobate mind, to do those things which are not convenient; [29]Being filled with all *unrighteousness*, fornication, wickedness, covetousness, maliciousness; full of envy, murder, debate, deceit, malignity; whisperers, [30]Backbiters, haters of God, despiteful, proud, boasters, inventors of evil things, disobedient to parents, [31]Without understanding, covenant breakers, without natural affection, implacable, unmerciful: [32]Who knowing the judgment of God, that they which commit such things are worthy of death, not only do the same, but have pleasure in them that do them.

Romans 2: [1]Therefore thou art inexcusable, O man, whosoever thou art that judgest: for wherein thou judgest another, thou condemnest thyself; for thou that judgest doest the same things. [2]But we are sure that the judgment of God is according to truth against them which commit such things. [3]And thinkest thou this, O man, that judgest them which do such things, and doest the same, that thou shalt escape the judgment of God? [4]Or despisest thou the riches of his goodness and forbearance and longsuffering; not knowing that the goodness of God leadeth thee to repentance? *[5]But after thy hardness and impenitent heart treasurest up unto thyself wrath against the day of wrath and revelation of the righteous judgment of God; [6]Who will render to every man according to his deeds: [7]To them who by patient continuance in well doing seek for glory and honour and immortality, eternal life:* [8]But unto them that are contentious, and do not obey the truth, but obey *unrigh-*

teousness, indignation and wrath, ⁹Tribulation and anguish, upon every soul of man that doeth evil, of the Jew first, and also of the Gentile;

2 Thessalonians 2: ¹Now we beseech you, brethren, by the coming of our Lord Jesus Christ, and by our gathering together unto him, ²That ye be not soon shaken in mind, or be troubled, neither by spirit, nor by word, nor by letter as from us, as that the day of Christ is at hand. ³Let no man deceive you by any means: for that day shall not come, except there come a falling away first, and that man of sin be revealed, the son of perdition; ⁴Who opposeth and exalteth himself above all that is called God, or that is worshipped; so that he as God sitteth in the temple of God, shewing himself that he is God. ⁵Remember ye not, that, when I was yet with you, I told you these things? ⁶And now ye know what withholdeth that he might be revealed in his time. ⁷For the mystery of iniquity doth already work: only he who now letteth will let, until he be taken out of the way. ⁸And then shall that Wicked be revealed, whom the Lord shall consume with the spirit of his mouth, and shall destroy with the brightness of his coming: ⁹Even him, whose coming is after the working of Satan with all power and signs and lying wonders, ¹⁰And with all deceivableness of *unrighteousness* in them that perish; because they received not the love of the truth, that they might be saved. ¹¹And for this cause God shall send them strong delusion, that they should believe a lie: ¹²That they all might be damned who believed not the truth, but had pleasure in *unrighteousness*. ¹³But we are bound to give thanks alway to God for you, brethren beloved of the Lord, because God hath from the beginning chosen you to salvation through sanctification of the Spirit and belief of the truth: ¹⁴Whereunto he called you by our gospel, to the obtaining of the glory of our Lord Jesus Christ. ¹⁵Therefore, brethren, stand fast, and hold the traditions which ye have been taught, whether by word, or our epistle. ¹⁶Now our Lord Jesus Christ himself, and God, even our Father, which hath loved us, and hath given us everlasting consolation and good hope through grace, ¹⁷Comfort your hearts, and stablish you in every good word and work.

1 Corinthians 6: ⁸Nay, ye do wrong, and defraud, and that your brethren. *⁹Know ye not that the unrighteous shall not inherit the kingdom of God?* Be not deceived: neither fornicators, nor idolaters, nor adulterers, nor effeminate, nor abusers of themselves with mankind, ¹⁰Nor thieves, nor covetous, nor drunkards, nor revilers, nor extortioners, shall inherit the kingdom of God.

1 Corinthians 15: ⁴⁹And as we have borne the image of the earthy, we shall also bear the image of the heavenly. *⁵⁰Now this I say, brethren, that flesh and blood cannot inherit the kingdom of God; neither doth corruption inherit incorruption.* ⁵¹Behold, I shew you a mystery; We shall not all sleep, but we shall all be changed, ⁵²In a moment, in the twinkling of an eye, at the last trump: for the trumpet shall sound, and the dead shall be raised incorruptible, and we shall be changed. *⁵³ For this corruptible must put on incorruption, and this mortal must put on immortality. ⁵⁴ So when this corruptible shall have put on incorruption, and this mortal shall have put on immortality, then shall be brought to pass the saying that is written, Death is swallowed up in victory. ⁵⁵ O death, where is thy sting? O grave, where is thy victory? ⁵⁶ The sting of death is sin; and the strength of sin is the law. ⁵⁷ But thanks be to God, which giveth us the victory through our Lord Jesus Christ. ⁵⁸ Therefore, my beloved brethren, be ye stedfast, unmoveable, always abounding in the work of the Lord, forasmuch as ye know that your labour is not in vain in the Lord.*

2 Corinthians 6: [13]Now for a recompence in the same, (I speak as unto my children,) be ye also enlarged. [14]Be ye not unequally yoked together with unbelievers: for what fellowship hath *righteousness* with *unrighteousness*? and what communion hath light with darkness? [15]And what concord hath Christ with Belial? or what part hath he that believeth with an infidel?

2 Corinthians 9: [1]For as touching the ministering to the saints, it is superfluous for me to write to you: [2]For I know the forwardness of your mind, for which I boast of you to them of Macedonia, that Achaia was ready a year ago; and your zeal hath provoked very many. [3]Yet have I sent the brethren, lest our boasting of you should be in vain in this behalf; that, as I said, ye may be ready: [4]Lest haply if they of Macedonia come with me, and find you unprepared, we (that we say not, ye) should be ashamed in this same confident boasting. [5]Therefore I thought it necessary to exhort the brethren, that they would go before unto you, and make up beforehand your bounty, whereof ye had notice before, that the same might be ready, as a matter of bounty, and not as of covetousness. *[6]But this I say, He which soweth sparingly shall reap also sparingly; and he which soweth bountifully shall reap also bountifully. [7]Every man according as he purposeth in his heart, so let him give; not grudgingly, or of necessity: for God loveth a cheerful giver. [8]And God is able to make all grace abound toward you; that ye, always having all sufficiency in all things, may abound to every good work: [9](As it is written, He hath dispersed abroad; he hath given to the poor: his righteousness remaineth forever. [10]Now he that ministereth seed to the sower both minister bread for your food, and multiply your seed sown, and increase the fruits of your righteousness;) [11]Being enriched in everything to all bountifulness, which causeth through us thanksgiving to God. [12]For the administration of this service not only supplieth the want of the saints, but is abundant also by many thanksgivings unto God; [13]Whiles by the experiment of this ministration they glorify God for your professed subjection unto the gospel of Christ, and for your liberal distribution unto them, and unto all men; [14]And by their prayer for you, which long after you for the exceeding grace of God in you. [15]Thanks be unto God for his unspeakable gift.*

Galatians (KJV) 5: [16]This I say then, Walk in the Spirit, and ye shall not fulfil the lust of the flesh. [17]For the flesh lusteth against the Spirit, and the Spirit against the flesh: and these are contrary the one to the other: so that ye cannot do the things that ye would. [18]But if ye be led of the Spirit, ye are not under the law. [19]Now the works of the flesh are manifest, which are these; Adultery, fornication, uncleanness, lasciviousness, [20]Idolatry, witchcraft, hatred, variance, emulations, wrath, strife, seditions, heresies,[21]Envyings, murders, drunkenness, revellings, and such like: of the which I tell you before, as I have also told you in time past, *that they which do such things shall not inherit the kingdom of God.* [22]But the fruit of the Spirit is love, joy, peace, longsuffering, gentleness, goodness, faith, [23]Meekness, temperance: against such there is no law. [24]And they that are Christ's have crucified the flesh with the affections and lusts. [25]If we live in the Spirit, let us also walk in the Spirit.

Ephesians 5: *[4]Neither filthiness, nor foolish talking, nor jesting, which are not convenient: but rather giving of thanks. [5]For this ye know, that no whoremonger, nor unclean person, nor covetous man, who is an idolater, hath any inheritance in the kingdom of Christ and of God. [6]Let no man deceive you with vain words: for because of these things cometh the wrath of God upon the children of disobedience.*

Hebrews 8: [10]For this is the covenant that I will make with the house of Israel after those days, saith the Lord; I will put my laws into their mind, and write them in their hearts: and I will be to them a God, and they shall be to me a people: [11]And they shall not teach every man his neighbour, and every man his brother, saying, Know the Lord: for all shall know me, from the least to the greatest. *[12]For I will be merciful to their unrighteousness,* and their sins and their iniquities will I remember no more. [13]In that he saith, A new covenant, he hath made the first old. Now that which decayeth and waxeth old is ready to vanish away.

1 John 1: [8]If we say that we have no sin, we deceive ourselves, and the truth is not in us. [9]If we confess our sins, he is faithful and just to forgive us our sins, and to cleanse us from all *unrighteousness*. [10]If we say that we have not sinned, we make him a liar, and his word is not in us.

Revelation 21: [6]And he said unto me, It is done. I am Alpha and Omega, the beginning and the end. I will give unto him that is athirst of the fountain of the water of life freely. *[7]He that overcometh shall inherit all things; and I will be his God, and he shall be my son. [8]But the fearful, and unbelieving, and the abominable, and murderers, and whoremongers, and sorcerers, and idolaters, and all liars, shall have their part in the lake which burneth with fire and brimstone: which is the second death.*

1 Corinthians 15: [20]But now is Christ risen from the dead, and become the first fruits of them that slept. [21]For since by man came death, by man came also the resurrection of the dead. [22]For as in Adam all die, even so in Christ shall all be made alive. [23]But every man in his own order: Christ the first fruits; afterward they that are Christ's at his coming. *[24]Then cometh the end, when he shall have delivered up the kingdom to God, even the Father; when he shall have put down all rule and all authority and power.* [25]For he must reign, till he hath put all enemies under his feet.

Hebrews 1: [8]But unto the Son he saith, Thy throne, O God, is forever and ever: a sceptre of *righteousness* is the sceptre of thy kingdom. [9]Thou hast loved *righteousness*, and hated iniquity; therefore God, even thy God, hath anointed thee with the oil of gladness above thy fellows. [10]And, Thou, Lord, in the beginning hast laid the foundation of the earth; and the heavens are the works of thine hands: [11]They shall perish; but thou remainest; and they all shall wax old as doth a garment; [12]And as a vesture shalt thou fold them up, and they shall be changed: but thou art the same, and thy years shall not fail.

An unrighteous lifestyle locks us out of the Kingdom of God. Righteousness unlocks the Kingdom of Heaven. Seek it.

Matt. (KJV) 5: [6]Blessed are they which do hunger and thirst after *righteousness*: for they shall be filled.

Matt. (KJV) 5: [10]Blessed are they which are persecuted for *righteousness'* sake: for theirs is the *kingdom of heaven*.

Figure 5.5

Jesus giving to St. Peter the keys and giving to St. Paul the Doctrine's Book, ca. 1540

The Next Key to the Kingdom of God is Peace

Isaiah (KJV)11 And there shall come forth a rod out of the stem of Jesse, and a Branch shall grow out of his roots: *² And the spirit of the Lord shall rest upon him, the spirit of wisdom and under-standing, the spirit of counsel and might, the spirit of knowledge and of the fear of the Lord; ³ And shall make him of quick understanding in the fear of the Lord: and he shall not judge after the sight of his eyes, neither reprove after the hearing of his ears: ⁴ But with righteousness shall he judge the poor, and reprove with equity for the meek of the earth: and he shall smite the earth: with the rod of his mouth, and with the breath of his lips shall he slay the wicked. ⁵ And righteousness shall be the girdle of his loins, and faithfulness the girdle of his reins.* ⁶ The wolf also shall dwell with the lamb, and the leopard shall lie down with the kid; and the calf and the young lion and the fatling together; and a little child shall lead them. ⁷ And the cow and the bear shall feed; their young ones shall lie down together: and the lion shall eat straw like the ox. ⁸ And the sucking child shall play on the hole of the asp, and the weaned child shall put his hand on the cockatrice' den. ⁹They shall not hurt nor destroy in all my holy mountain: for the earth shall be full of the knowledge of the LORD, as the waters cover the sea. ¹⁰And in that day there shall be a root of Jesse, which shall stand for an ensign of the people; to it shall the Gentiles seek: and his rest shall be glorious.

Figure 5.6 Lion and the lamb by Jeff Miztah Rogers, Yahoo! Contributor Network.

Isaiah 26: ²Open ye the gates, that the righteous nation which keepeth the truth may enter in. *³Thou wilt keep him in perfect peace, whose mind is stayed on thee:* because he trusteth in thee. ⁴Trust ye in the LORD forever: for in the LORD JEHOVAH is everlasting strength:

Isaiah 32: *¹⁶Then judgment shall dwell in the wilderness, and righteousness remain in the fruitful field. ¹⁷And the work of righteousness shall be peace; and the effect of righteousness quietness and assurance forever. ¹⁸And my people shall dwell in a peaceable habitation, and in sure dwellings, and in quiet resting places;*

Isaiah 48: ¹⁷Thus saith the LORD, thy Redeemer, the Holy One of Israel; I am the LORD thy God which teacheth thee to profit, which leadeth thee by the way that thou shouldest go. ¹⁸O that thou hadst hearkened to my commandments! *then had thy peace been as a river, and thy righteousness as the waves of the sea:* ¹⁹Thy seed also had been as the sand, and the offspring of thy bowels like the gravel thereof; his name should not have been cut off nor destroyed from before me.

Matt. 6: ⁹ *Blessed are the peacemakers*: for they shall be called the children of God.

Psalm 34:14 Depart from evil, and do good; *seek peace,* and pursue it.

Psalm 85:10 Mercy and truth are met together; *righteousness* and *peace* have kissed each other.

Psalm 119:165 *Great peace* have they which love thy law: and nothing shall offend them.

Proverbs 3: [1]My son, forget not my law; but let thine heart keep my commandments: [2]For length of days, and long life, and *peace,* shall they add to thee. [3]Let not mercy and truth forsake thee: bind them about thy neck; write them upon the table of thine heart:

Proverbs 16: [6]By mercy and truth iniquity is purged: and by the fear of the LORD men depart from evil. [7]When a man's ways please the LORD, he maketh even his enemies to be *at* peace with him. [8]Better is a little with righteousness than great revenues without right.

Isaiah 52: [6]Therefore my people shall know my name: therefore they shall know in that day that I am he that doth speak: behold, it is I. [7]*How beautiful upon the mountains are the feet of him that bringeth good tidings, that publisheth peace; that bringeth good tidings of good, that publisheth salvation; that saith unto Zion, Thy God reigneth!* [8]Thy watchmen shall lift up the voice; with the voice together shall they sing: for they shall see eye to eye, when the LORD shall bring again Zion

Zephaniah 1: [5]And them that worship the host of heaven upon the housetops; and them that worship and that swear by the LORD, and that swear by Malcham; [6]*And them that are turned back from the LORD; and those who have not sought the LORD, nor enquired for him.* [7]*Hold thy peace at the presence of the Lord GOD: for the day of the LORD is at hand: for the LORD hath prepared a sacrifice, he hath bid his guests.* [8]*And it shall come to pass in the day of the LORD's sacrifice, that I will punish the princes, and the king's children, and all such as are clothed with strange apparel.*

Malachi 2: [4]And ye shall know that I have sent this commandment unto you, that my covenant might be with Levi, saith the LORD of hosts. [5]*My covenant was with him of life and peace; and I gave them to him for the fear wherewith he feared me, and was afraid before my name.* [6]*The law of truth was in his mouth, and iniquity was not found in his lips: he walked with me in peace and equity, and did turn many away from iniquity.*

Luke 1: [75]*In holiness and righteousness before him, all the days of our life.* [76]And thou, child, shalt be called the prophet of the Highest: for thou shalt go before the face of the Lord to prepare his ways; [77]To give knowledge of salvation unto his people by the remission of their sins, [78]*Through the tender mercy of our God; whereby the dayspring from on high hath visited us,* [79]*To give light to them that sit in darkness and in the shadow of death, to guide our feet into the way of peace.* [80]And the child grew, and waxed strong in spirit, and was in the deserts till the day of his shewing unto Israel.

The Next Key is Joy

Figure 5.7 Christ surrendering the keys to St. Peter by Peter Paul Rubens

Isaiah (KJV) 35: The wilderness and the solitary place shall be glad for them; and the desert shall rejoice, and blossom as the rose. [2] It shall blossom abundantly, and rejoice even with joy and singing: the glory of Lebanon shall be given unto it, the excellency of Carmel and Sharon, they shall see the glory of the LORD, and the excellency of our God. [3] Strengthen ye the weak hands, and confirm the feeble knees.[4] Say to them that are of a fearful heart, Be strong, fear not: behold, your God will come with vengeance, even God with a recompence; he will come and save you.[5] Then the eyes of the blind shall be opened, and the ears of the deaf shall be unstopped.[6] Then shall the lame man leap as an hart, and the tongue of the dumb sing: for in the wilderness shall waters break out, and streams in the desert. [7] And the parched ground shall become a pool, and the thirsty land springs of water: in the habitation of dragons, where each lay, shall be grass with reeds and rushes. [8] And an highway shall be there, and a way, and it shall be called The way of holiness; the unclean shall not pass over it; but it shall be for those: the wayfaring men, though fools, shall not err therein. [9] No lion shall be there, nor any ravenous beast shall go up thereon, it shall not be found there; but the redeemed shall walk there: [10] *And the ransomed of the LORD shall return, and come* *to Zion with songs and everlasting joy upon their heads: they shall obtain joy and gladness, and sorrow and sighing shall flee away.*

Proverbs 12: [19]The lip of truth shall be established for ever: but a lying tongue is but for a moment. [20]Deceit is in the heart of them that imagine evil: *but to the counsellors of peace is joy.*[21]There shall no evil happen to the just: but the wicked shall be filled with mischief.

1 Thessalonians (KJV) 2: [18] Wherefore we would have come unto you, even I Paul, once and again; but Satan hindered us. [19] For what is our hope, or joy, or crown of rejoicing? Are not even ye in the presence of our Lord Jesus Christ at his coming? [20] *For ye are our glory and joy.*

Psalm 16: [10]For thou wilt not leave my soul in hell; neither wilt thou suffer thine Holy One to see corruption. *[11]Thou wilt shew me the path of life: in thy presence is fullness of joy; at thy right hand there are pleasures forever more.*

Psalm 16: 11 *Thou wilt shew me the path of life; in thy presence is fullness of joy; at thy right hand there are pleasures forever more.*

As discussed earlier the only way to get into the presence of God as we saw in the Old Testament is that you have to be a Priest. Then it is the priests' responsibility to purity themselves from all sins of omission and commission.

Colossians 1: *[11]Strengthened with all might, according to his glorious power, unto all patience and longsuffering with joyfulness;* [12]Giving thanks unto the Father, which hath made us meet to be partakers of the inheritance of the saints in light: [13]Who hath delivered us from the power of darkness, and hath translated us into the kingdom of his dear Son:

Jeremiah (KJV) 33 Moreover the word of the LORD came unto Jeremiah the second time, while he was yet shut up in the court of the prison, saying,

Figure 5.8 Jeremiah lamenting the destruction of Jerusalem (1630) by Rembrandt.

2 Thus saith the LORD the maker thereof, the LORD that formed it, to establish it; the LORD is his name; ³ Call unto me, and I will answer thee, and show thee great and mighty things, which thou knowest not. ⁴ For thus saith the LORD, the God of Israel, concerning the houses of this city, and concerning the houses of the kings of Judah, which are thrown down by the mounts, and by the sword; ⁵ They come to fight with the Chaldeans, but it is to fill them with the dead bodies of men, whom I have slain in mine anger and in my fury, and for all whose wickedness I have hid my face from this city. ⁶ Behold, I will bring it health and cure, and I will cure them, and will reveal unto them the abundance of peace and truth. ⁷ And I will cause the captivity of Judah and the captivity of Israel to return, and will build them, as at the first. ⁸ And I will cleanse them from all their iniquity, whereby they have sinned against me; and I will pardon all their iniquities, whereby they have sinned, and whereby they have transgressed against me. *⁹ And it shall be to me a name of joy, a praise and an honour before all the nations of the earth, which shall hear all the good that I do unto them: and they shall fear and tremble for all the goodness and for all the prosperity that I procure unto it. ¹⁰ Thus saith the LORD; Again there shall be heard in this place, which ye say shall*

be desolate without man and without beast, even in the cities of Judah, and in the streets of Jerusalem, that are desolate, without man, and without inhabitant, and without beast, ¹¹ The voice of joy, and the voice of gladness, the voice of the bridegroom, and the voice of the bride, the voice of them that shall say, Praise the LORD of hosts: for the LORD is good; for his mercy endureth for ever: and of them that shall bring the sacrifice of praise into the house of the LORD. For I will cause to return the captivity of the land, as at the first, saith the LORD.

Joy is a major key to the Kingdom of God. It is a force that is so powerful that it can reverse a situation that has turned negative in our favor with a simple prayer from verse 11. If we don't let the devil steal our joy, he cannot keep our goods. Jerry Savelle preached this sermon many years ago. And my wife and I have never forgotten it. You make the devil pay back seven times what he has stolen with the next scripture:

Proverbs 6:³⁰ Men do not despise a thief, if he steal to satisfy his soul when he is hungry; ³¹ But if he be found, he shall restore sevenfold; he shall give all the substance of his house.

Whenever we allow negative circumstances to draw us into depression and thoughts of defeat, we have just locked ourselves out of the Kingdom of God because we have shut down our faith, which is another key. Satan knows this and that is why the attacks come; either we know how the keys to the Kingdom work and apply them to our spiritual walk and overcome, or we will fail and be locked out of the Kingdom of God.

There are two more keys that we will look at next: the love and faith of God.

Figure 5.9 Ancient statue of St. Peter in St. Peter's Basilica, Rome, possibly the work of Atnolfo di Cambio, Photographer: Mattana

The love and faith of God are the main keys to the Kingdom, because they come out of the heart of God and do two things. The fruit of love and the fruit of faith start out as seeds. These two seeds, must be cultivated before they can mature and become the fruit of the Spirit. Next, they will empower the rest of the other fruits of the Spirit and they also become the keys to the Kingdom. They are what we inherited when we were born of God. It is the same in the natural; we are a product of our parent's genetic make-up. Just as we expect our children to mature, our Heavenly Father is the same way. We are not the children of wrath which are the very opposite, we are the children of God. We must grow and mature spiritually; God gave us a tutor the Holy Spirit to lead and guide us.

1 Thessalonians (KJV) 5: [4] But ye, brethren, are not in darkness, that that day should overtake you as a thief. [5] Ye are all the children of light, and the children of the day: we are not of the night, nor of darkness. [6] Therefore let us not sleep, as do others; but let us watch and be sober. [7] *For they that* *sleep sleep in the night; and they that be drunken are drunken in the night.*[8] *But let us, who are of the day, be sober, putting on the breastplate of **faith and love;** and for an helmet, the hope of salvation.* [9] *For God hath not appointed us to wrath, but to obtain salvation by our Lord Jesus Christ,* [10] *Who died for us, that, whether we wake or sleep, we should live together with him.* [11] *Wherefore comfort yourselves together, and edify one another, even as also ye do.*

1Timothy (KJV) 6: [10] For the love of money is the root of all evil: which while some coveted after, they have erred from the faith, and pierced themselves through with many sorrows. [11] *But thou, O man of God, flee these things; and follow after righteousness, godliness, faith, love, patience, meekness.* [12] *Fight the good fight of faith, lay hold on eternal life, whereunto thou art also called, and hast professed a good profession before many witnesses.*

Notice how the Fruit of the Spirit perform many functions once they mature.

Ephesians (KJV) 1: [10] That in the dispensation of the fulness of times he might gather together in one all things in Christ, both which are in heaven, and which are on earth; even in him: [11] In whom also we have obtained an inheritance, being predestinated according to the purpose of him who worketh all things after the counsel of his own will: [12] That we should be to the praise of his glory, who first trusted in Christ.[13] In whom ye also trusted, after that ye heard the word of truth, the gospel of your salvation: in whom also after that ye believed, ye were sealed with that holy Spirit of promise, [14] Which is the earnest of our inheritance until the redemption of the purchased possession, unto the praise of his glory. [15] Wherefore I also, after I heard of your faith in the Lord Jesus, and love unto all the saints, [16] Cease not to give thanks for you, making mention of you in my prayers; [17] *That the God of our Lord Jesus Christ, the Father of glory, may give unto you the spirit of wisdom and revelation in the knowledge of him:* [18] *The eyes of your understanding being enlightened; that ye may know what is the hope of his calling, and what the riches of the glory of his inheritance in the saints,* [19] *And what is the exceeding greatness of his power to us-ward who believe, according to the working of his mighty power,* [20] *Which he wrought in Christ, when he raised him from the dead, and set him at his own right hand in the heavenly places,* [21] *Far above all principality, and power, and might, and dominion, and every name that is named, not only in this world, but also in that which is to come:* [22] *And hath put all things under his feet, and gave him to be the head over all things to the church,* [23] *Which is his body, the fulness of him that filleth all in all.*

Ephesians (KJV) 4: I therefore, the prisoner of the Lord, beseech you that ye walk worthy of the vocation wherewith ye are called, [2] *With all lowliness and meekness, with longsuffering, forbearing one another in love;* [3] *Endeavouring to keep the unity of the Spirit in the bond of peace.*

Colossians (KJV) 1: [10] That ye might walk worthy of the Lord unto all pleasing, being fruitful in every good work, and increasing in the knowledge of God; [11] *Strengthened with all might, according to his glorious power, unto all patience and longsuffering with joyfulness;* [12] *Giving thanks unto the Father, which hath made us meet to be partakers of the inheritance of the saints in light:*

Colossians (KJV) 3: [11] Where there is neither Greek nor Jew, circumcision nor uncircumcision, Barbarian, Scythian, bond nor free: *but Christ is all, and in all.* [12] *Put on therefore, as the elect of God, holy and beloved, bowels of mercies, kindness, humbleness of mind, meekness, longsuffering;*

[13] Forbearing one another, and forgiving one another, if any man have a quarrel against any: even as Christ forgave you, so also do ye. [14] And above all these things put on charity, which is the bond of perfectness. [15] And let the peace of God rule in your hearts, to the which also ye are called in one body; and be ye thankful. [16] Let the word of Christ dwell in you richly in all wisdom; teaching and admonishing one another in psalms and hymns and spiritual songs, singing with grace in your hearts to the Lord.

Galatians (KJV) 5: [18] But if ye be led of the Spirit, ye are not under the law. [19] Now the works of the flesh are manifest, which are these; Adultery, fornication, uncleanness, lasciviousness, [20] Idolatry, witchcraft, hatred, variance, emulations, wrath, strife, seditions, heresies, [21] Envyings, murders, drunkenness, revellings, and such like: *of the which I tell you before, as I have also told you in time past, that they which do such things shall not inherit the kingdom of God.[22] But the fruit of the Spirit is love, joy, peace, longsuffering, gentleness, goodness, faith,[23] Meekness, temperance: against such there is no law.*

Romans (KJV) 5: [2] By whom also we have access by faith into this grace wherein we stand, and rejoice in hope of the glory of God. *[3] And not only so, but we glory in tribulations also: knowing that tribulation worketh patience; [4] And patience, experience; and experience, hope: [5] And hope maketh not ashamed; because the love of God is shed abroad in our hearts by the Holy Ghost which is given unto us.*

2 Thessalonians (KJV) 1: *[3] We are bound to thank God always for you, brethren, as it is meet, because that your faith groweth exceedingly, and the charity of every one of you all toward each other aboundeth; [4] So that we ourselves glory in you in the churches of God for your patience and faith in all your persecutions and tribulations that ye endure: [5] Which is a manifest token of the righteous judgment of God, that ye may be counted worthy of the kingdom of God, for which ye also suffer: [6] Seeing it is a righteous thing with God to recompense tribulation to them that trouble you; And to you who are troubled rest with us, when the Lord Jesus shall be revealed from heaven with his mighty angels, [8] In flaming fire taking vengeance on them that know not God, and that obey not the gospel of our Lord Jesus Christ: [9] Who shall be punished with everlasting destruction from the presence of the Lord, and from the glory of his power; [10] When he shall come to be glorified in his saints, and to be admired in all them that believe (because our testimony among you was believed) in that day.*

These verses say it all: do not seek money seek the Kingdom of God first.

1Timothy (KJV) 6: *[10] For the love of money is the root of all evil: which while some coveted after, they have erred from the faith, and pierced themselves through with many sorrows. [11] But thou, O man of God, flee these things; and follow after righteousness, godliness, faith, love, patience, meekness. [12] Fight the good fight of faith, lay hold on eternal life, whereunto thou art also called, and hast professed a good profession before many witnesses.*

Hebrews (KJV) 6: [11] And we desire that every one of you do shew the same diligence to the full assurance of hope unto the end: *[12] That ye be not slothful, but followers of them who through faith and patience inherit the promises. [13] For when God made promise to Abraham, because he could* *swear by no greater, he sware by himself,* [14] *Saying, Surely blessing I will bless thee, and multiplying I will multiply thee.* [15] *And so, after he had patiently endured, he obtained the promise.*

Hebrews (KJV) 12: Wherefore seeing we also are compassed about with so great a cloud of witnesses, let us lay aside every weight, and the sin which doth so easily beset us, and let us run with patience the race that is set before us, [2] *Looking unto Jesus the author and finisher of our faith; who for the joy that was set before him endured the cross, despising the shame, and is set down at the right hand of the throne of God.* [3] *For consider him that endured such contradiction of sinners against himself, lest ye be wearied and faint in your minds.* [4] *Ye have not yet resisted unto blood, striving against sin.*

James (KJV) 1: [3] *Knowing this, that the trying of your faith worketh patience.* [4] *But let patience have her perfect work, that ye may be perfect and entire, wanting nothing.* [5] *If any of you lack wisdom, let him ask of God, that giveth to all men liberally, and upbraideth not; and it shall be given him.* [6] *But let him ask in faith, nothing wavering. For he that wavereth is like a wave of the sea driven with the wind and tossed.*

James (KJV) 5: [7] *Be patient therefore, brethren, unto the coming of the Lord. Behold, the husbandman waiteth for the precious fruit of the earth, and hath long patience for it, until he receive the early and latter rain.* [8] *Be ye also patient; stablish your hearts: for the coming of the Lord draweth nigh.*

It is not a coincidence that the keys to the Kingdom of God are the same as the Fruit of the Spirit which are: love, joy, peace, longsuffering, gentleness, goodness, faith, meekness, temperance: against such there is no law. It is also not a coincidence that the definition of the Kingdom of God is righteousness, peace, and joy in the Holy Spirit; the fruit of the Spirit functions as the keys that allow entrance into the Kingdom of God. The seeds, fruit, the keys, all work together in the Kingdom of Heaven and are all created and birthed by God. This is why Jesus commanded us to seek the Kingdom first and not to go after wealth. The wealth will come once you understand who your Heavenly Father is and how His Kingdom functions and the part that God has pre-ordained for you to walk in. More on this is in the chapter "The Garden of Whatever Your Name Is."

Figure 5.10 A sculpture of Saint Peter, Author Jean-noël Lafargue Date 24 July 2006

There are many other keys but one of the biggest for me has been asking questions. I never stop asking God questions about the Bible. I don't stop until He gives me the answer that I am looking for. Then after that I ask for a deeper understanding because we are never going to stop learning, and I know that there is always more.

Luke (KJV) 11: [7] And he from within shall answer and say, Trouble me not: the door is now shut, and my children are with me in bed; I cannot rise and give thee. [8] I say unto you, Though he will not rise and give him, because he is his friend, yet because of his importunity he will rise and give him as many as he needeth. *[9] And I say unto you, Ask, and it shall be given you; seek, and ye shall find; knock, and it shall be opened unto you. [10] For every one that asketh receiveth; and he that seeketh findeth; and to him that knocketh it shall be opened.* [11] If a son shall ask bread of any of you that is a father, will he give him a stone? or if he ask a fish, will he for a fish give him a serpent? [12] Or if he shall ask an egg, will he offer him a scorpion? [13] If ye then, being evil, know how to give good gifts unto your children: **how much more shall your heavenly Father give the Holy Spirit to them that ask him?**

James (KJV) 1: [5] If any of you lack wisdom, let him ask of God, that giveth to all men liberally, and upbraideth not; and it shall be given him. [6] But let him ask in faith, nothing wavering. For he that wavereth is like a wave of the sea driven with the wind and tossed. [7] For let not that man think that he shall receive anything of the Lord

CHAPTER 6

The Garden of Whatever Your Name Is

Psalm 57 Be merciful unto me, O God, be merciful unto me: for my soul trusteth in thee: yea, in the shadow of thy wings will I make my refuge, until these calamities be overpast.

Genesis (KJV) 2: Thus the heavens and the earth were finished, and all the host of them.[2] And on the seventh day God ended his work which he had made; and he rested on the seventh day from all his work which he had made. [3] And God blessed the seventh day, and sanctified it: because that in it he had rested from all his work which God created and made. [4] These are the generations of the heavens and of the earth when they were created, in the day that the LORD God made the earth and the heavens, [5] And every plant of the field before it was in the earth, and every herb of the field before it grew: for the LORD God had not caused it to rain upon the earth, and there was not a man to till the ground. [6] But there went up a mist from the earth, and watered the whole face of the ground. [7] And the LORD God formed man of the dust of the ground, and breathed into his nostrils the breath of life; and man became a living soul.

Ruth 2:[12] The LORD recompense thy work, and a full reward be given thee of the LORD God of Israel, under whose wings thou art come to trust.

Figure 6.1 Elohim Creating Adam, by William Blake (1757–1827)

[8] And the LORD God planted a garden eastward in Eden; and there he put the man whom he had formed. [9] And out of the ground made the LORD God to grow every tree that is pleasant to the sight, and good for food; the tree of life also in the midst of the garden, and the tree of knowledge of good and evil. [10] And a river went out of Eden to water the garden; and from thence it was parted, and became into four heads. [11] The name of the first is Pison: that is it which compasseth the whole land of Havilah, where there is gold; [12] And the gold of that land is good: there is bdellium and the onyx stone. [13] And the name of the second river is Gihon: the same is it that compasseth the whole land of Ethiopia. [14] And the name of the third river is Hiddekel: that is it which goeth toward the east of Assyria. And the fourth river is Euphrates. [15] And the LORD God took the man, and put him into the Garden of Eden to dress it and to keep it. [16] And the LORD God commanded the man, saying, Of every tree of the garden thou mayest freely eat: [17] But of the tree of the knowledge of good and evil, thou shalt not eat of it:for in the day that thou eatest thereof thou shalt surely die. [18] And the LORD God said, It is not good that the man should be alone; I will make him an help meet for him. [19] And out of the ground the LORD God formed every beast of the field, and every fowl of the air; and brought them unto Adam to see what he would call them: and whatsoever Adam called every living creature, that was the name thereof.

Figure 6.2 The Creation of Adam in Paradise by Jan Brueghel (II) (1601-1678).

[20] And Adam gave names to all cattle, and to the fowl of the air, and to every beast of the field; but for Adam there was not found an help meet for him. [21] And the LORD God caused a deep sleep to fall upon Adam, and he slept: and he took one of his ribs, and closed up the flesh instead thereof; [22] And the rib, which the LORD God had taken from man, made he a woman, and brought her unto the man.

Figure 6.3 Creation of Eve; marble relief on the left pier of the façade of the cathedral by Georges Jansoone Photographer (JoJan)

[23] And Adam said, This is now bone of my bones, and flesh of my flesh: she shall be called Woman, because she was taken out of Man.

[24] Therefore shall a man leave his father and his mother, and shall cleave unto his wife: and they shall be one flesh. [25] And they were both naked, the man and his wife, and were not ashamed.

Figure 6.4 The Garden of Eden (1601) by Jacob Savery the Elder.

Figure 6.5 The Garden of Eden (c. 1860) by Erastus Salisbury Field.

Genesis (KJV) 3: Now the serpent was more subtil than any beast of the field which the LORD God had made. And he said unto the woman, Yea, hath God said, Ye shall not eat of every tree of the garden? [2] And the woman said unto the serpent, We may eat of the fruit of the trees of the garden:

Figure 6.6 The Temptation of Adam (c. 1551–1552) by Tintoretto

[3] But of the fruit of the tree which is in the midst of the garden, God hath said, Ye shall not eat of it, neither shall ye touch it, lest ye die. [4] And the serpent said unto the woman, Ye shall not surely die: [5] For God doth know that in the day ye eat thereof, then your eyes shall be opened, and ye shall be as gods, knowing good and evil. [6] And when the woman saw that the tree was good for food, and that it was pleasant to the eyes, and a tree to be desired to make one wise, she took of the fruit thereof, and did eat, and gave also unto her husband with her; and he did eat.

[7] And the eyes of them both were opened, and they knew that they were naked; and they sewed fig leaves together, and made themselves aprons.

Figure 6.7 Description: Paradise tree and Maria in the Apocalypse,

(Artist: Melchior Steidl)

[8]And they heard the voice of the LORD God walking in the garden in the cool of the day: and Adam and his wife hid themselves from the presence of the LORD God amongst the trees of the garden. [9] And the LORD God called unto Adam, and said unto him, Where art thou? [10] And he said, I heard thy voice in the garden, and I was afraid, because I was naked; and I hid myself. [11] And he said, Who told thee that thou wast naked? Hast thou eaten of the tree, whereof I commanded thee that thou shouldest not eat? [12] And the man said, The woman whom thou gavest to be with me, she gave me of the tree, and I did eat. [13] And the LORD God said unto the woman, What is this that thou hast done? And the woman said, The serpent beguiled me, and I did eat. [14] And the LORD God said unto the serpent, Because thou hast done this, thou art cursed above all cattle, and above every beast of the field; upon thy belly shalt thou go, and dust shalt thou eat all the days of thy life: [15] And I will put enmity between thee and the woman, and between thy seed and her seed; it shall bruise thy head, and thou shalt bruise his heel. [16] Unto the woman he said, I will greatly multiply thy sorrow

and thy conception; in sorrow thou shalt bring forth children; and thy desire shall be to thy husband, and he shall rule over thee. [17] And unto Adam he said, Because thou hast hearkened unto the voice of thy wife, and hast eaten of the tree, of which I commanded thee, saying, Thou shalt not eat of it: cursed is the ground for thy sake; in sorrow shalt thou eat of it all the days of thy life; [18] Thorns also and thistles shall it bring forth to thee; and thou shalt eat the herb of the field; [19] In the sweat of thy face shalt thou eat bread, till thou return unto the ground; for out of it wast thou taken: for dust thou art, and unto dust shalt thou return. [20] And Adam called his wife's name Eve; because she was the mother of all living. [21] Unto Adam also and to his wife did the LORD God make coats of skins, and clothed them.

Figure 6.8 The Expulsion of Adam and Eve from Paradise (1791) by Benjamin West.

[22] And the LORD God said, Behold, the man is become as one of us, to know good and evil: and now, lest he put forth his hand, and take also of the tree of life, and eat, and live forever:

[23] Therefore the LORD God sent him forth from the Garden of Eden, to till the ground from whence he was taken. [24] So he drove out the man; and he placed at the east of the garden of Eden Cherubims, and a flaming sword which turned every way, to keep the way of the tree of life.

Figure 6.9 Expulsion from Paradise, marble bas-relief by Lorenzo Maitani on the Orvieto Cathedral, Italy. Photographer Georges Jansoone (JoJan).

Figure 6.10 Expulsions from the Garden of Eden (1828) by Thomas Cole.

Adam and Eve missed out on the opportunity of an eternity to live on earth, which was at that time a carbon copy of Heaven. Adam's responsibility was to dress and keep the garden. They also were warned not to eat from one tree but they could eat freely from all the other trees in the garden. Fruit like all food is a source life. Eden was a type of sanctuary where everything that was needed to survive in peace and harmony was right at hand. There were no problems with violence, jealousy, or corruption of any kind before Adam failed to do his job. There was peace of mind, contentment, and serenity. Eden was Paradise.

Genesis (AMP) 2: [15] And the Lord God took the man and put him in the Garden of Eden to tend and guard and keep it.

The fruit of the Spirit is love, joy, peace, longsuffering, gentleness, goodness, faith, meekness, kindness, temperance, and righteousness: against such there is no law. We are God's garden today, according to the parable about the vineyard owner. We have been given the same responsibility to tend, develop, cultivate, and guard the fruit of the Spirit that Adam and Eve had over the Garden of Eden. Most of all, we are to keep the serpent out of our innermost being, our (garden) our spirit, soul (which consist of our mind, our will, and our emotions) and body. Each fruit of the Spirit: love, joy, peace, longsuffering, gentleness, goodness, faith, kindness, meekness, temperance, and righteousness, has an opposite twin which represents corruption, ungodliness, and sin: everything that will keep us from God's presence at His return.

1 John (KJV)1: [7] But if we walk in the light, as he is in the light, we have fellowship one with another, and the blood of Jesus Christ his Son cleanseth us from all sin.

Adam and Eve were pure, unpolluted, and untainted in their thoughts and deeds until they ate fruit from the tree of knowledge of good and evil; then they immediately died spiritually. They did not die physically until nine hundred years later, but the corruption and death separated them from God and caused them to be cast out of the garden. Their face-to-face relationship with God ended.

2 Corinthians (KJV) 6:[13] Now for a recompence in the same, (I speak as unto my children,) be ye also enlarged. [14]Be ye not unequally yoked together with unbelievers: for what fellowship hath righteousness with unrighteousness? and what communion hath light with darkness? [15] And what concord hath Christ with Belial? or what part hath he that believeth with an infidel? [16] And what agreement hath the temple of God with idols? for ye are the temple of the living God; as God hath said, I will dwell in them, and walk in them; and I will be their God, and they shall be my people. *[17] Wherefore come out from among them, and be ye separate, saith the Lord, and touch not the unclean thing; and I will receive you. [18] And will be a Father unto you, and ye shall be my sons and daughters, saith the Lord Almighty.*

Our Heavenly Father is trying to get us to separate ourselves from the latter, the sins of this worldly system that Satan has set up, because we are totally different from Adam. Adam was created out of the dust of the ground; we are born of the Holy Spirit. Adam could never pray the Lord's prayer, Adam could not say "our Father" because he was created by God and not born of God. We are the children of God, and He is expecting more out of us.

As we learned earlier, the fruit of the Spirit is a source of nutrition for our spirit man, and once they mature they also become the armor of God against attacks of Satan and also become the keys that allow us to enter the Kingdom of God. So if we walk in the Spirit and not in the flesh we can walk in the power of God. And we will not yield to the arm of the flesh. This will cause us to grow up to the measure and statue of Jesus Christ.

The Cause of Unfruitfulness

Luke (KJV) 8: [11] Now the parable is this: The seed is the word of God.

Figure 6.11 An icon depicting the Sower. Photographer: Sulfababy of en.wiki.

Mark (KJV) 4: [2] And he taught them many things by parables, and said unto them in his doctrine, [3] *Hearken; Behold, there went out a sower to sow:* [4] And it came to pass, as he sowed, some fell by the way side, and the fowls of the air came and devoured it up. [5] *And some fell on stony ground,* where it had not much earth; and immediately it sprang up, because it had no depth of earth: [6] But when the sun was up, it was scorched; and because it had no root, it withered away. [7] *And some fell among thorns, and the thorns grew up, and choked it, and it yielded no fruit.* [8] *And other fell on good ground, and did yield fruit that sprang up and increased; and brought forth, some thirty and some sixty and some an hundred.* [9] *And he said unto them, He that hath ears to hear, let him hear.*

1 Corinthians (KJV) 3: [6] I have planted, Apollos watered; but God gave the increase. [7] So then neither is he that planteth anything, neither he that watereth; but God that giveth the increase. [8] Now he that planteth and he that watereth are one: and every man shall receive his own reward according to his own labour. [9] For we are labourers together with God: ye are God's husbandry, ye are God's building. [10] According to the grace of God which is given unto me, as a wise master builder, I have laid the foundation, and another buildeth thereon. But let every man take heed how he buildeth thereupon. [11] For other foundation can no man lay than that is laid, which is Jesus Christ. [12] Now if any man build upon this foundation gold, silver, precious stones, wood, hay, stubble; *[13] Every man's work shall be made manifest: for the day shall declare it, because it shall be revealed by fire; and the fire shall try every man's work of what sort it is. [14] If any man's work abide which he hath built thereupon, he shall receive a reward. [15] If any man's work shall be burned, he shall suffer loss: but he himself shall be saved; yet so as by fire. [16] Know ye not that ye are the Temple of God, and that the Spirit of God dwelleth in you? [17] If any man defile the Temple of God, him shall God destroy; for the Temple of God is holy, which Temple ye are.* [18] Let no man deceive himself. If any man among you seemeth to be wise in this world, let him become a fool, that he may be wise. [19] For the wisdom of this world is foolishness with God. For it is written, He taketh the wise in their own craftiness. [20] And again, The Lord knoweth the thoughts of the wise, that they are vain. [21] Therefore let no man glory in men. For all things are your's; [22] Whether Paul, or Apollos, or Cephas, or the world, or life, or death, or things present, or things to come; all are your's; [23] And ye are Christ's; and Christ is God's.

Ephesians (KJV) 3: [16] That he would grant you, according to the riches of his glory, to be strengthened with might by his Spirit in the inner man; *[17] That Christ may dwell in your hearts by faith; that ye, being rooted and grounded in love,* [18] May be able to comprehend with all saints what is the breadth, and length, and depth, and height; [19] And to know the love of Christ, which passeth knowledge, that ye might be filled with all the fullness of God.

In order for any seed to grow, it must be planted in the right soil. The Bible tells us that God has given us the right soil. The love of God has been spread abroad in our heart by the Holy Spirit, and as stated above we must be rooted and grounded in love.

God placed His love in our hearts which forms the basis (or the soil) for which the seeds of joy, peace, longsuffering, gentleness, kindness, goodness, faith, meekness, temperance, and righteousness are to be planted and take root. Love empowers all the other seeds. You have to have love to be able to walk in peace when situations could turn violent. You have to know the love that God has for us and that nothing can separate us from it to be victorious in our quest to overcome. We have to allow that love of God to become *one* with us and not be conformed to the world or react the same way the world would in the same situation.

We must learn to die to our own selfish desires of choosing when and to whom we extend our false love to, and allow our love to be replaced with the *agape* love of God for all people. We have to love and be merciful to homosexuals, murderers, your siblings, people that are living together, ex-wives and husbands, the child abusers, and so forth. We have to look past the surface and see what God saw when He found us. We cannot allow hatred or any other type of corruption to reign in our hearts.

Even faith works by love. The righteousness of God is a free gift from Him out of His love for us even though we did not earn it or deserve it. He gave it to us any way. We have to maintain our righteousness because Jesus will establish His Kingdom in righteousness.

Gentleness, meekness, goodness, longsuffering, and temperance all stem, or get their roots from, the love of God. Our hearts are full of the love of God, and we make choices about when and to whom we dispense it to. God wants us to be a constant flow of His agape love through our giving and ministering to the needs of others—even to the people that we come across every day that may not have the best of favor for us.

Mark (KJV) 4: [10] And when he was alone, they that were about him with the twelve asked of him the parable. [11] And he said unto them, Unto you it is given to know the mystery of the kingdom of God: but unto them that are without, all these things are done in parables: [12] That seeing they may see, and not perceive; and hearing they may hear, and not understand; lest at any time they should be converted, and their sins should be forgiven them. *[13] And he said unto them, Know ye not this parable? and how then will ye know all parables?*

Verse 13 says, if you understand how seed time and harvest time works, then you will understand all the parables, including the parable about the ten virgins. You will also understand the mystery of the Kingdom of God and how it functions. You will also understand God's purpose for your existence in the earth because it all revolves around seed time and harvest time.

Mark (KJV) 4: [14] The sower soweth the word. [15] And these are they by the way side, where the word is sown; but when they have heard, Satan cometh immediately, and taketh away the word that was sown in their hearts. [16] And these are they likewise which are sown on stony ground; who, when they have heard the word, immediately receive it with gladness; [17] And have no root in themselves, and so endure but for a time: afterward, when affliction or persecution ariseth for the word's sake, immediately they are offended.

[One function of the love of God is the ability to forgive when you are offended, but you have to be taught that. You have to walk in love on a daily basis, and God will increase the fruit of love. And when you practice it, the love of God has the power to grow as it becomes a part of us if we let it. We cannot make people love us (Jesus proved that with His ministry) but we have the God-given responsibility to love people whether they love us or not. We cannot afford to allow the root of bitterness to corrupt our (garden) heart.

Jesus was beaten all night long and was crucified on the cross, but before He died, He asked the Father to forgive them because they did not know what they were doing. We have been given the same capacity to forgive that Jesus has, but we have to choose to forgive. With Jesus it was automatic. We have to yield our will to agree with the Word of God, just like Jesus did in the Garden of Gethsemane.

This is just one example of how the fruit of the Spirit functions and you can apply this to all the fruit (joy, peace, longsuffering, temperance, gentleness, faith, kindness, meekness, righteousness) and then apply them to your spiritual life.]

The Stony Heart

A person with a "stony heart," will not allow the "seed" of the love of God to penetrate into their heart; they have the seeds of un-forgiveness, hatred, anger, revenge, etc. reigning in their heart. Jesus said that Satan literally reaches inside that person's heart and takes out the seed, or Word of forgiveness and the love of God that was sown in their heart. That Word which starts out as a seed is never able to take root and grow and manifest itself as the fruit of love which comes from our Heavenly Father. But by the same token, the seeds of un-forgiveness, anger, hatred, etc., will develop, and be cultivated into corrupt fruit.

Luke (KJV) 6: [43] **For a good tree bringeth not forth corrupt fruit; neither doth a corrupt tree bring forth good fruit.** [44] **For every tree is known by his own fruit. For of thorns men do not gather figs, nor of a bramble bush gather they grapes.** [45] **A good man out of the good treasure of his heart bringeth forth that which is good; and an evil man out of the evil treasure of his heart bringeth forth that which is evil: for of the abundance of the heart his mouth speaketh.** [46] **And why call ye me, Lord, Lord, and do not the things which I say?**

That person, even though they are saved, has to make the decision to not be conformed to the world but be transformed into the image of Christ. And if not they will eventually become just like they were before they were saved. They are still filled with un-forgiveness, which breeds hatred. If you hate someone, the Bible says that now you are no different than a murderer.

But when your heart is filled with the Word of God (which is the Sword of the Spirit) it will quench the thoughts of un-forgiveness and allow the seeds of God's Word to be cultivated in our heart. This is how the seed of the Word of God, once it is cultivated, becomes the sword of the Spirit in the Armor of God and unlocks and allows entrances into the Kingdom of God.

Matthew (KJV) 24: [11] And many false prophets shall rise, and shall deceive many. [12] And because iniquity shall abound, the love of many shall wax cold. [13] But he that shall endure unto the end, the same shall be saved.

Ezekiel (KVJ) 11: [17] Therefore say, Thus saith the Lord GOD; I will even gather you from the people, and assemble you out of the countries where ye have been scattered, and I will give you the land of Israel. [18] And they shall come thither, and they shall take away all the detestable things thereof and all the abominations thereof from thence. *[19] And I will give them one heart, and I will put a new spirit within you; and I will take the "Stony Heart" out of their flesh, and will give them an heart of flesh: [20] That they may walk in my statutes, and keep mine ordinances, and do them: and they shall be my people, and I will be their God.*

Thorns

Mark (AMP) 4: [18] And the ones sown among the thorns are others who hear the Word; [19] Then the cares and anxieties of the world and distractions of the age, and the pleasure and delight and false glamour and deceitfulness of riches, and the craving and passionate desire for other things creep in and choke and suffocate the Word, and it becomes fruitless.

The Word of God is sown in their heart, but it cannot develop into fruit because the person spent their increase on themselves, thinking that was God's way of blessing them. They prospered for a while but they never experienced the true riches that God has stored up for them. God wants us wealthy, but He wants our priorities to be identical with His—then wealth will be added to us.

Matthew (KJV) 6: [19] Lay not up for yourselves treasures upon earth, where moth and rust doth corrupt, and where thieves break through and steal: [20] But lay up for yourselves treasures in heaven, where neither moth nor rust doth corrupt, and where thieves do not break through nor steal: [21] For where your treasure is, there will your heart be also.

God's heart is toward the poor, those that are lacking spiritually, physically, or financially and He wants our heart to be the same as His.

James (KJV) 5:[2] Your riches are corrupted, and your garments are moth eaten. [3] Your gold and silver is cankered; and the rust of them shall be a witness against you, and shall eat your flesh as it were fire. Ye have heaped treasure together for the last days.

God showed me a vision of this scripture; on the Day of Judgment when it was our turn He showed me all the clothes that I did not need were standing next to me talking like Baalam's ass, witnessing about how they were sitting in my closet becoming moth eaten. My wife and I were looking in our closets and saw that it was wasteful. We were convicted in our hearts that we had become a reservoir instead a channel God could use to allow blessing to flow to the needy. We have to remember the rich young ruler.

We are all going to have to get real with the Word of God because it is going to get real with us on the Day of Judgment. Do not let the thorns of wanting wealth just for you keep you from the true riches of God.

The book of James says that the rust of wasted wealth will witness against us. Instead of giving more with the increase that God blesses us with and being sensible with it, we should pay off debts, put some aside for emergencies, and live within or below our means so we can give more into the Kingdom of God.

When the Word is sown among thorns, the individual allows the cares of this world to choke the seed of the Word of God and prevent it from germinating and producing the fruit of the Spirit. The cares of this world could be problems, or what is going on with our economy. People worrying whether or not they are going to lose their jobs and become homeless are just some examples of how the cares of this world can enter into our heart, and choke the seed or the Word of faith and prevent it from maturing into the fruit of faith. The devil knows that if he can keep the seed, which is the same as the Word of God, from reaching maturity and developing in your heart into the Fruit of the spirit called faith or any of the other fruits, he can keep us defeated, spiritually weak, unfruitful, and in bondage to him.

Fear is the opposite of faith. It says that you have not fully developed your trust in God's ability to deliver you out of every negative situation or the attacks of Satan. Nearly every Christian faces this dilemma daily. We are all faced with situations that require our faith to carry us to our next victory. You cannot allow fear (which is a demonic force) to grip your heart, or the Word of faith, or better yet the seed of faith, and it will never become rooted and grounded in the love of God that has already been spread abroad or sown in your heart by the Holy Spirit. The book of Hebrews calls it, an "evil heart of unbelief," which should never be a part of us or in us. Fear is a feeling that comes when we think we are going to fail, and those are thoughts that Satan places in our mind which most of the time never happens anyway. Satan does this because of the Word, or seeds, that are sown in our heart, and he does not want to see it manifested into fruit because if it does he is defeated. Is it easier to cut a tree down that is 200 feet high or prevent the seed from growing in the first place?

Another source of thorns comes from individuals that are more concerned about keeping up with the world; the glamour and the fascination of it are dangerous. If you think that you can use the Gospel to pour prosperity on yourself, by just giving more and more so that one day you can buy a bigger house and a car, then you have the wrong idea about God. His desire is for everyone on this planet to prosper. Prosperity is not just to lavish on yourself, while people not even ten or fifteen minutes from your home are without warm clothes and food. This is the wisdom that Jesus was trying to get into the "stony heart" of the rich young ruler. But the "thorns" that were getting in the way of him bearing fruit was that he had great possessions and he was not willing to let any of it go and give to someone else who he did not know or probably did not even care about. He turned down eternal life for the wealth and riches of the world, which made the Word of God unfruitful and barren in his heart. He turned it down and missed the true riches that God wanted him to have so that the purpose of the Kingdom of God could be established in the earth. God's will is for the quality of life on earth to be equal to that of Heaven.

Thorns have a double meaning. Thorns represent something that does not want to be touched and is self-sustaining like a weed. Thorns do not provide nutritional substance like fruit. They are like weeds which suck the life out of and away from flowers around them. They are like parasites or leeches which suck the life out of their hosts just to maintain themselves, and they are not concerned with the needs of others. They are Christians that never mature spiritually and never see or experience the thirty, sixty, or one hundred-fold return. Again, they are like the rich young ruler who did not want to give anything to the poor. He got lost in the transition, but he could have gotten back on the right path with just a little correction if he had just listened to Jesus. This is also the reason why Jesus will not allow any of us to remain connected to the "true vine," sucking the spiritual life out of Him.

Luke (KJV) 16:[10] He that is faithful in that which is least is faithful also in much: and he that is unjust in the least is unjust also in much. [11] If therefore ye have not been faithful in the unrighteous mammon, who will commit to your trust the true riches? [12] And if ye have not been faithful in that which is another man's, who shall give you that which is your own? [13] No servant can serve two masters: for either he will hate the one, and love the other; or else he will hold to the one, and despise the other. Ye cannot serve God and mammon.

Many Christians understand the importance of giving their tithes and offering and the importance of inheriting eternal life. There are many churches that have caught on to reaching out to the needy. They are fulfilling the quest to inherit eternal life which is awesome, and they are bringing glory to God by bearing fruit.

God wants to give us the *true riches*. He wants to make us richer than the lilies of the fields, which Jesus said were richer than Solomon. But God will only allow that kind of wealth to come into the hands of His children who understand how the Kingdom works: only His children that have become *one* with Him, the ones that know how God thinks and knows what He wants done with the money and have proven to God that they can be trusted with the true riches that God desires to give us—and that are committed to doing it God's way. The children who will say, like Jesus said, "I will only do what I see my Father doing. I will only give where He says to give," and follow after the ministry that Jesus laid the foundation for. God wants to bless His children that have matured and grown up to the statue of Jesus. That is why Jesus said seek the Kingdom first!

God already knows what each one of us will do with "real wealth" if He puts it in our hands right this very second. He has seen our past! If you will be honest with yourself, you know what you would do with it because you already have a checklist in the back of your mind (pay tithes and offerings, new house, car, etc.). The question is, do you understand the parable of the sower; do you have a stony heart, or is your garden full of thorns? Have you converted the soil in your garden (heart or spirit man) to the love of God and have broken through that stony heart?)

Jesus said the "deceitfulness of riches" will choke the Word that God has sown in your heart and make it unfruitful. Then you have become like the barren fig tree, unfruitful. Like the rich young ruler who was obedient to the commandments; you know he paid tithes and offerings because he was Jewish, and Jesus said that He loved the rich young ruler for his obedience. But Jesus said if he wanted to inherit eternal life, he had to sell what he had and give to the poor and follow Him.

If we want to obtain eternal life, we must take up the other end of the cross of Jesus and continue "His work," giving into the lives of others starting with salvation and whatever else that maybe lacking in their life.

Mark (KJV) 10: [29] And Jesus answered and said, Verily I say unto you, There is no man that hath left house, or brethren, or sisters, or father, or mother, or wife, or children, or lands, for my sake, and the gospel's, [30] But he shall receive an hundredfold now in this time, houses, and brethren, and sisters, But and mothers, and children, and lands, with persecutions; and in the world to come eternal life. [31] many that are first shall be last; and the last first.

Point of interest: did you know that you could buy a home for about $2,000 to $4,000 for a family of five or six in third-World nations? For someone who has been living in a grass hut all their life that would be a mansion. This is an example of raising the quality life for that person who, all their life, only knew a dirt floor and a mud hut..

In the book of Acts, the church caught on to what the Kingdom of God was all about. Giving to the poor started with the members of the church. They took care of the widows, the sick, and orphans. They fed the poor and clothed the naked. They understood the importance of inheriting eternal life. They were in the process of raising the quality of life to be equal among all the members as they went from house to house, preaching and teaching the Gospel of the Kingdom. They sold land and other processions and gave the money to the church, where it was redistributed to those who needed it most. Jesus said that those who gave out of obedience for His sake and the Gospel of the Kingdom received 100-fold now and eternal life in the world to come, along with **persecution**.

Acts (KJV) 4: [33] and with great power gave the apostles witness of the resurrection of the Lord Jesus: and great grace was upon them all. [34] Neither was there any among them that lacked: for as many as were possessors of lands or houses sold them, and brought the prices of the things that were sold, [35] And laid them down at the apostles' feet: and distribution was made unto every man according as he had need. [6] And Joses, who by the apostles was surnamed Barnabas, (which is, being interpreted, The son of consolation,) a Levite, and of the country of Cyprus, [37] Having land, sold it, and brought the money, and laid it at the apostles' feet.

Jesus dying on the "cross" represents the ultimate in giving in the Kingdom of God. When a person sacrifices their life so someone else can live, then that person makes a difference in the world by doing the same for the next person's life. If the rich young ruler had obeyed Jesus by selling what he had and giving to the poor, he would have received as much as 100-fold return in his lifetime and eternal life at the end. Whatever you sow will be multiplied back to you. If you are not sowing anything, don't expect anything back from God. This is one way the Kingdom of God works.

Receive the new heart that our Heavenly Father has promised in:

Ezekiel (KJV) 11: [18] And they shall come thither, and they shall take away all the detestable things thereof and all the abominations thereof from thence. *[19] And I will give them one heart, and I will put a new spirit within you; and I will take the stony heart out of their flesh, and will give them an heart of flesh: [20] That they may walk in my statutes, and keep mine ordinances, and do them: and they shall be my people, and I will be their God.*

Ezekiel (KJV) 36: [24] For I will take you from among the heathen, and gather you out of all countries, and will bring you into your own land. [25] Then will I sprinkle clean water upon you, and ye shall be clean: from all your filthiness, and from all your idols, will I cleanse you. *[26] A new heart also will I give you, and a new spirit will I put within you: and I will take away the "Stony Heart" out of your flesh, and I will give you an heart of flesh. [27] And I will put my spirit within you, and cause you to walk in my statutes, and ye shall keep my judgments, and do them.*

Genesis 8: [22] While the earth remaineth, seedtime and harvest, and cold and heat, and summer and winter, and day and night shall not cease.

The Process from Seed to Fruit

Figure 6.12 Image of the Sower Parable (1874) by Alexander Bida.

Mark (AMP) 4: [20] And these are they which are sown on good ground; such as hear the word, and receive it, and bring forth fruit, some thirtyfold, some sixty, and some an hundred. [21] And he said unto them, Is a candle brought to be put under a bushel, or under a bed?

Figure 6.13 Picture of the lamp on a stand and the parable of the growing seed (1695), by Johan Christoph Weigel.

and not to be set on a candlestick? [22] For there is nothing hid, which shall not be manifested; neither was anything kept secret, but that it should come abroad. [23] If any man have ears to hear, let him hear. [24] And he said unto them, Take heed what ye hear: with what measure ye mete, it shall be measured to you: and unto you that hear shall more be given. [25] For he that hath, to him shall be given: and he that hath not, from him shall be taken even that which he hath. [26] And he said, So is the kingdom of God, as if a man should cast seed into the ground; [27] And should sleep, and rise night and day, and the seed should spring and grow up, he knoweth not how. [28] For the earth bringeth forth fruit of herself; first the blade, then the ear, after that the full corn in the ear. [29] But when the fruit is brought forth, immediately he putteth in the sickle, because the harvest is come.

Ephesians (KJV) 3: [16] That he would grant you, according to the riches of his glory, to be strengthened with might by his Spirit in the inner man; [17] That Christ may dwell in your hearts by faith; that ye, being rooted and grounded in love, [18] May be able to comprehend with all saints what is the breadth, and length, and depth, and height; [19] And to know the love of Christ, which passeth knowledge, that ye might be filled with all the fulness of God.

[God's desire is that the seeds of the fruit of the Spirit will germinate and bear fruit inside of our hearts, because we are born of God and He is expecting us to do the same works that Jesus did. We have His DNA; the fruit of God's Spirit are His characteristics, or what makes Him God. This is what Satan is afraid of happening: the manifestation of the sons of God to come forth. As verse 19 says, God's desire is for us to be filled with the fullness of all that God is.

The desire of Satan is to take the seed of the Word of God out of our hearts and to keep it from maturing into fruit. Each time we do not allow the Word of God to take root in our hearts by being obedient to it, it will keep us barren and unfruitful. Satan knows we will never mature and that we will become like the barren fig tree which is a symbol of the foolish virgins that were left, because they never understood the basic principles of seed time and harvest time! Satan knows how the Kingdom of God works, and he knows what it will take to make you fail! Satan's main concern is to deceive us, and keep us ignorant of who we are in Christ Jesus. But as long as we are ignorant we are no threat to Satan or his kingdom. Next to the Father, Son, and the Holy Spirit, we are the most frightening beings on the planet to Satan, when we learn how to walk in the power of God. Satan is absolutely terrified that we will not only seek the Kingdom of God, but that we will comprehend and discern how the Kingdom of God works. He knows that day is coming when we will learn how the Kingdom of God operates. We must learn from the Garden of Eden. God already knows Satan's end. He has already declared and decreed Satan's destruction will come by the Blood of the Lamb and the Word of our testimony. The Body of Christ is waking up and taking their places as sons of God!]

Psalm (KJV) 127: Except the LORD build the house, they labour in vain that build it: except the LORD keep the city, the watchman waketh but in vain.

At least half of all Christians will fail because they did not realize they were God's garden, in which they failed to cultivate the seed of the Word of God into the fruit of the Spirit. I am praying that none of us will be lost or left behind. **God's desire is that all come to the knowledge of the truth!**

We have to fight daily.

2 Corinthians 10: [3] For though we walk in the flesh, we do not war after the flesh: [4] (For the weapons of our warfare are not carnal, but mighty through God to the pulling down of strong holds;)[5]Casting down imaginations, and every high thing that exalteth itself against the knowledge of God, and bringing into captivity every thought to the obedience of Christ; [6] And having in a readiness to revenge all disobedience, when your obedience is fulfilled.

We have to spend time in the Word and spend time in His presence and we have to decide what to do with our free time and then make time for God. You cannot sow mingled seed; you cannot sow a lot of corruption from television and the Internet, and maybe even wrong associations, and so on and expect to be transformed and grow in the grace of God. Not all television and Internet is bad or wrong. Each one of us knows what is right and what we should and should not be looking at and doing because we already have an inward witness from the Holy Spirit. So just do what you know is right before God. Your mind is the biggest battleground that Satan uses to keep you frustrated, upset, in doubt and unbelief, worried, fearful, oppressed, depressed, and defeated. Eventually we will begin to murmur and complain, which are all attacks on our spirit man to keep us in bondage, and to draw the Word and the spiritual life of God out of us.

Psalm 91

He that dwelleth in the secret place of the most High shall abide under the shadow of the Almighty. ²I will say of the LORD, He is my refuge and my fortress: my God; in him will I trust.³ Surely he shall deliver thee from the snare of the fowler, and from the noisome pestilence. ⁴He shall cover thee with his feathers, and under his wings shalt thou trust: his truth shall be thy shield and buckler.⁵Thou shalt not be afraid for the terror by night; nor for the arrow that flieth by day; ⁶ Nor for the pestilence that walketh in darkness; nor for the destruction that wasteth at noonday. ⁷A thousand shall fall at thy side, and ten thousand at thy right hand; but it shall not come nigh thee. ⁸ Only with thine eyes shalt thou behold and see the reward of the wicked. ⁹Because thou hast made the Lord, which is my refuge, even the most High, thy habitation; ¹⁰There shall no evil befall thee, neither shall any plague come nigh thy dwelling. ¹¹For he shall give his angels charge over thee, to keep thee in all thy ways. ¹²They shall bear thee up in their hands, lest thou dash thy foot against a stone. ¹³Thou shalt tread upon the lion and adder: the young lion and the dragon shalt thou trample under feet. ¹⁴Because he hath set his love upon me, therefore will I deliver him: I will set him on high, because he hath known my name. ¹⁵He shall call upon me, and I will answer him: I will be with him in trouble; I will deliver him, and honour him. ¹⁶With long life will I satisfy him, and shew him my salvation.

Put on the Whole Armor of God

1 Peter (KJV) 1: *¹²Unto whom it was revealed, that not unto themselves, but unto us they did minister the things, which are now reported unto you by them that have preached the gospel unto you with the Holy Ghost sent down from heaven; which things the angels desire to look into. ¹³ Wherefore gird up the loins of your mind, be sober, and hope to the end for the grace that is to be brought unto you at the revelation of Jesus Christ; ¹⁴ as obedient children, not fashioning yourselves according to the former lusts in your ignorance:*

The Garden of Eden was also the first sanctuary where God could meet and commune with the man and woman that He created. We are the temple of the Holy Spirit, which makes us the new sanctuary where God has come to make His abode within us. A garden has been planted within our soul and spirit by the Holy Spirit. Our soul consists of our mind, our will and our emotions. God has sown the seeds of His attributes (or His DNA), and His characteristics within us. We are responsible for developing and cultivating them. God has given us His Word to fill our mind and heart with His wisdom if we ask. He wants us to yield our will to be submitted to His will. He wants our emotions to be the by-products of the fruit of the Spirit, or the characteristics of God: love, joy, peace, etc.

In the parable of the barren fig tree, the gardener was given time to cultivate the tree by water and fertilize it to try and get it to bear fruit. The seed of the Word of God, as everything else in the Kingdom, has many functions.

1 Peter (KVJ) 2: ²As newborn babes, desire the sincere milk of the word, that ye may grow thereby:

Hebrews (KJV) 5: [12] For when for the time ye ought to be teachers, ye have need that one teach you again which be the first principles of the oracles of God; and are become such as have need of milk, and not of strong meat. [13] For every one that useth milk is unskilful in the word of righteousness: for he is a babe. [14] But strong meat belongeth to them that are of full age, even those who by reason of use have their senses exercised to discern both good and evil.

John (KJV) 16: [13] Howbeit when he, the Spirit of truth, is come, he will guide you into all truth: for he shall not speak of himself; but whatsoever he shall hear, that shall he speak: and he will shew you things to come.

God has given us the Holy Spirit to be our teacher and guide to lead us into all the truth about the Bible. You should take time to read and meditate the Bible daily, but you have to decide the direction that you are going to take. God wants only those that want Him, are you willing to be obedient and bear fruit and fulfill your destiny?

Hebrews (KJV) 12: [2] Looking unto Jesus the author and finisher of our faith; who for the joy that was set before him endured the cross, despising the shame, and is set down at the right hand of the throne of God

Jesus said if you are bearing fruit, He wants you to bear more fruit. That means He wants your love, joy, peace, longsuffering, gentleness, kindness, meekness, faith, and righteousness to increase more and more. Jesus said if we are producing fruit, we will be treated like a fruit tree in the natural because we are one in the spiritual realm. In the natural realm if you do not prune a fruit tree eventually that tree will dry up and die. The same thing will happen to us if we are not challenged to love more, to build a deeper walk of faith, to have a closer walk with God, to be kinder, to have more patience, to be more longsuffering, and so forth. This is why Jesus said He is the True Vine and we are the branches, and we must bear more fruit or we will be cut off from Him. All the spiritual life-giving resources flow out of Him and into and through us because we are the branches. Because of our connection with Jesus, we are to mimic Him by walking in His attributes (or by walking in the Spirit) by fulfilling His prayer request for us to be *one* with Him, the Father, and the Holy Spirit. That is why if you are born of God, you should get great joy from giving to someone else that is in need of the love that is flowing out of the True Vine and through us and into them.

Figure 6.14 Christ the True Vine and We are the Branches.
Author: Anonymous, Date: before 20 c

Mark 4:[30] And he said, Whereunto shall we liken the kingdom of God? or with what comparison shall we compare it? [31] It is like a grain of mustard seed, which, when it is sown in the earth, is less than all the seeds that be in the earth: [32] But when it is sown, it groweth up, and becometh greater than all herbs, and shooteth out great branches; so that the fowls of the air may lodge under the shadow of it.

[Like the mustard seed when it matures not only is it a very useful herb, it provides a source of habitation for many other animals. The Kingdom is the same way; God wants to bless us so much that we can become a source of supply and be able to give into every good and perfect work.

In order to get more fruit you have to prune the branches back on a fruit tree. When the tree is rejuvenated, the main trunk of the tree sends more life-giving resources to the pruned branches and more branches will sprout and more fruit will be produced.

You will experience challenging situations with your health, with your children, your finances, and so on. Jesus told Peter that Satan wanted to sift him like a brand-new bag of flour. Or in other words, Satan was going to do everything he could to destroy Peter's faith, love, joy, peace, and his ministry. This is all representative of your being pruned. God wants your faith, love, joy, and all the other fruit to grow stronger. Jesus wants us to bring defeat to the kingdom of darkness with the armor of God. Jesus told Peter that He was praying that Peter's faith would not fail him, and Jesus is saying the same thing to us. He is praying that our faith will not fail us, either. Jesus is the author and finisher of our faith but we have to do our part. With each new challenge our faith should grow stronger, and stronger. Faith comes by hearing and hearing by the Word of God over and over again. The just shall live by his faith!]

Ephesians 3: [19] *And to know the love of Christ, which passeth knowledge, that ye might be filled with all the fulness of God.* [20] *Now unto him that is able to do exceeding abundantly above all that we ask or think, according to the power that worketh in us,* [21] Unto him be glory in the church by Christ Jesus throughout all ages, world without end. Amen.

Proverbs (KJV) 4: [5] Get wisdom, get understanding: forget it not; neither decline from the words of my mouth. [6] Forsake her not, and she shall preserve thee: love her, and she shall keep thee. [7] Wisdom is the principal thing; therefore get wisdom: and with all thy getting get understanding. [8] Exalt her, and she shall promote thee: she shall bring thee to honour, when thou dost embrace her. [9] She shall give to thine head an ornament of grace: a crown of glory shall she deliver to thee. [10] Hear, O my son, and receive my sayings; and the years of thy life shall be many. [11] I have taught thee in the way of wisdom; I have led thee in right paths. [2] When thou goest, thy steps shall not be straitened; and when thou runnest, thou shalt not stumble. [13] Take fast hold of instruction; let her not go: keep her; for she is thy life. [14] Enter not into the path of the wicked, and go not in the way of evil men. [15] Avoid it, pass not by it, turn from it, and pass away. [16] For they sleep not, except they have done mischief; and their sleep is taken away, unless they cause some to fall. [17] For they eat the bread of wickedness, and drink the wine of violence. [18] *But the path of the just is as the shining light, that shineth more and more unto the perfect day.* [19] The way of the wicked is as darkness: they know not at what they stumble. [20] My son, attend to my words; incline thine ear unto my sayings. [21] Let them not depart from thine eyes; keep them in the midst of thine heart. [22] For they are life unto those who find them, and health to all their flesh. [23] Keep thy heart with all diligence; for out of it are the issues of life. [24] Put away from thee a froward mouth, and perverse lips put far from thee.

[The calmest place on earth should be your innermost being, inside your own mind and heart. Even in the midst of all kinds of turmoil going on around you, the peace of God should fill your heart, knowing that you are in the Kingdom of God and you understand its basic principles and you put them to work in your life. You have to establish your heart in knowing that the Kingdom of God is about you keeping your mind stayed on Jesus and He will keep you in perfect peace because you know everything is going to turn out in your favor. When the seed of joy takes root in the love of God, the fruit of joy will spring forth as the joy of the Lord which is your strength even at our weakest points. Just being in His (Jesus') presence is fullness of joy.

If we let patience have its perfect work, we will be perfect and entire not lacking or missing anything, whether it is healing, or other needs being met in our lives. Everything that you will ever need to be victorious is already inside of you, because the Kingdom is within you. We have to draw on our faith in God; it is one of our weapons. We have to know that God not only loves us, but He has given us His love, which empowers our faith that happens to come from Him.

God made our body the temple of the Holy Spirit; our body is now the sanctuary where His desire is to be *one* with us so that in the midst of trouble we can come boldly to the throne of grace to find help in a time of need as we are ministering to the homeless, to people who are sick and believing God for their healing. We can come to the throne of grace, and we do not have to get upset or be frustrated with negative situations and bad reports. The seed of the fruit of love will never fail if we will cultivate that seed along with the other seeds of the fruit of the Spirit.

We have it better than Adam and Eve could ever imagine. God built the Garden of Eden, and placed Adam and Eve in it. Then God would commune with the man and woman that He created out of the dust of the ground. The Garden was a sanctuary that was filled with everything that was needed for their spiritual growth. They had the fruit trees which God said was good for food and they had His presence to teach and guide them daily. If they had a concern especially about whether or not they should eat from the forbidden tree they could have waited until the "cool of the day" to get clarification on the matter. Jesus prayed that we would be *one* with the Trinity. Adam and Eve did not have that option, but they still could have waited to confer with God before they did anything rash.]

2 Corinthians (KJV) 3: [12] Seeing then that we have such hope, we use great plainness of speech: [13] And not as Moses, which put a veil over his face, that the children of Israel could not stedfastly look to the end of that which is abolished: [14] But their minds were blinded: for until this day remaineth the same vail untaken away in the reading of the old testament; which vail is done away in Christ. [15] But even unto this day, when Moses is read, the vail is upon their heart. [16] Nevertheless when it shall turn to the Lord, the vail shall be taken away. [17] Now the Lord is that Spirit: and where the Spirit of the Lord is, there is liberty. [18] But we all, with open face beholding as in a glass the glory of the Lord, are changed into the same image from glory to glory, even as by the Spirit of the Lord.

If we allow God free course in our lives, (which is why He moved inside of us) He will help us to be transformed into the image of Christ. But we have to have a hearing heart and be willing to change and obey the leading of the Holy Spirit. His desire for us is to glorify God, and we can glorify God in the earth the same way Jesus did when we work with God to fulfill His purpose for our destiny.

John 17: [3] *And this is life eternal*, that they might know thee the only true God, and Jesus Christ, whom thou hast sent. [4] *I have glorified thee on the earth: I have finished the work which thou gavest me to do.* [5] And now, O Father, glorify thou me with thine own self with the glory which I had with thee before the world was.

[A garden is a place of rest and rejuvenation, and we have a well of living water springing up into everlasting life. That well of water is the Word of God which should be flowing constantly within us. Water is necessary for the growth of all gardens. We are God's garden. My sister used to sing an old song that I think God really wrote for our generation; it's called "Mary, Mary Quite Contrary How Does Your Garden Grow?"]

What does your garden look like; which side of the picture represents your garden?

Figure 6.15 The Garden of Eden (1828) by Thomas Cole.

We are God's Garden

Genesis (KJV) 1: [8] And God called the firmament Heaven. And the evening and the morning were the second day. [9] And God said, Let the waters under the heaven be gathered together unto one place, and let the dry land appear: and it was so. [10] And God called the dry land Earth; and the gathering together of the waters called he Seas: and God saw that it was good. [11] And God said, Let the earth bring forth grass, the herb yielding seed, and the fruit tree yielding fruit after his kind, whose seed is in itself, upon the earth: and it was so. [12] And the earth brought forth grass, and herb yielding seed after his kind, and the tree yielding fruit, whose seed was in itself, after his kind: and God saw that it was good.

The Kingdom, The Keys, The Seed, The Fruit, The Garden and You, A Quick Review

The Kingdom of Heaven revolves around seed time and harvest time; it started in Genesis. Everything living that was created has the ability to reproduce itself, and it comes in the form of a seed. Within every seed lies its purpose that was placed there by God. The full and complete purpose for each seed will not be revealed until it reaches maturity. In case of a single kernel of corn, the fruit from it will not be revealed until the seed germinates and grows to maturity.

In the natural realm first the seed must die, then it is buried in the ground; next it needs water and energy from the sun to continue toward maturity. The next step after the seed is planted then is the blade, then the ear, after that the full corn in the ear. When the full ear comes forth then the fruit is ready to be harvested to be used for its main purpose or purposes. And that is to fulfill a need, in most cases to satisfy someone's hunger. Actually corn has many uses from food to an alternative fuel source. This is how God looks at us. He has preordained many functions and purposes for each of us.

It will really be sad if we do not fulfill God's purpose for our life. He has done everything possible to give us free access to the Father, the Son, and the Holy Spirit. But God's will is going to be done in those who are willing to mature and grow in grace and seek God with their whole heart and to please Him by reaching their destiny.

First of all it is not a coincidence that the definition of the Kingdom of God uses three of the fruit of the Spirit (joy, peace, and righteousness) to describe what the Kingdom of God is all about. The Kingdom of God revolves around the Body of Christ bearing fruit or fulfilling their divine purpose. Their divine purpose is already in the heart and mind of our Heavenly Father and was preordained before the foundation of the earth was laid. As we reach spiritual maturity He will reveal our purpose if we will be faithful enough to follow the simple instructions, starting with learning how to inherit or (obtain) eternal life and seeking first the Kingdom of God. As we prove to God that we are faithful to take hold of the responsibilities that He places before us now, with ministering eternal life to the people around us, God will reveal more and more of our divine purpose. The parable of the ten talents explains in detail how God judges and rewards faithfulness with more responsibility.

Seeking the Kingdom of God starts with us understanding how the fruit of righteousness, peace, and joy in the Holy Spirit functions. Which is all about the Body of Christ becoming *one* with the Father, the Son, and the Holy Spirit. This was done so that His power can flow through us and so He can live and move and have His being inside of us.

2 Corinthians (KJV) 5: [21] For he hath made him to be sin for us, who knew no sin; that we might be made the righteousness of God in him.

We have been made the righteousness of God in Christ Jesus. This means we have been set free from sin and guilt, and we are in right standing with God. When we commit sin, we lose our right standing status, and we separate ourselves from God. When we separate ourselves from God by committing unrighteous acts, we are no longer in the Kingdom of God. But God is faithful and just to forgive us of our sins when we ask. So when we ask God to forgive us and we repent, we are restored back into the Kingdom of God. God has made us priests and our bodies the temple which He has chosen to dwell in.

1 Corinthians (KJV) 6: [9] Know ye not that the unrighteous shall not inherit the kingdom of God? Be not deceived: neither fornicators, nor idolaters, nor adulterers, nor effeminate, nor abusers of themselves with mankind, [10] Nor thieves, nor covetous, nor drunkards, nor revilers, nor extortioners, shall inherit the kingdom of God. [11] And such were some of you: but ye are washed, but ye are sanctified, but ye are justified in the name of the Lord Jesus, and by the Spirit of our God

2 Corinthians (KJV) 9: [10] Now he that ministereth seed to the sower both minister bread for your food, and multiply your seed sown, and increase the fruits of your righteousness;

James (KJV) 3: [18] And the fruit of righteousness is sown in peace of them that make peace.

When we are seeking the Kingdom of God, the seed of the fruit of peace is the next step. The only way to have peace is to keep our mind stayed on Jesus. So when problems cause you to step outside of the comfort zone of being at peace in any situation, then you know that you just stepped outside of the Kingdom. You should know that Jesus will never leave you nor forsake you even unto the end of the world. There is no problem too big that the Kingdom of God cannot handle. But when you step over into worrying again then you have stepped out of the Kingdom of God and over into the kingdom of darkness. That is how the spirit of depression and oppression consumes our thinking. The fruit of peace becomes another key to the Kingdom of God, and without peace reigning in your heart you will become locked out of the Kingdom of God—and out of the Kingdom is where Satan wants to keep you. When the seed of the fruit of peace matures we no longer fall prey to worry, oppression, depression and failure.

1 John 5: [18] We know that whosoever is born of God sinneth not; but he that is begotten of God keepeth himself, and that wicked one toucheth him not.

Matthew (KJV) 5: [9] Blessed are the peacemakers: for they shall be called the children of God.

Hebrews (KJV) 12: [11] Now no chastening for the present seemeth to be joyous, but grievous: nevertheless afterward it yieldeth the peaceable fruit of righteousness unto them which are exercised thereby.

Romans (KLV) 5: [20] Moreover the law entered, that the offence might abound. But where sin abounded, grace did much more abound: [21] That as sin hath reigned unto death, even so might grace reign through righteousness unto eternal life by Jesus Christ our Lord.

The Kingdom of God is joy in the Holy Spirit; when the seed of joy matures it becomes the joy of the Lord, which is our strength. True joy can only be found in the presence of God.

John (KJV) 6: [52] The Jews therefore strove among themselves, saying, How can this man give us his flesh to eat? [53] Then Jesus said unto them, Verily, verily, I say unto you, Except ye eat the flesh of the Son of man, and drink his blood, ye have no life in you. [54] *Whoso eateth my flesh, and drinketh my blood, hath eternal life; and I will raise him up at the last day.*

1 Peter (KJV) 1: [14] As obedient children, not fashioning yourselves according to the former lusts in your ignorance: [15] But as he which hath called you is holy, so be ye holy in all manner of conversation; [16] Because it is written, Be ye holy; for I am holy. [17] And if ye call on the Father, who without respect of persons judgeth according to every man's work, pass the time of your sojourning here in fear: [18] Forasmuch as ye know that ye were not redeemed with corruptible things, as silver and gold, from your vain conversation received by tradition from your fathers; [19] But with the precious blood of Christ, as of a lamb without blemish and without spot: [20] Who verily was foreordained before the foundation of the world, but was manifest in these last times for you.

It is going to be the same way at the second coming of Jesus, only when He comes back all Christians that are found in sin will be left behind. This is what will happen to the foolish virgins because they never understood or knew what God was expecting from them at the time of the rapture. Now we are the temple of God, so when we ask Jesus to come into our heart, He was already *one* with God the Father and God the Holy Spirit, and Jesus prayed that we would become *one* with the Trinity, also. The foolish virgins did not understand why God made them priests nor did they walk in holiness. The only reason they did not understand is because they had not been taught nor did they seek God who gives wisdom.

These are the "Last Days" and God loves all people. Just as God sent angels to deliver Lot's family and He warned Noah and his family, God is warning us ahead of time.

Daniel (KJV) 12: [3] And they that be wise shall shine as the brightness of the firmament; and they that turn many to righteousness as the stars for ever and ever. [4] But thou, O Daniel, shut up the words, and seal the book, even to the time of the end: many shall run to and fro, and knowledge shall be increased.

Hebrews (KJV) 10: [19] Having therefore, brethren, boldness to enter into the holiest by the blood of Jesus, [20] By a new and living way, which he hath consecrated for us, through the veil, that is to say, his flesh; [21] And having an high priest over the house of God; [22] Let us draw near with a true heart in full assurance of faith, having our hearts sprinkled from an evil conscience, and our bodies washed with pure water. [23] Let us hold fast the profession of our faith without wavering; (for he is faithful that promised;)

1 Corinthians (KJV) 15: [23] But every man in his own order: Christ the first fruits; afterward they that are Christ's at his coming. [24] Then cometh the end, when he shall have delivered up the kingdom to God, even the Father; when he shall have put down all rule and all authority and power. [25] For he must reign, till he hath put all enemies under his feet.

[When the fruit of the Spirit are developed within the Body of Christ, they become providers for the physical and spiritual needs of the lost and unsaved. Bearing fruit also means being a source of food for the hungry and clothing for the naked; it means ministering to the needs of those who are in prison, and it is also a source of the prayer of faith for the sick and to bring destruction to the kingdom of darkness. The Body of Christ is responsible for laying the foundation for the will of God being done on earth as it is in Heaven. That is why Jesus asked us to pray the Lord's Prayer because it will cause the Kingdom to come and God's will to be done on Earth as it is in Heaven. (The Lord's Prayer is one of the most important prayers that can be found in the Bible because it covers all the bases—because it is the Lord's Prayer and every prayer that Jesus prayed God answered!)

Before fruit can come forth, the seeds that are sown in our hearts have to go through the process of germination before the manifestation of the fruit of the Spirit (love, joy, peace, longsuffering, and so on) can come forth. Every seed has a multitude of functions that it can perform once the fruit reaches maturity.

The Seed, the Fruit, and the Armor: Its Many Functions and You

Figure 6.16 Lucifer by Mihály Zichy

Revelation (KJV) 12: And there appeared a great wonder in heaven; a woman clothed with the sun, and the moon under her feet, and upon her head a crown of twelve stars:[2] And she being with child cried, travailing in birth, and pained to be delivered. [3] And there appeared another wonder in heaven; and behold a great red dragon, having seven heads and ten horns, and seven crowns upon his heads. [4] And his tail drew the third part of the stars of heaven, and did cast them to the earth: and the dragon stood before the woman which was ready to be delivered, for to devour her child as soon as it was born.

Figure 6.17 Woman of Apocalypse by Peter Paul Rubens (1577–1640)

[5] And she brought forth a man child, who was to rule all nations with a rod of iron: and her child was caught up unto God, and to his throne. [6] And the woman fled into the wilderness, where she hath a place prepared of God, that they should feed her there a thousand two hundred and three-score days.

[7] And there was war in heaven: Michael and his angels fought against the dragon; and the dragon fought and his angels, [8] And prevailed not; neither was their place found any more in heaven.

Notice the shield of faith in the left hand of God.

Figure 6.18 The Fall of Lucifer (early seventeenth century) by Peter Paul Rubens

[9]And the great dragon was cast out,

Figure 6.19 The fall of the rebel angels (after 1680) by Charles Le Brun.

that old serpent called the Devil, and Satan, which deceiveth the whole world: he was cast out into the earth, and his angels were cast out with him.

Figure 6.20 Fall of the Rebel Angels by Sebastiano Ricci (1659-1734).

Revelation (KJV) 12:10 And I heard a loud voice saying in heaven, Now is come salvation, and strength, and the kingdom of our God, and the power of his Christ: for the accuser of our brethren is cast down, which accused them before our God day and night.*¹¹ And they overcame him by the blood of the Lamb, and by the word of their testimony; and they loved not their lives unto the death.*
¹² Therefore rejoice, ye heavens, and ye that dwell in them. Woe to the inhabiters of the earth and of the sea! for the devil is come down unto you, having great wrath, because he knoweth that he hath but a short time.

[We are all here for a short time. We have to grow up in Christ, and our part in the Kingdom of God is vital because we were placed here for a specific purpose. Our Heavenly Father knows the end from the beginning, and most importantly He knows our end individually and He has given us the victory, but we have to line our life up with His Word. The Word of God is called a plum-line that a master builder uses to build a house, and we are God's house.

Jesus was thirty-three years old when He was crucified. His ministry only lasted three and half years, but He was born of the seed of God and he had to mature before He could walk in the power of His Father. It took time for Him to mature. Jesus spent time with the Holy Spirit who lead and guided him into the truth that He was Mary's son but His Father was the creator of the universe. And His purpose was to undo what Adam did which caused all people to be destined to spend an eternity in hell. Jesus came so we might inherit eternal life and the Kingdom of Heaven. I would hate to spend a lifetime in church and then spend an eternity suffering in hell with the individual that I have been trying to avoid. Especially when God already has our future planned out that was pre-ordained for us before the first particle of dust was collected to form the foundation of the earth. We have to be a giver of life to inherit eternal life.]

Revelation (KJV) 12: [13] And when the dragon saw that he was cast unto the earth, he persecuted the woman which brought forth the man child.

**Figure 6.21 The Great Red Dragon and the Woman Clothed with the Sun
(1805-1810) by William Blake.**

Revelation (KJV) 12:14 And to the woman were given two wings of a great eagle, that she might fly into the wilderness, into her place, where she is nourished for a time, and times, and half a time, from the face of the serpent.

[15] And the serpent cast out of his mouth water as a flood after the woman, that he might cause her to be carried away of the flood

Figure 6.22 Woman of the Apocalypse (1549)

[16] And the earth helped the woman, and the earth opened her mouth, and swallowed up the flood which the dragon cast out of his mouth. [17] **And the dragon was wroth with the woman, and went to make war with the remnant of her seed, which keep the commandments of God, and have the testimony of Jesus Christ.**

It is not another coincidence that the armor of God is made up of the Fruit of the Spirit!

St Michael the archangel, dressed somewhat like a Roman soldier, about to slay the devil (in the form of a dragon) with a fiery sword, by Michael Jaletzke Date 17 July 2007

Figure 6.23

We have been given the armor that God used when there was war in Heaven, when Lucifer tried to destroy the Man Child. But Lucifer and his angels lost in their attempt to kill the child and to take God's throne. God has given us everything we need to bring destruction to the kingdom of darkness. He has given us His armor, the name of Jesus, and at just the sound of His name demons tremble. We have been given the Blood of the Lamb and the word of our testimony to aid us in overcoming Satan. God has given us His love which can never fail and His faith. He has given us a promise that whatever we bind on earth He will bind in Heaven; in other words, God will stand behind us because Jesus said that the victory is ours and the battle is the Lord's. Michael, Gabriel, and all the angels are sent to minister to all the heirs of salvation.

Once the seeds of the fruit of the Spirit go from germination, to cultivation, to maturity, they become the weapons of our warfare which are mighty through God to the pulling down of Satan's strongholds. When we are walking in the power of love, joy, peace, longsuffering, gentleness, kindness, righteousness, and meekness, they become the armor of God.

They protect our mind from attacks of hatred, anger, rage, and violence when we want to strike out, or back against others who may have hurt us. When we are faced with a bad report of lost jobs, death in the family, rejoicing is our weapon of choice, because it is the joy of the Lord which is our strength. If we develop the other seeds of the fruit of the Spirit and walk in them we will not fulfill the lust of the flesh.

Galatians 5:[15] But if ye bite and devour one another, take heed that ye be not consumed one of another. [16] This I say then, *Walk in the Spirit, and ye shall not fulfil the lust of the flesh.* [17] *For the flesh lusteth against the Spirit, and the Spirit against the flesh: and these are contrary the one to the other: so that ye cannot do the things that ye would.*

Galatians (KJV) 5: [20] *Idolatry, witchcraft, hatred, variance, emulations, wrath, strife, seditions, heresies,* [21] *Envyings, murders, drunkenness, revellings, and such like: of the which I tell you before, as I have also told you in time past, that they which do such things shall not inherit the kingdom of God.* [22] *But the fruit of the Spirit is love, joy, peace, longsuffering, gentleness, goodness, faith,* [23] *Meekness, temperance: against such there is no law.* [24] *And they that are Christ's have crucified the flesh with the affections and lusts.* [25] *If we live in the Spirit, let us also walk in the Spirit.* [26] *Let us not be desirous of vain glory, provoking one another, envying one another.*

The warfare is over the control over our minds and over the spiritual and natural realms, but God gives us the victory if we walk in the Spirit.

Hebrews (KJV) 1 : [13] But to which of the angels said he at any time, Sit on my right hand, until I make thine enemies thy footstool? [14] Are they not all ministering spirits, sent forth to minister for them who shall be heirs of salvation?

Warfare is what angels do best, and that is what they were created for as we have just read. The war continues:

Matthew (KJV) 11: [12] *And from the days of John the Baptist until now the kingdom of heaven suffereth violence, and the violent take it by force.*

The Body of Christ is doing very little in taking part in the battle for causing the kingdoms of this world to become the Kingdoms of our God. The victory is ours, the battle is the Lord's, but daily intercessory prayer against the kingdom of darkness is more important than asking for wealth and riches (when God said they will be added to us when we seek His Kingdom first). There are some Christians today with the mentality of the rich young ruler.

Revelation (KJV) 11: [15] And the seventh angel sounded; and there were great voices in heaven, saying, *The kingdoms of this world are becoming the kingdoms of our Lord, and of his Christ; and he shall reign for ever and ever.*

[We should stop spending so much time praying for God to bless us with wealth, which is not going to be added to us anyway until we seek the Kingdom of God first, and get on with waging our warfare against the kingdom of darkness, which is another part of our divine destiny. We should be coming against the principalities, and the powers, and against the rulers of the darkness of this world and the wicked spirits in high places, which are the spirits that control all the violence and mayhem that is in the earth. We must loose the angels of Heaven against the god of this world who blinds the minds of those who do not believe in the Gospel of Jesus Christ so that all people can see, hear, and understand the message of salvation and the love of God. We are to loose the angels against the prince of the power of the air, the spirit that is operating in the children of disobedience. Those are the spirits that are taking control over our youth. And they are the controlling spirits that rule over the violence in the earth. If one person can put a 1,000 to flight and two can put 10 thousand to flight, what will happen when we come together in the unity of our faith and in the knowledge of the Son of God? The Body of Christ would take dominion over the kingdom of darkness and placed it under the feet of the Body of Christ. This is why God made us kings and priests. He made us priests so we could have unity with Him. He made us kings, which gives us power and authority over the kingdom of darkness. Kings have dominion over principalities, powers, and rulers of darkness, but the seeds have to mature.

Romans (KJV) 8: [17] And if children, then heirs; heirs of God, and joint-heirs with Christ; if so be that we suffer with him, that we may be also glorified together. [18] For I reckon that the sufferings of this present time are not worthy to be compared with the glory which shall be revealed in us. [19] For the earnest expectation of the creature waiteth for the manifestation of the sons of God.

Ephesians (KJV) 6: [11] Put on the whole armor of God, that ye may be able to stand against the wiles of the devil. [12] For we wrestle not against flesh and blood, but against principalities, against powers, against the rulers of the darkness of this world, against spiritual wickedness in high places. [13] Wherefore take unto you the whole armor of God, that ye may be able to withstand in the evil day, and having done all, to stand. [14] Stand therefore, having your loins girt about with truth, and having on the breastplate of righteousness; [15] And your feet shod with the preparation of the gospel of peace; [16] Above all, taking the shield of faith, wherewith ye shall be able to quench all the fiery darts of the wicked. [17] And take the helmet of salvation, and the sword of the Spirit, which is the word of God: [18] Praying always with all prayer and supplication in the Spirit, and watching thereunto with all perseverance and supplication for all saints; [19] And for me, that utterance may be given unto me, that I may open my mouth boldly, to make known the mystery of the gospel,

The Seed of Faith

When the fruit of the Spirit manifest or matures, the seed of faith becomes the shield of faith in the armor of God. Regardless of what Satan brings against you, the shield of faith, once it is developed, will quench all the fiery darts of the wicked one.

The Seed of Righteousness

When the seed of righteousness, with its many facets and functions, matures, it becomes the breastplate of righteousness in the armor of God. Righteousness means you are in agreement with

God and you understand the importance of being *one* with Him. We are also keeping ourselves holy before God, and not defiling His temple.

When the seed of righteousness matures, it also becomes a garment worn by the Lamb's wife:

Rev. 19: *⁸And to her was granted that she should be arrayed in fine linen, clean and white: for the fine linen is the righteousness of saints.*

When we become steadfast in our stand against sin and it becomes part of our spiritual lives, our salvation is sealed. When you understand this and walk in it, it becomes the helmet of salvation and we will not allow any negative thoughts to enter our mind.

The Seed of Peace

When the seed of peace matures and its fruit comes forth as the gospel of peace, it forms the covering for our feet, which we are to use to tread upon principalities, powers, and the rulers of the darkness of this world, and wicked spirits in high places.

Luke 8: 11 The Parable is This: The seed is the Word of God.

Like all seeds in the spirit and in the natural realm they all ultimately have many functions.

One function of the Seed of the Word is it also becomes the Belt of Truth:

Ephesians 6: ¹⁴Stand therefore, having your loins girt about with truth.

1 Peter (KJV) 1: *¹³ Wherefore gird up the loins of your mind*, be sober, and hope to the end for the grace that is to be brought unto you at the revelation of Jesus Christ; ¹⁴As obedient children, not fashioning yourselves according to the former lusts in your ignorance: ¹⁵But as he which hath called you is holy, so be ye holy in all manner of conversation; ¹⁶Because it is written, Be ye holy; for I am holy.

2 Corinthians (KJV) 10: ⁴ (For the weapons of our warfare are not carnal, but mighty through God to the pulling down of strong holds;) *⁵ Casting down imaginations, and every high thing that exalteth itself against the knowledge of God, and bringing into captivity every thought to the obedience of Christ.*

Proverbs (KJV) 4: *²⁰ My son, attend to my words; incline thine ear unto my sayings. ²¹ Let them not depart from thine eyes; keep them in the midst of thine heart. ²² For they are life unto those who find them, and health to all their flesh. ²³ Keep thy heart with all diligence; for out of it are the issues of life. ²⁴ Put away from thee a froward mouth, and perverse lips put far from thee.*

Philippians (KJV) 4: ⁷And the *peace of God*, which passeth all understanding, shall keep your hearts and minds through Christ Jesus. ⁸ Finally, brethren, whatsoever things are true, whatsoever things are honest, whatsoever things are just, whatsoever things are pure, whatsoever things are lovely, whatsoever things are of good report; if there be any virtue, and if there be any praise, think on these things. [9] Those things, which ye have both learned, and received, and heard, and seen in me, do: and the *God of peace* shall be with you.

When the seed of the Word of God matures in our hearts, it is bearing fruit and we will automatically know what to meditate on and not be consumed with worry.

When the seed of the Word of God is nurtured and cultivated, it also becomes a living thing; it becomes the sword of the spirit in the armor of God.

John (KJV) 6:[63] It is the spirit that quickeneth; the flesh profiteth nothing: *the words that I speak unto you, they are spirit, and they are life.*

Hebrews (KJV) 4:[12] *For the word of God is quick, and powerful, and sharper than any two edged sword, piercing even to the dividing asunder of soul and spirit, and of the joints and marrow, and is a discerner of the thoughts and intents of the heart.*

Isaiah (KJV) 55:[11] *So shall my word be that goeth forth out of my mouth: it shall not return unto me void, but it shall accomplish that which I please, and it shall prosper in the thing whereto I sent it.*

When the seed of the Word of God matures, it becomes the fruit that becomes a sword in the armor of God. The seed of the Word of God has many functions. Once the fruit manifests itself, it will be the instrument that will bring about the destruction of the kingdom of darkness.

John (KJV)1: [11] He came unto his own, and his own received him not. [12] But as many as received him, to them gave He the power to become the sons of God, even to them that believe on his name: [13] Which were born, not of blood, nor of the will of the flesh, nor of the will of man, but of God. [14] And the *Word* was made flesh, and dwelt among us, (and we beheld his glory, the glory as of the only begotten of the Father,) full of grace and truth.

Hebrews (KJV)13: [15] By him therefore let us offer the sacrifice of praise to God continually, that is, *the fruit of our lips* giving thanks to his name. [16] But to do good and to communicate (which means give) forget not: for with such sacrifices God is well pleased.

[The kingdom of darkness knows when the children of God really find out who they are and walk in the power of the Holy Spirit, their rule and control over the earth will be broken, and the Kingdom of God will come into manifestation.

Not only are we the temple of the Holy Spirit, we are the garden of God. It is so important that we grow up spiritually, because "the husband is waiting for the precious fruit." God is waiting for us to mature; remember, Satan's goal is to keep us from bearing fruit by removing the seed of the Word of God out of our heart or by preventing that seed from growing and maturing.

One way that prevents growth is a stony heart. A stony heart is where the seed of the Word of God is never allowed to penetrate into the heart of a believer. Some of the areas that causes a stony heart are pride, sin, arrogance, conceit, unwillingness to forgive. These are just some of the things that cause our hearts to become hard like stone so that the seed of the Word of God cannot enter into that person's heart and have the opportunity to take root and develop into fruit.

The Word that is sown among thorns is a person who has the Word in their heart, but the seed never produced fruit because they never fully understood the process of seed time to harvest time. The cares of this world, the deceitfulness of riches, and the lusts of other things enter in to choke the word, and became unfruitful to them because they wanted wealth more for themselves than they wanted to be a blessing to the men, women, and children who are dying by the thousands from starvation every day. Not only do they need food and shelter, they need to be taught the Gospel of the Kingdom of God. This is what Jesus has been trying to get through to us for over 2,000 years with the story about the rich man in Luke 16:19-31, and the rich man in Luke 12:15-21 who decided to tear down his barns and build bigger barns just so that he could live in luxury all the rest of his days. And he did, he died that night. Both men are still in hell today.

God wants us to be *one* with Him so that we will have the same heart of compassion for the poor financially and also for the poor in spirit that He has. So that our affections are identical to His to the point where we will do everything we can to reach out and make a difference in the world by our giving. God does not just want us to give financially alone, but also to teach this Gospel of the Kingdom of God to the world.

Matthew (KJV) 24:[14] *And this gospel of the kingdom shall be preached in all the world for a witness unto all nations; and then shall the end come.*

God wants us to be the good ground; such as hear the word, and receive it, and bring forth fruit, and be the ones who started out receiving thirtyfold return, then move to the sixtyfold return, and finally move into the category where we will even receive one hundredfold return. God wants us to prove to the world what the perfect will of God is.

Romans (KJV) 8: [8] So then they that are in the flesh cannot please God.[9] But ye are not in the flesh, but in the Spirit, if so be that the Spirit of God dwell in you. Now if any man have not the Spirit of Christ, he is none of his. [10] And if Christ be in you, the body is dead because of sin; but the Spirit is life because of righteousness.

Colossians (KJV) 3:[15] And let the peace of God rule in your hearts, to the which also ye are called in one body; and be ye thankful. [16] Let the word of Christ dwell in you richly in all wisdom; teaching and admonishing one another in psalms and hymns and spiritual songs, singing with grace in your hearts to the Lord. [17] And whatsoever ye do in word or deed, do all in the name of the Lord Jesus, giving thanks to God and the Father by him.

First, the Kingdom is about us becoming *one* with the Word of God by perfecting righteousness and keeping ourselves holy and keeping our minds stayed on Jesus, which will keep us in perfect peace at all times and in every situation. God made us priests and our bodies the temple of the Holy Spirit so we could come into the presence of the Holy Spirit where we can commune with the Trinity and be led daily into the destiny God has planned for each of us from the beginning. Second, they are the keys that allow us entrance into the Kingdom of God. Third, when the fruit matures, they form the armor of God. Lastly every seed or Word has a multitude of functions, but everything starts as a seed.

Revelation (KJV) 19: [11] And I saw heaven opened, and behold a white horse; and he that sat upon him was called Faithful and True, and in righteousness he doth judge and make war. [12] His eyes were as a flame of fire, and on his head were many crowns; and he had a name written, that no man knew, but he himself. [13] And he was clothed with a vesture dipped in blood: and his name is called **The Word of God.**

Blessed Be the Host of the King of Heaven

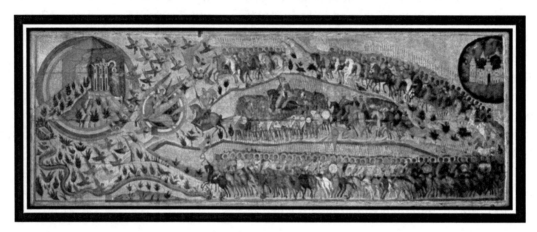

Figure 6.24 Blessed Be the Host of the King of Heaven (mid-sixteenth century) Artist: Anonymous, attributed to Athanasius

[14] And the armies which were in heaven followed him upon white horses, clothed in fine linen, white and clean. [15] And out of his mouth goeth a sharp sword, that with it he should smite the nations: and he shall rule them with a rod of iron: and he treadeth the winepress of the fierceness and wrath of Almighty God.

Figure 6.25 The Vision of the Seven Candlesticks, Revelation 1:12-20 by Matthias Gerung.

[16] And he hath on his vesture and on his thigh a name written, KING OF KINGS, AND LORD OF LORDS.

Luke (KJV) 21: [32] Verily I say unto you, This generation shall not pass away, till all be fulfilled. [33] Heaven and earth shall pass away: *but my words shall not pass away.* [34] And take heed to your-selves, lest at any time your hearts be overcharged with surfeiting, and drunkenness, and cares of this life, and so that day come upon you unawares. [35] For as a snare shall it come on all them that dwell on the face of the whole earth. [36] Watch ye therefore, and pray always, that ye may be accounted worthy to escape all these things that shall come to pass, and to stand before the Son of man.

The fruit of the Spirit are to bring about stabilization and to established our heart and mind, and to produce spiritual strength so that you can live in an atmosphere of God's presence and His power. Love, joy, peace, longsuffering, gentleness, righteousness, kindness, meekness, and faith are like the figs that would have been a source of food and life for Jesus if they had been present on the tree that He cursed. These fruit are the source of our spiritual life and the power of God, and they are the essence, the embodiment, and epitome of who God is and who He wants us to become.

This explains why the owner of the garden told the gardener to remove a nonproducing fruit tree and why Jesus commanded us to bear fruit; if not we would be cut off. Jesus is the ultimate giver of life because He gave his life so all could be saved and become partaker of His divine nature. He was the ultimate seed that was sown into the ground and His death brought everlasting life to all people who believe and accept Him as their Lord and Savior. But we must continue being a giver of life to others. A huge part of Jesus' ministry was giving to the poor and preaching the Gospel of the Kingdom of God to them. The Kingdom revolves around the developing of the owner's garden.

Isaiah (AMP) 58: *[10] And if you pour out that with which you sustain your own life for the hungry and satisfy the need of the afflicted, then shall your light rise in darkness, and your obscurity and gloom become like the noonday. [11] And the Lord shall guide you continually and satisfy you in drought and in dry places and make strong your bones. And you shall be like a watered garden and like a spring of water whose waters fail not. [12] And your ancient ruins shall be rebuilt; you shall raise up the foundations of [buildings that have laid waste for] many generations; and you shall be called Repairer of the Breach, Restorer of Streets to Dwell In.*

As Jesus said He wants to make us richer than the birds who He said were richer than Solomon so we could be called **"Repairer of the Breach and Restorer of Streets to Dwell in."** God wants to make us wealthy so we can raise the quality of life for a generation of people. Not just with food, clothing, and shelter only, but teaching the Kingdom of God principles concerning inheriting eternal life. God wants us so wealthy that we could buy houses and lands to give to the homeless all over the world.

Matthew 19: *[28] And Jesus said unto them, Verily I say unto you, That ye which have followed me, in the regeneration when the Son of man shall sit in the throne of his glory, ye also shall sit upon twelve thrones, judging the twelve tribes of Israel. [29] And every one that hath forsaken houses, or brethren, or sisters, or father, or mother, or wife, or children, or lands, for my name's sake, shall receive an hundredfold, and shall inherit everlasting life. [30]* But many that are first shall be last; and the last shall be first.

God wants us wealthier than we can imagine but not for the reasons that we are currently thinking unless we have absorbed the mind of Christ and we have truly become *one* in our actions, in our ways, and our thoughts line up with God's ways and thoughts.

Matthew (KJV) 6:.[25] Therefore I say unto you, Take no thought for your life, what ye shall eat, or what ye shall drink; nor yet for your body, what ye shall put on. Is not the life more than meat, and the body than raiment? [26] Behold the fowls of the air: for they sow not, neither do they reap, nor gather into barns; yet your heavenly Father feedeth them. Are ye not much better than they? [27] Which of you by taking thought can add one cubit unto his stature? [28] And why take ye thought for raiment? **Consider the lilies of the field, how they grow; they toil not, neither do they spin: [29] And yet I say unto you, That even Solomon in all his glory was not arrayed like one of these.[30] Wherefore, if God so clothe the grass of the field, which today is, and tomorrow is cast into the oven, shall he not much more clothe you, O ye of little faith? [31] Therefore take no thought, saying, What shall we eat? or, What shall we drink? or, Wherewithal shall we be clothed? [32] (For after all these things do the Gentiles seek:) for your heavenly Father knoweth that ye have need of all these things. [33] But seek ye first the kingdom of God, and his righteousness; and all these things shall be added unto you.** [34] Take therefore no thought for the morrow: for the morrow shall take thought for the things of itself. Sufficient unto the day is the evil thereof.

Psalm (KJV) 1 Blessed is the man that walketh not in the counsel of the ungodly, nor standeth in the way of sinners, nor sitteth in the seat of the scornful. [2] But his delight is in the law of the LORD; and in his law doth he meditate day and night. [3] **And he shall be like a tree planted by the rivers of water, that bringeth forth his fruit in his season; his leaf also shall not wither; and whatsoever he doeth shall prosper.** [4] The ungodly are not so: but are like the chaff which the wind driveth away. [5] Therefore the ungodly shall not stand in the judgment, nor sinners in the congregation of the righteous. [6] For the LORD knoweth the way of the righteous: but the way of the ungodly shall perish.

Isaiah (AMP) 58: [9] Then you shall call, and the Lord will answer; you shall cry, and He will say, Here I am. If you take away from your midst yokes of oppression [wherever you find them], the finger pointed in scorn [toward the oppressed or the godly], and every form of false, harsh, unjust, *and* wicked speaking, [10] And if you pour out that with which you sustain your own life for the hungry and satisfy the need of the afflicted, then shall your light rise in darkness, and your obscurity *and* gloom become like the noonday. [11] **And the Lord shall guide you continually and satisfy you in drought and in dry places and make strong your bones. And you shall be like a watered garden and like a spring of water whose waters fail not.** [12] And your ancient ruins shall be rebuilt; you shall raise up the foundations of [buildings that have laid waste for] many generations; and you shall be called Repairer of the Breach, Restorer of Streets to Dwell In. [13] If you turn away your foot from [traveling unduly on] the Sabbath, from doing your own pleasure on My holy day, and call the Sabbath a [spiritual] delight, the holy day of the Lord honorable, and honor Him *and* it, not going your own way or seeking *or* finding your own pleasure or speaking with your own [idle] words, [14] Then will you delight yourself in the Lord, and I will make you to ride on the high places of the earth, and I will feed you with the heritage [promised for you] of Jacob your father; for the mouth of the Lord has spoken it.

Isaiah 61: The Spirit of the Lord GOD is upon me; because the LORD hath anointed me to preach good tidings unto the meek; he hath sent me to bind up the brokenhearted, to proclaim liberty to the captives, and the opening of the prison to them that are bound; *[2] To proclaim the acceptable year of the LORD, and the day of vengeance of our God; to comfort all that mourn; [3] To appoint unto them that mourn in Zion, to give unto them beauty for ashes, the oil of joy for mourning, the garment of praise for the spirit of heaviness;* **that they might be called trees of righteousness, the planting of the LORD, that he might be glorified.**

Isaiah (KJV) 61: [10] I will greatly rejoice in the LORD, my soul shall be joyful in my God; for he hath clothed me with the garments of salvation, he hath covered me with the robe of righteousness, as a bridegroom decketh himself with ornaments, and as a bride adorneth herself with her jewels. [11] **For as the earth bringeth forth her bud, and as the garden causeth the things that are sown in it to spring forth; so the Lord GOD will cause righteousness and praise to spring forth before all the nations.**

CHAPTER 7

"The Power and Force of One"

1 Corinthians 6: [15] Know ye not that your bodies are the members of Christ? shall I then take the members of Christ, and make them the members of an harlot? God forbid. [16] What? Know ye not that he which is joined to an harlot is one body? for two, saith he, shall be one flesh. [17] **But he that is joined unto the Lord is one spirit.**

Matthew (KJV) 7: [15] Beware of false prophets, which come to you in sheep's clothing, but inwardly they are ravening wolves. [16] Ye shall know them by their fruits. Do men gather grapes of thorns, or figs of thistles? [17] Even so every good tree bringeth forth good fruit; but a corrupt tree bringeth forth evil fruit. [18] A good tree cannot bring forth evil fruit, neither can a corrupt tree bring forth good fruit. [19] Every tree that bringeth not forth good fruit is hewn down, and cast into the fire. [20] Wherefore by their fruits ye shall know them. [21] **Not every one that saith unto me, Lord, Lord, shall enter into the kingdom of heaven; but he that doeth the will of my Father which is in heaven. [22] Many will say to me in that day, Lord, Lord, have we not prophesied in thy name? and in thy name have cast out devils? and in thy name done many wonderful works? [23] And then will I profess unto them, I never knew you: depart from me, ye that work iniquity.**

Jesus made the statement "I never knew you" to the foolish virgins, and to the man that did not fulfill his responsibilities, and finally to the individuals who were judged as being goats in the twenty-fifth chapter of Matthew.

Being *one* with someone means you know them so well and you have been with them so long that you know how they think and they know how you think. You understand what they would do in every situation because you both have been through so many difficult and seemingly impossible situations together. The two of you have developed a deep trust and have enough confidence in each other to know that no matter what, you have each other's support. The bond between you is so strong that nothing can separate you, because you have made a commitment to stand by each other through thick and thin.

The relationship that we should develop between ourselves and the Trinity is similar to the oneness between a husband and wife who have been together after thirty, forty, or fifty years of marriage, but our relation to the Trinity is deeper and broader than that.

The meaning of oneness is solidarity, unanimity, singleness of heart, unison, and harmony, which is the relationship that God wants between the Trinity and His children.

The Bible says we have been given the mind of Christ. Our mind is like a computer which will not do anything until it is programmed. Our mind is the same way it has been programmed by this ungodly worldly system that Satan has put in place. We have enormous amounts of knowledge stored in our mind: some of it is good and some of it is evil. There is nothing wrong with the good because Jesus told the rich young ruler that there is none good except God. But from the Garden of Eden, we learned when you mix good and evil you get corruption. We have to put the Word of God in our mind and heart if we want to understand how God thinks and acts so we can come in agreement with Him. His thoughts are higher than our thoughts; His ways are higher than our ways. He wants our thoughts and ways to be on the same level with His.

God wants our actions, emotions, compassion, passions, and our sensitivity to be a byproduct of the fruit of the Spirit; Love, joy, peace, longsuffering, gentleness, kindness, meekness, faith, and righteousness which are the attributes that we see in Christ's ministry. Thomas asked Jesus to show him the Father. Jesus as much as said if God had showed up in person, He would not have talked, touched, preached, healed, or ministered any differently because Jesus was God in the flesh and because they both, including the Holy Spirit, were one. Jesus came in a flesh-and-bone body. His mother was Mary, but He knew who His Father was. And that His Father's seed, His Father's DNA, His purpose and divine destiny were already implanted within Him. There are many prophecies in the Old Testament that tells us all, Jews and Gentiles alike, how to recognize the Messiah. And when Jesus returns the second time everyone will know that He was and is the Messiah because the wounds in His hands and feet from the cross will be proof that He is the Savior. We know Jesus began studying the Old Testament long before the age of twelve because He was found in the synagogue asking questions and answering them at that age.

**Figure 7.1 Jesus Found in the Temple by His Parents at the Age of Twelve (1860)
by William Brassey Hole.**

When He grew up, He was the image of His Father inside and out, His actions, what He did, and what He said were exactly the same as His Father because they were ONE. Jesus is our pattern, the blueprint of His life is found in the New Testament. Our ultimate desire should be to follow after the same pattern of being in unity with the Spirit of God because we have the same Father.

Like Adam and Eve, we have been given the same charge to guard and protect the garden. We have been given the same charge to guard and protect our access to our only source of spiritual life, which is our connection between the Father, the Son, the Holy Spirit, and our spirit man. God warned Adam and Eve to stay away from corruption because it would kill them, and Jesus is saying the same thing to us. We are God's garden so we have to be careful about what goes into our spirits, souls, and bodies. Enjoy life while avoiding sin, especially sexual sins, because they defile the body. We have to take time to feed our spirits and souls with the Word of God, through studying, meditation and prayer **DAILY**.

1 Thessalonians (KJV) 5: [14] Now we exhort you, brethren, warn them that are unruly, comfort the feebleminded, support the weak, be patient toward all men. [15] See that none render evil for evil unto any man; but ever follow that which is good, both among yourselves, and to all men. [16] Rejoice evermore. [17] Pray without ceasing. [18] In everything give thanks: for this is the will of God in Christ Jesus concerning you. [19] Quench not the Spirit. [20] Despise not prophesyings. [21] Prove all things; hold fast that which is good. [22] Abstain from all appearance of evil. *And the very God of peace sanctify you wholly; and I pray God your whole spirit and soul and body be preserved blameless unto the coming of our Lord Jesus Christ.* [24] *Faithful is he that calleth you, who also will do it.*

Philippians (KJV) 4: [5] *Let your moderation be known unto all men. The Lord is at hand.* [6] Be careful for nothing; but in everything by prayer and supplication with thanksgiving let your requests be made known unto God. [7] And the peace of God, which passeth all understanding, shall keep your hearts and minds through Christ Jesus. [8] *Finally, brethren, whatsoever things are true, whatsoever things are honest, whatsoever things are just, whatsoever things are pure, whatsoever things are lovely, whatsoever things are of good report; if there be any virtue, and if there be any praise, think on these things.* [9] *Those things, which ye have both learned, and received, and heard, and seen in me, do: and the God of peace shall be with you.*

For the most part we have had a one-sided relationship with God, that must go deeper than a relationship between a husband and wife or two very close friends who grew up with each other. God has made a covenant with us to take care of us, to heal us, to bless us, and to make us to be a blessing in the earth. He promised to never leave or forsake us even until the end of the world. Man unsaved and unredeemed is able to do very little against the kingdom of darkness in their own strength and really they can do very little for the Kingdom of God until they have the knowledge or know how to use the authority from God to do so. But when we become *one* with the Trinity, it will be God working in us and through us to do His will on the Earth. When we become *one* with God it means we think the way He thinks, we act and say only what we sense, hear, feel, and see in our spirit to do. Jesus said in:

John 14: [10] Believest thou not that I am in the Father, and the Father in me? The words that I speak unto you I speak not of myself: but the Father that dwelleth in me, he doeth the works.

Philippians (KJV) 2: ⁵Let this mind be in you, which was also in Christ Jesus: ⁶Who, being in the form of God, thought it not robbery to be equal with God: ⁷But made himself of no reputation, and took upon him the form of a servant, and was made in the likeness of men:

John (KJV) 14: *Let not your heart be troubled: ye believe in God, believe also in me. ²In my Father's house are many mansions: if it were not so, I would have told you. I go to prepare a place for you. ³And if I go and prepare a place for you, I will come again, and receive you unto myself; that where I am, there ye may be also. ⁴And whither I go ye know, and the way ye know.* ⁵Thomas saith unto him, Lord, we know not whither thou goest; and how can we know the way? ⁶Jesus saith unto him, I am the way, the truth, and the life: no man cometh unto the Father, but by me. ⁷If ye had known me, ye should have known my Father also: and from henceforth ye know him, and have seen him. ⁸Philip saith unto him, Lord, show us the Father, and it sufficeth us. ⁹Jesus saith unto him, Have I been so long time with you, and yet hast thou not known me, Philip? he that hath seen me hath seen the Father; and how sayest thou then, Show us the Father? ¹⁰Believest thou not that I am in the Father, and the Father in me? the words that I speak unto you I speak not of myself: but the Father that dwelleth in me, he doeth the works. ¹¹Believe me that I am in the Father, and the Father in me: or else believe me for the very works' sake.¹² **Verily, verily, I say unto you, He that believeth on me, the works that I do shall he do also; and greater works than these shall he do; because I go unto my Father.** ¹³And whatsoever ye shall ask in my name, that will I do, that the Father may be glorified in the Son. ¹⁴If ye shall ask any thing in my name, I will do it. ¹⁵If ye love me, keep my commandments. ¹⁶And I will pray the Father, and he shall give you another Comforter that he may abide with you forever; ¹⁷Even the Spirit of truth; whom the world cannot receive, because it seeth him not, neither knoweth him: but ye know him; for he dwelleth with you, and shall be in you. ¹⁸I will not leave you comfortless: I will come to you. ¹⁹Yet a little while, and the world seeth me no more; but ye see me: because I live, ye shall live also. **²⁰At that day ye shall know that I am in my Father, and ye in me, and I in you.** ²¹He that hath my commandments, and keepeth them, he it is that loveth me: and he that loveth me shall be loved of my Father, and I will love him, and will manifest myself to him. ²²Judas saith unto him, not Iscariot, Lord, how is it that thou wilt manifest thyself unto us, and not unto the world? ²³Jesus answered and said unto him, If a man love me, he will keep my words: and my Father will love him, and we will come unto him, and make our abode with him. ²⁴He that loveth me not keepeth not my sayings: and the word which ye hear is not mine, but the Father's which sent me.²⁵These things have I spoken unto you, being yet present with you.

Being *one* with God is what we should be striving for daily because John 14: 20 says that in the Day of the Lord, you will have to be *one* with the Trinity. He is going to manifest (which means to make visible or reveal) Himself only to those who are keeping His commandments; the rest of the world along with the foolish virgins will not even know what has happened until it is over. You cannot really love God if you do not keep the commandments, so lip service will not work. You can say how much you think you love Him, but is it love or agape that you have for Him? We can sing songs and roll around under the pews and even cry. But the bottom line is, obedience and manifestation of the fruit of the Spirit is what Jesus and the angels will be looking for at the time of His return.

There has been a great deal of emphasis placed on being *one* throughout the Bible. We have established that it is the definition of the Kingdom of God. Jesus prayed to the Father that we would become *one* with the Trinity. God wants us as the Body of Christ to come together in the unity of our faith and of the knowledge of the Son of God unto a perfect man.

God is also *one* with us from another standpoint, we have learned that when we feed the hungry, clothe the naked, visit the sick and those who are in prison, we are ministering to Jesus. When the church is being persecuted (for the cause of the ministry) Jesus takes that just as personal because it is an attack against His Body. We saw this when Saul was holding the coats of the men who were stoning Stephen for ministering the Gospel of the Kingdom; we see Jesus was standing up to receive Stephen into Heaven. When you get a chance, you should read the powerful sermon that Stephen preached in Acts 6 and 7; it is very moving.

Acts 7: [47] But Solomon built him an house. [48] Howbeit the most High dwelleth not in temples made with hands; as saith the prophet, [49] Heaven is my throne, and earth is my footstool: what house will ye build me? saith the Lord: or what is the place of my rest? [50] Hath not my hand made all these things? **[51] Ye stiff necked and uncircumcised in heart and ears, ye do always resist the Holy Ghost: as your fathers did, so do ye. [52] Which of the prophets have not your fathers persecuted? and they have slain them which shewed before of the coming of the Just One; of whom ye have been now the betrayers and murderers:** [53] Who have received the law by the disposition of angels, and have not kept it. [54] When they heard these things, they were cut to the heart, and they gnashed on him with their teeth. [55] But he, being full of the Holy Ghost, looked up stedfastly into heaven, and saw the glory of God, and Jesus standing on the right hand of God, [56] And said, Behold, I see the heavens opened, and the Son of man standing on the right hand of God. [57] Then they cried out with a loud voice, and stopped their ears, and ran upon him with one accord, [58] And cast him out of the city, and stoned him: and the witnesses laid down their clothes at a young man's feet, whose name was Saul. [59] And they stoned Stephen, calling upon God, and saying, Lord Jesus, receive my spirit. [60] And he kneeled down, and cried with a loud voice, Lord, lay not this sin to their charge. And when he had said this, he fell asleep.

Figure 7.2 Stoning of Saint Stephen (1660) by Pietro da Cortona.

Whatever happens to the members of Jesus Body, whether it is individually or collectively, it affects Him. Especially if they are ministering the Gospel. Saul continued persecuting Christians when Jesus intervened and spoke aloud and said to Saul, "Why do you persecute Me?" That is personal. He did not say, why are you persecuting Christians or religious people; He said why do you persecute "Me," because Jesus completely identifies with the members of His Body.

Acts (KJV) 9 And Saul, yet breathing out threatenings and slaughter against the disciples of the Lord, went unto the high priest,[2] And desired of him letters to Damascus to the synagogues, that if he found any of this way, whether they were men or women, he might bring them bound unto Jerusalem.[3] And as he journeyed, he came near Damascus: and suddenly there shined round about him a light from heaven: [4] *And he fell to the earth, and heard a voice saying unto him, Saul, Saul, why persecutest thou me?*

Figure 7.3 The Conversion of Paul (1690s) by Luca Giordano. Photographer Vassil

[5] And he said, Who art thou, Lord? And the Lord said, I am Jesus whom thou persecutest: it is hard for thee to kick against the pricks. [6] And he trembling and astonished said, Lord, what wilt thou have me to do? And the Lord said unto him, Arise, and go into the city, and it shall be told thee what thou must do. [7] And the men which journeyed with him stood speechless, hearing a voice, but seeing no man.

The Conversion of Paul

Figure 7.4 Paul on the Road to Damascus (between 1570 and 1577) by Hans Speckaert.

[8] And Saul arose from the earth; and when his eyes were opened, he saw no man: but they led him by the hand, and brought him into Damascus. [9] And he was three days without sight, and neither did eat nor drink. [10] And there was a certain disciple at Damascus, named Ananias; and to him said the Lord in a vision, Ananias. And he said, Behold, I am here, Lord. [11] And the Lord said unto him, Arise, and go into the street which is called Straight, and enquire in the house of Judas for one called Saul, of Tarsus: for, behold, he prayeth, [12] And hath seen in a vision a man named Ananias coming in, and putting his hand on him, that he might receive his sight. [13] Then Ananias answered, Lord, I have heard by many of this man, how much evil he hath done to thy saints at Jerusalem: [14] And here he hath authority from the chief priests to bind all that call on thy name. [15] But the Lord said unto him, Go thy way: for he is a chosen vessel unto me, to bear my name before the Gentiles, and kings, and the children of Israel: [16] For I will shew him how great things he must suffer for my name's sake.

Figure 7.5 Ananias restoring the sight of St Paul (1631) by Pietro da Cortona.

[17] And Ananias went his way, and entered into the house; and putting his hands on him said, Brother Saul, the Lord, even Jesus, that appeared unto thee in the way as thou camest, hath sent me, that thou mightest receive thy sight, and be filled with the Holy Ghost. [18] And immediately there fell from his eyes as it had been scales: and he received sight forthwith, and arose, and was baptized. [19] And when he had received meat, he was strengthened. Then was Saul certain days with the disciples which were at Damascus. [20] And straightway he preached Christ in the synagogues, that he is the Son of God. [21] But all that heard him were amazed, and said; Is not this he that destroyed them which called on this name in Jerusalem, and came hither for that intent, that he might bring them bound unto the chief priests? [22] But Saul increased the more in strength, and confounded the Jews which dwelt at Damascus, proving that this is very Christ.

After Saul's Damascus Road experience, Jesus changed Saul's life forever. Saul repented; he received the Holy Spirit and became *one* with Christ. He became a member of the Body that he once tried to destroy. He walked in the power of the Holy Spirit and began fulfilling his divine purpose. Saul became the Apostle Paul who wrote a large portion of the New Testament. Paul's writings are still changing the lives of people to this very day.

I Cor. 12: *²⁵ That there should be no schism in the body;* but that the members should have the same care one for another. ²⁶And whether one member suffer, all the members suffer with it; or one member be honoured, all the members rejoice with it. *²⁷Now ye are the body of Christ, and members in particular.*

[Jesus will be judging each of us based on our obedience, and He will separate us according to whether or not He knows us or not. **As we have seen, the foolish virgins who had no oil in their lamps were walking in darkness because the Word of God was not in their heart.** The individuals who did not minister to the needy were cast out because Jesus said that He did not know them. They were given the means and the resources with which to start the Kingdom of God principles of sowing and reaping to begin operating in their life. But for whatever reason they did not apply the principles and they reaped the consequences. Even if we are less fortunate ourselves like the widow with two mites, the Word of God will work anywhere and for anyone.

But by the same token, the foolish virgins, the man with one talent, and the individuals who did not minister to the less fortunate did not know Jesus, and Jesus did not know them, either. Knowing and becoming *one* with the Trinity both work together; there has to be a meeting of the minds and an agreement between both parties. And the agreement has to be on the side of the Word of God. That is why the Bible says we have been given the mind of Christ. And when we put the Word of God in our heart by reading, etc., then God fulfills His part of the covenant.]

Hebrews (KJV) 8:¹⁰ For this is the covenant that I will make with the house of Israel after those days, saith the Lord; I will put my laws into their mind, and write them in their hearts: and I will be to them a God, and they shall be to me a people.

The Lord's Prayer for All Christians

John (KJV) 17: 1These words spake Jesus, and lifted up his eyes to heaven, and said, Father, the hour is come; glorify thy Son, that thy Son also may glorify thee:²As thou hast given him power over all flesh, that he should give eternal life to as many as thou hast given him. ³And this is life eternal, that they might know thee the only true God, and Jesus Christ, whom thou hast sent. ⁴I have glorified thee on the earth: I have finished the work which thou gavest me to do. ⁵And now, O Father, glorify thou me with thine own self with the glory which I had with thee before the world was. ⁶I have manifested thy name unto the men which thou gavest me out of the world: thine they were, and thou gavest them me; and they have kept thy word. ⁷Now they have known that all things whatsoever thou hast given me are of thee. ⁸For I have given unto them the words which thou gavest me; and they have received them, and have known surely that I came out from thee, and they have believed that thou didst send me. ⁹I pray for them: I pray not for the world, but for them which thou hast given me; for they are thine. ¹⁰And all mine are thine, and thine are mine; and I am glorified in them. ¹¹And now I am no more in the world, but these are in the world, and I come to thee. Holy Father, keep through thine own name those whom thou hast given me, that they may be one, as we are. ¹²While I was with them in the world, I kept them in thy name: those that thou gavest me I have kept, and none of them is lost, but the son of perdition; that the scripture might be fulfilled. ¹³ And now come I to thee; and these things I speak in the world, that they might have my joy fulfilled in themselves. ¹⁴ I have given them thy word; and the world hath hated them, because they are not of the world, even as I am not of the world. ¹⁵ I pray not that thou shouldest take them out of the world, but that thou shouldest keep them from the evil. ¹⁶ They are not of the world, even as I am not of the world.¹⁷ Sanctify them through thy truth: thy word is truth. ¹⁸ As thou hast sent me into the world, even so have I also sent them into the world. ¹⁹ And for their sakes I sanctify myself, that they also might be sanctified through the truth. **²⁰ Neither pray I for these alone, but for them also which shall believe on me through their word; ²¹ That they all may be one; as thou, Father, art in me, and I in thee, that they also may be one in us: that the world may believe that thou hast sent me. ²² And the glory which thou gavest me I have given them; that they may be one, even as we are one: ²³ I in them, and thou in me, that they may be made perfect in one; and that the world may know that thou hast sent me, and hast loved them, as thou hast loved me. ²⁴ Father, I will that they also, whom thou hast given me, be with me where I am; that they may behold my glory, which thou hast given me: for thou lovedst me before the foundation of the world. ²⁵ O righteous Father, the world hath not known thee: but I have known thee, and these have known that thou hast sent me.²⁶ And I have declared unto them thy name, and will declare it: that the love wherewith thou hast loved me may be in them, and I in them.**

The Foolish Virgins Did Not Understand the Office of the Priest

The Day of the Lord in the Old Testament is the same in the New Testament

Malachi (KJV) 3 Behold, I will send my messenger, and he shall prepare the way before me: and the LORD, whom ye seek, shall suddenly come to his temple, even the messenger of the covenant, whom ye delight in: behold, he shall come, saith the LORD of hosts. ² But who may abide the day of his coming? and who shall stand when he appeareth? for he is like a refiner's fire, and like fullers' soap: ³ And he shall sit as a refiner and purifier of silver: and he shall purify the sons of Levi, and purge them as gold and silver, that they may offer unto the LORD an offering in righteousness.

It is important that we study Malachi because it brings together several truths that we need to understand. It is a transitioning point between the Old Testament and the New Testament. It is a crossover from the Old Testament priesthood to the New Testament priesthood. It's placement at the end of the Old Testament and at the beginning of the New Testament is not a coincidence. It lays the foundation for the New Testament temple, because God chose to move His residence from the Old Testament tabernacle to live inside of us, therefore making our body the temple of the Holy Spirit. And He made our spirit man the priest.

Figure 7.6 The Tabernacle in the Wilderness; illustration from the 1890 Holman Bible.

Malachi 3: *1 Behold, I will send my messenger, and he shall prepare the way before me: and, the LORD, whom ye seek, shall suddenly come to his temple even the messenger of the covenant, whom ye delight in: behold, he shall come, saith the LORD of hosts.*

In the Old Testament, the tabernacle was a structure that God had the people to build using wood and gold, etc., (see Figure 7.6). The tabernacle was a place where God could meet (or commune) with His people but only the High Priest could go beyond the second veil into the Holy of Holies. Now we are the temple of God. In the Old Testament the priest had the responsibility to purify himself with the blood of a lamb or a young bull, which had to be spotless, before it could be sacrificed. In the New Testament we have been given the Blood of the Lamb of God (Jesus Christ) with which to cleanse ourselves so we can have boldness in the Day of Judgment. The priest knew that he had to be pure and holy before he could go into the temple and enter into the Holy of Holies into the Presence of the Lord, or he would die instantly (Figure 7.7).

In the New Testament, whether we know it or not, if we are not living a holy life when Jesus returns we will be left. That is another reason why Jesus said five out of every ten Christians will be left. We are born of God, He decided to live in us but we have to obey His Word in order to maintain our union with Him. This is what Adam and Eve could not do. Our obedience is a demonstration of our love for Him and it allows us to maintain our unity with God.

Figure7.7 The Holy of Holies; illustration from the 1890 Holman Bible

John (KJV) 14: [23] Jesus answered and said unto him, If a man love me, he will keep my words: and my Father will love him, and we will come unto him, and make our abode with him.

Malachi 3: *[2] But who may abide the day of his coming? and who shall stand when he appeareth? for he is like a refiner's fire, and like fullers' soap:[3] And he shall sit as a refiner and purifier that they may offer unto the Lord an offering in righteousness. [4] Then shall the offering of Judah and Jerusalem be pleasant unto the Lord, as in the days of old, and as in former years.[5] And I will come near to you to judgment; and I will be a swift witness against the sorcerers, and against the adulterers, and against false swearers, and against those that oppress the hireling in his wages, the widow, and the fatherless, and that turn aside the stranger from his right, and fear not me, saith the Lord of hosts.[6] For I am the Lord, I change not; therefore ye sons of Jacob are not consumed.[7] Even from the days of your fathers ye are gone away from mine ordinances, and have not kept them.*

Malachi 4 gives us a prelude to the "The Day of the Lord".

Malachi 4: *For, behold, the day cometh, that shall burn as an oven; and all the proud, yea, and all that do wickedly, shall be stubble: and the day that cometh shall burn them up, saith the Lord of hosts, that it shall leave them neither root nor branch. [2] But unto you that fear my name shall the Sun of righteousness arise with healing in his wings; and ye shall go forth, and grow up as calves of the stall.[3] And ye shall tread down the wicked; for they shall be ashes under the soles of your feet in the day that I shall do this, saith the Lord of hosts. [4] Remember ye the law of Moses my servant,*

292

which I commanded unto him in Horeb for all Israel, with the statutes and judgments. [5] *Behold, I will send you Elijah the prophet before the coming of the great and dreadful day of the* LORD: [6] *And he shall turn the heart of the fathers to the children, and the heart of the children to their fathers, lest I come and smite the earth with a curse.*

The foolish virgins did not understand that on Judgment Day, God is going to judge the motives and the intentions of our hearts and He wants them to be pure and holy because He is holy. There is no fellowship between righteousness and unrighteousness. God knew that we are not perfect so He made us priests and our bodies are the temple of the Holy Spirit so when we make mistakes we can come to God and ask for and receive forgiveness. Our purpose is to finish what Jesus started and that is to destroy the works of the devil. That is why Jesus said that in the end it will be Kingdom against kingdom, and the kingdoms of this world are becoming the Kingdom of our God. It will happen by God working through us.

Since the death, burial, and resurrection of Jesus, a new covenant has come forth, a new way of access to God for all people who are willing to accept Jesus Christ as their Lord and Savior. When Jesus comes into our hearts He brings the Kingdom of God with Him and we become the temple of God. Now everyone can have a personal relationship with God.

Luke (KJV) 17: [20] And when he was demanded of the Pharisees, when the kingdom of God should come, he answered them and said, The kingdom of God cometh not with observation: [21] Neither shall they say, Lo here! or, lo there! for, behold, *the kingdom of God is within you.*

James (KJV) 4: [4] Ye adulterers and adulteresses, know ye not that the friendship of the world is enmity with God? whosoever therefore will be a friend of the world is the enemy of God. [5] Do ye think that the scripture saith in vain, The spirit that dwelleth in us lusteth to envy? [6] But he giveth more grace. Wherefore he saith, God resisteth the proud, but giveth grace unto the humble. [7] Submit yourselves therefore to God. Resist the devil, and he will flee from you. **[8] Draw nigh to God, and he will draw nigh to you. Cleanse your hands, ye sinners; and purify your hearts, ye double minded. [9] Be afflicted, and mourn, and weep: let your laughter be turned to mourning, and your joy to heaviness. [10] Humble yourselves in the sight of the Lord, and he shall lift you up. [11] Speak not evil one of another, brethren. He that speaketh evil of his brother, and judgeth his brother, speaketh evil of the law, and judgeth the law: but if thou judge the law, thou art not a doer of the law, but a judge. [12] There is one lawgiver, who is able to save and to destroy: who art thou that judgest another?**

Communion is the next source that God uses to draw us closer to becoming *one with Him*.

Communion, Communication, Close Association, Unity, Relationship

Figure 7.8 Behold the Lamb of God (1432) by Jan van Eyck. Plot to kill Jesus

Luke 22 (CEB) The Festival of Unleavened Bread, which is called Passover, was approaching. [2] The chief priests and the legal experts were looking for a way to kill Jesus, because they were afraid of the people. [3] Then Satan entered Judas, called Iscariot, who was one of the Twelve. [4] He went out and discussed with the chief priests and the officers of the temple guard how he could hand Jesus over to them. [5] They were delighted and arranged payment for him. [6] He agreed and began looking for an opportunity to hand Jesus over to them—a time when the crowds would be absent.

Figure 7.9 The Israelites eat the Passover, as in Exodus 12:1-8, 27b: "And the Lord spake unto Moses and Aaron in the land of Egypt, saying, This month shall be unto you the beginning of months: it shall be the first month of the year to you. Speak ye unto all the congregation of Israel, saying, In the tenth day of this month they shall take to them every man a lamb, according to the house of their fathers, a lamb for an house: And if the household be too little for the lamb, let him and his neighbour next unto his house take it according to the number of the souls; every man according to his eating shall make your count for the lamb. Your lamb shall be without blemish, a male of the first year: ye shall take it out from the sheep, or from the goats: And ye shall keep it up until the fourteenth day of the same month: and the whole assembly of the congregation of Israel shall kill it in the evening. And they shall take of the blood, and strike it on the two side posts and on the upper door post of the houses, wherein they shall eat it. And they shall eat the flesh in that night, roast with fire, and unleavened bread; and with bitter herbs they shall eat it. . . . It is the sacrifice of the Lord's passover, who passed over the houses of the children of Israel in Egypt, when he smote the Egyptians, and delivered our houses. And the people bowed the head and worshipped.";illustration from the 1728 Figures de la Bible; illustrated by Gerard Hoet (1648–1733) and others, and published by P. de Hondt in The Hague; image courtesy Bizzell Bible Collection, University of Oklahoma Libraries.

295

[7] The Day of Unleavened Bread arrived, when the Passover had to be sacrificed. [8] Jesus sent Peter and John with this task: "Go and prepare for us to eat the Passover meal." [9] They said to him, "Where do you want us to prepare it?" [10] Jesus replied, "When you go into the city, a man carrying a water jar will meet you. Follow him to the house he enters. [11] Say to the owner of the house, 'The teacher says to you, "Where is the guestroom where I can eat the Passover meal with my disciples?" ' [12] He will show you a large upstairs room, already furnished. Make preparations there." [13] They went and found everything just as he had told them, and they prepared the Passover meal.

The Passover meal

Figure 7.10 The Last Supper by Joan de Joanes (1523–1579).

[14] When the time came, Jesus took his place at the table, and the apostles joined him. [15] He said to them, "I have earnestly desired to eat this Passover with you before I suffer. [16] I tell you, I won't eat it until it is fulfilled in God's kingdom." [17] After taking a cup and giving thanks, he said, "Take this and share it among yourselves. [18] I tell you that from now on I won't drink from the fruit of the vine until God's kingdom has come." [19] After taking the bread and giving thanks, he broke it and gave it to them, saying, "This is my body, which is given for you. Do this in remembrance of me." [20] In the same way, he took the cup after the meal and said, "This cup is the new covenant by my blood, which is poured out for you. [21] "But look! My betrayer is with me; his hand is on this table. [22] The Human One (the Son of Man) goes just as it has been determined. But how terrible it is for that person who betrays him."

2 Corinthians (KJV) 4: [10] Always bearing about in the body the dying of the Lord Jesus, that the life also of Jesus might be made manifest in our body. [11] For we which live are always delivered unto death for Jesus' sake, that the life also of Jesus might be made manifest in our mortal flesh.

Hebrews (CEB) Chapter 9

Christ's service in the heavenly meeting tent

1So then the first covenant had regulations for the priests' service and the holy place on earth. [2] They pitched the first tent called the holy place. It contained the lampstand, the table, and the loaves of bread presented to God. [3] There was a tent behind the second curtain called the holy of holies. [4] It had the gold altar for incense and the chest containing the covenant, which was covered with gold on all sides. In the chest there was a gold jar containing manna, Aaron's rod that budded, and the stone tablets of the covenant. [5] Above the chest there were magnificent winged creatures casting their shadow over the seat of the chest, where sin is taken care of. Right now we can't talk about these things in detail. [6] When these things have been prepared in this way, priests enter the first tent all the time as they perform their service.

Communion started here in the Old Testament: once the Priest purified himself with the blood of a spotless lamb or goat he could go beyond the second veil into the Presence of God. Our bodies are the temple of the Holy Spirit. Jesus' flesh is the veil (Heb. 10:20), which makes Him the Holy of Holies and because the Holy Spirit and God are *one* with Him. Jesus prayed that we would be *one* also. Communion is a one-to-one, face-to-face relationship that God, Jesus, and the Holy Spirit desire to have with us individually.

Communion Started Here with the High Priest

Exodus 25: [16] And thou shalt put into the ark the testimony which I shall give thee. [17] And thou shalt make a mercy seat of pure gold: two cubits and a half shall be the length thereof, and a cubit and a half the breadth thereof. [18] And thou shalt make two cherubims of gold, of beaten work shalt thou make them, in the two ends of the mercy seat. [19] And make one cherub on the one end, and the other cherub on the other end: even of the mercy seat shall ye make the cherubims on the two ends thereof. [20] And the cherubims shall stretch forth their wings on high, covering the mercy seat with their wings, and their faces shall look one to another; toward the mercy seat shall the faces of the cherubims be. [21] And thou shalt put the mercy seat above upon the ark; and in the ark thou shalt put the testimony that I shall give thee. **[22] And there I will meet with thee, and I will commune with thee from above the mercy seat, from between the two cherubims which are upon the ark of the testimony, of all things which I will give thee in commandment unto the children of Israel.**

Leviticus (KJV) 16: 1: [14] And he shall take of the blood of the bullock, and sprinkle it with his finger upon the mercy seat eastward; and before the mercy seat shall he sprinkle of the blood with his finger seven times. [15] Then shall he kill the goat of the sin offering, that is for the people, and bring his blood within the vail, and do with that blood as he did with the blood of the bullock, and sprinkle it upon the mercy seat, and before the mercy seat: [16] And he shall make an atonement for the holy place, because of the uncleanness of the children of Israel, and because of their transgressions in all their sins: and so shall he do for the tabernacle of the congregation, that remaineth among them in the midst of their uncleanness. [17] And there shall be no man in the tabernacle of the congregation when he goeth in to make an atonement in the holy place, until he come out, and have made an atonement for himself, and for

his household, and for all the congregation of Israel. [33] And he shall make an atonement for the holy sanctuary, and he shall make an atonement for the tabernacle of the congregation, and for the altar, and he shall make an atonement for the priests, and for all the people of the congregation. [34] And this shall be an everlasting statute unto you, to make an atonement for the children of Israel for all their sins once a year. And he did as the LORD commanded Moses.

Figure 7.11 The Shekinah Glory Enters the Tabernacle (1908), illustration from the The Bible and Its Story Taught by One Thousand Picture Lessons.

Hebrews (CEV) 9: [7] But only the high priest enters the second tent once a year. He never does this without blood, which he offers for himself and for the sins the people committed in ignorance. [8] With this, the Holy Spirit is showing that the way into the holy place hadn't been revealed yet while the first tent was standing. [9] This is a symbol for the present time. It shows that the gifts and sacrifices that are being offered can't perfect the conscience of the one who is serving. [10] These are superficial regulations that are only about food, drink, and various ritual ways to wash with water. They are regulations that have been imposed until the time of the new order. [11] **But Christ has appeared as the high priest of the good things that have happened. He passed through the greater and more perfect meeting tent, which isn't made by human hands (that is, it's not a part of this world). [12] He entered the holy of holies once for all by his own blood, not by the blood of goats or calves, securing our deliverance for all time. [13] If the blood of goats and bulls and the sprinkled ashes of cows made spiritually contaminated people holy and clean, [14] how much more will the blood of Jesus wash our consciences clean from dead works in order to serve the living God? He offered himself to God through the eternal Spirit as a sacrifice without any flaw.**

Christ's Death and the New Covenant

[15] This is why he's the mediator of a new covenant (which is a will): so that those who are called might receive the promise of the eternal inheritance on the basis of his death. His death occurred to set them free from the offenses committed under the first covenant. [16] When there is a will, you need to confirm the death of the one who made the will. [17] This is because a will takes effect only after a death, since it's not in force while the one who made the will is alive. **[18] So not even the first covenant was put into effect without blood.**

Hebrews 10 (CEB)

Christ's Once-for-All Sacrifice

The Law is a shadow of the good things that are coming, not the real things themselves. It never can perfect the ones who are trying to draw near to God through the same sacrifices that are offered continually every year. [2] Otherwise, wouldn't they have stopped being offered? If the people carrying out their religious duties had been completely cleansed once, no one would have been aware of sin anymore. [3] Instead, these sacrifices are a reminder of sin every year, [4] because it's impossible for the blood of bulls and goats to take away sins. [5] Therefore, when he comes into the world he says,

> *You didn't want a sacrifice or an offering,*
> *but you prepared a body for me;*
> [6] *you weren't pleased with entirely burned offerings or a sin offering.*
> [7] *So then I said,*
> *"Look, I've come to do your will, God.*
> *This has been written about me in the scroll."*

[8] He says above, *You didn't want* and *you weren't pleased with a sacrifice or an offering* or *with entirely burned offerings or a purification offering,* which are offered because the Law requires them. **[9] Then he said,** *Look, I've come to do your will.* **He puts an end to the first to establish the second.** [10] **We have been made holy by God's will through the offering of Jesus Christ's body once for all.** [11] Every priest stands every day serving and offering the same sacrifices over and over, sacrifices that can never take away sins. [12] But when this priest offered one sacrifice for sins for all time, he sat down at the right side of God. [13] Since then, he's waiting until his enemies are made into a footstool for his feet, [14] because he perfected the people who are being made holy with one offering for all time. [15] The Holy Spirit affirms this when saying,

> [16] *This is the covenant that I will make with them.*
> *After these days, says the Lord,*
> *I will place my laws in their hearts*
> *and write them on their minds.*
> [17] *And I won't remember their sins*

[18] When there is forgiveness for these things, there is no longer an offering for sin.
> *and their lawless behavior anymore.*

(CEV) Second summary of the message

Hebrews (KJV) 10: [19] Having therefore, brethren, boldness to enter into the holiest by the blood of Jesus, [20] *By a new and living way, which he hath consecrated for us, through the veil, that is to say, his flesh;* [21] *And having an high priest over the house of God;* [22] *Let us draw near with a true heart in full assurance of faith, having our hearts sprinkled from an evil conscience, and our bodies washed with pure water.* [23] *Let us hold fast the profession of our faith without wavering; (for he is faithful that promised;)* [24] *And let us consider one another to provoke unto love and to good works:* [25] *Not forsaking the assembling of ourselves together, as the manner of some is; but exhorting one another: and so much the more, as ye see the day approaching.*

Judgment for intentional sin

Hebrews (CEB) 10: [26] If we make the decision to sin after we receive the knowledge of the truth, there isn't a sacrifice for sins left any longer. [27] There's only a scary expectation of judgment and of a burning fire that's going to devour God's opponents. [28] When someone rejected the Law from Moses, they were put to death without mercy on the basis of the testimony of two or three witnesses. [29] How much worse punishment do you think is deserved by the person who walks all over God's Son, who acts as if the blood of the covenant that made us holy is just ordinary blood, and who insults the Spirit of grace? [30] We know the one who said, *Judgment is mine; I will pay people back.* And he also said, *The Lord will judge his people.* [31] It's scary to fall into the hands of the living God!

Confidence and Faith to Endure

[32] **But remember the earlier days, after you saw the light.** You stood your ground while you were suffering from an enormous amount of pressure. [33] Sometimes you were exposed to insults and abuse in public. Other times you became partners with those who were treated that way. [34] You even showed sympathy toward people in prison and accepted the confiscation of your possessions with joy, since you knew that you had better and lasting possessions. [35] So don't throw away your confidence—it brings a great reward. **[36] You need to endure so that you can receive the promises after you do God's will.**

[37] *In a little while longer,*
the one who is coming will come and won't delay;
[38] *but my righteous one will live by faith,*
and my whole being won't be pleased with anyone who shrinks back.

[39] But we aren't the sort of people who timidly draw back and end up being destroyed. We're the sort of people who have faith so that our whole beings are preserved.

2 Corinthians (KJV) 6: [16] And what agreement hath the temple of God with idols? **for ye are the temple of the living God; as God hath said, I will dwell in them, and walk in them; and I will be their God, and they shall be my people.**

Everything in the New Testament points to us becoming *one* with the Trinity. It also completes the definition of the Kingdom of God which also means becoming *one* with God. God made our bodies His Temple so He could dwell within us and our spirit man was made the priest over that temple. The priest is totally responsible for maintaining and keeping their temple from being defiled.

1 Corinthians (KJV) 3: [17] **If any man defile the temple of God, him shall God destroy; for the temple of God is holy, which temple ye are.**

Mark (KJV) 7: [20] **And he said, That which cometh out of the man, that defileth the man.** [21] **For from within, out of the heart of men, proceed evil thoughts, adulteries, fornications, murders,** [22] **Thefts, covetousness, wickedness, deceit, lasciviousness, an evil eye, blasphemy, pride, foolishness:** [23] **All these evil things come from within, and defile the man.**

1 Timothy (KJV)1: [9] **Knowing this, that the law is not made for a righteous man, but for the lawless and disobedient, for the ungodly and for sinners, for unholy and profane, for murderers of fathers and murderers of mothers, for manslayers,** [10] **For whoremongers, for them that defile themselves with mankind, for menstealers, for liars, for perjured persons, and if there be any other thing that is contrary to sound doctrine;** [11] **According to the glorious gospel of the blessed God, which was committed to my trust.**

The Blood of Jesus was left in the earth because it is the only suitable sacrifice that is able to cleanse us from our sins and purge even our conscience and our minds from dead works, so that we can stand blameless before the Lord. Jesus' flesh is the "veil," and God dwells in Him which makes Jesus the Holy of Holies. Again we are the temple of God, and he wants to be *one* with us. The foolish virgins did not understand the purpose and function of the office of the priest.

Hebrews 10 explains why Jesus was called the Lamb that was slain before the foundation of the earth was laid. The blood of bulls and goats could never take away the sins of the people. It only covered them. It explains why His Blood was left in the earth so we can have access to the presence of God and a personal relationship with the Trinity.

John (KJV) 6: [45] It is written in the prophets, And they shall be all taught of God. Every man therefore that hath heard, and hath learned of the Father, cometh unto me. [46] Not that any man hath seen the Father, save he which is of God, he hath seen the Father. [47] Verily, verily, I say unto you, He that believeth on me hath everlasting life. [48] I am that bread of life. [49] Your fathers did eat manna in the wilderness, and are dead. [50] This is the bread which cometh down from heaven, that a man may eat thereof, and not die. [51] **I am the living bread which came down from heaven: if any man eat of this bread, he shall live forever: and the bread that I will give is my flesh, which I will give for the life of the world.** [52] The Jews therefore strove among themselves, saying, How can this man give us his flesh to eat? [53] Then Jesus said unto them, *Verily, verily, I say unto you, Except ye eat the flesh of the Son of man, and drink his blood, ye have no life in you.* [54] *Whoso eateth my flesh, and drinketh my blood, hath eternal life; and I will raise him up at the last day.* [55] *For my flesh is meat indeed, and my blood is drink indeed.* [56] *He that eateth my flesh, and drinketh my blood, dwelleth in me, and I in him.* [57] *As the living Father hath sent me, and I live by the Father: so he that eateth me, even he shall live by me.* [58] *This is that bread which came down from heaven: not as your fathers* *did eat manna, and are dead: he that eateth of this bread shall live forever.* [59] *These things said he in the synagogue, as he taught in Capernaum.*

The Record in Heaven and the Witness in the Earth agree together as *one*.

1 John (KJV) 5: Whosoever believeth that Jesus is the Christ is born of God: and every one that loveth him that begat loveth him also that is begotten of him. [2] By this we know that we love the children of God, when we love God, and keep his commandments. [3] *For this is the love of God, that we keep his commandments: and his commandments are not grievous.* [4] *For whatsoever is born of God overcometh the world: and this is the victory that overcometh the world, even our faith.* [5] *Who is he that overcometh the world, but he that believeth that Jesus is the Son of God?* [6] *This is he that came by water and blood, even Jesus Christ; not by water only, but by water and blood.* And it is the Spirit that beareth witness, because the Spirit is truth. [7] For there are three that bear record in heaven, the Father, the Word, and the Holy Ghost: and these three are one. [8] And there are three that bear witness in earth, the Spirit, and the water, and the blood: and these three agree in one. [9] If we receive the witness of men, the witness of God is greater: for this is the witness of God which he hath testified of his Son. [10] He that believeth on the Son of God hath the witness in himself: he that believeth not God hath made him a liar; because he believeth not the record that God gave of his Son. [11] And this is the record, that God hath given to us eternal life, and this life is in his Son. [12] **He that hath the Son hath life; and he that hath not the Son of God hath not life.** [13] These things have I written unto you that believe on the name of the Son of God; that ye may know that ye have eternal life, and that ye may believe on the name of the Son of God. [14] And this is the confidence that we have in him, that, if we ask any thing according to his will, he heareth us: [15] And if we know that he hear us, whatsoever we ask, we know that we have the petitions that we desired of him. [16] If any man see his brother sin a sin which is not unto death, he shall ask, and he shall give him life for them that sin not unto death. There is a sin unto death: I do not say that he shall pray for it. [17] All unrighteousness is sin: and there is a sin not unto death. [18] We know that whosoever is born of God sinneth not; but he that is begotten of God keepeth himself, and that wicked one toucheth him not. [19] And we know that we are of God, and the whole world lieth in wickedness. [20] **And we know that the Son of God is come, and hath given us an understanding, that we may know him that is true, and we are in him that is true, even in his Son Jesus Christ. This is the true God, and eternal life.** [21] **Little children, keep yourselves from idols. Amen.**

2 Corinthians (KJV) 13: [14] The grace of the Lord Jesus Christ, and the love of God, and **the Communion of the Holy Ghost, be with you all. Amen.**

1 Corinthians (KJV) 11: [33] For I have received of the Lord that which also I delivered unto you, that the Lord Jesus the same night in which he was betrayed took bread: [24] And when he had given thanks, he brake it, and said, Take, eat: this is my body, which is broken for you: this do in remembrance of me. [25] After the same manner also he took the cup, when he had supped, saying, this cup is the new testament in my blood: this do ye, as oft as ye drink it, in remembrance of me. [26] *For as often as ye eat this bread, and drink this cup, ye do shew the Lord's death till he come.* [27] Wherefore whosoever shall eat this bread, and drink this cup of the Lord, unworthily, shall be guilty of the body and blood of the Lord. [8] But let a man examine himself, and so let him eat of that bread, and drink of that cup. [29] For he that eateth and drinketh unworthily, eateth and drinketh damnation to himself, **not discerning the Lord's body. [30] For this cause many are weak and sickly among you, and many sleep. [31] For if we would judge ourselves, we should not be judged. [32] But when we are judged, we are chastened of the Lord, that we should not be condemned with the world.**

When we are taking communion, God asked us to judge ourselves. We are to examine our walk with God and His Word and be honest with ourselves before God, because He already knows our weaknesses and sins. We acknowledge those weaknesses and become sincere and repent and receive our forgiveness. And ask God to help us to overcome our weakness, by the power of the Holy Spirit so that we do not bring damnation on ourselves and be condemned with the world.

Discerning the Lord's Body means we understand fully the reason we are already healed is that Jesus became our scapegoat. He did it so that our sins, sickness, poverty, ungodliness, and diseases could be done away with, because He took our place on the cross. He bore our sins in His own body. He was buried and spent three days in hell so we could become separated from our sins. By the same token we are now able to become *one* with the Trinity. (Review Chapter 3 The Fruit of Faith: Part I).

Just as Jesus totally identified with the Body of Christ when they were being persecuted by Saul mercilessly to death, to the point where He said to Saul, "Why are you persecuting Me?" Jesus felt their suffering, and pain because He discerned their body. Jesus was talking to Saul as if he literally was beating Him. The truth of the matter is Saul was beating Jesus. It is the same when Jesus said to the goats that were on the left, "depart from Me" because they did not feed the hungry, clothe the naked, visit the sick and those in prison and did not take the stranger in. It was because they did not care about anyone but themselves.

Jesus identifies with His Body the same way He wants us to identify with His Body which is healed from the beating He took for us. He is healed from the thirty-nine stripes and being crucified on the cross. He died and was raised from the dead by the power of the Holy Spirit. His body was healed from all of the torture, the stripes, and the sicknesses and diseases that had ravaged His body, all by the power of the Holy Spirit. And as He is so are we in this World, we are healed now!

1 Peter (KJV) 2: [20] For what glory is it, if, when ye be buffeted for your faults, ye shall take it patiently? but if, when ye do well, and suffer for it, ye take it patiently, this is acceptable with God. [21] For even hereunto were ye called: because Christ also suffered for us, leaving us an example, that ye should follow his steps: [22] *Who did no sin, neither was guile found in his mouth:* [23] *Who, when he was reviled, reviled not again; when he suffered, he threatened not; but committed himself to him that judgeth righteously:* [24] *Who his own self bare our sins in his own body on the tree, that we, being dead to sins, should live unto righteousness: by whose stripes ye were healed.*

Mark (KJV) 11: [24] *Therefore I say unto you, What things soever ye desire, when ye pray, believe that ye receive them, and ye shall have them.* [25] And when ye stand praying, forgive, if ye have ought against any: that your Father also which is in heaven may forgive you your trespasses. [26] But if ye do not forgive, neither will your Father which is in heaven forgive your trespasses.

Communion (drinking Christ's Blood and eating His flesh) is very important because if we do not, Jesus said we do not have eternal life. He also says when we partake of His flesh and drink His Blood, He lives and dwells in us and He will raise us up on the Last Day.

Important points to remember (or in remembrance of) about communion:

1. 1 Corinthians (KJV) 11:26 For as often as ye eat this bread, and drink this cup, ye do shew the Lord's death till he come.

2. 1 Corinthians (KJV) 11:32 For if we would judge ourselves, we should not be judged. But when we are judged, we are chastened of the Lord, that we should not be condemned with the world.

3. John (KJV) 6:54 Whoso eateth my flesh, and drinketh my blood, hath eternal life; and I will raise him up at the last day.

4. John (KJV) 6:56 He that eateth my flesh, and drinketh my blood, dwelleth in me, and I in him.

5. Health and healing will be restored to us when we discern the Body of Christ. [1 Corinthians (KJV) 11: 30]

6. The Blood of Jesus cleanses us from all sins because it was the innocent Blood of a man who never sinned, which was enough to erase all sin for everyone who would accept it. Hebrews (KJV) 10:19

7. It gives us access to go through the veil into the presence of the Holy Spirit so that we could be led and guided daily into our divine purpose and destiny. [Hebrews 10:20]

8. Satan spilled the innocent Blood of Jesus and its power will overcome and destroy the kingdom of darkness when we use it.

The Priest were commanded to keep themselves holy.

Exodus (KJV) 29: [35] And thus shalt thou do unto Aaron, and to his sons, according to all things which I have commanded thee: seven days shalt thou consecrate them. [36] And thou shalt offer every day a bullock for a sin offering for atonement: and thou shalt cleanse the altar, when thou hast made an atonement for it, and thou shalt anoint it, to sanctify it. [37] Seven days thou shalt make an atonement for the altar, and sanctify it; and it shall be an altar most holy: whatsoever toucheth the altar shall be holy. [38] Now this is that which thou shalt offer upon the altar; two lambs of the first year day by day continually. [39] **The one lamb thou shalt offer in the morning; and the other lamb thou shalt offer at even:** [40] And with the one lamb a tenth deal of flour mingled with the fourth part of an hin of beaten oil; and the fourth part of an hin of wine for a drink offering.

Years ago my wife and I were led to take communion daily, and lately we have been led to do it twice a day. Jesus said as often as we take communion we are to remember that these and many, many other blessing are the reasons that He left His Blood in the earth. We did not totally understand at first, but now we do. Communion is just part of our fulfilling Jesus' prayer to the Father for us to become *one*. God's thoughts and ways are higher than our ways, and He wants us to come up to His level. To do that we have to grow in our knowledge and understanding of how the Kingdom of Heaven functions. This is why He sent the Holy Spirit to lead us into all truths.

Romans (KJV) 5: [18] Therefore as by the offence of one judgment came upon all men to condemnation; even so by the righteousness of one the free gift came upon all men unto justification of life. [19] For as by one man's disobedience many were made sinners, so by the obedience of one shall many be made righteous.

God Orchestrates the Unity of the Kingdom

Ephesians (AMP) 2 And you [He made alive], when you were dead (slain) by [your] trespasses and sins ²In which at one time you walked [habitually]. You were following the course *and* fashion of this world [were under the sway of the tendency of this present age], following the prince of the power of the air. [You were obedient to and under the control of] the [demon] spirit that still constantly works in the sons of disobedience [the careless, the rebellious, and the unbelieving, who go against the purposes of God].³Among these we as well as you once lived *and* conducted ourselves in the passions of our flesh [our behavior governed by our corrupt and sensual nature], obeying the impulses of the flesh and the thoughts of the mind [our cravings dictated by our senses and our dark imaginings]. We were then by nature children of [God's] wrath *and* heirs of [His] indignation, like the rest of mankind. **⁴But God—so rich is He in His mercy! Because of *and* in order to satisfy the great *and* wonderful *and* intense love with which He loved us, ⁵Even when we were dead (slain) by [our own] shortcomings *and* trespasses, He made us alive together in fellowship *and* in union with Christ; [He gave us the very life of Christ Himself, the same new life with which He quickened Him, for] it is by grace (His favor and mercy which you did not deserve) that you are saved (delivered from judgment and made partakers of Christ's salvation). ⁶And He raised us up together with Him and made us sit down together [giving us joint seating with Him] in the heavenly sphere [by virtue of our being] in Christ Jesus (the Messiah, the Anointed One). ⁷He did this that He might clearly demonstrate through the ages to come the immeasurable (limitless, surpassing) riches of His free grace (His unmerited favor) in [His] kindness *and* goodness of heart toward us in Christ Jesus.⁸For it is by free grace (God's unmerited favor) that you are saved (delivered from judgment *and* made partakers of Christ's salvation) through [your] faith. And this [salvation] is not of yourselves [of your own doing, it came not through your own striving], but it is the gift of God; ⁹Not because of works [not the fulfillment of the Law's demands], lest any man should boast. [It is not the result of what anyone can possibly do, so no one can pride himself in it or take glory to himself.] ¹⁰For we are God's [own] handiwork (His workmanship), recreated in Christ Jesus, [born anew] that we may do those good works which God predestined (planned beforehand) for us [taking paths which He prepared ahead of time], that we should walk in them [living the good life which He prearranged and made ready for us to live]. ¹¹Therefore, remember that at one time you were Gentiles (heathens) in the flesh, called Uncircumcision by those who called themselves Circumcision, [itself a mere mark] in the flesh made by human hands.¹² [Remember] that you were at that time separated (living apart) from Christ [excluded from all part in Him], utterly estranged *and* outlawed from the rights of Israel as a nation, and strangers with no share in the sacred compacts of the [Messianic] promise [with no knowledge of or right in God's agreements, His covenants]. And you had no hope (no promise); you were in the world without God. ¹³But now in Christ Jesus, you who once were [so] far away, through (by, in) the blood of Christ have been brought near. ¹⁴For He is [Himself] our peace (our bond of unity and harmony). He has made us both [Jew and Gentile] one [body], and has broken down (destroyed, abolished) the hostile dividing wall between us, ¹⁵By abolishing in His [own crucified] flesh the enmity [caused by] the Law with its decrees and ordinances [which He annulled]; that He from the two might create in Himself one new man [one new quality of humanity out of the two], so making peace. ¹⁶And [He designed] to reconcile to God both [Jew and Gentile, united] in a single body by means of His cross, thereby killing the**

mutual enmity *and* bringing the feud to an end. [17] And He came and preached the glad tidings of peace to you who were afar off and [peace] to those who were near. [18] For it is through Him that we both [whether far off or near] now have an introduction (access) by one [Holy] Spirit to the Father [so that we are able to approach Him]. [19] Therefore you are no longer outsiders (exiles, migrants, and aliens, excluded from the rights of citizens), but you now share citizenship with the saints (God's own people, consecrated and set apart for Himself); and you belong to God's [own] household. [20] You are built upon the foundation of the apostles and prophets with Christ Jesus Himself the chief Cornerstone. [21] In Him the whole structure is joined (bound, welded) together harmoniously, and it continues to rise (grow, increase) into a holy temple in the Lord [a sanctuary dedicated, consecrated, and sacred to the presence of the Lord]. [22] In Him [and in fellowship with one another] you yourselves also are being built up [into this structure] with the rest, to form a fixed abode (dwelling place) of God in (by, through) the Spirit.

Ephesians (AMP) 3: For this reason [because I preached that you are thus built up together], I, Paul, [am] the prisoner of Jesus the Christ for the sake *and* on behalf of you Gentiles— [2] Assuming that you have heard of the stewardship of God's grace (His unmerited favor) that was entrusted to me [to dispense to you] for your benefit, [3] **[And] that the mystery (secret) was made known to me *and* I was allowed to comprehend it by direct revelation, as I already briefly wrote you. [4] When you read this you can understand my insight into the mystery of Christ. [5] [This mystery] was never disclosed to human beings in past generations as it has now been revealed to His holy apostles (consecrated messengers) and prophets by the [Holy] Spirit. [6] [It is this:] that the Gentiles are now to be fellow heirs [with the Jews], members of the same body and joint partakers [sharing] in the same divine promise in Christ through [their acceptance of] the glad tidings (the Gospel). [7] Of this [Gospel] I was made a minister according to the gift of God's free grace (undeserved favor) which was bestowed on me by the exercise (the working in all its effectiveness) of His power. To me, though I am the very least of all the saints (God's consecrated people), this grace (favor, privilege) was granted *and* graciously entrusted: to proclaim to the Gentiles the unending (boundless, fathomless, incalculable, and exhaustless) riches of Christ [wealth which no human being could have searched out], [9] Also to enlighten all men *and* make plain to them what is the plan [regarding the Gentiles and providing for the salvation of all men] of the mystery kept hidden through the ages *and* concealed until now in [the mind of] God Who created all things *by Christ Jesus*. [10] [The purpose is] that through the church the complicated, many-sided wisdom of God in all its infinite variety *and* innumerable aspects might now be made known to the angelic rulers and authorities (principalities and powers) in the heavenly sphere. [11] This is in accordance with the terms of the eternal *and* timeless purpose which He has realized *and* carried into effect in [the person of] Christ Jesus our Lord, [12] In Whom, because of our faith in Him, we dare to have the boldness (courage and confidence) of free access (an unreserved approach to God with freedom and without fear). [13] So I ask you not to lose heart [not to faint or become despondent through fear] at what I am suffering in your behalf. [Rather glory in it] for it is an honor to you. [14] For this reason [seeing the greatness of this plan by which you are built together in Christ], I bow my knees before the Father *of our Lord Jesus Christ*, [15] For Whom every family in heaven and on earth is named [that Father from Whom all fatherhood takes its title and derives its name]. [16] May He grant you out of the rich treasury of His glory to be strengthened *and* reinforced with mighty** power in the inner man by the [Holy] Spirit [Himself indwelling your innermost being and personality]. [17] May Christ through your faith [actually] dwell (settle down, abide, make His permanent home) in your hearts! May you be rooted deep in love *and* founded securely on love, [18] That you may have the power *and* be strong to apprehend *and* grasp with all the saints [God's devoted people, the experience of that love] what is the breadth and length and height and depth [of it]; [19] [That you may really come] to know [practically, through experience for yourselves] the love of Christ, which far surpasses mere knowledge [without experience]; that you may be filled [through all your being] unto all the fullness of God [may have the richest measure of the divine Presence, and become a body wholly filled and flooded with God Himself]! [20] Now to Him Who, by (in consequence of) the [action of His] power that is at work within us, is able to [carry out His purpose and] do superabundantly, far over *and* above all that we [dare] ask or think [infinitely beyond our highest prayers, desires, thoughts, hopes, or dreams] [21] To Him be glory in the church and in Christ Jesus throughout all generations forever and ever. Amen (so be it).

Ephesians (AMP) 4:I therefore, the prisoner for the Lord, appeal to and beg you to walk (lead a life) worthy of the [divine] calling to which you have been called [with behavior that is a credit to the summons to God's service, [2] Living as becomes you] with complete lowliness of mind (humility) and meekness (unselfishness, gentleness, mildness), with patience, bearing with one another *and* making allowances because you love one another. 3Be eager *and* strive earnestly to guard *and* keep the harmony *and* oneness of [and produced by] the Spirit in the binding power of peace. [4] [There is] one body and one Spirit—just as there is also one hope [that belongs] to the calling you received—[5] [There is] one Lord, one faith, one baptism, [6] One God and Father of [us] all, Who is above all [Sovereign over all], pervading all and [living] in [us] all. [7] Yet grace (God's unmerited favor) was given to each of us individually [not indiscriminately, but in different ways] in proportion to the measure of Christ's [rich and bounteous] gift. [8] Therefore it is said, When He ascended on high, He led captivity captive [He led a train of vanquished foes] and He bestowed gifts on men. [9] [But He ascended?] Now what can this, He ascended, mean but that He had previously descended from [the heights of] heaven into [the depths], the lower parts of the earth? [10] He Who descended is the [very] same as He Who also has ascended high above all the heavens, that He [His presence] might fill all things (the whole universe, from the lowest to the highest). [11] And His gifts were [varied; He Himself appointed and gave men to us] some to be apostles (special messengers), some prophets (inspired preachers and expounders), some evangelists (preachers of the Gospel, traveling missionaries), some pastors (shepherds of His flock) and teachers. [12] His intention was the perfecting *and* the full equipping of the saints (His consecrated people), [that they should do] the work of ministering toward building up Christ's body (the church), [13] [That it might develop] until we all attain oneness in the faith and in the comprehension of the [full and accurate] knowledge of the Son of God, that [we might arrive] at really mature manhood (the completeness of personality which is nothing less than the standard height of Christ's own perfection), the measure of the stature of the fullness of the Christ *and* the completeness found in Him. [14] So then, we may no longer be children, tossed [like ships] to and fro between chance gusts of teaching *and* wavering with every changing wind of doctrine, [the prey of] the cunning *and* cleverness of unscrupulous men, [gamblers engaged] in every shifting form of trickery in inventing errors to mislead. [15] Rather, let our lives lovingly express truth [in all things, speaking truly, dealing truly, living truly]. Enfolded in love, let us grow up in every way *and* in all things into Him Who is the Head, [even] Christ (the Messiah, the Anointed One). [16] For because of Him the whole body (the church, in all its various parts), closely joined and firmly knit together by the joints *and* ligaments with which it is supplied, when each part [with power adapted to its need] is working properly [in all its functions], grows to full maturity, building itself up in love. [17] So this I say and solemnly testify in [the name of] the Lord [as in His presence], that you must no longer live as the heathen (the Gentiles) do in their perverseness [in the folly, vanity, and emptiness of their souls and the futility] of their minds. [18] Their moral understanding is darkened *and* their reasoning is beclouded. [They are] alienated (estranged, self-banished) from the life of God [with no share in it; this is] because of the ignorance (the want of knowledge and perception, the willful blindness) that is deep-seated in them, due to their hardness of heart [to the insensitiveness of their moral nature]. [19] In their spiritual apathy they have become callous *and* past feeling *and* reckless and have abandoned themselves [a prey] to unbridled sensuality, eager *and* greedy to indulge in every form of impurity [that their depraved desires may suggest and demand]. [20] But you did not so learn Christ! [21] Assuming that you have really heard Him *and* been taught by Him, as [all] Truth is in Jesus [embodied and personified in Him], [22] Strip yourselves of your former nature [put off and discard your old unrenewed self] which characterized your previous manner of life and becomes corrupt through lusts *and* desires that spring from delusion; [23] And be constantly renewed in the spirit of your mind [having a fresh mental and spiritual attitude], [24] And put on the new nature (the regenerate self) created in God's image, [Godlike] in true righteousness and holiness. [25] Therefore, rejecting all falsity *and* being done now with it, let everyone express the truth with his neighbor, for we are all parts of one body *and* members one of another. [26] When angry, do not sin; do not ever let your wrath (your exasperation, your fury or indignation) last until the sun goes down. [27] Leave no [such] room *or* foothold for the devil [give no opportunity to him]. [28] Let the thief steal no more, but rather let him be industrious, making an honest living with his own hands, so that he may be able to give to those in need. [29] Let no foul *or* polluting language, *nor* evil word *nor* unwholesome *or* worthless talk [ever] come out of your mouth, but only such [speech] as is good *and* beneficial to the spiritual progress of others, as is fitting to the need *and* the occasion, that it may be a blessing *and* give grace (God's favor) to those who hear it. [30] And do not grieve the Holy Spirit of God [do not offend or vex or sadden Him], by Whom you were sealed (marked, branded as God's own, secured) for the day of redemption (of final deliverance through Christ from evil and the consequences of sin). [31] Let all bitterness and indignation *and* wrath (passion, rage, bad temper) and resentment (anger, animosity) and quarreling (brawling, clamor, contention) and slander (evil-speaking, abusive or blasphemous language) be banished from you, with all malice (spite, ill will, or baseness of any kind). [32] And become useful *and* helpful *and* kind to one another, tenderhearted (compassionate, understanding, loving-hearted), forgiving one another [readily and freely], as God in Christ forgave you.

1 Corinthians (KJV) 6: [15] Know ye not that your bodies are the members of Christ? shall I then take the members of Christ, and make them the members of an harlot? God forbid. [16] What? know ye not that he which is joined to an harlot is one body? for two, saith he, shall be one flesh. [17] But he that is joined unto the Lord is one spirit.

Matthew (KJV) 19 : [4] And he answered and said unto them, Have ye not read, that he which made them at the beginning made them male and female, [5] And said, For this cause shall a man leave father and mother, and shall cleave to his wife: and they twain shall be one flesh? [6] Wherefore they are no more twain, but one flesh. What therefore God hath joined together, let not man put asunder.

CHAPTER 8

Why the Foolish Virgins Had No Oil in Their Lamps

The seed of the Word of God performs one more function as it matures: it becomes light.

Acts (KJV) 26: [10] Which thing I also did in Jerusalem: and many of the saints did I shut up in prison, having received authority from the chief priests; and when they were put to death, I gave my voice against them. [11] And I punished them oft in every synagogue, and compelled them to blaspheme; and being exceedingly mad against them, I persecuted them even unto strange cities. [12] Whereupon as I went to Damascus with authority and commission from the chief priests,[13] At midday, O king, I saw in the way a light from heaven, above the brightness of the sun, shining round about me and them which journeyed with me.

Figure 8.1 Trial of the Apostle Paul (1875) by Nikolas Kornilievich Bodarevsky.

Acts (KJV) 26: [14] And when we were all fallen to the earth, I heard a voice speaking unto me, and saying in the Hebrew tongue, Saul, Saul, why persecutest thou me? it is hard for thee to kick against the pricks.[15] And I said, Who art thou, Lord? And he said, I am Jesus whom thou persecutest. [16] But rise, and stand upon thy feet: for I have appeared unto thee for this purpose, to make thee a minister and a witness both of these things which thou hast seen, and of those things in the which I will appear unto thee; [17] Delivering thee from the people, and from the Gentiles, unto whom now I send thee, **[18] To open their eyes, and to turn them from darkness to light, and from the power of Satan unto God, that they may receive forgiveness of sins, and inheritance among them which are sanctified by faith that is in me. [19] Whereupon, O king Agrippa, I was not disobedient unto the heavenly vision:**

Figure 8.2 The Light of the World (1853–1854) by William Holman Hunt.

The picture above is a symbol of Jesus knocking on the door of our heart and His desire is that we fill our heart with the Word of God. Because whatever is in your heart in abundance will eventually determine whether we are children of the light or we are children of the darkness.

2 Corinthians (KJV) 4: [6] For God, who commanded the light to shine out of darkness, hath shined in our hearts, to give the light of the knowledge of the glory of God in the face of Jesus Christ.[7] But we have this treasure in earthen vessels, that the excellency of the power may be of God, and not of us.

The foolish virgins fail to come to the knowledge of the truth.

Matthew (KJV) 4: [15] The land of Zabulon, and the land of Nephthalim, by the way of the sea, beyond Jordan, Galilee of the Gentiles; **[16] The people which sat in darkness saw great light; and to them which sat in the region and shadow of death light is sprung up. [17] From that time Jesus began to preach, and to say, Repent: for the kingdom of heaven is at hand.**

John (KJV) 1: 1 In the beginning was the Word, and the Word was with God, and the Word was God. [2] The same was in the beginning with God. [3] All things were made by him; and without him was not anything made that was made. **[4] In him was life; and the life was the light of men. [5] And the light shineth in darkness; and the darkness comprehended it not. [6] There was a man sent from God, whose name was John. [7] The same came for a witness, to bear witness of the Light, that all men through him might believe. [8] He was not that Light, but was sent to bear witness of that Light. [9] That was the true Light, which lighteth every man that cometh into the world. [10] He was in the world, and the world was made by him, and the world knew him not. [11] He came unto his own, and his own received him not. [12] But as many as received him, to them gave he power to become the sons of God, even to them that believe on his name: [13] Which were born, not of blood, nor of the will of the flesh, nor of the will of man, but of God. [14] And the Word was made flesh, and dwelt among us, (and we beheld his glory, the glory as of the only begotten of the Father,) full of grace and truth. [15] John bare witness of him, and cried, saying, This was he of whom I spake, He that cometh after me is preferred before me: for he was before me. [16] And of his fulness have all we received, and grace for grace.**

John (KJV) 8 Jesus went unto the mount of Olives. [2] And early in the morning he came again into the temple, and all the people came unto him; and he sat down, and taught them. [3] And the scribes and Pharisees brought unto him a woman taken in adultery; and when they had set her in the midst, [4] They say unto him, Master, this woman was taken in adultery, in the very act. [5] Now Moses in the law commanded us, that such should be stoned: but what sayest thou?

Figure 8.3 The Woman Taken in Adultery (1644) by Rembrandt.

[6] This they said, tempting him, that they might have to accuse him. But Jesus stooped down, and with his finger wrote on the ground, as though he heard them not.

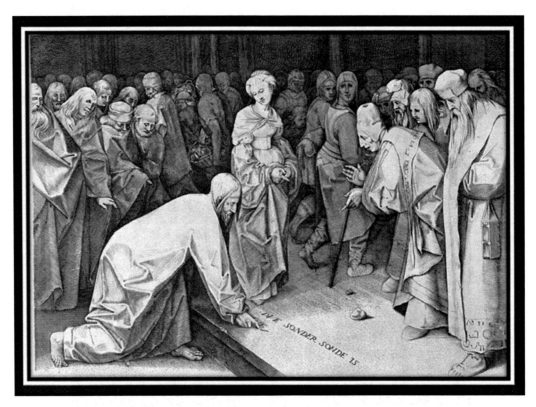

Figure 8.4 Christ begins writing on the Ground (post 1564–1565) by Paul Perret.

[7] So when they continued asking him, he lifted up himself, and said unto them, He that is without sin among you, let him first cast a stone at her. [8] And again he stooped down, and wrote on the ground. [9] And they which heard it, being convicted by their own conscience, went out one by one, beginning at the eldest, even unto the last: and Jesus was left alone, and the woman standing in the midst. [10] When Jesus had lifted up himself, and saw none but the woman, he said unto her, Woman, where are those thine accusers? hath no man condemned thee? [11] She said, No man, Lord. And Jesus said unto her, Neither do I condemn thee: go, and sin no more. **[12] Then spake Jesus again unto them, saying, I am the light of the world: he that followeth me shall not walk in darkness, but shall have the light of life.**

The Foolish Virgins Were Walking in Darkness

Figure 8.5 Christ as the True Light (1526) by Hans Holbein the Younger.

Psalm 119: [130] The entrance of thy words giveth light; it giveth understanding unto the simple.

John (KJV)8 [13] The Pharisees therefore said unto him, Thou bearest record of thyself; thy record is not true. [14] Jesus answered and said unto them, Though I bear record of myself, yet my record is true: for I know whence I came, and whither I go; but ye cannot tell whence I come, and whither I go. [15] Ye judge after the flesh; I judge no man. [16] And yet if I judge, my judgment is true: for I am not alone, but I and the Father that sent me. [17] It is also written in your law, that the testimony of two men is true. [18] I am one that bear witness of myself, and the Father that sent me beareth witness of me. [19] Then said they unto him, Where is thy Father? Jesus answered, Ye neither know me, nor my Father: if ye had known me, ye should have known my Father also. [20] These words spake Jesus in the treasury, as he taught in the Temple: and no man laid hands on him; for his hour was not yet come. [21] Then said Jesus again unto them, I go my way, and ye shall seek me, and shall die in your sins: whither I go, ye cannot come. [22] Then said the Jews, Will he kill himself? because he saith, Whither I go, ye cannot come. [23] And he said unto them, Ye are from beneath; I am from above: ye are of this world; I am not of this world. [24] I said therefore unto you, that ye shall die in your sins: for if ye believe not that I am he, ye shall die in your sins. [25] Then said they unto him, Who art thou? And Jesus saith unto them, Even the same that I said unto you from the beginning. [26] I have many things to say and to judge of you: but he that sent me is true; and I speak to the world those things which I have heard of him. [27] They understood not that he spake to them of the Father. [28] Then said Jesus unto them, When ye have lifted up the Son of man, then shall ye know that I am he, and that I do nothing of myself; but as my Father hath taught me, I speak these things. [29] And he that sent me is with me: the Father hath not left me alone; for I do always those things that please him. [30] As he spake these words, many believed on him. [31] Then said Jesus to those Jews which believed on him, If ye continue in my word, then are ye my disciples indeed; [32] And ye shall know the truth, and the truth shall make you free. [33] They answered him, We be Abraham's seed, and were never in bondage to any man: how sayest thou, Ye shall be made free? [34] Jesus answered them, Verily, verily, I say unto you, Whosoever committeth sin is the servant of sin. [35] And the servant abideth not in the house for ever: but the Son abideth ever. [36] If the Son therefore shall make you free, ye shall be free indeed.

John (AMP) 3: [11] I assure you, most solemnly I tell you, We speak only of what we know [we know absolutely what we are talking about]; we have actually seen what we are testifying to [we were eyewitnesses of it]. And still you do not receive our testimony [you reject and refuse our evidence—that of Myself and of all those who are born of the Spirit]. [12] If I have told you of things that happen right here on the earth and yet none of you believes Me, how can you believe (trust Me, adhere to Me, rely on Me) if I tell you of heavenly things? [13] And yet no one has ever gone up to heaven, but there is One Who has come down from heaven—the Son of Man [Himself], Who is (dwells, has His home) in heaven. [14] And as Moses lifted up the serpent in the wilderness,,

Figure 8.6 Moses Pointing to a Great Snake (1897) illustration in Bible Pictures and What They Teach Us: Containing 400 Illustrations from the Old and New Testaments. Moses is standing up and pointing to a great snake, or serpent. The serpent is made of brass. It is fastened to the top of a pole. Moses is telling the people to look at it. For some live serpents have come among the people and are biting them. The serpents are poisonous. They are biting both men and women, and whoever is bitten by them dies. And God has told Moses to make this serpent out of brass, and to set it up on a pole, and whoever looks at it, God says, shall get well. And now Moses is pointing to the serpent of brass, and telling the people who are bitten to look at it, so that they may get well. It was because the people had done wrong and disobeyed God, that the poisonous serpents came into the camp and bit them.

even so must the Son of man be lifted up: [15] That whosoever believeth in him should not perish, but have eternal life. [16] For God so loved the world, that he gave his only begotten Son, that whosoever believeth in him should not perish, but have everlasting life. [17] For God sent not his Son into the world to condemn the world; but that the world through him might be saved. [18] **He that believeth on him is not condemned: but he that believeth not is condemned already, because he hath not believed in the name of the only begotten Son of God. [19] And this is the condemnation, that light is come into the world, and men loved darkness rather than light, because their deeds were evil. [20] For every one that doeth evil hateth the light, neither cometh to the light,**

lest his deeds should be reproved. [21] But he that doeth truth cometh to the light, that his deeds may be made manifest, that they are wrought in God.

1 John (KJV): [1]That which was from the beginning, which we have heard, which we have seen with our eyes, which we have looked upon, and our hands have handled, of the Word of life; [2](For the life was manifested, and we have seen it, and bear witness, and shew unto you that eternal life, which was with the Father, and was manifested unto us;) [3]That which we have seen and heard declare we unto you, that ye also may have fellowship with us: and truly our fellowship is with the Father, and with his Son Jesus Christ. [4]And these things write we unto you, that your joy may be full. **[5]This then is the message which we have heard of him, and declare unto you, that God is light, and in him is no darkness at all. [6]If we say that we have fellowship with him, and walk in darkness, we lie, and do not the truth: [7]But if we walk in the light, as he is in the light, we have fellowship one with another, and the blood of Jesus Christ his Son cleanseth us from all sin. [8]If we say that we have no sin, we deceive ourselves, and the truth is not in us. [9]If we confess our sins, he is faithful and just to forgive us our sins, and to cleanse us from all unrighteousness. [10]If we say that we have not sinned, we make him a liar, and his word is not in us.**

1 John (KJV) 2: [1]My little children, these things write I unto you, that ye sin not. And if any man sin, we have an advocate with the Father, Jesus Christ the righteous: [2]And he is the propitiation for our sins: and not for ours only, but also for the sins of the whole world. **[3]And hereby we do know that we know him, if we keep his commandments. [4]He that saith, I know him, and keepeth not his commandments, is a liar, and the truth is not in him. [5]But whoso keepeth his word, in him verily is the love of God perfected: hereby know we that we are in him. [6]He that saith he abideth in him ought himself also so to walk, even as he walked. [7]Brethren, I write no new commandment unto you, but an old commandment which ye had from the beginning. The old commandment is the word which ye have heard from the beginning. [8]Again, a new commandment I write unto you, which thing is true in him and in you: because the darkness is past, and the true light now shineth. [9]He that saith he is in the light, and hateth his brother, is in darkness even until now. [10]He that loveth his brother abideth in the light, and there is none occasion of stumbling in him. [11]But he that hateth his brother is in darkness, and walketh in darkness, and knoweth not whither he goeth, because that darkness hath blinded his eyes. [12]I write unto you, little children, because your sins are forgiven you for his name's sake. [13]I write unto you, fathers, because ye have known him that is from the beginning. I write unto you, young men, because ye have overcome the wicked one. I write unto you, little children, because ye have known the Father.** [14]I have written unto you, fathers, because ye have known him that is from the beginning. I have written unto you, young men, because ye are strong, and the word of God abideth in you, and ye have overcome the wicked one. [15]Love not the world, neither the things that are in the world. If any man love the world, the love of the Father is not in him. [16]For all that is in the world, the lust of the flesh, and the lust of the eyes, and the pride of life, is not of the Father, but is of the world. [17]And the world passeth away, and the lust thereof: but he that doeth the will of God abideth forever. [18]Little children, it is the last time: and as ye have heard that antichrist shall come, even now are there many antichrists; whereby we know that it is the last time. [19]They went out from us, but they were not of us; for if they had been of us, they would no doubt have continued with us: but they went out, that they might be made manifest that they were not all of us. [20]But ye have an unction from the Holy One, and ye know all things. [21]I have not written unto you because ye know not the truth, but because ye know it, and that no lie is of the truth. ²²Who is a liar but he that denieth that Jesus is the Christ? He is antichrist, that denieth the Father and the Son. ²³Whosoever denieth the Son, the same hath not the Father: he that acknowledgeth the Son hath the Father also. ²⁴Let that therefore abide in you, which ye have heard from the beginning. If that which ye have heard from the beginning shall remain in you, ye also shall continue in the Son, and in the Father. ²⁵And this is the promise that he hath promised us, even eternal life. ²⁶These things have I written unto you concerning them that seduce you. **²⁷But the anointing which ye have received of him abideth in you, and ye need not that any man teach you: but as the same anointing teacheth you of all things, and is truth, and is no lie, and even as it hath taught you, ye shall abide in him. ²⁸And now, little children, abide in him; that, when he shall appear, we may have confidence, and not be ashamed before him at his coming. ²⁹If ye know that he is righteous, ye know that every one that doeth righteousness is born of him.**

John (KJV) 3: ¹Behold, what manner of love the Father hath bestowed upon us, that we should be called the sons of God: therefore the world knoweth us not, because it knew him not. *²Beloved, now are we the sons of God, and it doth not yet appear what we shall be: but we know that, when he shall appear, we shall be like him; for we shall see him as he is. ³And every man that hath this hope in him purifieth himself, even as he is pure.* ⁴Whosoever committeth sin transgresseth also the law: for sin is the transgression of the law. ⁵And ye know that he was manifested to take away our sins; and in him is no sin. ⁶Whosoever abideth in him sinneth not: whosoever sinneth hath not seen him, neither known him. ⁷Little children, let no man deceive you: he that doeth righteousness is righteous, even as he is righteous. ⁸He that committeth sin is of the devil; for the devil sinneth from the beginning. For this purpose the Son of God was manifested, that he might destroy the works of the devil. ⁹Whosoever is born of God doth not commit sin; for his seed remaineth in him: and he cannot sin, because he is born of God. ¹⁰In this the children of God are manifest, and the children of the devil: whosoever doeth not righteousness is not of God, neither he that loveth not his brother. ¹¹For this is the message that ye heard from the beginning, that we should love one another. *¹²Not as Cain, who was of that wicked one, and slew his brother. And wherefore slew he him? Because his own works were evil, and his brother's righteous. ¹³Marvel not, my brethren, if the world hate you. ¹⁴We know that we have passed from death unto life, because we love the brethren. He that loveth not his brother abideth in death. ¹⁵Whosoever hateth his brother is a murderer: and ye know that no murderer hath eternal life abiding in him. ¹⁶Hereby perceive we the love of God, because he laid down his life for us: and we ought to lay down our lives for the brethren. ¹⁷But whoso hath this world's good, and seeth his brother have need, and shutteth up his bowels of compassion from him, how dwelleth the love of God in him? ¹⁸My little children, let us not love in word, neither in tongue; but in deed and in truth. ¹⁹And hereby we know that we are of the truth, and shall assure our hearts before him. ²⁰For if our heart condemn us, God is greater than our heart, and knoweth all things. ²¹Beloved, if our heart condemn us not, then have we confidence toward God. ²²And whatsoever we ask, we receive of him, because we keep his commandments, and do those things that are pleasing in his sight. ²³And this is his commandment, That we should believe on the name of his Son Jesus Christ, and love one another, as he gave us commandment. ²⁴And he that keepeth his commandments dwelleth in him, and he in him. And hereby we know that he abideth in us, by the Spirit which he hath given us.*

Matthew (KJV) 6: [20] But lay up for yourselves treasures in heaven, where neither moth nor rust doth corrupt, and where thieves do not break through nor steal: [21] For where your treasure is, there will your heart be also. **[22] The light of the body is the eye: if therefore thine eye be single, thy whole body shall be full of light. [23] But if thine eye be evil, thy whole body shall be full of darkness. If therefore the light that is in thee be darkness, how great is that darkness!**

Notice the function of the Fruit of the Spirit.

Colossians (KJV) 1: [5] For the hope which is laid up for you in heaven, whereof ye heard before in the word of the truth of the gospel; [6] Which is come unto you, as it is in all the world; and bringeth forth fruit, as it doth also in you, since the day ye heard of it, and knew the grace of God in truth: [7] As ye also learned of Epaphras our dear fellowservant, who is for you a faithful minister of Christ; [8] Who also declared unto us your love in the Spirit. [9] For this cause we also, since the day we heard it, do not cease to pray for you, and to desire that ye might be filled with the knowledge of his will in all wisdom and spiritual understanding; [10] That ye might walk worthy of the Lord unto all pleasing, being fruitful in every good work, and increasing in the knowledge of God; [11] Strengthened with all might, according to his glorious power, unto all patience and longsuffering with joyfulness; **[12] Giving thanks unto the Father, which hath made us meet to be partakers of the inheritance of the saints in light: [13] Who hath delivered us from the power of darkness, and hath translated us into the kingdom of his dear Son: [14] In whom we have redemption through his blood, even the forgiveness of sins: [15] Who is the image of the invisible God, the firstborn of every creature: [16] For by him were all things created, that are in heaven, and that are in earth, visible and invisible, whether they be thrones, or dominions, or principleities, or powers: all things were created by him, and for him: [17] And he is before all things, and by him all things consist. [18] And he is the head of the body, the church: who is the beginning, the firstborn from the dead; that in all things he might have the preeminence. [19] For it pleased the Father that in him should all fulness dwell; [20] And, having made peace through the blood of his cross, by him to reconcile all things unto himself; by him, I say, whether they be things in earth, or things in heaven.**

Ephesians (AMP) 5: Therefore be imitators of God [copy Him and follow His example], as well-beloved children [imitate their father]. [2] And walk in love, [esteeming and delighting in one another] as Christ loved us and gave Himself up for us, a slain offering and sacrifice to God [for you, so that it became] a sweet fragrance. [3] But immorality (sexual vice) and all impurity [of lustful, rich, wasteful living] or greediness must not even be named among you, as is fitting and proper among saints (God's consecrated people). [4] Let there be no filthiness (obscenity, indecency) nor foolish and sinful (silly and corrupt) talk, nor coarse jesting, which are not fitting or becoming; but instead voice your thankfulness [to God]. [5] For be sure of this: that no person practicing sexual vice or impurity in thought or in life, or one who is covetous [who has lustful desire for the property of others and is greedy for gain]—for he [in effect] is an idolater—has any inheritance in the kingdom of Christ and of God. [6] Let no one delude and deceive you with empty excuses and groundless arguments [for these sins], for through these things the wrath of God comes upon the sons of rebellion and disobedience. [7] So do not associate or be sharers with them. **[8] For once you were darkness, but now you are light in the Lord; walk as children of Light [lead the lives of those native-born to the Light]. [9] For the fruit (the effect, the product) of the Light or the**

Spirit [consists] in every form of kindly goodness, uprightness of heart, and trueness of life. [10] And try to learn [in your experience] what is pleasing to the Lord [let your lives be constant proofs of what is most acceptable to Him]. [11] Take no part in and have no fellowship with the fruitless deeds and enterprises of darkness, but instead [let your lives be so in contrast as to] expose and reprove and convict them. [12] For it is a shame even to speak of or mention the things that [such people] practice in secret. [13] But when anything is exposed and reproved by the light, it is made visible and clear; and where everything is visible and clear there is light. [14] Therefore He says, Awake, O sleeper, and arise from the dead, and Christ shall shine (make day dawn) upon you and give you light. [15] Look carefully then how you walk! Live purposefully and worthily and accurately, not as the unwise and witless, but as wise (sensible, intelligent people), [16] Making the very most of the time [buying up each opportunity], because the days are evil. [17] Therefore do not be vague and thoughtless and foolish, but understanding and firmly grasping what the will of the Lord is. [18] And do not get drunk with wine, for that is debauchery; but ever be filled and stimulated with the [Holy] Spirit. [19] Speak out to one another in psalms and hymns and spiritual songs, offering praise with voices [and instruments] and making melody with all your heart to the Lord, [20] At all times and for everything giving thanks in the name of our Lord Jesus Christ to God the Father. [21] Be subject to one another out of reverence for Christ (the Messiah, the Anointed One).

1 Thessalonians (AMP) 5: But as to the suitable times and the precise seasons and dates, brethren, you have no necessity for anything being written to you. [2] For you yourselves know perfectly well that the day of the [return of the] Lord will come [as unexpectedly and suddenly] as a thief in the night. [3] When people are saying, All is well and secure, and, There is peace and safety, then in a moment unforeseen destruction (ruin and death) will come upon them as suddenly as labor pains come upon a woman with child; and they shall by no means escape, for there will be no escape. [4] But you are not in [given up to the power of] darkness, brethren, for that day to overtake you by surprise like a thief. [5] For you are all sons of light and sons of the day; we do not belong either to the night or to darkness. [6] Accordingly then, let us not sleep, as the rest do, but let us keep wide awake (alert, watchful, cautious, and on our guard) and let us be sober (calm, collected, and circumspect). [7] For those who sleep, sleep at night, and those who are drunk, get drunk at night. [8] But we belong to the day; therefore, let us be sober and put on the breastplate (corslet) of faith and love and for a helmet the hope of salvation. [9] For God has not appointed us to [incur His] wrath [He did not select us to condemn us], but [that we might] obtain [His] salvation through our Lord Jesus Christ (the Messiah) [10] Who died for us so that whether we are still alive or are dead [at Christ's appearing], we might live together with Him and share His life. [11] Therefore encourage (admonish, exhort) one another and edify (strengthen and build up) one another, just as you are doing. [12] Now also we beseech you, brethren, get to know those who labor among you [recognize them for what they are, acknowledge and appreciate and respect them all]—your leaders who are over you in the Lord and those who warn and kindly reprove and exhort you. [13] And hold them in very high and most affectionate esteem in [intelligent and sympathetic] appreciation of their work. Be at peace among yourselves. [14] And we earnestly beseech you, brethren, admonish (warn and seriously advise) those who are out of line [the loafers, the disorderly, and the unruly]; encourage the timid and fainthearted, help and give your support to the weak souls, [and] be very patient with everybody [always keeping your temper]. [15] See that none of you repays another with evil for evil, but always aim to show kindness and seek to do good to one another and to everybody. [16] Be happy [in your faith] and rejoice and be glad-hearted continually (always); [17] Be unceasing in prayer [praying perseveringly]; [18] Thank [God] in everything [no matter what the circumstances may be, be thankful and give thanks], for this is the will of God for you [who are] in Christ Jesus [the Revealer and Mediator of that will]. [19] Do not quench (suppress or subdue) the [Holy] Spirit; [20] Do not spurn the gifts and utterances of the prophets [do not depreciate prophetic revelations nor despise inspired instruction or exhortation or warning].[21] But test and prove all things [until you can recognize] what is good; [to that] hold fast. [22] Abstain from evil [shrink from it and keep aloof from it] in whatever form or whatever kind it may be.[23] And may the God of peace Himself sanctify you through and through [separate you from profane things, make you pure and wholly consecrated to God]; and may your spirit and soul and body be preserved sound and complete [and found] blameless at the coming of our Lord Jesus Christ (the Messiah). [24] Faithful is He Who is calling you [to Himself] and utterly trustworthy, and He will also do it [fulfill His call by hallowing and keeping you]. [25] Brethren, pray for us.[26] Greet all the brethren with a sacred kiss. [27] I solemnly charge you [in the name of] the Lord to have this letter read before all the brethren.[28] The grace (the unmerited favor and blessings) of our Lord Jesus Christ (the Messiah) be with you all. Amen, (so be it).

1 John (KJV) 4:[1]Beloved, believe not every spirit, but try the spirits whether they are of God: because many false prophets are gone out into the world. [2]Hereby know ye the Spirit of God: Every spirit that confesseth that Jesus Christ is come in the flesh is of God: [3]And every spirit that confesseth not that Jesus Christ is come in the flesh is not of God: and this is that spirit of antichrist, whereof ye have heard that it should come; and even now already is it in the world. [4]Ye are of God, little children, and have overcome them: because greater is he that is in you, than he that is in the world. [5]They are of the world: therefore speak they of the world, and the world heareth them. [6]We are of God: he that knoweth God heareth us; he that is not of God heareth not us. Hereby know we the spirit of truth, and the spirit of error. [7]Beloved, let us love one another: for love is of God; and every one that loveth is born of God, and knoweth God. [8]He that loveth not knoweth not God; for God is love. [9]In this was manifested the love of God toward us, because that God sent his only begotten Son into the world, that we might live through him. [10]Herein is love, not that we loved God, but that he loved us, and sent his Son to be the propitiation for our sins. [11]Beloved, if God so loved us, we ought also to love one another. [12]No man hath seen God at any time. If we love one another, God dwelleth in us, and his love is perfected in us. [13]Hereby know we that we dwell in him, and he in us, because he hath given us of his Spirit. [14]And we have seen and do testify that the Father sent the Son to be the Saviour of the world. [15]Whosoever shall confess that Jesus is the Son of God, God dwelleth in him, and he in God. [16]And we have known and believed the love that God hath to us. God is love; and he that dwelleth in love dwelleth in God, and God in him. [17]Herein is our love made perfect, that we may have boldness in the day of judgment: because as he is, so are we in this world. [18]There is no fear in love; but perfect love casteth out fear: because fear hath torment. He that feareth is not made perfect in love. [19]We love him, because he first loved us. [20]If a man say, I love God, and hateth his brother, he is a liar: for he that loveth not his brother whom he hath seen, how can he love God whom he hath not seen? [21]And this commandment have we from him, That he who loveth God love his brother also.

1 John (KJV) 5: ¹Whosoever believeth that Jesus is the Christ is born of God: and everyone that loveth him that begat loveth him also that is begotten of him. ²By this we know that we love the children of God, when we love God, and keep his commandments. ³For this is the love of God, that we keep his commandments: and his commandments are not grievous. ⁴For whatsoever is born of God overcometh the world: and this is the victory that overcometh the world, even our faith. ⁵Who is he that overcometh the world, but he that believeth that Jesus is the Son of God? ⁶This is he that came by water and blood, even Jesus Christ; not by water only, but by water and blood. And it is the Spirit that beareth witness, because the Spirit is truth. ⁷For there are three that bear record in heaven, the Father, the Word, and the Holy Ghost: and these three are one. ⁸And there are three that bear witness in earth, the Spirit, and the water, and the blood: and these three agree in one. ⁹If we receive the witness of men, the witness of God is greater: for this is the witness of God which he hath testified of his Son. ¹⁰He that believeth on the Son of God hath the witness in himself: he that believeth not God hath made him a liar; because he believeth not the record that God gave of his Son. ¹¹And this is the record, that God hath given to us eternal life, and this life is in his Son. ¹²He that hath the Son hath life; and he that hath not the Son of God hath not life. ¹³These things have I written unto you that believe on the name of the Son of God; that ye may know that ye have eternal life, and that ye may believe on the name of the Son of God. ¹⁴And this is the confidence that we have in him, that, if we ask any thing according to his will, he heareth us: ¹⁵And if we know that he hear us, whatsoever we ask, we know that we have the petitions that we desired of him. ¹⁶If any man see his brother sin a sin which is not unto death, he shall ask, and he shall give him life for them that sin not unto death. There is a sin unto death: I do not say that he shall pray for it. ¹⁷All unrighteousness is sin: and there is a sin not unto death. ¹⁸We know that whosoever is born of God sinneth not; but he that is begotten of God keepeth himself, and that wicked one toucheth him not. ¹⁹And we know that we are of God, and the whole world lieth in wickedness. ²⁰And we know that the Son of God is come, and hath given us an understanding, that we may know him that is true, and we are in him that is true, even in his Son Jesus Christ. This is the true God, and eternal life. ²¹Little children, keep yourselves from idols. Amen.

2 Corinthians (KJV) 4: Therefore seeing we have this ministry, as we have received mercy, we faint not; ²But have renounced the hidden things of dishonesty, not walking in craftiness, nor handling the word of God deceitfully; but by manifestation of the truth commending ourselves to every man's conscience in the sight of God.³But if our gospel be hid, it is hid to them that are lost: ⁴In whom the god of this world hath blinded the minds of them which believe not, lest the light of the glorious gospel of Christ, who is the image of God, should shine unto them. ⁵For we preach not ourselves, but Christ Jesus the Lord; and ourselves your servants for Jesus' sake.⁶For God, who commanded the light to shine out of darkness, hath shined in our hearts, to give the light of the knowledge of the glory of God in the face of Jesus Christ.⁷But we have this treasure in earthen vessels, that the excellency of the power may be of God, and not of us. *We are troubled on every side, yet not distressed; we are perplexed, but not in despair; ⁹ Persecuted, but not forsaken; cast down, but not destroyed; ¹⁰ Always bearing about in the body the dying of the Lord Jesus, that the life also of Jesus might be made manifest in our body. ¹¹ For we which live are always delivered unto death for Jesus' sake, that the life also of Jesus might be made manifest in our mortal flesh. ¹² So then death worketh in us, but life in you.¹³ We having the same spirit of faith, according as it is written, I believed, and therefore have I spoken; we also believe, and therefore speak; ¹⁴ Knowing that he which raised up the Lord Jesus shall raise up us also by Jesus, and shall present us with* *you.[15] For all things are for your sakes, that the abundant grace might through the thanksgiving of many redound to the glory of God.[16] For which cause we faint not; but though our outward man perish, yet the inward man is renewed day by day. [17] For our light affliction, which is but for a moment, worketh for us a far more exceeding and eternal weight of glory; [18] While we look not at the things which are seen, but at the things which are not seen: for the things which are seen are temporal; but the things which are not seen are eternal.*

Romans (KJV) 13: [5] Wherefore ye must needs be subject, not only for wrath, but also for conscience sake.[6] For for this cause pay ye tribute also: for they are God's ministers, attending continually upon this very thing. [7] Render therefore to all their dues: tribute to whom tribute is due; custom to whom custom; fear to whom fear; honour to whom honour. [8] Owe no man anything, but to love one another: for he that loveth another hath fulfilled the law. [9] For this, Thou shalt not commit adultery, Thou shalt not kill, Thou shalt not steal, Thou shalt not bear false witness, Thou shalt not covet; and if there be any other commandment, it is briefly comprehended in this saying, namely, Thou shalt love thy neighbour as thyself.[10] Love worketh no ill to his neighbour: therefore love is the fulfilling of the law. **[11] And that, knowing the time, that now it is high time to awake out of sleep: for now is our salvation nearer than when we believed. [12] The night is far spent, the day is at hand: let us therefore cast off the works of darkness, and let us put on the armour of light. [13] Let us walk honestly, as in the day; not in rioting and drunkenness, not in chambering and wantonness, not in strife and envying. [14] But put ye on the Lord Jesus Christ, and make not provision for the flesh, to fulfil the lusts thereof.**

***2 John (KJV) 1 :** [1] The elder unto the elect lady and her children, whom I love in the truth; and not I only, but also all they that have known the truth; [2] For the truth's sake, which dwelleth in us, and shall be with us forever. [3] Grace be with you, mercy, and peace, from God the Father, and from the Lord Jesus Christ, the Son of the Father, in truth and love. [4] I rejoiced greatly that I found of thy children walking in truth, as we have received a commandment from the Father. [5] And now I beseech thee, lady, not as though I wrote a new commandment unto thee, but that which we had from the beginning, that we love one another. [6] And this is love, that we walk after his commandments. This is the commandment, That, as ye have heard from the beginning, ye should walk in it. [7] For many deceivers are entered into the world, who confess not that Jesus Christ is come in the flesh. This is a deceiver and an antichrist. [8] Look to yourselves, that we lose not those things which we have wrought, but that we receive a full reward. 9 Whosoever transgresseth, and abideth not in the doctrine of Christ, hath not God. He that abideth in the doctrine of Christ, he hath both the Father and the Son. [10] If there come any unto you, and bring not this doctrine, receive him not into your house, neither bid him God speed: [11] For he that biddeth him God speed is partaker of his evil deeds. [12] Having many things to write unto you, I would not write with paper and ink: but I trust to come unto you, and speak face to face, that our joy may be full. [13] The children of thy elect sister greet thee. Amen.*

3 John (KJV) 1: [1] The elder unto the well beloved Gaius, whom I love in the truth. [2] Beloved, I wish above all things that thou mayest prosper and be in health, even as thy soul prospereth. [3] For I rejoiced greatly, when the brethren came and testified of the truth that is in thee, even as thou walkest in the truth. [4] I have no greater joy than to hear that my children walk in truth. [5] Beloved, thou doest faithfully whatsoever thou doest to the brethren, and to strangers; [6] Which have borne witness of thy charity before the church: whom if thou bring forward on their journey after a godly sort, thou shalt do well: ⁷Because that for his name's sake they went forth, taking nothing of the Gentiles. ⁸We therefore ought to receive such, that we might be fellowhelpers to the truth. ⁹I wrote unto the church: but Diotrephes, who loveth to have the preeminence among them, receiveth us not. ¹⁰Wherefore, if I come, I will remember his deeds which he doeth, prating against us with malicious words: and not content therewith, neither doth he himself receive the brethren, and forbiddeth them that would, and casteth them out of the church. ¹¹Beloved, follow not that which is evil, but that which is good. He that doeth good is of God: but he that doeth evil hath not seen God. ¹²Demetrius hath good report of all men, and of the truth itself: yea, and we also bear record; and ye know that our record is true. ¹³I had many things to write, but I will not with ink and pen write unto thee: ¹⁴But I trust I shall shortly see thee, and we shall speak face to face. Peace be to thee. Our friends salute thee. Greet the friends by name.

Jude (KJV): *¹ Jude, the servant of Jesus Christ, and brother of James, to them that are sanctified by God the Father, and preserved in Jesus Christ, and called: ² Mercy unto you, and peace, and love, be multiplied. ³ Beloved, when I gave all diligence to write unto you of the common salvation, it was needful for me to write unto you, and exhort you that ye should earnestly contend for the faith which was once delivered unto the saints. ⁴ For there are certain men crept in unawares, who were before of old ordained to this condemnation, ungodly men, turning the grace of our God into lasciviousness, and denying the only Lord God, and our Lord Jesus Christ. ⁵ I will therefore put you in remembrance, though ye once knew this, how that the Lord, having saved the people out of the land of Egypt, afterward destroyed them that believed not.*

Figure 8.7 Joshua and the Israelites crossing the Jordan (Gustave Doré)

Jude (KJV): *⁶ And the angels which kept not their first estate, but left their own habitation, he hath reserved in everlasting chains under darkness unto the judgment of the great day.*

Figure 8.8 Fallen Angels Chained in Hell (c. 1841) by John Martin.

Jude (KJV): [7] Even as Sodom and Gomorrha, and the cities about them in like manner, giving themselves over to fornication, and going after strange flesh, are set forth for an example, suffering the vengeance of eternal fire.

Figure 8.9 Lot Fleeing with his Daughters from Sodom (c. 1498) by Albrecht Dürer.

Jude (KJV): [8] Likewise also these filthy dreamers defile the flesh, despise dominion, and speak evil of dignities.[9] Yet Michael the archangel, when contending with the devil he disputed about the body of Moses, durst not bring against him a railing accusation, but said The Lord rebuke thee.

Figure 8.10 The Death of Moses illustration from the 1890 Holman Bible, Date 1890

Jude (KJV): *¹⁰ But these speak evil of those things which they know not: but what they know naturally, as brute beasts, in those things they corrupt themselves. ¹¹ Woe unto them! for they have gone in the way of Cain, and ran greedily after the error of Balaam for reward, and perished in the gainsaying of Core. ¹² These are spots in your feasts of charity, when they feast with you, feeding themselves without fear:*

The second part of verse 12 is about the foolish virgins who did not understand the importance and purpose of all Christians is to obtain eternal life by being a giver of life. We have to extend charity (the love of God) to the people that are hurting around us because God has given us the power to obtain wealth. God wants to make us so wealthy that we will be able to give into every good and perfect work. Whether it is distributing food, clothing, or visiting and ministering to the sick and those in prison, we are actually ministering to Jesus. Obtaining eternal life is not just about giving financially to the needy; there are also people who are poor in their spirit. They lack the understanding of the Kingdom of God principles, and it has to be taught to them, which is what Jesus commissioned all of us to do.

Matthew (KJV) 24: ¹⁰ And then shall many be offended, and shall betray one another, and shall hate one another. ¹¹ And many false prophets shall rise, and shall deceive many. ¹² And because iniquity shall abound, the love of many shall wax cold.*[13] But he that shall endure unto the end, the same shall be saved.[14] And this gospel of the kingdom shall be preached in all the world for a witness unto all nations; and then shall the end come.*

Jude 1:12 . . . *clouds they are without water, carried about of winds; trees whose fruit withereth, without fruit, twice dead, plucked up by the roots;*

The foolish virgins are like the fig tree that Jesus cursed. The only difference is, in the verse above, these Christians were bearing fruit at one time but now they stopped bearing fruit. They became distracted. They were ministering to the needs of others, but they stopped so suddenly that their fruit withered while it was still on the vine, (Jesus True Vine). These branches were cut off because they quit providing life to others. Twice dead means when Jesus realized these branches just stopped producing, He cut them off. They died spiritually again. We are to be found faithful to the end! This is why some people lose their jobs. They started out working hard, going beyond what was expected, but later became lazy.

This is a perfect example of the virgins; they were all saved at one time, but as Jesus puts it, half lost their way. They were drawn back into their old ways. When He saved them the first time they were brought to life spiritually and they were doing the will of the Lord. But because they stop producing, He cut them off and they died spiritually again because they separated themselves from the life of Christ by not giving life. Hence the phase "twice dead." The foolish virgins lost their salvation because they became lukewarm. They stopped doing the things that were required to obtain and maintain eternal life.

Jude (KJV): *[13] Raging waves of the sea, foaming out their own shame; wandering stars, to whom is reserved the blackness of darkness forever.[14] And Enoch also, the seventh from Adam, prophesied of these, saying, Behold, the Lord cometh with ten thousands of his saints,*

Figure 8.11 A Vision of the Last Judgment (1808) by William Blake.

Jude (KJV): *[15] To execute judgment upon all, and to convince all that are ungodly among them of all their ungodly deeds which they have ungodly committed, and of all their hard speeches which ungodly sinners have spoken against him. [16] These are murmurers, complainers, walking after their own lusts; and their mouth speaketh great swelling words, having men's persons in admiration because of advantage. [17] But, beloved, remember ye the words which were spoken before of the apostles of our Lord Jesus Christ; [18] How that they told you there should be mockers in the last time, who should walk after their own ungodly lusts. [19] These be they who separate themselves, sensual, having not the Spirit.[20] But ye, beloved, building up yourselves on your most holy faith, praying in the Holy Ghost, [21] Keep yourselves in the love of God, looking for the mercy of our Lord Jesus Christ unto eternal life.[22] And of some have compassion, making a difference: [23] And others save with fear, pulling them out of the fire; hating even the garment spotted by the flesh. [24] Now unto him that is able to keep you from falling, and to present you faultless before the presence of his glory with exceeding joy, [25] To the only wise God our Saviour, be glory and majesty, dominion and power, both now and ever. Amen.*

Figure 8.12 Detail on stained glass depicting Jesus: I am the light of the world, <u>Bantry</u>, Ireland. Photographer Andreas Borchert

Isaiah 58 summarizes why the foolish virgins were walking in darkness and why they were not bearing fruit.

Isaiah (AMP) 58: Cry aloud, spare not. Lift up your voice like a trumpet and declare to My people their transgression and to the house of Jacob their sins! [2] Yet they seek, inquire for, *and* require Me daily and delight [externally] to know My ways, as [if they were in reality] a nation that did righteousness and forsook not the ordinance of their God. They ask of Me righteous judgments, they delight to draw near to God [in visible ways]. [3] Why have we fasted, they say, and You do not see it? Why have we afflicted ourselves, and You take no knowledge [of it]? Behold [O Israel], on the day of your fast [when you should be grieving for your sins], you find profit in your business, and [instead of stopping all work, as the law implies you and your workmen should do] you extort from your hired servants a full amount of labor. [4] [The facts are that] you fast only for strife and debate and to smite with the fist of wickedness. Fasting as you do today will not cause your voice to be heard on high. [5] Is such a fast as yours what I have chosen, a day for a man to humble himself with sorrow in his soul? [Is true fasting merely mechanical?] Is it only to bow down his head like a bulrush and to spread sackcloth and ashes under him [to indicate a condition of heart that he does not have]? Will you call this a fast and an acceptable day to the Lord? [6] [Rather] is not this the fast that I have chosen: to loose the bonds of wickedness, to undo the bands of the yoke, to let the oppressed go free, and that you break every [enslaving] yoke? [7] Is it not to divide your bread with the hungry and bring the homeless poor into your house—when you see the naked, that you cover him, and that you hide not yourself from [the needs of] your own flesh *and* blood?

The purpose of true fasting is to completely search your heart before God, fasting with the sincere desire and mindset of separating ourselves from sin. We do not want anything to stand between us and our relationship with God.

Next, ministering the seven works of mercy, or the giving into the lives of others by giving food, clothing, and shelter did not start with Jesus' ministry. It started in the Old Testament, and it shows us the heart of God from the beginning to the end. God's perfect will is for earth and Heaven to be identical. His love and sensitivity is towards all people. This is what He has been trying to get across to us: to love what He loves and hate and separate ourselves from sin. When we do this, the wisdom and understanding of God will come forth. When we become a giver of life, life starts flowing again through us and our healing will spring forth. Our relationship with God will be re-established, prosperity will be restored, and God will be our protection.

Isaiah (AMP) 58: [8] Then shall your light break forth like the morning, and your healing (your restoration and the power of a new life) shall spring forth speedily; your righteousness (your rightness, your justice, and your right relationship with God) shall go before you [conducting you to peace and prosperity], and the glory of the Lord shall be your rear guard. [9] Then you shall call, and the Lord will answer; you shall cry, and He will say, here I am. If you take away from your midst yokes of oppression [wherever you find them], the finger pointed in scorn [toward the oppressed or the godly], and every form of false, harsh, unjust, *and* wicked speaking, [10] **And if you pour out that with which you sustain your own life for the hungry and satisfy the need of the afflicted, then shall your light rise in darkness, and your obscurity *and* gloom become like the noonday.** [11] And the Lord shall guide you continually and satisfy you in drought *and* in dry places and make strong your bones. And you shall be like a watered garden and like a spring of water whose waters fail not. [12] And your ancient ruins shall be rebuilt; you shall raise up the foundations of [buildings that have laid waste for] many generations; and you shall be called Repairer of the Breach, Restorer of Streets to Dwell In.

God wants to bless us more than He blessed Solomon so that we could raise the quality of life for the poorest of the poor no matter where they are found. We hear and see every day people who live in unbelievable poverty, but God provides us with the resources to help them. However, most of our income is tied up in paying off our own selfish desires, debts, and foolish, wasteful spending habits.

Isaiah (AMP) 58: [13] If you turn away your foot from [traveling unduly on] the Sabbath, from doing your own pleasure on My holy day, and call the Sabbath a [spiritual] delight, the holy day of the Lord honorable, and honor Him *and* it, not going your own way or seeking *or* finding your own

Why The Foolish Virgins Had No Oil In Their Lamps

pleasure or speaking with your own [idle] words, [14] Then will you delight yourself in the Lord, and I will make you to ride on the high places of the earth, and I will feed you with the heritage [promised for you] of Jacob your father; for the mouth of the Lord has spoken it.

Isaiah (AMP) 58 summarizes the Kingdom of Heaven's desire to be manifested in the earth and the part each one of us plays in causing it to come to pass. God is expecting His children to follow after the footsteps of Jesus' ministry. We have to walk in the wisdom, knowledge, and the power of God. The foolish virgins were left because they did not understand their purpose nor did they understand what the will of the Lord was.

The reason the Foolish Virgin had no Oil in their Lamps

They were void of the Word of God and darkness filled their heart because they just did not know what God was expecting of them. God loves us, and He wants to fill our heart and mind with the wisdom and knowledge of the glory of God that He promised to give us in:

2 Corinthians (KJV) 4: Therefore seeing we have this ministry, as we have received mercy, we faint not; [2] But have renounced the hidden things of dishonesty, not walking in craftiness, nor handling the word of God deceitfully; but by manifestation of the truth commending ourselves to every man's conscience in the sight of God. [3] But if our gospel be hid, it is hid to them that are lost: [4] In whom the god of this world hath blinded the minds of them which believe not, lest the light of the glorious gospel of Christ, who is the image of God, should shine unto them. [5] For we preach not ourselves, but Christ Jesus the Lord; and ourselves your servants for Jesus' sake. [6] For God, who commanded the light to shine out of darkness, hath shined in our hearts, to give the light of the knowledge of the glory of God in the face of Jesus Christ. [7] But we have this treasure in earthen vessels, that the excellency of the power may be of God, and not of us. [8] We are troubled on every side, yet not distressed; we are perplexed, but not in despair; [9] Persecuted, but not forsaken; cast down, but not destroyed; [10] **Always bearing about in the body the dying of the Lord Jesus, that the life also of Jesus might be made manifest in our body.**

But we have to "Seek God" on a daily basis for ourselves.
We have to have a hunger and a thirst for righteousness.

Ephesians (KJV) 1: [6] Cease not to give thanks for you, making mention of you in my prayers; [17] That the God of our Lord Jesus Christ, the Father of glory, may give unto you the spirit of wisdom and revelation in the knowledge of him: [18] *The eyes of your understanding being enlightened; that ye may know what is the hope of his calling, and what the riches of the glory of his inheritance in the saints,* [19] *And what is the exceeding greatness of his power to us-ward who believe, according to the working of his mighty power,* [20] *Which he wrought in Christ, when he raised him from the dead, and set him at his own right hand in the heavenly places,* [21] *Far above all principality, and power, and might, and dominion, and every name that is named, not only in this world, but also in that which is to come:* [22] *And hath put all things under his feet, and gave him to be the head over all things to the church,* [23] *Which is his body, the fulness of him that filleth all in all.*

333

CHAPTER 9

The Parable of the Ten Virgins Five Were Wise and Five Were Foolish

Figure 9.1 The Parable of the Ten Virgins by St. Anselm.

The main purpose of this book is to give insight into some very important statements that Jesus made about the Body of Christ, which are very vital to all of us because of the times that we are living in now. I have spent several years trying to understand what "seeking the Kingdom of God" meant because Jesus said that is mandatory for all Christians. I know He asked us to do that because there is a wealth of knowledge that God wants to give us concerning who we are and what He is expecting out of us as His children. I have already discussed many of the principles concerning the Kingdom of God so hopefully understanding this parable will be easier.

One Sunday morning as I was meditating on seed time and harvest time, God spoke into my heart about harvest time. And when He did, everything fell into place. Everything in the Kingdom of Heaven revolves around seed time and harvest time. God brought to my mind the scripture where Jesus said that he will send the angels to bring in "the harvest" at the end of the world. God brought to my mind again what Jesus said about how there would be two people working at the mill. One would be taken, and the other one would be left. Then He said that there would be two working in the field; one would be taken and the other one would be left. Then there was one more, there would be two lying in bed; one would be taken and the other one would be left. Then the next thing that God brought to my mind was the parable of the ten virgins; five were wise and five were foolish. Then it came to me, Jesus is not just throwing out numbers and just talking. He is trying to get a point across to us. At His second coming, half of the Body of Christ will be left; five out of every ten Christians will miss the Lord. We have already covered many of the reasons why, but next I want to cover with the Lord's help specifically why the foolish were "foolish" and what the wise knew that allowed them to enter into the Kingdom of Heaven.

The end of the world is imminent, so do not even try to guess or figure out when it will happen; that is not important. What is imperative is that we are found doing what God has created us to do and that is fulfilling our potential, because that is what Jesus will be looking for at His return. Jesus begins in Matthew 24 to lay out the foundation for which the end will come and even though these words were spoken over 2,000 years ago and I know most people are tired of hearing about it, there are those of us who sense deep in our spirits that something is about to happen. On one side there is so much violence, destruction, and moral decay that we see in the natural realm but on the other side, it seems like salvation and deliverance is just around the corner.

2 Peter 3: *⁸But, beloved, be not ignorant of this one thing, that one day is with the Lord as a thousand years, and a thousand years as one day. ⁹The Lord is not slack concerning his promise, as some men count slackness; but is longsuffering to us-ward, not willing that any should perish, but that all should come to repentance.*

apud: phillip medhurst   PARABLE OF THE LOST SHEEP. MATTHEW 18:12. JAN LUYKEN   excudit: harry kossuth

**Figure 9.2 Etching illustrating Parable of the lost sheep Matthew 18:12
by Jan Luyken in Bowyer Bible.**

If you do not know your purpose, God gives it to you.

In Matthew Chapters 24 and 25 Jesus goes into detail in explaining that when He returns, He will be looking for a bride, and only virgins will qualify. Also to qualify, Jesus will be looking for those who are doing the will of God and those who are walking in faith. For Christians who are searching for their purpose and destiny, Jesus gives us the first stages of reaching our destiny in the parable about the ten talents. In the Kingdom, God judges by seeing if we are willing to follow instructions, which was the first requirement for remaining in the Garden of Eden. The men with the talents all knew what their lord required, but one was lazy and rebellious and he was cast into hell. The two men who were faithful with their talents and doubled them were given more responsibility. And we have to prove that we can be trusted and understand what the will of the Lord is, and be willing to do whatever it takes to fulfill our destiny. Then God will continue to increase our responsibilities in serving Him, and as Jesus told the rich young ruler, if he wanted to lay hold of eternal life, he had to be a giver of life. And if we are not giving into the lives of others in the form of meeting a spiritual or physical need, it is the same as not sowing seed and if you are not sowing, you are not bearing fruit. God multiplies the seed you sow and He will increase the fruit of righteousness in your life. But if you are not giving life, it is because you don't know Him, and neither will He know you, because you are already disconnected from your source of everlasting life which is Jesus Christ. Or the other reason that you are not sowing is that you were not told why it is so important to give life. The man who did not do anything with the one talent, and the person who did not minister to the needy and the foolish virgins, were cast into hell because they were disobedient and rebellious they were all the same.

Matthew (KJV) 24: [1]And Jesus went out, and departed from the temple: and his disciples came to him for to shew him the buildings of the temple. [2]And Jesus said unto them, See ye not all these things? verily I say unto you, There shall not be left here one stone upon another, that shall not be thrown down. [3]And as he sat upon the mount of Olives, the disciples came unto him privately, saying, Tell us, when shall these things be? and what shall be the sign of thy coming, and of the end of the world? [4]And Jesus answered and said unto them, Take heed that no man deceive you. [5]For many shall come in my name, saying, I am Christ; and shall deceive many. [6]And ye shall hear of wars and rumours of wars: **see that ye be not troubled**:

The point here is regardless of all the bad news that you hear, stay focused on your assignment; most of all do not worry. Worry is a sin and it means that you do not have your mind stayed on Jesus. One definition of the Kingdom of God is peace.

If your own circumstances keep you frustrated, that also means that you are out of the presence of God. Because in His presence is fullness of joy, which is another meaning of the Kingdom of God (joy in the Holy Spirit). This is a personal battle for me daily that I have to overcome myself. But understanding the principles helps to establish my heart.

The next point to remember is to maintain our right-standing (righteousness) with God because sin will automatically separate you from God. Righteousness is another definition of the Kingdom of God.

Matthew (KJV) 24:6 for all these things must come to pass, but the end is not yet.[7]For nation shall rise against nation, and kingdom against kingdom: and there shall be famines, and pestilences, and earthquakes, in divers places. [8]All these are the beginning of sorrows. [9]Then shall they deliver you up to be afflicted, and shall kill you: and ye shall be hated of all nations for my name's sake. [10]And then shall many be offended, and shall betray one another, and shall hate one another. [11]And many false prophets shall rise, and shall deceive many. [12]**And because iniquity shall abound, the love of many shall wax cold.**

There are two kinds of love, one is from the world which is selfish and devilish, and the other is the love of God which was given to us by the Holy Spirit. The love of God is powerful, and it will never fail. We must learn how to walk in that love in every situation, good or bad. Faith works by and it is powered by love; it is one of the fruit of the Spirit that has to be cultivated, as we have learned. Without it wisdom will disappear, and faith will stop working,

Figure.9.3 Cellar painting in Peace church in Schweidnitz (an apocalyptic scene)

Matthew (KJV) 24: *¹³But he that shall endure unto the end, the same shall be saved.¹⁴And this gospel of the kingdom shall be preached in all the world for a witness unto all nations; and then shall the end come.*

More and more the teaching of the Gospel of the Kingdom of God is going to spread to all nations. I am not talking about preaching about money, or family, but preaching about understanding how the Kingdom functions and the importance of all Christians reaching their potential. All of the other things family, money, what we are going to put on, and so forth, will be added to us when we get our priorities straight.

Matthew (KJV) 24: *¹⁵When ye therefore shall see the abomination of desolation, spoken of by Daniel the prophet, stand in the holy place, (whoso readeth, let him understand:)*

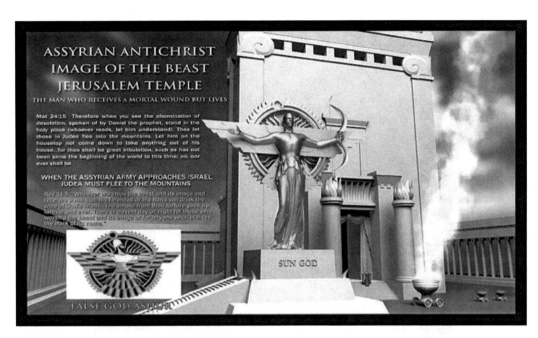

Figure 9.4 Antichrist, beast, image of the beast, 666 by John reve

[16]Then let them which be in Judaea flee into the mountains: [17]Let him which is on the housetop not come down to take anything out of his house: [18]Neither let him which is in the field return back to take his clothes. [19]And woe unto them that are with child, and to them that give suck in those days! [20]But pray ye that your flight be not in the winter, neither on the sabbath day: [21]For then shall be great tribulation, such as was not since the beginning of the world to this time, no, nor ever shall be. [22]And except those days should be shortened, there should no flesh be saved: but for the elect's sake those days shall be shortened. [23]Then if any man shall say unto you, Lo, here is Christ, or there; believe it not. [24]For there shall arise false Christs, and false prophets, and shall shew great signs and wonders; insomuch that, if it were possible, they shall deceive the very elect. [25]Behold, I have told you before. [26]Wherefore if they shall say unto you, Behold, he is in the desert; go not forth: behold, he is in the secret chambers; believe it not. [27]For as the lightning cometh out of the east, and shineth even unto the west; so shall also the coming of the Son of man be. [28]For wheresoever the carcase is, there will the eagles be gathered together. [29]Immediately after the tribulation of those days shall the sun be darkened, and the moon shall not give her light, and the stars shall fall from heaven,

Figure 9.5 The most famous depiction of the 1833 meteor storm actually produced in 1889 for the Adventist book *Bible Readings for the Home Circle*—the engraving is by Adolf Vollmy based upon an original painting by the Swiss artist Karl Jauslin, that is in turn based on a first-person account of the 1833 storm by a minister, Joseph Harvey Waggoner on his way from Florida to New Orleans.

and the powers of the heavens shall be shaken: [30]And then shall appear the sign of the Son of man in heaven: and then shall all the tribes of the earth mourn, and they shall see the Son of man coming in the clouds of heaven with power and great glory.

Figure 9.6 Angels Holding the Four Winds/The Sealing of the 144,000, Revelation 7:1-8 (1530–1532) by Matthias Gerung.

[31]And he shall send his angels with a great sound of a trumpet, and they shall gather together his elect from the four winds, from one end of heaven to the other. [32]Now learn a parable of the fig tree; When his branch is yet tender, and putteth forth leaves, ye know that summer is nigh:

James 5: [7] Be patient therefore, brethren, unto the coming of the Lord. Behold, the husbandman waiteth for the precious fruit of the earth, and hath long patience for it, until he receive the early and latter rain.

As we have learned previously from the parable of the fig tree, God is waiting for His sons and daughters to reach maturity. The wise virgins understood the principles of seed time and harvest time, and they knew why it is so crucial that they must be bearing fruit, or in other words, they knew they must be found doing what God created and pre-ordained for them to do. They had taken the seeds of the fruit of the Spirit and developed them into maturity. The fruit became the keys which allow us access into the Kingdom of Heaven; they also become the armor of God. Also, when the seeds mature, we develop and form the attributes of our Heavenly Father. Our physical body came from the earth, but our spiritual man was born of God and the whole creation is groaning and travailing in pain waiting for the sons and daughters of God to reach maturity or come up to the measure and statue of Jesus Christ.

We have to become *one* with the Father, Son, and Holy Spirit by allowing the seed of the Word of God to take root in our hearts and develop into the fruit of the Spirit, the attributes, and the characteristics of God, which is one way of becoming *one* with God. The characteristics of God are righteousness, love, joy, peace, longsuffering, gentleness, kindness, goodness, faith, meekness, and temperance. And God's desire is for us to bear much fruit.

Matthew 24: [32] says; "learn the Parable of the fig tree," as discussed earlier is a warning not be like the fig tree that Jesus found that had leaves but no fruit. Which means that some Christians were not doing anything for the Lord, or for the Kingdom of God. When the branch becomes tender and puts forth leaves, that means fruit is present. The foolish virgins were the same way they were dressed like the wise virgins but they did not have oil in their lamps. Which meant the foolish virgins did not have the Wisdom of God in their heart. But God made provision for us to receive wisdom, James 5: says, all we have to do is ask in faith.

2 Corinthians 4: [4]But if our gospel be hid, it is hid to them that are lost: [4]In whom the god of this world hath blinded the minds of them which believe not, lest the light of the glorious gospel of Christ, who is the image of God, should shine unto them. [5]For we preach not ourselves, but Christ Jesus the Lord; and ourselves your servants for Jesus' sake. [6]For God, who commanded the light to shine out of darkness, hath shined in our hearts, to give the light of the knowledge of the glory of God in the face of Jesus Christ. [7]But we have this treasure in earthen vessels, that the Excellency of the power may be of God, and not of us. [8]We are troubled on every side, yet not distressed; we are perplexed, but not in despair; [9]Persecuted, but not forsaken; cast down, but not destroyed; [10]Always bearing about in the body the dying of the Lord Jesus, that the life also of Jesus might be made manifest in our body.

We learned previously from John the Baptist that the ax is laid at the root of all the trees; we are the trees John was warning us about. We are the garden of God. Being born again is not going to mean anything if we are not living the life from which Jesus laid the foundation for. It is not going to matter how long we have been in the church or what position we hold; it will all be determined by our obedience or by our rebellion to God's Word.

2 Peter (KJV) 1:1 Simon Peter, a servant and an apostle of Jesus Christ, to them that have obtained like precious faith with us through the righteousness of God and our Saviour Jesus Christ: *[2] Grace and peace be multiplied unto you through the knowledge of God, and of Jesus our Lord,[3] According as his divine power hath given unto us all things that pertain unto life and godliness, through the knowledge of him that hath called us to glory and virtue: [4] Whereby are given unto us exceeding great and precious promises: that by these ye might be partakers of the divine nature, having escaped the corruption that is in the world through lust. [5] And beside this, giving all diligence, add to your faith virtue; and to virtue knowledge; [6] And to knowledge temperance; and to temperance patience; and to patience godliness; [7] And to godliness brotherly kindness; and to brotherly kindness charity.[8] For if these things be in you, and abound, they make you that ye shall neither be barren nor unfruitful in the knowledge of our Lord Jesus Christ.[9] But he that lacketh these things is blind, and cannot see afar off, and hath forgotten that he was purged from his old sins.[10] Wherefore the rather, brethren, give diligence to make your calling and election sure: for if ye do these things, ye shall never fall: [11] For so an entrance shall be ministered unto you abundantly into the* *everlasting kingdom of our Lord and Saviour Jesus Christ.[12] Wherefore I will not be negligent to put you always in remembrance of these things, though ye know them, and be established in the present truth.*

Matthew (KJV) 24: [33]So likewise ye, when ye shall see all these things, know that it is near, even at the doors. [34]Verily I say unto you, This generation shall not pass, till all these things be fulfilled. [35]Heaven and earth shall pass away, but my words shall not pass away. **And of that day and hour knoweth no man, no, not the angels of heaven, but my Father only.**

Figure 9.7 The Earth was corrupt before God and filled with violence (right plate); as in Genesis 6:5: "And God saw that the wickedness of man was great in the earth, and that every imagination of the thoughts of his heart was only evil continually."; illustration from the 1728 *Figures de la Bible*; **illustrated by Gerard Hoet (1648–1733) and others, and published by P. de Hondt in The Hague; image courtesy Bizzell Bible Collection, University of Oklahoma Libraries.**

Matthew (KJV) 24: [37]But as the days of Noah were, so shall also the coming of the Son of man be. [38]For as in the days that were before the flood they were eating and drinking, marrying and giving in marriage, until the day that Noe entered into the ark,

Figure 9.8 The Eve of the Deluge (1840) by Artist John Martin.

Matthew (KJV) 24: [39]And knew not until the flood came, and took them all away; so shall also the coming of the Son of man be.

Figure 9.9 "The Deluge," frontispiece to Gustave Doré's illustrated edition of the Bible. Based on the story of Noah's Ark, this shows humans and a tiger doomed by the flood futilely attempting to save their children and cubs. Date The first edition was 1866.

[40]Then shall two be in the field; the one shall be taken, and the other left.

**Figure 9.10 "The Rapture: One in the Field",
Etching by Jan Luyken illustrating Matthew 24:40 in the Bowyer Bible.**

[41]Two women shall be grinding at the mill; the one shall be taken, and the other left.

apud: phillip medhurst   THE RAPTURE: ONE AT THE MILL. MATTHEW 24:41. JAN LUYKEN   excudit: harry kossuth

**Figure 9.11 "The Rapture: One at the Mill",
Etching by Jan Luyken illustrating Matthew 24:41 in the Bowyer Bible.**

[42]Watch therefore: for ye know not what hour your Lord doth come. [43]But know this, that if the goodman of the house had known in what watch the thief would come, he would have watched, and would not have suffered his house to be broken up. [44]Therefore be ye also ready: for in such an hour as ye think not the Son of man cometh.

Figure 9.12"The Faithful and Wise Servant", Etching by Jan Luyken illustrating Matt. 24: 45 is the correct scripture reference in the Bowyer Bible.

The book of Luke gives the same account; the Bible says, "out of the mouth of two or three witnesses shall every word be established." In Luke Jesus adds one more scene:

Luke (KJV) 17: [30]Even thus shall it be in the day when the Son of man is revealed. [31]In that day, he which shall be upon the housetop, and his stuff in the house, let him not come down to take it away: and he that is in the field, let him likewise not return back. [32] Remember Lot's wife. [33]Whosoever shall seek to save his life shall lose it; and whosoever shall lose his life shall preserve it. [34]I tell you, in that night there shall be two men in one bed; the one shall be taken, and the other shall be left.

apud: phillip medhurst THE RAPTURE: ONE IN THE BED. LUKE 17:34. JAN LUYKEN excudit: harry kossuth

Figure 9.13 "The Rapture: One in Bed".
etching by Jan Luyken illustrating Luke 17:34 in the Bowyer Bible.

Matthew 24: [45] Who then is a faithful and wise servant, whom his lord hath made ruler over his household, to give them meat in due season?

The "meat" that Jesus is talking about is the Word of God, or as Hebrews 5 says, the Word of righteousness, once it is cultivated into fruit, it becomes the robe or the garments of righteousness, which make us eligible to be called the Bride of Christ. The faithful and wise servants are the pastors, teachers, evangelists, prophets, and apostles who have been given rule over His household, which is the Body of Christ. The due season is now and they should be teaching the Gospel of the Kingdom.

Hebrews (KJV) 5: [12] For when for the time ye ought to be teachers, ye have need that one teach you again which be the first principles of the oracles of God; and are become such as have need of milk, and not of strong meat. [13] For every one that useth milk is unskillful in the word of righteousness: for he is a babe. *[14] But strong meat belongeth to them that are of full age, even those who by reason of use have their senses exercised to discern both good and evil.*

Matthew 24: *[46]Blessed is that servant, whom his lord when he cometh shall find so doing. [47]Verily I say unto you, That he shall make him ruler over all his goods. [48]But and if that evil servant shall say in his heart, My lord delayeth his coming; [49]And shall begin to smite his fellow servants, and to eat and drink with the drunken; [50]The lord of that servant shall come in a day when he looketh not for him, and in an hour that he is not aware of, [51]And shall cut him asunder, and appoint him his portion with the hypocrites: there shall be weeping and gnashing of teeth.*

Figure 9.14 Triptych: The Last Judgment (c. 1450) by Fra. Angelico.

Matthew 25 (KJV) 1 Then shall the kingdom of heaven be likened unto ten virgins, which took their lamps, and went forth to meet the bridegroom. 2 And five of them were wise, and five were foolish.

**Figure 9.15 Parable of the Wise and Foolish Virgins (c. 1616)
by Hieronymus Francken (II).**

[3] They that were foolish took their lamps, and took no oil with them: [4] But the wise took oil in their vessels with their lamps. [5] While the bridegroom tarried, they all slumbered and slept.

[6] And at midnight there was a cry made, Behold, the bridegroom cometh; go ye out to meet him.

Figure 9.16 The Parable of the Wise and Foolish Virgins (c. 1838–1842)
Friedrich Wilhelm Schadow

Matthew (KJV) 25: 7: ⁷Then all those virgins arose, and trimmed their lamps. ⁸And the foolish said unto the wise, Give us of your oil; for our lamps are gone out. ⁹But the wise answered, saying, Not so; lest there be not enough for us and you: but go ye rather to them that sell, and buy for yourselves. ¹⁰And while they went to buy, the bridegroom came; and they that were ready went in with him to the marriage: and the door was shut. ¹¹Afterward came also the other virgins, saying, Lord, Lord, open to us. ¹²But he answered and said, Verily I say unto you, I know you not. *¹³Watch therefore, for ye know neither the day nor the hour wherein the Son of man cometh. ¹⁴For the kingdom of heaven is as a man travelling into a far country, who called his own servants, and delivered unto them his goods. ¹⁵And unto one he gave five talents, to another two, and to another one; to every man according to his several ability; and straightway took his journey. ¹⁶Then he that had received the five talents went and traded with the same, and made them other five talents. ¹⁷And likewise he that had received two, he also gained other two. ¹⁸But he that had received one went and digged in the earth, and hid his lord's money. ¹⁹After a long time the lord of those servants cometh, and reckoneth with them. ²⁰And so he that had received five talents came and brought other five talents, saying, Lord, thou deliveredst unto me five talents: behold, I have gained beside them five talents more. ²¹His lord said unto him, Well done, thou good and faithful servant: thou hast been faithful over a few things, I will make thee ruler over many things: enter thou into the joy of thy lord. ²²He also that had received two talents came and said, Lord, thou deliveredst unto me two talents: behold, I have gained two other talents beside them. ²³His lord said unto him, Well done, good and faithful servant; thou hast been faithful over a few things, I will make thee ruler over many things: enter thou into the joy of thy lord.*

[24]Then he which had received the one talent came and said, Lord, I knew thee that thou art an hard man, reaping where thou hast not sown, and gathering where thou hast not strawed: [25]And I was afraid, and went and hid thy talent in the earth: lo, there thou hast that is thine. [26]His lord answered and said unto him, Thou wicked and slothful servant, thou knewest that I reap where I sowed not, and gather where I have not strawed: [27]Thou oughtest therefore to have put my money to the exchangers, and then at my coming I should have received mine own with usury. [28]Take therefore the talent from him, and give it unto him which hath ten talents. [29]For unto every one that hath shall be given, and he shall have abundance: but from him that hath not shall be taken away even that which he hath. [30]And cast ye the unprofitable servant into outer darkness: there shall be weeping and gnashing of teeth. [31]When the Son of man shall come in his glory, and all the holy angels with him, then shall he sit upon the throne of his glory:

Figure 9.17 The Last Judgment is attributed to German painter Hans Memling, Date 1466-1473

Matt. (KJV) 25: *[32]And before him shall be gathered all nations: and he shall separate them one from another, as a shepherd divideth his sheep from the goats: [33]And he shall set the sheep on his right hand, but the goats on the left.*

Figure 9.18 The Separation of the Sheep and the Goats by Fra. Angelico.

³⁴Then shall the King say unto them on his right hand, Come, ye blessed of my Father, inherit the kingdom prepared for you from the foundation of the world:

The parables of the ten virgins, the ten talents, and the separation of the sheep from the goats and the seven works of mercy come together as one to make a huge statement about the kingdom authority of God. The ten talents explain how the Kingdom of Heaven operates on instruction, obedience, and reward. Failure to obey resulted in the individual who hid his one talent and the person who did not give to the poor, or visit the sick, and so forth; both were cast into hell for eternity. The foolish virgins fell into this same category of disobedience because they were foolish like the man with one talent who knew that his lord expected a return on his investment. The man with one talent was given the resources, and he should have had at least doubled the talent like the other men did. The ten virgins, the sheep and the goats and the seven works of mercy are a more direct account into the Kingdom of God authority on instruction, obedience, and reward. The relationship is a more direct way of what God is telling us exactly what He is expecting from us as Christians, because we are part of His Body.

1 Corinthians (KJV) 12: ²⁵ That there should be no schism in the body; but that the members should have the same care one for another. ²⁶ And whether one member suffer, all the members suffer with it; or one member be honoured, all the members rejoice with it. ²⁷ Now ye are the secondarily prophets, thirdly teachers, after that miracles, then gifts of healings, helps, governments, diversities of tongues. 28 And God hath set some in the church, first apostles, secondarily prophets, thirdly teachers, after that miracles, then gifts of healings, helps, governments, diversities of tongues. ²⁹ Are all apostles? are all prophets? are all teachers? are all workers of miracles? ³⁰ Have all the gifts of healing? do all speak with tongues? do all interpret? ³¹ But covet earnestly the best gifts: and yet shew I unto you a more excellent way.

The Body gets instruction from the Head, and in Revelation the members of the Body of Christ who were lukewarm were cast out or spewed out of His mouth. In other words, Jesus cast them out of His Body. (They were just happy churchgoers who did not dig deep enough into the Word of God to find out their purpose and work to fulfill that purpose.) We all have a divine destiny; God starts by giving us instructions that sits at His very heart—and that is the spiritual, physical, financial, and mental condition of the everyone. We are all blind spiritually or lacking in some form, God wants to fill all of the voids in our spirit, soul, and body. But God was trying to give them insight, guidance, and direction concerning the Kingdom of God, so we are working with Jesus, and not against Him.

Matthew (KJV) 4: [15] The land of Zabulon, and the land of Nephthalim, by the way of the sea, beyond Jordan, Galilee of the Gentiles; [16] *The people which sat in darkness saw great light; and to them which sat in the region and shadow of death light is sprung up.* [17] *From that time Jesus began to preach, and to say, Repent: for the kingdom of heaven is at hand.*

Figure 9.19 The Blind Leading the Blind by Sebastian Vrancx (1573–1647).

Revelation (KJV) 3:[15] I know thy works, that thou art neither cold nor hot: I would thou wert cold or hot. [16] So then because thou art lukewarm, and neither cold nor hot, I will spue thee out of my mouth. [17] Because thou sayest, I am rich, and increased with goods, and have need of nothing; and knowest not that thou art wretched, and miserable, and poor, and blind, and naked:[18] I counsel thee to buy of me gold tried in the fire, that thou mayest be rich; and white raiment, that thou mayest be clothed, and that the shame of thy nakedness do not appear; and anoint thine eyes with eyesalve, that thou mayest see. [19] As many as I love, I rebuke and chasten: be zealous therefore, and repent. [20] Behold, I stand at the door, and knock: if any man hear my voice, and open the door, I will come in to him, and will sup with him, and he with me. [21] To him that overcometh will I grant to sit with me in my throne, even as I also overcame, and am set down with my Father in his throne. [22] He that hath an ear, let him hear what the Spirit saith unto the churches.

The saddest thing is the person who never allowed the seven works of mercy to become part of their own personal ministry. I hate to sound like a parakeet, but God's original intention for earth was for it to be an exact copy of Heaven, and we are to play a major part in that. This is why God wants to bless us greater than He blessed Solomon. We have to get our priorities lined up with God's Word. Heaven is a place of tranquility, peace, joy there is no poverty, sickness, nor violence there. The seven works of mercy are a symbol of the Kingdom of God coming into manifestation; our destiny and divine purpose is centered on the Lord's Prayer. Jesus placed so much importance on raising the quality of life for everyone that He judged and condemned individuals who did not have compassion on the less fortunate because they were given the resources just like the men who were given the talents. The talents were given out according to each man's ability; the man who received one talent had the one talent taken from him and given to the man who gained five more because he knew what to do with responsibility.

It is not all about money, we can visit the sick to minister to their needs and to pray for their total restoration. We can visit those who are in prison and preach, and teach the Gospel of the Kingdom and minister salvation to them. Most of us have clothes that are either too big or too small that we can give to someone in need. Just as the widow with two mites, who Jesus said gave more than the people who were wealthy. It is not so much the size of the gift but the motive of the heart that God weighs, and God will multiply seed back to us if our motives are pure. Some received thirty, sixty, and one hundred-fold returns. But beware Jesus also warns us that along with the increase will come persecution.

To become *one* with the Trinity as we have discussed is to know how God thinks and be in agreement with Him because He created the Heavens and the earth, and doing it His way is the only way that it will work. In the past, we just did not understand because we failed to seek and to know or understand the Kingdom of Heaven or the Kingdom of God. That is why Jesus said He never knew the people that did not have compassion on the less fortunate. Jesus spoke of the people (the Pharisees and Sadducees) who spent all this time going to church, however long or short it has been, that they were forever hearing but they never learned anything.

2 Timothy (KJV) 3: [7] Ever learning, and never able to come to the knowledge of the truth.

In the book of Acts they caught on to what Jesus was preaching:

Acts (KJV) 4:[33] And with great power gave the apostles witness of the resurrection of the Lord Jesus: and great grace was upon them all. [34] Neither was there any among them that lacked: for as many as were possessors of lands or houses sold them, and brought the prices of the things that were sold,[35] And laid them down at the apostles' feet: and distribution was made unto every man according as he had need. [36] And Joses, who by the apostles was surnamed Barnabas, (which is, being interpreted, The son of consolation,) a Levite, and of the country of Cyprus,[37] Having land, sold it, and brought the money, and laid it at the apostles' feet.

[The first thing that they did was to take the money that was taken in from the sale of land and houses and gave it to the apostles who distributed it to everyone according to what they needed. What is so amazing is that they made sure that the poorest members of their church were not lacking financially; their debts were paid off. Those members who were poor in that church had their quality of life elevated. Jesus was compassionate; he was easily touched by the feelings of their infirmities. Jesus hurts when we are hurting. He became *one* with us when we became part of His Body.

If you have ever hit your finger with a hammer hard enough you felt it all over your body, including your head because it knew the finger was hurting. You did everything you could to stop the pain and that is what Jesus was saying about us.

When you become *one* with God, you know how He thinks, and He knows what you think and what you need; that is when our thoughts and ways come up to the level of His thoughts and ways because we have been given the Mind of Christ. The apostles understood about the rich young ruler; they were there when Jesus was ministering to him. There are many who believe that Barnabus was the rich young ruler who Jesus ministered to earlier in His ministry.

The reasons the foolish virgins missed the wedding and the Kingdom of Heaven is that they never took the opportunity to get to know Jesus and find out what God meant by His will being done on earth as it is in Heaven.

Matthew (KJV) 25: *[35]For I was an hungred, and ye gave me meat: I was thirsty, and ye gave me drink: [36]Naked, and ye clothed me I was sick, and ye visited me I was in prison, and ye came unto me. [37]Then shall the righteous answer him, saying, Lord, when saw we thee an hungred, and fed thee? or thirsty, and gave thee drink? [38]When saw we thee a stranger, and took thee in? or naked, and clothed thee? [39]Or when saw we thee sick, or in prison, and came unto thee? [40]And the King shall answer and say unto them, Verily I say unto you, Inasmuch as ye have done it unto one of the least of these my brethren, ye have done it unto me.*

Figure 9.20 The works of mercy by Pieter Brueghel the younger (1564-1637) and involving Cornelis Mahu (1613-1689)

Matthew (KJV) 25: *[41]Then shall he say also unto them on the left hand, Depart from me, ye cursed, into everlasting fire, prepared for the devil and his angels: [42]For I was an hungred, and ye gave me no meat: I was thirsty, and ye gave me no drink: [43]I was a stranger, and ye took me not in: naked, and ye clothed me not: sick, and in prison, and ye visited me not. [44]Then shall they also answer him, saying, Lord, when saw we thee an hungred, or athirst, or a stranger, or naked, or sick, or in prison, and did not minister unto thee?*

Figure 9.21 Last Judgment and the Wise and Foolish Virgins (1450s)
by unknown Flemish master.

Matthew (KJV) 25: *⁴⁵Then shall he answer them, saying, Verily I say unto you, Inasmuch as ye did it not to one of the least of these, ye did it not to me. ⁴⁶And these shall go away into everlasting punishment: but the righteous into life eternal.*

Matthew (KJV) 7: 7 Judge not, that ye be not judged. ² For with what judgment ye judge, ye shall be judged: and with what measure ye mete, it shall be measured to you again. ³ And why beholdest thou the mote that is in thy brother's eye, but considerest not the beam that is in thine own eye?

Figure 22 The bar and the splinter Date (c. 1700)
by Dutch artist: possible B. Picart, Jan Luyken or G. Hoet.

[4] Or how wilt thou say to thy brother, Let me pull out the mote out of thine eye; and, behold, a beam is in thine own eye? [5] Thou hypocrite, first cast out the beam out of thine own eye; and then shalt thou see clearly to cast out the mote out of thy brother's eye. [6] Give not that which is holy unto the dogs, neither cast ye your pearls before swine, lest they trample them under their feet, and turn again and rend you. [7] Ask, and it shall be given you; seek, and ye shall find; knock, and it shall be opened unto you: [8] For every one that asketh receiveth; and he that seeketh findeth; and to him that knocketh it shall be opened. [9] Or what man is there of you, whom if his son ask bread, will he give him a stone? [10] Or if he ask a fish, will he give him a serpent? [11] If ye then, being evil, know how to give good gifts unto your children, how much more shall your Father which is in heaven give good things to them that ask him? [12] Therefore all things whatsoever ye would that men should do to you, do ye even so to them: for this is the law and the prophets. [13] Enter ye in at the strait gate: for wide is the gate, and broad is the way, that leadeth to destruction, and many there be which go in thereat:

Figure 9.23 The Broad and the Narrow Way, a popular German Pietist painting (1866)

[14] Because strait is the gate, and narrow is the way, which leadeth unto life, and few there be that find it. [15] Beware of false prophets, which come to you in sheep's clothing, but inwardly they are ravening wolves. [16] Ye shall know them by their fruits. Do men gather grapes of thorns, or figs of thistles? [17] Even so every good tree bringeth forth good fruit; but a corrupt tree bringeth forth evil fruit. [18] A good tree cannot bring forth evil fruit, neither can a corrupt tree bring forth good fruit. [19] Every tree that bringeth not forth good fruit is hewn down, and cast into the fire. [20] Wherefore by their fruits ye shall know them. *[21] Not every one that saith unto me, Lord, Lord, shall enter into the kingdom of heaven; but he that doeth the will of my Father which is in heaven.* [22] Many will say to me in that day, Lord, Lord, have we not prophesied in thy name? and in thy name have cast out devils? and in thy name done many wonderful works? *[23] And then will I profess unto them, I never knew you: depart from me, ye that work iniquity.* [24] Therefore whosoever heareth these sayings of mine, and doeth them, I will liken him unto a wise man, which built his house upon a rock:

Figure 9.24 Bell Rock Lighthouse, illustration by "Miss Stevenson."

[25] And the rain descended, and the floods came, and the winds blew, and beat upon that house; and it fell not: for it was founded upon a rock. [26] And every one that heareth these sayings of mine, and doeth them not, shall be likened unto a foolish man, which built his house upon the sand: [27] And the rain descended, and the floods came, and the winds blew, and beat upon that house; and it fell: and great was the fall of it. [28] And it came to pass, when Jesus had ended these sayings, the people were astonished at his doctrine: [29] For he taught them as one having authority, and not as the scribes.

Summary

As we started out, Jesus goes into detail in explaining that when He returns He will be looking for His Bride and only virgins will qualify, because the next great event after the rapture will be the wedding supper of the Lamb. If we do not understand how the Kingdom of God operates and apply it to our life, then we will be judged a foolish virgin. Everyone is invited but not everyone will meet the requirements. The individuals who did not meet the requirements were the foolish ones who did not lay the foundation of their spiritual life on the seed of the Word of God maturing and bearing fruit in their lives. The wise virgins knew that they had to fulfill their potential and their divine purpose.

The foolish virgins did not understand the importance of separating themselves from sin. Keeping ourselves holy before the Lord is why God made our bodies the temple of the Holy Spirit,

362

and our spiritual man was made the priest of that Temple. All Old Testament priests knew that they had to be holy before they could come into the presence of the Lord.

Everything that was done in the Old Testament was to prepare us for the return of Jesus, the destruction of the kingdom of darkness and the Kingdom of God being re-established in the earth. The foolish virgins did not understand or take part in these events. The foolish virgins did not become *one* with God nor did they know God; neither did He know them, and they were not doing the will of God. If you do not know your purpose for being in the earth, God gives us our purpose in the seven works of mercy. As in the parable of the ten talents, every Christian has a responsibility to minister to the needs of the less fortunate. So if you do not know your purpose, God gives it to us. Our responsibility is to raise the quality of life for the people around us to be equal to that of Heaven! Not just giving them things but most importantly giving them the Gospel of the kingdom of God.

The person with five talents was found faithful when his lord came back to check, and his lord gave him more responsibility. And when God sees us faithful, then he will give us greater responsibility because He sees us faithful and we can be trusted to obey and be willing to do whatever we are told to do. Never let anyone sidetrack you from obeying God. That is the first lesson everyone should have learned from the Garden of Eden. God told Adam what not to do, the devil told Eve not to listen to God, and well you know what happened.

When you are giving your time, your money, your resources, or the Word of God into the lives of others, you are giving them a portion of your life. You are giving them something that they could not do for themselves. Just like Jesus gave His life for us, we are giving life to others who need it. That was Jesus' life and ministry from beginning to end. And we have inherited His ministry from Him. He came that we might have life and have it more abundantly so we can allow that abundant (or eternal) life to flow from us to others.

Just as important, we have been called to walk in the Spirit, so that we will not fulfill the lust of the flesh. When we are walking in the Spirit, it is a sign that the seeds of the fruit of the Spirit are maturing in our lives and we are growing up to the measure and statue of Christ. It also says that the life of God is being manifested in our lives.

Every time we choose to walk in the love of God instead of hate or anger, we are bearing the fruit of love. When we yield to walking in the faith of God instead of being defeated by the spirit of fear, the fruit of the faith of God has matured in our lives.

And lastly we have to bear the fruit of the Spirit. The fruit starts out as seeds that have to be cultivated and once they mature, each fruit performs many functions. They become the keys to the Kingdom they become the armor of God, and the life-giving resources that we sow into the lives of the less fortunate.

We must learn how the Kingdom of God functions so we can be ready when Jesus delivers up the Kingdom.

CHAPTER 10

The Heavenly Wedding—Do Not Miss It!

**Figure 10.1 An 1880 Baxter process illustration of Revelation 22:17
by Joseph Martin Kronheim.**

Before God brings destruction, He always warns His people first so they will not be caught off guard. From Noah's flood to the destruction of Sodom and Gomorrah God warned His people before the destruction actually occurred. These are all examples for us to make note of because whatever God says is going to happen; it will happen because He is not a liar! He is warning us because He loves us and He does not want to see anyone perish because hell is forever.

It took one hundred years for Noah to build the ark as God instructed him. Noah also preached righteousness to the people during that one hundred year period because there was so much moral decay. He warned them that God was going to destroy every living thing on the earth by water. But if the people repented and follow him into the ark they would be saved. The people did not listen to Noah. His family went inside and the doors of the ark were closed and it started raining. Only Noah and his family were saved.

This time, God is going to destroy the heavens and the earth by fire and create a new Heaven and earth. But this time there will be more than just one family going into the New Heaven and earth. The people that will be saved will all be of one mind and one spirit and one body. The two shall become "one flesh." God started the preparation for this union in the Old Testament.

Isaiah 61: The Spirit of the Lord GOD is upon me; because the LORD hath anointed me to preach good tidings unto the meek; he hath sent me to bind up the brokenhearted, to proclaim liberty to the captives, and the opening of the prison to them that are bound; ² To proclaim the acceptable year of the LORD, and the day of vengeance of our God; to comfort all that mourn; ³ To appoint unto them that mourn in Zion, to give unto them beauty for ashes, the oil of joy for mourning, the garment of praise for the spirit of heaviness; that they might be called trees of righteousness, the planting of the LORD, that he might be glorified. ⁴ And they shall build the old wastes, they shall raise up the former desolations, and they shall repair the waste cities, the desolations of many generations. ⁵ And strangers shall stand and feed your flocks, and the sons of the alien shall be your plowmen and your vinedressers. **⁶ But ye shall be named the Priests of the LORD: men shall call you the Ministers of our God: ye shall eat the riches of the Gentiles, and in their glory shall ye boast yourselves. ⁷ For your shame ye shall have double; and for confusion they shall rejoice in their portion: therefore in their land they shall possess the double: everlasting joy shall be unto them. ⁸ For I the LORD love judgment, I hate robbery for burnt offering; and I will direct their work in truth, and I will make an everlasting covenant with them. ⁹ And their seed shall be known among the Gentiles, and their offspring among the people: all that see them shall acknowledge them, that they are the seed which the LORD hath blessed. ¹⁰ I will greatly rejoice in the LORD, my soul shall be joyful in my God; for he hath clothed me with the garments of salvation, he hath covered me with the robe of righteousness, as a bridegroom decketh himself with ornaments, and as a bride adorneth herself with her jewels. ¹¹ For as the earth bringeth forth her bud, and as the garden causeth the things that are sown in it to spring forth; so the Lord GOD will cause righteousness and praise to spring forth before all the nations.**

apud: phillip medhurst   THE MAN WITHOUT A WEDDING GARMENT. MATTHEW 22:11-14. JAN LUYKEN   excudit: harry kossuth

**Figure 10.2 The Man without a Wedding Garment,
Etching by Jan Luyken illustrating Matthew 22:11-14 in the Bowyer Bible**

Isaiah (KJV) 62: For Zion's sake will I not hold my peace, and for Jerusalem's sake, I will not rest, until the righteousness thereof go forth as brightness, and the salvation thereof as a lamp that burneth. ² And the Gentiles shall see thy righteousness, and all kings thy glory: and thou shalt be called by a new name, which the mouth of the LORD shall name. ³ Thou shalt also be a crown of glory in the hand of the LORD, and a royal diadem in the hand of thy God. ⁴ Thou shalt no more be termed Forsaken; neither shall thy land any more be termed Desolate: but thou shalt be called Hephzibah, and thy land Beulah: for the LORD delighteth in thee, and thy land shall be married. ⁵ For as a young man marrieth a virgin, so shall thy sons marry thee: and as the bridegroom rejoiceth over the bride, so shall thy God rejoice over thee. ⁶ I have set watchmen upon thy walls, O Jerusalem, which shall never hold their peace day nor night: ye that make mention of the LORD, keep not silence, ⁷ And give him no rest, till he establish, and till he make Jerusalem a praise in the earth. ⁸ The LORD hath sworn by his right hand, and by the arm of his strength, Surely I will no more give thy corn to be meat for thine enemies; and the sons of the stranger shall not drink thy wine, for the which thou hast laboured: ⁹ But they that have gathered it shall eat it, and praise the LORD; and they that have brought it together shall drink it in the courts of my holiness. **¹⁰ Go through, go through the gates; prepare ye the way of the people; cast up, cast up the highway; gather out the stones; lift up a standard for the people. ¹¹ Behold, the LORD hath proclaimed unto the end of the world, Say ye to the daughter of Zion, Behold, thy salvation cometh; behold, his reward is with him, and**

his work before him.[12] **And they shall call them, The holy people, The redeemed of the** L**ORD**: **and thou shalt be called, Sought out, A city not forsaken.**

Matthew (KJV) 5: [17] Think not that I am come to destroy the law, or the prophets: I am not come to destroy, but to fulfil. *[18] For verily I say unto you, Till heaven and earth pass, one jot or one tittle shall in no wise pass from the law, till all be fulfilled.* [19] Whosoever therefore shall break one of these least commandments, and shall teach men so, he shall be called the least in the kingdom of heaven: but whosoever shall do and teach them, the same shall be called great in the kingdom of heaven.

Revelation (KJV) 21: [5] And he that sat upon the throne said, Behold, I make all things new. And he said unto me, Write: for these words are true and faithful.[6] And he said unto me, It is done. I am Alpha and Omega, the beginning and the end. I will give unto him that is athirst of the fountain of the water of life freely. [7] He that overcometh shall inherit all things; and I will be his God, and he shall be my son.

The universe is set on course for a major makeover at the hand of God. This transformation was pre-ordained by God from the beginning that is why He is Alpha and the Omega. God is in the process of purging out everything that offends, corrupts, and defiles. He is going to create a new Heaven and a new earth for His children. Most people want to go to a place where there is peace and harmony, a place where there is no sickness, pain, or suffering. A place where we can live throughout eternity in the presence of the Lord, continuing to grow in grace. God places before us hope and gives us a promise of a future of ruling and reigning with Him forever. He has been preparing the church for this event for over two thousand years. The invitation is open to everyone regardless of their race, creed, or color.

**Figure 10.3 Invitation to the Great Banquet,
Etching by Jan Luyken illustrating Luke 14:16-24 in the Bowyer Bible.**

Hebrews (KJV) **1** God, who at sundry times and in divers manners spake in time past unto the fathers by the prophets, [2] Hath in these last days spoken unto us by his Son, whom he hath appointed heir of all things, by whom also he made the worlds; [3] Who being the brightness of his glory, and the express image of his person, and upholding all things by the word of his power, when he had by himself purged our sins, sat down on the right hand of the Majesty on high: [4] Being made so much better than the angels, as he hath by inheritance obtained a more excellent name than they. [5] For unto which of the angels said he at any time, Thou art my Son, this day have I begotten thee? And again, I will be to him a Father, and he shall be to me a Son? [6] And again, when he bringeth in the firstbegotten into the world, he saith, And let all the angels of God worship him. [7] And of the angels he saith, Who maketh his angels spirits, and his ministers a flame of fire. **[8] But unto the Son he saith, Thy throne, O God, is for ever and ever: a sceptre of righteousness is the sceptre of thy kingdom. [9] Thou hast loved righteousness, and hated iniquity; therefore God, even thy God, hath anointed thee with the oil of gladness above thy fellows. [10] And, Thou, Lord, in the beginning hast laid the foundation of the earth; and the heavens are the works of thine hands: [11] They shall perish; but thou remainest; and they all shall wax old as doth a garment; [12] And as a vesture shalt thou fold them up, and they shall be changed: but thou art the same, and thy years shall not fail. [13] But to which of the angels said he at any time, Sit on my right hand, until I make thine enemies thy footstool? [14] Are they not all ministering spirits, sent forth to minister for them who shall be heirs of salvation?**

John (KJV) 3: *[15] That whosoever believeth in him should not perish, but have eternal life. [16] For God so loved the world, that he gave his only begotten Son, that whosoever believeth in him should not perish, but have everlasting life. [17] For God sent not his Son into the world to condemn the world; but that the world through him might be saved. [18] He that believeth on him is not condemned: but he that believeth not is condemned already, because he hath not believed in the name of the only begotten Son of God. [19] And this is the condemnation, that light is come into the world, and men loved darkness rather than light, because their deeds were evil. [20] For every one that doeth evil hateth the light, neither cometh to the light, lest his deeds should be reproved. [21] But he that doeth truth cometh to the light, that his deeds may be made manifest, that they are wrought in God.* [22] After these things came Jesus and his disciples into the land of Judaea; and there he tarried with them, and baptized. [23] And John also was baptizing in Aenon near to Salim, because there was much water there: and they came, and were baptized. [24] For John was not yet cast into prison. [25] Then there arose a question between some of John's disciples and the Jews about purifying. [26] And they came unto John, and said unto him, Rabbi, he that was with thee beyond Jordan, to whom thou barest witness, behold, the same baptizeth, and all men come to him. [27] John answered and said, A man can receive nothing, except it be given him from heaven. [28] Ye yourselves bear me witness, that I said, I am not the Christ, but that I am sent before him. **[29] He that hath the bride is the bridegroom: but the friend of the bridegroom, which standeth and heareth him, rejoiceth greatly because of the bridegroom's voice: this my joy therefore is fulfilled. [30] He must increase, but I must decrease. [31] He that cometh from above is above all: he that is of the earth is earthly, and speaketh of the earth: he that cometh from heaven is above all. [32] And what he hath seen and heard, that he testifieth; and no man receiveth his testimony. [33] He that hath received his testimony hath set to his seal that God is true. [34] For he whom God hath sent speaketh the words of God: for God giveth not the Spirit by measure unto him. [35] The Father loveth the Son, and hath given all things into his hand. [36] He that believeth on the Son hath everlasting life: and he that believeth not the Son shall not see life; but the wrath of God abideth on him.**

2 Corinthians (KJV) 11: [1]Would to God ye could bear with me a little in my folly: and indeed bear with me. [2]For I am jealous over you with godly jealousy: for I have espoused you to one husband, that I may present you as a chaste virgin to Christ. [3]But I fear, lest by any means, as the serpent beguiled Eve through his subtilty, so your minds should be corrupted from the simplicity that is in Christ.

Ephesians (KJV) 5: [14] Wherefore he saith, Awake thou that sleepest, and arise from the dead, and Christ shall give thee light. [15]See then that ye walk circumspectly, not as fools, but as wise, [16]Redeeming the time, because the days are evil. [17]Wherefore be ye not unwise, but understanding what the will of the Lord is. [18]And be not drunk with wine, wherein is excess; but be filled with the Spirit; [19]Speaking to yourselves in psalms and hymns and spiritual songs, singing and making melody in your heart to the Lord; [20]Giving thanks always for all things unto God and the Father in the name of our Lord Jesus Christ; [21]Submitting yourselves one to another in the fear of God. [22]Wives, submit yourselves unto your own husbands, as unto the Lord. [23]For the husband is the head of the wife, even as Christ is the head of the church: and he is the saviour of the body. [24]Therefore as the church is subject unto Christ, so let the wives be to their own husbands in everything. **[25]Husbands, love your wives, even as Christ also loved the church, and gave himself for it; [26]That he might sanctify and cleanse it with the washing of water by the word, [27]That he**

might present it to himself a glorious church, not having spot, or wrinkle, or any such thing; but that it should be holy and without blemish. [28]So ought men to love their wives as their own bodies. He that loveth his wife loveth himself.[29]For no man ever yet hated his own flesh; but nourisheth and cherisheth it, even as the Lord the church: [30]For we are members of his body, of his flesh, and of his bones. [31]For this cause shall a man leave his father and mother, and shall be joined unto his wife, and they two shall be one flesh. [32]This is a great mystery: but I speak concerning Christ and the church. [33]Nevertheless let every one of you in particular so love his wife even as himself; and the wife see that she reverence her husband.

1 Corinthians (KJV) 15: [33]Be not deceived: evil communications corrupt good manners. [34]Awake to righteousness, and sin not; for some have not the knowledge of God: I speak this to your shame. [35]But some man will say, How are the dead raised up? and with what body do they come? [36]Thou fool, that which thou sowest is not quickened, except it die: [37]And that which thou sowest, thou sowest not that body that shall be, but bare grain, it may chance of wheat, or of some other grain: [38]But God giveth it a body as it hath pleased him, and to every seed his own body. [39]All flesh is not the same flesh: but there is one kind of flesh of men, another flesh of beasts, another of fishes, and another of birds.[40]There are also celestial bodies, and bodies terrestrial: but the glory of the celestial is one, and the glory of the terrestrial is another.[41]There is one glory of the sun, and another glory of the moon, and another glory of the stars: for one star differeth from another star in glory. [42]*So also is the resurrection of the dead. It is sown in corruption; it is raised in incorruption:* [43]*It is sown in dishonour; it is raised in glory: it is sown in weakness; it is raised in power:* [44]*It is sown a natural body; it is raised a spiritual body. There is a natural body, and there is a spiritual body.* [45]*And so it is written, The first man Adam was made a living soul; the last Adam was made a quickening spirit.* [46]*Howbeit that was not first which is spiritual, but that which is natural; and afterward that which is spiritual.* [47]*The first man is of the earth, earthy; the second man is the Lord from heaven.* [48]*As is the earthy, such are they also that are earthy: and as is the heavenly, such are they also that are heavenly.* [49]*And as we have borne the image of the earthy, we shall also bear the image of the heavenly.* [50]*Now this I say, brethren, that flesh and blood cannot inherit the kingdom of God; neither doth corruption inherit incorruption.* [51]*Behold, I shew you a mystery; We shall not all sleep, but we shall all be changed,* [52]*In a moment, in the twinkling of an eye, at the last trump: for the trumpet shall sound, and the dead shall be raised incorruptible, and we shall be changed.* [53]*For this corruptible must put on incorruption, and this mortal must put on immortality.* [54]*So when this corruptible shall have put on incorruption, and this mortal shall have put on immortality, then shall be brought to pass the saying that is written, Death is swallowed up in victory.* [55]*O death, where is thy sting? O grave, where is thy victory?* [56]*The sting of death is sin; and the strength of sin is the law.* [57]*But thanks be to God, which giveth us the victory through our Lord Jesus Christ.*[58] *Therefore, my beloved brethren, be ye stedfast, unmoveable, always abounding in the work of the Lord, forasmuch as ye know that your labour is not in vain in the Lord.*

Romans (KJV) 8: [28]And we know that all things work together for good to them that love God, to them who are the called according to his purpose. [29]For whom he did foreknow, he also did predestinate to be conformed to the image of his Son, that he might be the firstborn among many brethren. [30]Moreover whom he did predestinate, them he also called: and whom he called, them he also justified: and whom he justified, them he also glorified. [31]What shall we then say to these things? If God be for us, who can be against us? [32]He that spared not his own Son, but delivered him up for us all, how shall he not with him also freely give us all things? [33] Who shall lay anything to the charge of God's elect? It is God that justifieth. [34] Who is he that condemneth? It is Christ that died, yea rather, that is risen again, who is even at the right hand of God, who also maketh intercession for us.

We are in this world, but we are not of this world. The Bible tells us not be conformed to this world, but we must be transformed into the image of Christ by the Word of God: Heaven is our real home. The whole purpose for the church being called the Bride of Christ is that they must be virgins. The Kingdom of God sets in place all the criteria for being called the wise virgins. Now either we are virgins or we are not, we know the qualifications. Jesus has already said that half of the Body of Christ, or five out of ten virgins, will not qualify. There will not be any middle of the road, or shades of gray or grandfathering clauses. Everything about the Kingdom of God is done in preparation so we will not miss this event which is called the wedding supper of the Lamb and the new world to come.

Christ requires that all Christians must seek the Kingdom of God first so we would understand how Heaven functions and what He is expecting from His children. God did not just send His Son to the cross to die for us just so He could make us rich, and then we go to Heaven when we die. We are much more valuable than that to the Kingdom of God. If that was all being born again meant, then every time someone gave their heart to Christ they would be taken straight to Heaven, never to be seen again on this side. There would be no need for you to be hanging around if you are not going do anything else with your life. But God has a plan!

Seeking the Kingdom prepares us for reigning (which is why He made us kings) with Christ in the future and becoming His Bride. He made us priests because the purpose of the office of the priesthood is to keep ourselves holy and pure. We have to keep ourselves holy before God because God chose to live and dwell within us by making our bodies the temple of the Holy Spirit. We must separate ourselves from sin and not allow sin to rule (or reign) over us. And if we make a mistake, we have the Blood of Jesus available to cleanse us again.

Revelation 7: [9] After this I beheld, and, lo, a great multitude, which no man could number, of all nations, and kindreds, and people, and tongues, stood before the throne, and before the Lamb, clothed with white robes, and palms in their hands; [10] And cried with a loud voice, saying, Salvation to our God which sitteth upon the throne, and unto the Lamb. [11] And all the angels stood round about the throne, and about the elders and the four beasts, and fell before the throne on their faces, and worshipped God, [12] Saying, Amen: Blessing, and glory, and wisdom, and thanksgiving, and honour, and power, and might, be unto our God for ever and ever. Amen. [13] And one of the elders answered, saying unto me, What are these which are arrayed in white robes? and whence came they? *And I said unto him, Sir, thou knowest. And he said to me, These are they which came out of great tribulation, and have washed their robes, and made them white in the blood of the Lamb.* [15] *Therefore are they before the throne of God, and serve him day and night in his temple: and he that sitteth on the throne shall dwell among them.* [16] *They shall hunger no more, neither thirst anymore; neither shall the sun light on them, nor any heat.* [17] *For the Lamb which is in the midst of the throne shall feed them, and shall lead them unto living fountains of waters: and God shall wipe away all tears from their eyes.*

The wise virgins understood the office of the priest, because they knew only the righteous shall see God. These that have come have washed their robes (of righteousness) in the Blood of the Lamb. The wise virgins understand that Jesus is not going to be wed to Christians that are in bed with the world. We have to choose; we have to make a decision because whichever way we decide to go will last for an eternity, so choose life.

Matthew 22: [10] So those servants went out into the highways, and gathered together all as many as they found, both bad and good: and the wedding was furnished with guests. [11] And when the king came in to see the guests, he saw there a man which had not on a wedding garment: [12] And he saith unto him, Friend, how camest thou in hither not having a wedding garment? And he was speechless.[13] Then said the king to the servants, Bind him hand and foot, and take him away, and cast him into outer darkness, there shall be weeping and gnashing of teeth. [14] For many are called, but few are chosen.

Ultimately Being *One* with God Means

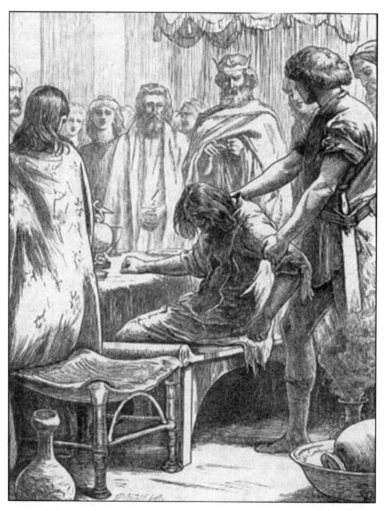

Figure 10.4 The Marriage Feast by John Everett Millais, from "Illustrations to 'The parables of our Lord," engraved by the Dalziel Brothers, 1864.

The wise virgins understand the importance of being *one* with God because the two shall become "one flesh." Our ways and thoughts should be a mirror image of God's thoughts because we have the mind of Christ. Jesus Christ, the Holy Spirit, and our Heavenly Father lives and dwells inside of us for the purpose of us uniting as *one* so God can minister through us. The purpose of making our bodies the temple was that we could be filled with the fullness of God. **2 Corinthians 4;** says that we have this treasure in earthen vessels. We have to wake up to righteousness, and God will give us understanding and enlightenment. We are headed for a wedding, We are the Bride of Christ and God wants us to prepare ourselves for this event. This is why Jesus warns us through the parable of the ten virgins, that half of the Body of Christ will not make it to the wedding. I know that none of us want to miss this event.

Ephesians (AMP) 3:18-21 [That you may really come] to know [practically, through experience for yourselves] the love of Christ, which far surpasses mere knowledge [without experience]; that you may be filled [through all your being] unto all the fullness of God [may have the richest measure of the divine Presence, and become a body wholly filled and flooded with God Himself]! Now to Him Who, by (in consequence of) the [action of His] power that is at work within us, is able to [carry out His purpose and] do superabundantly, far over *and* above all that we [dare] ask or think [infinitely beyond our highest prayers, desires, thoughts, hopes, or dreams] To Him be glory in the church and in Christ Jesus throughout all generations forever and ever. Amen (so be it).

Ephesians (KJV) 4:13 Till we all come in the unity of the faith, and of the knowledge of the Son of God, unto a perfect man, unto the measure of the stature of the fullness of Christ.

Always bearing about in the body the dying of the Lord Jesus, that the life also of Jesus might be made manifest in our body. For we which live are always delivered unto death for Jesus' sake, that the life of Jesus might be manifested in our mortal flesh.

I am not, and none of us are, so special that we can think that we can live our lives and not obey God's Word and expect to be accepted. God performed great and mighty deeds on the behalf of His children by working with and through Moses. Because of disobedience neither he nor any of his generation except Joshua and Caleb made it to the Promised Land. . Only Joshua and Caleb out of three million or more people that were delivered out of Egypt and entered into the land of milk and honey, because of their hard-heartedness, unbelief, and rebellion.

Lot's wife was consumed with Sodom and Gomorrah, because she looked back in disobedience and was turned to a pillar of salt.

Jesus said that the foolish virgins did not make it to the wedding because of their lack of knowledge of the Word of God. But we have to make up our minds to find out as much as we can about the Kingdom of God and put it into practice, because we do not want to fail God. We do not want Him to say to us that He never knew us.

Seed Time to Maturity

As the Bride, we must understand that we must take the Word of God, which starts out as a seed, and allow it to be sown into our spirit man or our hearts, and cultivate it until it matures into fruit. The entire Kingdom of God operates on seed time and harvest time, and God is waiting for us to mature in our spiritual walk with Him.

The seeds that we are to cultivate are the fruit of the Spirit; which are righteousness, love, joy, peace, longsuffering, gentleness, kindness, meekness, and faith. When they mature into fruit, they perform many functions. They become the armor of God. They also become the keys to the Kingdom of God. They are also the divine characteristics and the power and force of God.

Things that will keep us out of the Kingdom

1 Corinthians 6 : [9] Know ye not that the unrighteous shall not inherit the kingdom of God? Be not deceived: neither fornicators, nor idolaters, nor adulterers, nor effeminate, nor abusers of themselves with mankind, [10] Nor thieves, nor covetous, nor drunkards, nor revilers, nor extortioners, shall inherit the kingdom of God. [11] **And such were some of you: but ye are washed, but ye are sanctified, but ye are justified in the name of the Lord Jesus, and by the Spirit of our God.**

Galatians (KJV) 5: [19] Now the works of the flesh are manifest, which are these; Adultery, fornication, uncleanness, lasciviousness, [20] Idolatry, witchcraft, hatred, variance, emulations, wrath, strife, seditions, heresies, [21] Envyings, murders, drunkenness, revellings, and such like: of the which I tell you before, as I have also told you in time past, that they which do such things shall not inherit the kingdom of God. [22] But the (or The Keys to the Kingdom are the) fruit of the Spirit is love, joy, peace, longsuffering, gentleness, goodness, faith, [23] Meekness, temperance: against such there is no law. [24] And they that are Christ's have crucified the flesh with the affections and lusts. [25] If we live in the Spirit, let us also walk in the Spirit. [26] Let us not be desirous of vain glory, provoking one another, envying one another.

The seeds of the Word of God fail to reach maturity because they could not penetrate into a stony heart. This is a person who will not forgive. For example, a Christian who refuses to forgive an offense will not allow the seed of the love of God to take root in their heart and grow and mature into the fruit of love. When that fruit manifests itself, it gives them the ability to say, as Jesus said without any bitterness in their heart, Father forgive them. If they don't forgive, something else more sinister will take root and will grow in their heart and that will be hate and the other fruits of unrighteousness.

Matthew 12: [32] And whosoever speaketh a word against the Son of man, it shall be forgiven him: but whosoever speaketh against the Holy Ghost, it shall not be forgiven him, neither in this world, neither in the world to come. [33] Either make the tree good, and his fruit good; or else make the tree corrupt, and his fruit corrupt: for the tree is known by his fruit. [34] O generation of vipers, how can ye, being evil, speak good things? for out of the abundance of the heart the mouth speaketh. [35] A good man out of the good treasure of the heart bringeth forth good things: and an evil man out of the evil treasure bringeth forth evil things. [36] But I say unto you, That every idle word that men shall speak, they shall give account thereof in the day of judgment. [37] For by thy words thou shalt be justified, and by thy words thou shalt be condemned.

Thorns are the next obstacles that will prevent the growth of the seed of the Word of God. The thorns are the lust of satisfying one's own fleshly desires, preventing the maturity of the Seed. The seeds are in their heart, but the growth process was stunted because the lust for other things choked the Word and they never became fruitful. They wanted things more for themselves than they did for others who had greater needs. The desire to reach out with the love of God to help someone else in need like the Good Samaritan was far from them.

Figure 10.5 Parable of the Good Samaritan (1670) by Jan Wiinants

The proper soil for the seed of the Word of God to mature in us is the love of God, which was placed there by the Holy Spirit when we asked God to fill us with the gift of the Holy Spirit. When the fruit of love matures, it covers a multitude of functions in the Kingdom of Heaven.

Ephesians (KJV) 3: [16]That he would grant you, according to the riches of his glory, to be strengthened with might by his Spirit in the inner man; *[17] That Christ may dwell in your hearts by faith; that ye, being rooted and grounded in love,* [18] May be able to comprehend with all saints what is the breadth, and length, and depth, and height; [19] And to know the love of Christ, which passeth knowledge, that ye might be filled with all the fulness of God. [20] Now unto him that is able to do exceeding abundantly above all that we ask or think, according to the power that worketh in us.

When the love of God grows in our heart, the seeds of the fruit of the Spirit (righteousness, love, joy, peace, longsuffering, gentleness, kindness, meekness, and faith) will begin to manifest in our life as the characteristics of our Heavenly Father.

Another function of the fruit of the Spirit is that we must bear fruit, or in other words be productive on behalf of the Kingdom of Heaven. That means doing the will of the Father. When we are doing what we were created to do, we are glorifying God. Doing the will of the Father is "the seven works of mercy" giving food to the hungry, clothing to the naked, visiting the sick, visiting those in prison, taking in the stranger, giving water to the thirsty, and sowing the Gospel of the Kingdom of God into the lives of people around the world.

Jesus said in one of His last prayers to the Father was "I have glorified You in the earth; I have finished your work." Or in other words, Jesus fulfilled the first part of His destiny for being in the earth. And when it is our turn we want to be able to say the same thing. We all want to hear "thou good and faithful servant"; none of us want to miss God.

The Revelation (KJV) 20: 1 And I saw an angel come down from heaven, having the key of the bottomless pit and a great chain in his hand. ²And he laid hold on the dragon, that old serpent, which is the Devil, and Satan, and bound him a thousand years,₃ And cast him into the bottomless pit, and shut him up, and set a seal upon him, that he should deceive the nations no more, till the thousand years should be fulfilled: and after that he must be loosed a little season.

Union of the Bride and the Bridegroom

⁴And I saw thrones, and they sat upon them, and judgment was given unto them: and I saw the souls of them that were beheaded for the witness of Jesus, and for the word of God, and which had not worshipped the beast, neither his image, neither had received his mark upon their foreheads, or in their hands; and they lived and reigned with Christ a thousand years. ⁵But the rest of the dead lived not again until the thousand years were finished. This is the first resurrection.⁶Blessed and holy is he that hath part in the first resurrection: on such the second death hath no power, but they shall be priests of God and of Christ, and shall reign with him a thousand years.

Ephesians 5: ³¹For this cause shall a man leave his father and mother, and shall be joined unto his wife, and they two shall be one flesh. ³²This is a great mystery: but I speak concerning Christ and the church. ³³Nevertheless let every one of you in particular so love his wife even as himself; and the wife see that she reverence her husband.

The Book of Revelation

Revelation (KJV) 1: 1 The Revelation of Jesus Christ, which God gave unto him, to shew unto his servants things which must shortly come to pass; and he sent and signified it by his angel unto his servant John: ²Who bare record of the word of God, and of the testimony of Jesus Christ, and of all things that he saw. ³Blessed is he that readeth, and they that hear the words of this prophecy, and keep those things which are written therein: for the time is at hand. ⁴John to the seven churches which are in Asia: Grace be unto you, and peace, from him which is, and which was, and which is to come; and from the seven Spirits which are before his throne; ⁵And from Jesus Christ, who is the faithful witness, and the first begotten of the dead, and the prince of the kings of the earth. Unto him that loved us, and washed us from our sins in his own blood, [6] And hath made us kings and priests unto God and his Father; to him be glory and dominion for ever and ever. Amen. [7] Behold, he cometh with clouds; and every eye shall see him, and they also which pierced him: and all kindreds of the earth shall wail because of him. Even so, Amen. [8] I am Alpha and Omega, the beginning and the ending, saith the Lord, which is, and which was, and which is to come, the Almighty. [9] I John, who also am your brother, and companion in tribulation, and in the kingdom and patience of Jesus Christ, was in the isle that is called Patmos, for the word of God, and for the testimony of Jesus Christ. [10] I was in the Spirit on the Lord's day, and heard behind me a great voice, as of a trumpet, [11] Saying, I am Alpha and Omega, the first and the last: and, What thou seest, write in a book, and send it unto the seven churches which are in Asia; unto Ephesus, and unto Smyrna, and unto Pergamos, and unto Thyatira, and unto Sardis, and unto Philadelphia, and unto Laodicea. [12] And I turned to see the voice that spake with me. And being turned, I saw seven golden candlesticks;

Figure 10.6 Illustration to Revelation of St. John, Book printed in 1893.

[13] And in the midst of the seven candlesticks one like unto the Son of man, clothed with a garment down to the foot, and girt about the paps with a golden girdle. [14] His head and his hairs were white like wool, as white as snow; and his eyes were as a flame of fire; [15] And his feet like unto fine brass, as if they burned in a furnace; and his voice as the sound of many waters. [16] And he had in his right hand seven stars: and out of his mouth went a sharp twoedged sword: and his countenance was as the sun shineth in his strength. [17] And when I saw him, I fell at his feet as dead. And he laid his right hand upon me, saying unto me, Fear not; I am the first and the last: [18] I am he that liveth, and was dead; and, behold, I am alive for evermore, Amen; and have the keys of hell and of death. [19] Write the things which thou hast seen, and the things which are, and the things which shall be hereafter; [20] The mystery of the seven stars which thou sawest in my right hand, and the seven golden candlesticks. The seven stars are the angels of the seven churches: and the seven candlesticks which thou sawest are the seven churches.

Revelation (KJV) 2: Unto the angel of the church of Ephesus write; These things saith he that holdeth the seven stars in his right hand, who walketh in the midst of the seven golden candlesticks; [2] I know thy works, and thy labour, and thy patience, and how thou canst not bear them which are evil: and thou hast tried them which say they are apostles, and are not, and hast found them liars: [3] And hast borne, and hast patience, and for my name's sake hast laboured, and hast not fainted. [4] Nevertheless I have somewhat against thee, because thou hast left thy first love. [5] Remember therefore from whence thou art fallen, and repent, and do the first works; or else I will come unto thee quickly, and will remove thy candlestick out of his place, except thou repent. [6] But this thou hast, that thou hatest the deeds of the Nicolaitanes, which I also hate. [7] He that hath an ear, let him hear what the Spirit saith unto the churches; To him that overcometh will I give to eat of the tree of life, which is in the midst of the paradise of God. [8] And unto the angel of the church in Smyrna write; These things saith the first and the last, which was dead, and is alive; [9] I know thy works, and tribulation, and poverty, (but thou art rich) and I know the blasphemy of them which say they are Jews, and are not, but are the synagogue of Satan. [0] Fear none of those things which thou shalt suffer: behold, the devil shall cast some of you into prison, that ye may be tried; and ye shall have tribulation ten days: be thou faithful unto death, and I will give thee a crown of life. [11] He that hath an ear, let him hear what the Spirit saith unto the churches; He that overcometh shall not be hurt of the second death. [12] And to the angel of the church in Pergamos write; These things saith he which hath the sharp sword with two edges; [13] I know thy works, and where thou dwellest, even where Satan's seat is: and thou holdest fast my name, and hast not denied my faith, even in those days wherein Antipas was my faithful martyr, who was slain among you, where Satan dwelleth. [14] But I have a few things against thee, because thou hast there them that hold the doctrine of Balaam, who taught Balac to cast a stumblingblock before the children of Israel, to eat things sacrificed unto idols, and to commit fornication. [15] So hast thou also them that hold the doctrine of the Nicolaitanes, which thing I hate. [16] Repent; or else I will come unto thee quickly, and will fight against them with the sword of my mouth. [17] He that hath an ear, let him hear what the Spirit saith unto the churches; To him that overcometh will I give to eat of the hidden manna, and will give him a white stone, and in the stone a new name written, which no man knoweth saving he that receiveth it. [18] And unto the angel of the church in Thyatira write; These things saith the Son of God, who hath his eyes like unto a flame of fire, and his feet are like fine brass; [19] I know thy works, and charity, and service, and faith, and thy patience, and thy works; and the last to be more than the first. [20] Notwithstanding I have a few things against thee, because thou sufferest that woman

Jezebel, which calleth herself a prophetess, to teach and to seduce my servants to commit fornication, and to eat things sacrificed unto idols. [21] And I gave her space to repent of her fornication; and she repented not. [22] Behold, I will cast her into a bed, and them that commit adultery with her into great tribulation, except they repent of their deeds. [23] And I will kill her children with death; and all the churches shall know that I am he which searcheth the reins and hearts: and I will give unto every one of you according to your works. [24] But unto you I say, and unto the rest in Thyatira, as many as have not this doctrine, and which have not known the depths of Satan, as they speak; I will put upon you none other burden. [25] But that which ye have already hold fast till I come. [26] And he that overcometh, and keepeth my works unto the end, to him will I give power over the nations: [27] And he shall rule them with a rod of iron; as the vessels of a potter shall they be broken to shivers: even as I received of my Father. [28] And I will give him the morning star. [29] He that hath an ear, let him hear what the Spirit saith unto the churches.

Revelation 3: And unto the angel of the church in Sardis write; These things saith he that hath the seven Spirits of God, and the seven stars; I know thy works, that thou hast a name that thou livest, and art dead. [2] Be watchful, and strengthen the things which remain, that are ready to die: for I have not found thy works perfect before God. [3] Remember therefore how thou hast received and heard, and hold fast, and repent. If therefore thou shalt not watch, I will come on thee as a thief, and thou shalt not know what hour I will come upon thee. [4] Thou hast a few names even in Sardis which have not defiled their garments; and they shall walk with me in white: for they are worthy. [5] He that overcometh, the same shall be clothed in white raiment; and I will not blot out his name out of the book of life, but I will confess his name before my Father, and before his angels. [6] He that hath an ear, let him hear what the Spirit saith unto the churches. [7] And to the angel of the church in Philadelphia write; These things saith he that is holy, he that is true, he that hath the key of David, he that openeth, and no man shutteth; and shutteth, and no man openeth; [8] I know thy works: behold, I have set before thee an open door, and no man can shut it: for thou hast a little strength, and hast kept my word, and hast not denied my name. [9] Behold, I will make them of the synagogue of Satan, which say they are Jews, and are not, but do lie; behold, I will make them to come and worship before thy feet, and to know that I have loved thee. [10] Because thou hast kept the word of my patience, I also will keep thee from the hour of temptation, which shall come upon all the world, to try them that dwell upon the earth. [11] Behold, I come quickly: hold that fast which thou hast, that no man take thy crown. [12] Him that overcometh will I make a pillar in the temple of my God, and he shall go no more out: and I will write upon him the name of my God, and the name of the city of my God, which is new Jerusalem, which cometh down out of heaven from my God: and I will write upon him my new name. [13] He that hath an ear, let him hear what the Spirit saith unto the churches. [14] And unto the angel of the church of the Laodiceans write; These things saith the Amen, the faithful and true witness, the beginning of the creation of God; [15] I know thy works, that thou art neither cold nor hot: I would thou wert cold or hot. [16] So then because thou art lukewarm, and neither cold nor hot, I will spue thee out of my mouth. [17] Because thou sayest, I am rich, and increased with goods, and have need of nothing; and knowest not that thou art wretched, and miserable, and poor, and blind, and naked: [18] I counsel thee to buy of me gold tried in the fire, that thou mayest be rich; and white raiment, that thou mayest be clothed, and that the shame of thy nakedness do not appear; and anoint thine eyes with eyesalve, that thou mayest see. [19] As many as I love, I rebuke and chasten: be zealous therefore, and repent. [20] Behold, I stand at the door, and knock: if any man hear my voice, and open the door, I will come in to him, and will sup with him, and he with me. [21] To him that overcometh will I grant to sit with me in my throne, even as I also overcame, and am set down with my Father in his throne. [22] He that hath an ear, let him hear what the Spirit saith unto the churches.

Revelation 4: After this I looked, and, behold, a door was opened in heaven: and the first voice which I heard was as it were of a trumpet talking with me; which said, Come up hither, and I will shew thee things which must be hereafter. [2] And immediately I was in the spirit: and, behold, a throne was set in heaven, and one sat on the throne. [3] And he that sat was to look upon like a jasper and a sardine stone: and there was a rainbow round about the throne, in sight like unto an emerald.

Figure 10.7 Saint John on Patmos by the Limbourg Brothers. Date: between 1411 and 1416

[4] And round about the throne were four and twenty seats: and upon the seats I saw four and twenty elders sitting, clothed in white raiment; and they had on their heads crowns of gold. [5] And out of the throne proceeded lightnings and thunderings and voices: and there were seven lamps of fire burning before the throne, which are the seven Spirits of God. [6] And before the throne there was a

sea of glass like unto crystal: and in the midst of the throne, and round about the throne, were four beasts full of eyes before and behind. [7] And the first beast was like a lion, and the second beast like a calf, and the third beast had a face as a man, and the fourth beast was like a flying eagle. [8] And the four beasts had each of them six wings about him; and they were full of eyes within: and they rest not day and night, saying, Holy, holy, holy, LORD God Almighty, which was, and is, and is to come. [9] And when those beasts give glory and honour and thanks to him that sat on the throne, who liveth for ever and ever, [10] The four and twenty elders fall down before him that sat on the throne, and worship him that liveth for ever and ever, and cast their crowns before the throne, saying, [11] Thou art worthy, O Lord, to receive glory and honour and power: for thou hast created all things, and for thy pleasure they are and were created.

Revelation 5 And I saw in the right hand of him that sat on the throne a book written within and on the backside, sealed with seven seals. [2] And I saw a strong angel proclaiming with a loud voice, Who is worthy to open the book, and to loose the seals thereof? [3] And no man in heaven, nor in earth, neither under the earth, was able to open the book, neither to look thereon. [4] And I wept much, because no man was found worthy to open and to read the book, neither to look thereon. [5] And one of the elders saith unto me, Weep not: behold, the Lion of the tribe of Judah, the Root of David, hath prevailed to open the book, and to loose the seven seals thereof. [6] And I beheld, and, lo, in the midst of the throne and of the four beasts, and in the midst of the elders, stood a Lamb as it had been slain, having seven horns and seven eyes, which are the seven Spirits of God sent forth into all the earth. [7] And he came and took the book out of the right hand of him that sat upon the throne.

Figure 10.8 John's Vision of Heaven, Revelation 4:1-11, 5:1-14 by Matthias Gerung.

[8] And when he had taken the book, the four beasts and four and twenty elders fell down before the Lamb, having every one of them harps, and golden vials full of odours, which are the prayers of saints. [9] And they sung a new song, saying, Thou art worthy to take the book, and to open the seals thereof: for thou wast slain, and hast redeemed us to God by thy blood out of every kindred, and tongue, and people, and nation; [10] And hast made us unto our God kings and priests: and we shall reign on the earth. [11] And I beheld, and I heard the voice of many angels round about the throne and the beasts and the elders: and the number of them was ten thousand times ten thousand, and thousands of thousands; [12] Saying with a loud voice, Worthy is the Lamb that was slain to receive power, and riches, and wisdom, and strength, and honour, and glory, and blessing. [13] And every creature which is in heaven, and on the earth, and under the earth, and such as are in the sea, and all that are in them, heard I saying, Blessing, and honour, and glory, and power, be unto him that sitteth upon the throne, and unto the Lamb for ever and ever. [14] And the four beasts said, Amen. And the four and twenty elders fell down and worshipped him that liveth for ever and ever.

Revelation 6: And I saw when the Lamb opened one of the seals, and I heard, as it were the noise of thunder, one of the four beasts saying, Come and see. [2] And I saw, and behold a white horse: and he that sat on him had a bow; and a crown was given unto him: and he went forth conquering, and to conquer. [3] And when he had opened the second seal, I heard the second beast say, Come and see.

Figure 10.9 Four Horsemen of Apocalypse (1887), by Viktor Vasnetsov

[4] And there went out another horse that was red: and power was given to him that sat thereon to take peace from the earth, and that they should kill one another: and there was given unto him a great sword.

Figure 10.10 Death on a Pale Horse (1796) by Benjamin West.

[5] And when he had opened the third seal, I heard the third beast say, Come and see. And I beheld, and lo a black horse; and he that sat on him had a pair of balances in his hand. [6] And I heard a voice in the midst of the four beasts say, A measure of wheat for a penny, and three measures of barley for a penny; and see thou hurt not the oil and the wine. [7] And when he had opened the fourth seal, I heard the voice of the fourth beast say, Come and see. [8] And I looked, and behold a pale horse: and his name that sat on him was Death, and Hell followed with him. And power was given unto

them over the fourth part of the earth, to kill with sword, and with hunger, and with death, and with the beasts of the earth. [9] And when he had opened the fifth seal, I saw under the altar the souls of them that were slain for the word of God, and for the testimony which they held: [10] And they cried with a loud voice, saying, How long, O Lord, holy and true, dost thou not judge and avenge our blood on them that dwell on the earth? [11] And white robes were given unto every one of them; and it was said unto them, that they should rest yet for a little season, until their fellowservants also and their brethren, that should be killed as they were, should be fulfilled. [12] And I beheld when he had opened the sixth seal, and, lo, there was a great earthquake; and the sun became black as sackcloth of hair, and the moon became as blood; [3] And the stars of heaven fell unto the earth, even as a fig tree casteth her untimely figs, when she is shaken of a mighty wind. [14] And the heaven departed as a scroll when it is rolled together; and every mountain and island were moved out of their places. [15] And the kings of the earth, and the great men, and the rich men, and the chief captains, and the mighty men, and every bondman, and every free man, hid themselves in the dens and in the rocks of the mountains; [16] And said to the mountains and rocks, Fall on us, and hide us from the face of him that sitteth on the throne, and from the wrath of the Lamb: [17] For the great day of his wrath is come; and who shall be able to stand?

Revelation 7 And after these things I saw four angels standing on the four corners of the earth, holding the four winds of the earth, that the wind should not blow on the earth, nor on the sea, nor on any tree. [2] And I saw another angel ascending from the east, having the seal of the living God: and he cried with a loud voice to the four angels, to whom it was given to hurt the earth and the sea, [3] Saying, Hurt not the earth, neither the sea, nor the trees, till we have sealed the servants of our God in their foreheads.

**Figure 10.11 Angels Holding the Four Winds / The Sealing of the 144,000,
Revelation 7:1-8 by Matthias Gerung.**

[4] And I heard the number of them which were sealed: and there were sealed an hundred and forty and four thousand of all the tribes of the children of Israel. [5] Of the tribe of Juda were sealed twelve thousand. Of the tribe of Reuben were sealed twelve thousand. Of the tribe of Gad were sealed twelve thousand. [6] Of the tribe of Aser were sealed twelve thousand. Of the tribe of Nephthalim were sealed twelve thousand. Of the tribe of Manasses were sealed twelve thousand. [7] Of the tribe of Simeon were sealed twelve thousand. Of the tribe of Levi were sealed twelve thousand. Of the tribe of Issachar were sealed twelve thousand. [8] Of the tribe of Zabulon were sealed twelve thousand. Of the tribe of Joseph were sealed twelve thousand. Of the tribe of Benjamin were sealed twelve thousand. [9] After this I beheld, and, lo, a great multitude, which no man could number, of all nations, and kindreds, and people, and tongues, stood before the throne, and before the Lamb, clothed with white robes, and palms in their hands; [10] And cried with a loud voice, saying, Salvation to our God which sitteth upon the throne, and unto the Lamb. [11] And all the angels stood round about the throne, and about the elders and the four beasts, and fell before the throne on their faces, and worshipped God, [12] Saying, Amen: Blessing, and glory, and wisdom, and thanksgiving, and honour, and power, and might, be unto our God for ever and ever. Amen. [13] And one of the elders answered, saying unto me, What are these which are arrayed in white robes? and whence came they? [14] And I said unto him, Sir, thou knowest. And he said to me, These are they which came out of great tribulation, and have washed their robes, and made them white in the blood of the Lamb.

[15] Therefore are they before the throne of God, and serve him day and night in his temple: and he that sitteth on the throne shall dwell among them. [16] They shall hunger no more, neither thirst any more; neither shall the sun light on them, nor any heat. [17] For the Lamb which is in the midst of the throne shall feed them, and shall lead them unto living fountains of waters: and God shall wipe away all tears from their eyes.

Revelation 8 And when he had opened the seventh seal, there was silence in heaven about the space of half an hour. [2] And I saw the seven angels which stood before God; and to them were given seven trumpets. [3] And another angel came and stood at the altar, having a golden censer; and there was given unto him much incense, that he should offer it with the prayers of all saints upon the golden altar which was before the throne.

[4] And the smoke of the incense, which came with the prayers of the saints, ascended up before God out of the angel's hand.

Figure 10.12 The Opening of the Seventh Seal and the First Four Sounding Trumpets (1530–1532) by Matthias Gerung

[5] And the angel took the censer, and filled it with fire of the altar, and cast it into the earth: and there were voices, and thunderings, and lightnings, and an earthquake. [6] And the seven angels which had the seven trumpets prepared themselves to sound. [7] The first angel sounded, and there followed hail and fire mingled with blood, and they were cast upon the earth: and the third part of trees was burnt up, and all green grass was burnt up. [8] And the second angel sounded, and as it were a great mountain burning with fire was cast into the sea: and the third part of the sea became blood; [9] And the third part of the creatures which were in the sea, and had life, died; and the third part of the ships were destroyed. [10] And the third angel sounded, and there fell a great star from heaven, burning as it were a lamp, and it fell upon the third part of the rivers, and upon the fountains of waters; [11] And the name of the star is called Wormwood: and the third part of the waters became wormwood; and many men died of the waters, because they were made bitter. [12] And the fourth angel sounded, and the third part of the sun was smitten, and the third part of the moon, and the third part of the stars; so as the third part of them was darkened, and the day shone not for a third part of it, and the night likewise. [13] And I beheld, and heard an angel flying through the midst of heaven, saying with a loud voice, Woe, woe, woe, to the inhabiters of the earth by reason of the other voices of the trumpet of the three angels, which are yet to sound!

Revelation 9 And the fifth angel sounded, and I saw a star fall from heaven unto the earth: and to him was given the key of the bottomless pit. [2] And he opened the bottomless pit; and there arose a smoke out of the pit, as the smoke of a great furnace; and the sun and the air were darkened by reason of the smoke of the pit. [3] And there came out of the smoke locusts upon the earth: and unto them was given power, as the scorpions of the earth have power. [4] And it was commanded them that they should not hurt the grass of the earth, neither any green thing, neither any tree; but only those men which have not the seal of God in their foreheads. [5] And to them it was given that they should not kill them, but that they should be tormented five months: and their torment was as the torment of a scorpion, when he striketh a man. [6] And in those days shall men seek death, and shall not find it; and shall desire to die, and death shall flee from them. [7] And the shapes of the locusts were like unto horses prepared unto battle; and on their heads were as it were crowns like gold, and their faces were as the faces of men. [8] And they had hair as the hair of women, and their teeth were as the teeth of lions.

[9] And they had breastplates, as it were breastplates of iron; and the sound of their wings was as the sound of chariots of many horses running to battle. [10] And they had tails like unto scorpions, and there were stings in their tails: and their power was to hurt men five months.

Figure 10.13 The Fifth and Sixth Trumpets, Revelation 9:1-12 by Matthias Gerung.

[11] And they had a king over them, which is the angel of the bottomless pit, whose name in the Hebrew tongue is Abaddon, but in the Greek tongue hath his name Apollyon. [12] One woe is past; and, behold, there come two woes more hereafter. [13] And the sixth angel sounded, and I heard a voice from the four horns of the golden altar which is before God, [14] Saying to the sixth angel which had the trumpet, Loose the four angels which are bound in the great river Euphrates. [15] And the four angels were loosed, which were prepared for an hour, and a day, and a month, and a year, for to slay the third part of men. [16] And the number of the army of the horsemen were two hundred thousand thousand: and I heard the number of them. [17] And thus I saw the horses in the vision, and them that sat on them, having breastplates of fire, and of jacinth, and brimstone: and the heads of the horses were as the heads of lions; and out of their mouths issued fire and smoke and brimstone. [18] By these three was the third part of men killed, by the fire, and by the smoke, and by the brimstone, which issued out of their mouths. [19] For their power is in their mouth, and in their tails: for their tails were like unto serpents, and had heads, and with them they do hurt. [20] And the rest of the men which were not killed by these plagues yet repented not of the works of their hands, that they

should not worship devils, and idols of gold, and silver, and brass, and stone, and of wood: which neither can see, nor hear, nor walk: [21] Neither repented they of their murders, nor of their sorceries, nor of their fornication, nor of their thefts.

Revelation 10 And I saw another mighty angel come down from heaven, clothed with a cloud: and a rainbow was upon his head, and his face was as it were the sun, and his feet as pillars of fire: [2] And he had in his hand a little book open: and he set his right foot upon the sea, and his left foot on the earth, [3] And cried with a loud voice, as when a lion roareth: and when he had cried, seven thunders uttered their voices. [4] And when the seven thunders had uttered their voices, I was about to write: and I heard a voice from heaven saying unto me, Seal up those things which the seven thunders uttered, and write them not.

[5] And the angel which I saw stand upon the sea and upon the earth lifted up his hand to heaven, [6] And sware by him that liveth for ever and ever, who created heaven, and the things that therein are, and the earth, and the things that therein are, and the sea, and the things which are therein, that there should be time no longer:

Figure 10.14 St. John devouring the book, Rev 10:1-11 by Matthias Gerung.

[7] But in the days of the voice of the seventh angel, when he shall begin to sound, the mystery of God should be finished, as he hath declared to his servants the prophets. [8] And the voice which I heard from heaven spake unto me again, and said, Go and take the little book which is open in the hand of the angel which standeth upon the sea and upon the earth. [9] And I went unto the angel, and said unto him, Give me the little book. And he said unto me, Take it, and eat it up; and it shall make thy belly bitter, but it shall be in thy mouth sweet as honey. [10] And I took the little book out of the angel's hand, and ate it up; and it was in my mouth sweet as honey: and as soon as I had eaten it,

my belly was bitter. [11] And he said unto me, Thou must prophesy again before many peoples, and nations, and tongues, and kings.

Revelation 11 And there was given me a reed like unto a rod: and the angel stood, saying, Rise, and measure the temple of God, and the altar, and them that worship therein. [2] But the court which is without the leave out, and measure it not; for it is given unto the Gentiles: and the holy city shall they tread under foot forty and two months. [3] And I will give power unto my two witnesses, and they shall prophesy a thousand two hundred and threescore days, clothed in sackcloth.

Figure 10.15 The measurement of the temple and the testimony of the two prophets, Rev. 11:1-14 by Matthias Gerung.

[4] These are the two olive trees, and the two candlesticks standing before the God of the earth. [5] And if any man will hurt them, fire proceedeth out of their mouth, and devoureth their enemies: and if any man will hurt them, he must in this manner be killed. [6] These have power to shut heaven, that it rain not in the days of their prophecy: and have power over waters to turn them to blood, and

to smite the earth with all plagues, as often as they will. [7] And when they shall have finished their testimony, the beast that ascendeth out of the bottomless pit shall make war against them, and shall overcome them, and kill them. [8] And their dead bodies shall lie in the street of the great city, which spiritually is called Sodom and Egypt, where also our Lord was crucified. [9] And they of the people and kindreds and tongues and nations shall see their dead bodies three days and an half, and shall not suffer their dead bodies to be put in graves. [10] And they that dwell upon the earth shall rejoice over them, and make merry, and shall send gifts one to another; because these two prophets tormented them that dwelt on the earth. [11] And after three days and an half the spirit of life from God entered into them, and they stood upon their feet; and great fear fell upon them which saw them. [12] And they heard a great voice from heaven saying unto them, Come up hither. And they ascended up to heaven in a cloud; and their enemies beheld them. [13] And the same hour was there a great earthquake, and the tenth part of the city fell, and in the earthquake were slain of men seven thousand: and the remnant were affrighted, and gave glory to the God of heaven. [14] The second woe is past; and, behold, the third woe cometh quickly. [15] And the seventh angel sounded; and there were great voices in heaven, saying, The kingdoms of this world are become the kingdoms of our Lord, and of his Christ; and he shall reign for ever and ever. [16] And the four and twenty elders, which sat before God on their seats, fell upon their faces, and worshipped God, [17] Saying, We give thee thanks, O LORD God Almighty, which art, and wast, and art to come; because thou hast taken to thee thy great power, and hast reigned. [18] And the nations were angry, and thy wrath is come, and the time of the dead, that they should be judged, and that thou shouldest give reward unto thy servants the prophets, and to the saints, and them that fear thy name, small and great; and shouldest destroy them which destroy the earth. [19] And the temple of God was opened in heaven, and there was seen in his the ark of his testament: and there were lightnings, and voices, and thunderings, and an earthquake, and great hail.

Revelation 12 And there appeared a great wonder in heaven; a woman clothed with the sun, and the moon under her feet, and upon her head a crown of twelve stars: [2] And she being with child cried, travailing in birth, and pained to be delivered. [3] And there appeared another wonder in heaven; and behold a great red dragon, having seven heads and ten horns, and seven crowns upon his heads. [4] And his tail drew the third part of the stars of heaven, and did cast them to the earth: and the dragon stood before the woman which was ready to be delivered, for to devour her child as soon as it was born. [5] And she brought forth a man child, who was to rule all nations with a rod of iron: and her child was caught up unto God, and to his throne. [6] And the woman fled into the wilderness, where she hath a place prepared of God, that they should feed her there a thousand two hundred and threescore days.

**Figure 10.16 Landscape with St John the Evangelist at Patmos (1598)
by Tobias Verhaecht (1561–1631)**

[7] And there was war in heaven: Michael and his angels fought against the dragon; and the dragon fought and his angels, [8] And prevailed not; neither was their place found any more in heaven. [9] And the great dragon was cast out, that old serpent, called the Devil, and Satan, which deceiveth the whole world: he was cast out into the earth, and his angels were cast out with him. [10] And I heard a loud voice saying in heaven, Now is come salvation, and strength, and the kingdom of our God, and the power of his Christ: for the accuser of our brethren is cast down, which accused them before our God day and night. [11] And they overcame him by the blood of the Lamb, and by the word of their testimony; and they loved not their lives unto the death. [12] Therefore rejoice, ye heavens, and ye that dwell in them. Woe to the inhabiters of the earth and of the sea! for the devil is come down unto you, having great wrath, because he knoweth that he hath but a short time. [13] And when the dragon saw that he was cast unto the earth, he persecuted the woman which brought forth the man child. [14] And to the woman were given two wings of a great eagle, that she might fly into the wilderness, into her place, where she is nourished for a time, and times, and half a time, from the face of the serpent. [15] And the serpent cast out of his mouth water as a flood after the woman, that he might cause her to be carried away of the flood. [16] And the earth helped the woman, and the earth opened her mouth, and swallowed up the flood which the dragon cast out of his mouth. [17] And the dragon was wroth with the woman, and went to make war with the remnant of her seed, which keep the commandments of God, and have the testimony of Jesus Christ.

Revelation 13 And I stood upon the sand of the sea, and saw a beast rise up out of the sea, having seven heads and ten horns, and upon his horns ten crowns, and upon his heads the name of blasphemy. [2] And the beast which I saw was like unto a leopard, and his feet were as the feet of a bear, and his mouth as the mouth of a lion: and the dragon gave him his power, and his seat, and great authority. [3] And I saw one of his heads as it were wounded to death; and his deadly wound was healed: and all the world wondered after the beast. [4] And they worshipped the dragon which gave power unto the beast: and they worshipped the beast, saying, Who is like unto the beast? who is able to make war with him?

Figure 10.17 The Sea Monster and the Beast with the Lamb's Horn by Albrecht Dürer.

[5] And there was given unto him a mouth speaking great things and blasphemies; and power was given unto him to continue forty and two months. [6] And he opened his mouth in blasphemy against God, to blaspheme his name, and his tabernacle, and them that dwell in heaven. [7] And it was given unto him to make war with the saints, and to overcome them: and power was given him over all kindreds, and tongues, and nations. [8] And all that dwell upon the earth shall worship him, whose names are not written in the book of life of the Lamb slain from the foundation of the world. [9] If any man have an ear, let him hear.[10] He that leadeth into captivity shall go into captivity: he that

killeth with the sword must be killed with the sword. Here is the patience and the faith of the saints. [11] And I beheld another beast coming up out of the earth; and he had two horns like a lamb, and he spake as a dragon.

Figure 10.18 The Beast by William Blake (1757–1827).

[12] And he exerciseth all the power of the first beast before him, and causeth the earth and them which dwell therein to worship the first beast, whose deadly wound was healed. [13] And he doeth great wonders, so that he maketh fire come down from heaven on the earth in the sight of men, [14] And deceiveth them that dwell on the earth by the means of those miracles which he had power to do in the sight of the beast; saying to them that dwell on the earth, that they should make an image to the beast, which had the wound by a sword, and did live. [15] And he had power to give life unto the image of the beast, that the image of the beast should both speak, and cause that as many as would not worship the image of the beast should be killed. [16] And he causeth all, both small and great, rich and poor, free and bond, to receive a mark in their right hand, or in their foreheads: [17] And that no man might buy or sell, save he that had the mark, or the name of the beast, or the

number of his name. [18] Here is wisdom. Let him that hath understanding count the number of the beast: for it is the number of a man; and his number is Six hundred threescore and six.

Revelation 14 And I looked, and, lo, a Lamb stood on the mount Sion, and with him an hundred forty and four thousand, having his Father's name written in their foreheads. [2] And I heard a voice from heaven, as the voice of many waters, and as the voice of a great thunder: and I heard the voice of harpers harping with their harps: [3] And they sung as it were a new song before the throne, and before the four beasts, and the elders: and no man could learn that song but the hundred and forty and four thousand, which were redeemed from the earth. [4] These are they which were not defiled with women; for they are virgins. These are they which follow the Lamb whithersoever he goeth. These were redeemed from among men, being the firstfruits unto God and to the Lamb. [5] And in their mouth was found no guile: for they are without fault before the throne of God. [6] And I saw another angel fly in the midst of heaven, having the everlasting gospel to preach unto them that dwell on the earth, and to every nation, and kindred, and tongue, and people, [7] Saying with a loud voice, Fear God, and give glory to him; for the hour of his judgment is come: and worship him that made heaven, and earth, and the sea, and the fountains of waters. [8] And there followed another angel, saying, Babylon is fallen, is fallen, that great city, because she made all nations drink of the wine of the wrath of her fornication. [9] And the third angel followed them, saying with a loud voice, If any man worship the beast and his image, and receive his mark in his forehead, or in his hand, [10] The same shall drink of the wine of the wrath of God, which is poured out without mixture into the cup of his indignation; and he shall be tormented with fire and brimstone in the presence of the holy angels, and in the presence of the Lamb: [11] And the smoke of their torment ascendeth up for ever and ever: and they have no rest day nor night, who worship the beast and his image, and whosoever receiveth the mark of his name. [12] Here is the patience of the saints: here are they that keep the commandments of God, and the faith of Jesus. [13] And I heard a voice from heaven saying unto me, Write, Blessed are the dead which die in the Lord from henceforth: Yea, saith the Spirit, that they may rest from their labours; and their works do follow them. [14] And I looked, and behold a white cloud, and upon the cloud one sat like unto the Son of man, having on his head a golden crown, and in his hand a sharp sickle. [15] And another angel came out of the temple, crying with a loud voice to him that sat on the cloud, Thrust in thy sickle, and reap: for the time is come for thee to reap; for the harvest of the earth is ripe. [16] And he that sat on the cloud thrust in his sickle on the earth; and the earth was reaped. [17] And another angel came out of the temple which is in heaven, he also having a sharp sickle. [18] And another angel came out from the altar, which had power over fire; and cried with a loud cry to him that had the sharp sickle, saying, Thrust in thy sharp sickle, and gather the clusters of the vine of the earth; for her grapes are fully ripe. [19] And the angel thrust in his sickle into the earth, and gathered the vine of the earth, and cast it into the great winepress of the wrath of God. [20] And the winepress was trodden without the city, and blood came out of the winepress, even unto the horse bridles, by the space of a thousand and six hundred furlongs.

Revelation 15 And I saw another sign in heaven, great and marvellous, seven angels having the seven last plagues; for in them is filled up the wrath of God. [2] And I saw as it were a sea of glass mingled with fire: and them that had gotten the victory over the beast, and over his image, and over his mark, and over the number of his name, stand on the sea of glass, having the harps of God. [3] And they sing the song of Moses the servant of God, and the song of the Lamb, saying, Great and marvellous are thy works, Lord God Almighty; just and true are thy ways, thou King of saints. [4]

Who shall not fear thee, O Lord, and glorify thy name? for thou only art holy: for all nations shall come and worship before thee; for thy judgments are made manifest. [5]And after that I looked, and, behold, the temple of the tabernacle of the testimony in heaven was opened: [6]And the seven angels came out of the temple, having the seven plagues, clothed in pure and white linen, and having their breasts girded with golden girdles. [7]And one of the four beasts gave unto the seven angels seven golden vials full of the wrath of God, who liveth for ever and ever. [8]And the temple was filled with smoke from the glory of God, and from his power; and no man was able to enter into the temple, till the seven plagues of the seven angels were fulfilled.

Revelation 16 And I heard a great voice out of the temple saying to the seven angels, Go your ways, and pour out the vials of the wrath of God upon the earth. [2]And the first went, and poured out his vial upon the earth; and there fell a noisome and grievous sore upon the men which had the mark of the beast, and upon them which worshipped his image. [3]And the second angel poured out his vial upon the sea; and it became as the blood of a dead man: and every living soul died in the sea. [4]And the third angel poured out his vial upon the rivers and fountains of waters; and they became blood. [5]And I heard the angel of the waters say, Thou art righteous, O Lord, which art, and wast, and shalt be, because thou hast judged thus.

Figure 10.19 The Giving of the Seven Bowls of Wrath/The First Six Plagues, Revelation 16:1-16 by Matthias Gerung.

⁶ For they have shed the blood of saints and prophets, and thou hast given them blood to drink; for they are worthy. ⁷ And I heard another out of the altar say, Even so, Lord God Almighty, true and righteous are thy judgments. ⁸ And the fourth angel poured out his vial upon the sun; and power was given unto him to scorch men with fire. ⁹ And men were scorched with great heat, and blasphemed the name of God, which hath power over these plagues: and they repented not to give him glory. ¹⁰ And the fifth angel poured out his vial upon the seat of the beast; and his kingdom was full of darkness; and they gnawed their tongues for pain, ¹¹ And blasphemed the God of heaven because of their pains and their sores, and repented not of their deeds. ¹² And the sixth angel poured out his vial upon the great river Euphrates; and the water thereof was dried up, that the way of the kings of the east might be prepared. ¹³ And I saw three unclean spirits like frogs come out of the mouth of the dragon, and out of the mouth of the beast, and out of the mouth of the false prophet. ¹⁴ For they are the spirits of devils, working miracles, which go forth unto the kings of the earth and of the whole world, to gather them to the battle of that great day of God Almighty. ¹⁵ Behold, I come as a thief. Blessed is he that watcheth, and keepeth his garments, lest he walk naked, and they see his shame. ¹⁶ And he gathered them together into a place called in the Hebrew tongue Armageddon. ¹⁷ And the seventh angel poured out his vial into the air; and there came a great voice out of the temple of heaven, from the throne, saying, It is done.

Figure 10.20 The Giving of the Seventh Bowl of Wrath, Revelation 16:17-21 by Matthias Gerung.

[18] And there were voices, and thunders, and lightnings; and there was a great earthquake, such as was not since men were upon the earth, so mighty an earthquake, and so great. [19] And the great city was divided into three parts, and the cities of the nations fell: and great Babylon came in remembrance before God, to give unto her the cup of the wine of the fierceness of his wrath. [20] And every island fled away, and the mountains were not found. [21] And there fell upon men a great hail out of heaven, every stone about the weight of a talent: and men blasphemed God because of the plague of the hail; for the plague thereof was exceeding great.

Revelation 17 And there came one of the seven angels which had the seven vials, and talked with me, saying unto me, Come hither; I will shew unto thee the judgment of the great whore that sitteth upon many waters: [2] With whom the kings of the earth have committed fornication, and the inhabitants of the earth have been made drunk with the wine of her fornication. [3] So he carried me away in the spirit into the wilderness: and I saw a woman sit upon a scarlet coloured beast, full of names of blasphemy, having seven heads and ten horns. [4] And the woman was arrayed in purple and scarlet colour, and decked with gold and precious stones and pearls, having a golden cup in her hand full of abominations and filthiness of her fornication: [5] And upon her forehead was a name written, MYSTERY, BABYLON THE GREAT, THE MOTHER OF HARLOTS AND ABOMINATIONS OF THE EARTH. [6] And I saw the woman drunken with the blood of the saints, and with the blood of the martyrs of Jesus: and when I saw her, I wondered with great admiration. [7] And the angel said unto me, Wherefore didst thou marvel? I will tell thee the mystery of the woman, and of the beast that carrieth her, which hath the seven heads and ten horns. [8] The beast that thou sawest was, and is not; and shall ascend out of the bottomless pit, and go into perdition: and they that dwell on the earth shall wonder, whose names were not written in the book of life from the foundation of the world, when they behold the beast that was, and is not, and yet is. [9] And here is the mind which hath wisdom. The seven heads are seven mountains, on which the woman sitteth. [10] And there are seven kings: five are fallen, and one is, and the other is not yet come; and when he cometh, he must continue a short space. [11] And the beast that was, and is not, even he is the eighth, and is of the seven, and goeth into perdition. [12] And the ten horns which thou sawest are ten kings, which have received no kingdom as yet; but receive power as kings one hour with the beast. [13] These have one mind, and shall give their power and strength unto the beast. [14] These shall make war with the Lamb, and the Lamb shall overcome them: for he is Lord of lords, and King of kings: and they that are with him are called, and chosen, and faithful. [15] And he saith unto me, The waters which thou sawest, where the whore sitteth, are peoples, and multitudes, and nations, and tongues. [16] And the ten horns which thou sawest upon the beast, these shall hate the whore, and shall make her desolate and naked, and shall eat her flesh, and burn her with fire. [17] For God hath put in their hearts to fulfil his will, and to agree, and give their kingdom unto the beast, until the words of God shall be fulfilled. [18] And the woman which thou sawest is that great city, which reigneth over the kings of the earth.

Revelation 18 And after these things I saw another angel come down from heaven, having great power; and the earth was lightened with his glory. [2] And he cried mightily with a strong voice, saying, Babylon the great is fallen, is fallen, and is become the habitation of devils, and the hold of every foul spirit, and a cage of every unclean and hateful bird. [3] For all nations have drunk of the wine of the wrath of her fornication, and the kings of the earth have committed fornication with her, and the merchants of the earth are waxed rich through the abundance of her

**Figure 10.21 Colored version of the Whore of Babylon illustration
from Martin Luther's 1534 translation of the Bible.**

delicacies. [4] And I heard another voice from heaven, saying, Come out of her, my people, that ye be not partakers of her sins, and that ye receive not of her plagues. [5] For her sins have reached unto heaven, and God hath remembered her iniquities. [6] Reward her even as she rewarded you, and double unto her double according to her works: in the cup which she hath filled fill to her double. [7] How much she hath glorified herself, and lived deliciously, so much torment and sorrow give her: for she saith in her heart, I sit a queen, and am no widow, and shall see no sorrow. [8] Therefore shall her plagues come in one day, death, and mourning, and famine; and she shall be utterly burned with fire: for strong is the Lord God who judgeth her. [9] And the kings of the earth, who have committed fornication and lived deliciously with her, shall bewail her, and lament for her, when they shall see the smoke of her burning, [10] Standing afar off for the fear of her torment, saying, Alas, alas that great city Babylon, that mighty city! for in one hour is thy judgment come. [11] And the merchants of the earth shall weep and mourn over her; for no man buyeth their merchandise any more: [12] The merchandise of gold, and silver, and precious stones, and of pearls, and fine linen, and purple, and silk, and scarlet, and all thyine wood, and all manner vessels of ivory, and all manner vessels of most precious wood, and of brass, and iron, and marble, [13] And cinnamon, and odours, and ointments, and frankincense, and wine, and oil, and fine flour, and wheat, and beasts, and sheep, and horses, and chariots, and slaves, and souls of men. [14] And the fruits that thy soul lusted after are departed from thee, and all things which were dainty and goodly are departed from thee, and thou shalt find them no more at all. [15] The merchants of these things, which were made rich by her, shall stand afar off for the fear of her torment, weeping and wailing,

[#22] Figure10.22 The Fall of Babylon, Revelation 18:9-24, 19:11-21 (1530-1532) by Matthias Gerung.

[16] And saying, Alas, alas that great city, that was clothed in fine linen, and purple, and scarlet, and decked with gold, and precious stones, and pearls! [17] For in one hour so great riches is come to nought. And every shipmaster, and all the company in ships, and sailors, and as many as trade by sea, stood afar off, [18] And cried when they saw the smoke of her burning, saying, What city is like unto this great city! [19] And they cast dust on their heads, and cried, weeping and wailing, saying, Alas, alas that great city, wherein were made rich all that had ships in the sea by reason of her costliness! for in one hour is she made desolate. [20] Rejoice over her, thou heaven, and ye holy apostles and prophets; for God hath avenged you on her. [21] And a mighty angel took up a stone like a great millstone, and cast it into the sea, saying, Thus with violence shall that great city Babylon be thrown down, and shall be found no more at all. [22] And the voice of harpers, and musicians, and of pipers, and trumpeters, shall be heard no more at all in thee; and no craftsman, of whatsoever craft he be, shall be found any more in thee; and the sound of a millstone shall be heard no more at all in thee; [23] And the light of a candle shall shine no more at all in thee; and the voice of the bridegroom

and of the bride shall be heard no more at all in thee: for thy merchants were the great men of the earth; for by thy sorceries were all nations deceived. [24] And in her was found the blood of prophets, and of saints, and of all that were slain upon the earth.

Revelation 19 (KJV) And after these things I heard a great voice of much people in heaven, saying, Alleluia; Salvation, and glory, and honour, and power, unto the Lord our God: [2] For true and righteous are his judgments: for he hath judged the great whore, which did corrupt the earth with her fornication, and hath avenged the blood of his servants at her hand.[3] And again they said, Alleluia And her smoke rose up for ever and ever. [4] And the four and twenty elders and the four beasts fell down and worshipped God that sat on the throne, saying, Amen; Alleluia. [5] And a voice came out of the throne, saying, Praise our God, all ye his servants, and ye that fear him, both small and great. [6] And I heard as it were the voice of a great multitude, and as the voice of many waters, and as the voice of mighty thunderings, saying, Alleluia: for the Lord God omnipotent reigneth. [7] Let us be glad and rejoice, and give honour to him: for the marriage of the Lamb is come, and his wife hath made herself ready. [8] And to her was granted that she should be arrayed in fine linen, clean and white: **for the fine linen is the righteousness of saints.**

**Figure 10.23 Woodcut for "the Bride of Christ" (1860)
by Julius Schnorr von Carolsfeld (1794–1872)**

[9]And he saith unto me, Write, Blessed are they which are called unto the marriage supper of the Lamb. And he saith unto me, These are the true sayings of God [10]And I fell at his feet to worship him. And he said unto me, See thou do it not: I am thy fellowservant, and of thy brethren that have the testimony of Jesus: worship God: for the testimony of Jesus is the spirit of prophecy. [11]And I saw heaven opened, and behold a white horse; and he that sat upon him was called Faithful and True, and in righteousness he doth judge and make war. [12]His eyes were as a flame of fire, and on his head were many crowns; and he had a name written, that no man knew, but he himself. [13]And he was clothed with a vesture dipped in blood: and his name is called The Word of God. [14]And the armies which were in heaven followed him upon white horses, clothed in fine linen, white and clean. [15]And out of his mouth goeth a sharp sword, that with it he should smite the nations: and he shall rule them with a rod of iron: and he treadeth the winepress of the fierceness and wrath of Almighty God. [16]And he hath on his vesture and on his thigh a name written, KING OF KINGS, AND LORD OF LORDS. [17]And I saw an angel standing in the sun; and he cried with a loud voice, saying to all the fowls that fly in the midst of heaven, Come and gather yourselves together unto the supper of the great God; [18]That ye may eat the flesh of kings, and the flesh of captains, and the flesh of mighty men, and the flesh of horses, and of them that sit on them, and the flesh of all men, both free and bond, both small and great. [19]And I saw the beast, and the kings of the earth, and their armies, gathered together to make war against him that sat on the horse, and against his army. [20]And the beast was taken, and with him the false prophet that wrought miracles before him, with which he deceived them that had received the mark of the beast, and them that worshipped his image. These both were cast alive into a lake of fire burning with brimstone. [21]And the remnant were slain with the sword of him that sat upon the horse, which sword proceeded out of his mouth: and all the fowls were filled with their flesh.

Revelation 20: And I saw an angel come down from heaven, having the key of the bottomless pit and a great chain in his hand. [2]And he laid hold on the dragon, that old serpent, which is the Devil, and Satan, and bound him a thousand years,

Figure 10.24 The Bound Devil, Revelation 20:1-3 and 21:9-27 by Matthias Gerung.

³ And cast him into the bottomless pit, and shut him up, and set a seal upon him, that he should deceive the nations no more, till the thousand years should be fulfilled: and after that he must be loosed a little season.

Figure 10.25 Pandemonium—a print (c. 1825) by John Martin.

[4] And I saw thrones, and they sat upon them, and judgment was given unto them: and I saw the souls of them that were beheaded for the witness of Jesus, and for the word of God, and which had not worshipped the beast, neither his image, neither had received his mark upon their foreheads, or in their hands; and they lived and reigned with Christ a thousand years. [5] But the rest of the dead lived not again until the thousand years were finished. This is the first resurrection. [6] Blessed and holy is he that hath part in the first resurrection: on such the second death hath no power, but they shall be priests of God and of Christ, and shall reign with him a thousand years. [7] And when the thousand years are expired, Satan shall be loosed out of his prison, [8] And shall go out to deceive the nations which are in the four quarters of the earth, Gog, and Magog, to gather them together to battle: the number of whom is as the sand of the sea. [9] And they went up on the breadth of the earth, and compassed the camp of the saints about, and the beloved city: and fire came down from God out of heaven, and devoured them. [10] And the devil that deceived them was cast into the lake of fire and brimstone, where the beast and the false prophet are, and shall be tormented day and night for ever and ever. [11] And I saw a great white throne, and him that sat on it, from whose face the earth and the heaven fled away; and there was found no place for them. [12] And I saw the dead, small and great, stand before God; and the books were opened: and another book was opened, which is the book of life: and the dead were judged out of those things which were written in the books, according to their works. [13] And the sea gave up the dead which were in it; and death and hell delivered up the dead which were in them: and they were judged every man according to their works. [14] And death and hell were cast into the lake of fire. This is the second death. [15] And whosoever was not found written in the book of life was cast into the lake of fire.

404

Revelation 21 And I saw a new heaven and a new earth: for the first heaven and the first earth were passed away; and there was no more sea. [2] And I John saw the holy city, new Jerusalem,

Figure 10.26 The New Jerusalem (1865) by Gustave Doré.

coming down from God out of heaven, prepared as a bride adorned for her husband. [3] And I heard a great voice out of heaven saying, Behold, the tabernacle of God is with men, and he will dwell with them, and they shall be his people, and God himself shall be with them, and be their God. [4] And God shall wipe away all tears from their eyes; and there shall be no more death, neither sorrow, nor crying, neither shall there be any more pain: for the former things are passed away. [5] And he that sat upon the throne said, Behold, I make all things new. And he said unto me, Write: for these words are true and faithful. [6] And he said unto me, It is done. I am Alpha and Omega, the beginning and the end. I will give unto him that is athirst of the fountain of the water of life freely. [7] He that overcometh shall inherit all things; and I will be his God, and he shall be my son. [8] But the fearful, and unbelieving, and the abominable, and murderers, and whoremongers, and sorcerers, and idolaters, and all liars, shall have their part in the lake which burneth with fire and brimstone: which is the second death. [9]And there came unto me one of the seven angels which had the seven vials full of the seven last plagues, and talked with me, saying, Come hither, I will shew thee the bride, the Lamb's wife. [10]And he carried me away in the spirit to a great and high mountain, and shewed me that great city, the holy Jerusalem, descending out of heaven from God, [11]Having the glory of God: and her light was like unto a stone most precious, even like a jasper stone, clear as crystal; [12]And had a wall great and high, and had twelve gates, and at the gates twelve angels, and names written thereon, which are the names of the twelve tribes of the children of Israel: [13]On the east three gates; on the north three gates; on the south three gates; and on the west three gates. [14]And the wall of the city had twelve foundations, and in them the names of the twelve apostles of the Lamb. [15]And he that talked with me had a golden reed to measure the city, and the gates thereof, and the wall thereof. [16]And the city lieth foursquare, and the length is as large as the breadth: and he measured the city with the reed, twelve thousand furlongs. The length and the breadth and the height of it are equal. [17]And he measured the wall thereof, an hundred and forty and four cubits, according to the measure of a man, that is, of the angel. [18]And the building of the wall of it was of jasper: and the city was pure gold, like unto clear glass. [19]And the foundations of the wall of the city were garnished with all manner of precious stones. The first foundation was jasper; the second, sapphire; the third, a chalcedony; the fourth, an emerald; [20]The fifth, sardonyx; the sixth, sardius; the seventh, chrysolyte; the eighth, beryl; the ninth, a topaz; the tenth, a chrysoprasus; the eleventh, a jacinth; the twelfth, an amethyst. And the twelve gates were twelve pearls: every several gate was of one pearl: and the street of the city was pure gold, as it were transparent glass. [22]And I saw no temple therein: for the Lord God Almighty and the Lamb are the temple of it. [23]And the city had no need of the sun, neither of the moon, to shine in it: for the glory of God did lighten it, and the Lamb is the light thereof. [24]And the nations of them which are saved shall walk in the light of it: and the kings of the earth do bring their glory and honour into it. [25]And the gates of it shall not be shut at all by day: for there shall be no night there. [26]And they shall bring the glory and honour of the nations into it. [27]And there shall in no wise enter into it any thing that defileth, neither whatsoever worketh abomination, or maketh a lie: but they which are written in the Lamb's book of life.

Revelation (KJV) 22: [1]And he shewed me a pure river of water of life, clear as crystal, proceeding out of the throne of God and of the Lamb. 2 In the midst of the street of it, and on either side of the river, was there the tree of life, which bare twelve manner of fruits, and yielded her fruit every month: and the leaves of the tree were for the healing of the nations. [3]And there shall be no more curse: but the throne of God and of the Lamb shall be in it; and his servants shall serve him: [4]And they shall see his face; and his name shall be in their foreheads. [5]And there shall be no night there; and they need no candle, neither light of the sun; for the Lord God giveth them light: and they shall reign for ever and ever. [6]And he said unto me, These sayings are faithful and true: and the Lord God of the holy prophets sent his angel to shew unto his servants the things which must shortly be done. [7]Behold, I come quickly: blessed is he that keepeth the sayings of the prophecy of this book. [8]And I John saw these things, and heard them. And when I had heard and seen, I fell down to worship before the feet of the angel which shewed me these things. [9]Then saith he unto me, See thou do it not: for I am thy fellowservant, and of thy brethren the prophets, and of them which keep the sayings of this book: worship God. [10]And he saith unto me, Seal not the sayings of the prophecy of this book: for the time is at hand. [11]He that is unjust, let him be unjust still: and he which is filthy, let hi`m be filthy still: and he that is righteous, let him be righteous still: and he that is holy, let him be holy still. [12]And, behold, I come quickly; and my reward is with me, to give every man according as his work shall be. [13]I am Alpha and Omega, the beginning and the end, the first and the last. [14]Blessed are they that do his commandments, that they may have right to the tree of life, and may enter in through the gates into the city. [15]For without are dogs, and sorcerers, and whoremongers, and murderers, and idolaters, and whosoever loveth and maketh a lie. [16]I Jesus have sent mine angel to testify unto you these things in the churches. I am the root and the offspring of David, and the bright and morning star. [17]And the Spirit and the bride say, Come. And let him that heareth say, Come. And let him that is athirst come. And whosoever will, let him take the water of life freely. [18]For I testify unto every man that heareth the words of the prophecy of this book, If any man shall add unto these things, God shall add unto him the plagues that are written in this book: [19]And if any man shall take away from the words of the book of this prophecy, God shall take away his part out of the book of life, and out of the holy city, and from the things which are written in this book. [20]He which testifieth these things saith, Surely I come quickly. Amen. Even so, come, Lord Jesus. [21]The grace of our Lord Jesus Christ be with you all. Amen.

[The Kingdom of God is in the process of being birth into the earth. Just when things seem to be going in the wrong direction, a reversal is on the horizon. The Lord's Prayer is in the process of being manifested. Jesus gave us a prayer that is the answer to every problem that anyone could ever be faced with. Jesus asked us to pray that God's Kingdom would come and God's will would be done on Earth as it is in Heaven. Right now in the natural, things appear to be negative everywhere you look concerning the condition and state of the world. People are losing their moral compass, and the condition of the world today is similar to Noah's time.

The Armor of God was given to us so we can use it to guard our spirit, soul and body from the attacks of Satan, from depression, oppression, etc.. It was given to prevent the "spirit of fear" and defeat and failure from entering into our innermost being to choke the seed of faith, love, and all the other fruit of the Spirit out of our heart (or Spiritual Garden).

Remember, all of this is taking place right in the presence of God because you are temple of the Holy Spirit. I can remember when I was about eleven years old, I used to be picked on by two kids in my neighborhood. They would run me home every day after school. One day they decided to run me home, only this time one of them was going to use a brick and the other one had a tree branch and they were planning to kill me with them (so I thought). I ran home and went in the back door where my mother was in the kitchen. I told her what had happened, and you know how protective mothers are about their children when somebody is trying to hurt one of them. The two bullies had to cross in front of my house to get to their home so I told my mother that they were going to beat me to death with a brick and a branch. She went out the front door and met them as they were headed to their own homes. I don't remember everything she said but when they left they were really shaken up at what she had to say to them. And I was happy because I knew she had my back even though she was in front of me. I just knew that I was not going to have any more problems with those guys ever again. But what she said did not last long. My mother told my father that night and he talked to me. By the way he was the pastor of the church that I grew up in, and he told me if I let those boys run me home again he was going to punish me. So that weekend they cornered me two doors away from my house and they were going to kill me for squealing to my mother. I remembered what my father said so the fight was on. I did not know how to fight so I threw both fists at the same time. I hit one guy in the mouth and busted his lip. The other guy I hit in the eye and later I found out he had a black eye for a couple of weeks. Then they ran home crying, and I felt like I was the big shot in the neighborhood for about three hours until the mother of the boy with the black eye called to tell the pastor that his son was beating up kids in the neighborhood and that his son had given her son a black eye. So I was in for another lecture. I did remind my father that he was the one that told me to fight back, but he said I did not tell you to put someone's eye out. Although I don't think he was too upset, though, because I had been bullied.

My mother was willing to stand up and even go to battle for her baby, but my father wanted his son to stand up for himself. Parents cannot follow their children around all of their lives to provide protection for them. We all know babies require constant care, but as they grow they have to be taught to feed themselves, how to use the bathroom, and so forth. They have to be guided through the different stages of growth from babyhood, to adolescence, to young adulthood stages. God is the same way. He expects us to grow up in Christ Jesus and take up the fight against the kingdom of darkness, not in our strength but in the power of the Holy Spirit, with the Blood of the Lamb and the faith of God. He has given us everything that we need to fight and defeat the kingdom of darkness. But if we do not know how to use the weapons of our warfare, which are mighty through God for the pulling down of strongholds, then we will be defeated. Jesus said that the Kingdom of God suffers violence but the violent will take it by force.

God gave us anger, hatred, and violence not to use against each other, but to use against the kingdom of the darkness of this world, against principalities, and powers, against the god of this worldly system that blinds the minds of people who do not believe in the Gospel of Jesus Christ. Our rage, anger, and hatred must be against the prince of the power of the air—the spirit that is operating in the children of disobedience. It's part of our warfare and part of our weaponry: it is our intercessory prayer life. God also gave us these attributes to wage war against the sin in our own lives. When we get to the place where we hate to lie, steal, cheat, commit adultery, even if it is just in our mind, to the point where we refuse to do those things that grieve the Spirit of God. Because we love Him and we love His Word so much that we refuse to let our sins separate us from His love. And therefore we set our affections on the will of the Lord.]

Luke (KJV) 19: And Jesus entered and passed through Jericho. ²And, behold, there was a man named Zacchaeus, which was the chief among the publicans, and he was rich. ³And he sought to see Jesus who he was; and could not for the press, because he was little of stature. ⁴And he ran before, and climbed up into a sycamore tree to see him: for he was to pass that way. And when Jesus came to the place, he looked up, and saw him, and said unto him, Zacchaeus, make haste, and come down; for today I must abide at thy house. ⁶And he made haste, and came down, and received him joyfully. ⁷And when they saw it, they all murmured, saying, That he was gone to be guest with a man that is a sinner. ⁸And Zacchaeus stood, and said unto the Lord: Behold, Lord, the half of my goods I give to the poor; and if I have taken anything from any man by false accusation, I restore him fourfold. ⁹And Jesus said unto him, This day is salvation come to this house, forsomuch as he also is a son of Abraham. ¹⁰For the Son of man is come to seek and to save that which was lost. ¹¹And as they heard these things, he added and spake a parable, because he was nigh to Jerusalem, and because they thought that the kingdom of God should immediately appear. ¹²He said therefore, A certain nobleman went into a far country to receive for himself a kingdom, and to return. ¹³And he called his ten servants, and delivered them ten pounds, and said unto them, Occupy till I come. ¹⁴But his citizens hated him, and sent a message after him, saying, We will not have this man to reign over us. ¹⁵And it came to pass, that when he was returned, having received the kingdom, then he commanded these servants to be called unto him, to whom he had given the money, that he might know how much every man had gained by trading. ¹⁶Then came the first, saying, Lord, thy pound hath gained ten pounds. ¹⁷And he said unto him, Well, thou good servant: because thou hast been faithful in a very little, have thou authority over ten cities. ¹⁸And the second came, saying, Lord, thy pound hath gained five pounds. ¹⁹And he said likewise to him, Be thou also over five cities. ²⁰And another came, saying, Lord, behold, here is thy pound, which I have kept laid up in a napkin: ²¹For I feared thee, because thou art an austere man: thou takest up that thou layedst not down, and reapest that thou didst not sow. ²²And he saith unto him, Out of thine own mouth will I judge thee, thou wicked servant. Thou knewest that I was an austere man, taking up that I laid not down, and reaping that I did not sow: ²³Wherefore then gavest not thou my money into the bank, that at my coming I might have required mine own with usury? ²⁴And he said unto them that stood by, Take from him the pound, and give it to him that hath ten pounds. ²⁵(And they said unto him, Lord, he hath ten pounds.) ²⁶For I say unto you, That unto every one which hath shall be given; and from him that hath not, even that he hath shall be taken away from him. ²⁷But those mine enemies, which would not that I should reign over them, bring hither, and slay them before me. ²⁸And when he had thus spoken, he went before, ascending up to Jerusalem.

Jesus is coming back; no one knows when this event is going to take place, because Jesus says that only the Father knows, so don't listen to any predictions from anybody. Jesus gave us some good advice until the appointed time comes. He said occupy until He returns. Until the rapture does happen, this is what God is expecting for us to be doing: occupying and overcoming. He is expecting us to be giving into the lives of the needy, ministering the seven works of mercy along with teaching the Gospel of the Kingdom of God.

Take the teaching of the Gospel of the Kingdom very seriously.

Matthew (KJV) 10: ⁶But go rather to the lost sheep of the house of Israel. ⁷And as ye go, preach, saying, **The kingdom of heaven is at hand.** ⁸Heal the sick, cleanse the lepers, raise the dead, cast out devils: freely ye have received, freely give. ⁹Provide neither gold, nor silver, nor brass in your purses, ¹⁰Nor scrip for your journey, neither two coats, neither shoes, nor yet staves: for the workman is worthy of his meat. ¹¹And into whatsoever city or town ye shall enter, enquire who in it is worthy; and there abide till ye go thence. ¹²And when ye come into an house, salute it. ¹³And if the house be worthy, let your peace come upon it: but if it be not worthy, let your peace return to you. ¹⁴**And whosoever shall not receive you, nor hear your words, when ye depart out of that house or city, shake off the dust of your feet. ¹⁵Verily I say unto you, It shall be more tolerable for the land of Sodom and Gomorrah in the day of judgment, than for that city. ¹⁶Behold, I send you forth as sheep in the midst of wolves: be ye therefore wise as serpents, and harmless as doves.**

When a person or even a church disregards the teaching of the Gospel of the Kingdom they are saying that they do not want to know, discern, understand, fathom or grasp who God is. And this grieves the Spirit of God; we all know what it feels like to be rejected by someone that you deeply love. And when they reject Him, He in turn will reject them and on Judgment Day. **Verse 15 says;** it will be more tolerable for the people of Sodom and Gomorrha then it will be for them. Just think about that for a minute or two. They will be sent to a worse part of hell. We already know that the foolish virgins were left because of this very point.

This verse says something even more important. What a church teaches will govern or determine the outcome of a city on judgment day. Now I understand why so many people are going from church to church trying to find the right one that will fill the spiritual void in their life. The church is supposed to be a beacon of light where people can be drawn to, and taught how to seek the Kingdom of God and learn how to fulfill their destiny. Jesus said if we lift Him up, He will draw the people. The five-fold ministry has a tremendous responsibility to preach the Gospel of the Kingdom. If the right teaching will change the spiritual complexion of a city, it will change a state, and it will change a nation.

1 John (KJV) 5: ³ For this is the love of God, that we keep his commandments: and his commandments are not grievous. ⁴ For whatsoever is born of God *overcometh* the world: and this is the victory that *overcometh* the world, even our faith. ⁵ Who is he that *overcometh* the world, but he that believeth that Jesus is the Son of God?

Revelation (KLV) 2: ⁷ He that hath an ear, let him hear what the Spirit saith unto the churches; to him that *overcometh* will I give to eat of the tree of life, which is in the midst of the paradise of God.

Revelation (KJV) 2: ¹¹ He that hath an ear, let him hear what the Spirit saith unto the churches; He that *overcometh* shall not be hurt of the second death.

Revelation (KJV) 2: ¹⁷ He that hath an ear, let him hear what the Spirit saith unto the churches; To him that *overcometh* will I give to eat of the hidden manna, and will give him a white stone, and in the stone a new name written, which no man knoweth saving he that receiveth it.

Revelation (KJV) 2: ²⁶ And he that *overcometh*, and keepeth my works unto the end, to him will I give power over the nations:

Revelation (KJV) 3: ⁵ He that *overcometh*, the same shall be clothed in white raiment; and I will not blot out his name out of the book of life, but I will confess his name before my Father, and before his angels.

Revelation (KJV) 3: ¹² Him that *overcometh* will I make a pillar in the temple of my God, and he shall go no more out: and I will write upon him the name of my God, and the name of the city of my God, which is new Jerusalem, which cometh down out of heaven from my God: and I will write upon him my new name.

Revelation (KJV) 3: ²¹ To him that *overcometh* will I grant to sit with me in my throne, even as I also overcame, and am set down with my Father in his throne.

Now why God made us kings and priest becomes clear, and our seeking (to understand) how the Kingdom functions and operates is so important. It is imperative that we mature in Christ. Everything that the Kingdom of Heaven teaches prepares us for ruling and reigning together with Christ Jesus.

The Kingdom of Heaven functions around cultivating the fruit of the Spirit which are the attributes (or the power of God, and the life of God being manifested in our mortal body) so that we would be empowered to overcome the kingdom of darkness. The only way that it could be done was by God recreating Himself in us by causing us to be born again. We are born of Him. That is why we are called children of God. Don't fall short of your calling or your birthright. He gave us His faith, His love, the name of His first Son Jesus Christ of Nazareth, His Blood, and all the angels for us to use in our God-given quest to destroy the kingdom of darkness. and to help raise the quality of life on earth to be equal to the quality of life in Heaven. God has given us His own personal armor with which He used to remove Lucifer and all his belongings (and his angels) quite effectively out of Heaven. We are to do the same; we are capable and well able to do the same with the same armor, to subdue the kingdom of darkness and undo what Satan has set up in the earth, to establish God's Will and the Kingdom of God in the earth.

"Above all else, find your purpose fulfill your destiny and do not miss the Wedding Supper of the Lamb"

Dedication

First I must dedicate this book to our Heavenly Father, our Lord and Savior Jesus Christ, and to the Holy Spirit. Second we want to Praise God, for the greatest experience of our lives has been to write this book. I pray that this book will be a blessing to you and that it will help you to walk with God. My wife and I dedicate this book to you. We hope that you will understand and seek your purpose.

I also dedicate this book to my loving wife Margie for her support and input into this work. She helped to keep me on target to reach this goal.

We want to dedicate this book to our sons Kenneth, Scott, and Keith, also to the loving memory of our daughter Wilma.

We want to also dedicate this book to our daughters-in-laws, grandchildren and great-grandchildren.

A special thanks to everyone that stood with us in prayer and encouragement (You Know Who You Are) during the development of this book.

Copyright License

Figure 1.4
Description: A very old sycamore tree - Ficus sycomorus, with hollow trunk. (השקמה פיקוס) - Ramat-Gan.
Date 31 May 2006
Source: Photo by Author Eitan f 14:23, 31 May 2006 (UTC)
Permission: PD

Figure 1.5
Description: English: Bud of *Ficus carica* L.
Date: 10 April 2010
Source: Own work
Author: Etienne
Licensing: Public Domain:
This picture is also found on the back cover center picture.

Figure 1.6
Description: English: Leaves and immature fruit of common fig tree
Date: May 31, 2010
(31 May 2010 (original upload date))
Source:Transferred from en.wikipedia; transferred to Commons by User:Woodlot using CommonsHelper.
(Original text: *My own work*.)
Author: Woodlot (talk) 13:01, 31 May 2010 (UTC). Original uploader was Woodlot at en.wikipedia
Permission: CC-BY-3.0.

Licensing
Woodlot at en.wikipedia, the copyright holder of this work, hereby publishes it under the following license:
This licensed under the Creative Commons Attribution 3.0 Unported ile license.
Picture also appears on back cover lower picture.

Figure 1.7
Description: The Vine and the Branches
Date: 1922
Source: The New Bible Symbols
Author: M. Bihn and J. Bealings
Permission: public domain due to age

Figure 1.8
James Joseph Jacques Tissot (1836–1902)
Location: Brooklyn Museum European Art Collection
Title: English: The Rich Young Man Went Away Sorrowful
Date: between 1886 and 1894
European Art collection ,

Accession Number: 00.159.159
Credit Line: purchase by public subscription
Note: Signature bottom: *J.J. Tissot*
Source/Photographer: Online Collection of Brooklyn Museum; Photo: Brooklyn Museum, 2007,
00.159.159_PS2.jpg
Permission: Public Domain

Figure 1.9
Visiting the Sick
Description: English: An etching by Jan Luyken illustrating Matthew 25:36 in the Bowyer Bible,
Bolton, England.
Date: 6 August 2009
Source: Photo by Harry Kossuth
Author: Phillip Medhurst
Permission: PD

Figure 1.10
Clothing the Naked
Description: English: An etching by Jan Luyken illustrating Matthew 25:36 in the Bowyer Bible,
Bolton, England.
Date: 6 August 2009
Source: Photo by Harry Kossuth
Author: Phillip Medhurst
Permission: PD

Figure 1.11
Satisfying the Thirsty
Description: English: An etching by Jan Luyken illustrating Matthew 25:35 in the Bowyer Bible,
Bolton, England.
Date: 6 August 2009
Source: Photo by Harry Kossuth
Author: Phillip Medhurst
Permission: PD

Figure 1.12
Feeding the Hungry
Description: English: An etching by Jan Luyken illustrating Luke 10:33-34 in the Bowyer Bible,
Bolton, England.
Date: 6 August 2009
Source: Photo by Harry Kossuth
Phillip Medhurst
Permission: PD

Figure 1.13
Visiting the Prisoner
Description: English: An etching by Jan Luyken illustrating Luke 10:33-34 in the Bowyer Bible, Bolton, England.
Date:6 August 2009
Source: Photo by Harry Kossuth
Author: Phillip Medhurst
Permission: PD

Figure 1:14
Summary
Artist João Zeferino da Costa (1840–1915)
Description Brazilian painter, draughtsman, decorator and teacher
Title: The widow's mite
Date 1876(1876)
Medium oil on canvas
Current location (Inventory)Museu Nacional de Belas Artes
Location Rio de Janeiro, Brazil
Established 1937(1937)
Website www.mnba.gov.br/
Source/Photographer [1]
Location: Rio de Janeiro, Brazil Established: 1937 Website: www.mnba.gov.br/
Licensing: Public Domain

Figure 1.15
Artist: Rembrandt (1606–1669)
Alternate title: The Money Changer.
Date: 1627 Medium: oil on panel
Dimensions: 32 × 42.5 cm (12.6 × 16.7 in)
Current location: Gemäldegalerie Berlin Source/Photographer: Unknown
Licensing: Public Domain

Figure 1.16
Parable of the Rich Man
Description: English: An etching by Jan Luyken illustrating Luke 12:12-21 in the Bowyer Bible, Bolton, England.
Date: 6 August 2009 Source: Photo by Harry Kossuth
Author: Phillip Medhurst
Permission: PD

Figure 1.17
Description English: Field of arum lilies Nooordhoek, Cape Town. South Africans call these Arum Lilies, although strictly speaking they are not. Other names: Pig lilly (UK): calla lilly.
Date: August 08
Source: Own work

Author: Andrew massyn Noordhoek, Cape Town
Licensing: Public Domain

Figure 1.18
Artist: Tintoretto (1518–1594)
Title: Five Wise Virgins and Five Foolish virgins
Date: second half of 16th century
Medium: oil on canvas
Current location: (Inventory) Museum Boijmans Van Beuningen
Source/Photographer: The Yorck Project: 10.000 Meisterwerke der Malerei. DVD-ROM, 2002.
ISBN 3936122202.
Distributed: by DIRECTMEDIA Publishing GmbH.
Permission: (Reusing this file) [1] Licensing: Public Domain

Figure 1.19
Artist: Anonymous (Northern Netherlands):
Formerly attributed: to Pieter Cornelisz. van Rijck Title: Kitchen interior with the parable of the rich man and the poor Lazarus.
Date: circa 1610 Current location: (Inventory) Rijksmuseum Amsterdam
Source/Photographer: www.geheugenvannederland.nl: Home : Info : Pic Licensing: Public Domain

Figure 1.20
Medium: painting
Source/Photographer:
Description: Beggar named Lazarus
Source: Own work
Author: JEBA 17 Licensing: Public Domain

Figure 1.21
Artist: Bartholomeus van Bassen (circa 1590–1652)
Description: The Parable of the Rich Man and Lazarus
Date: circa 1620-30
ArtDaily.org
Licensing: Public Domain

Figure 1.22
Artist: James Joseph Jacques Tissot (1836-1902)
Work location Paris, Londres, Palestine, Buillon (Doubs)
Title: The Bad Rich Man in Hell
Date between 1886 and 1894
Medium opaque watercolor over graphite on gray wove paper
Current location Brooklyn Museum
European Art collection
Credit line purchase by public subscription

Notes Signature top left: J.J. Tissot
Source/Photographer Online Collection of Brooklyn Museum; Photo: Brooklyn Museum, 2007, 00.159.136_PS2.jpg
Permission: PD

Figure 1.23
Description: English: Royal Military College of Canada memorial window to Ian Sutherland Brown Sir Lancelot whole armour of God
Date: 2 December 2011 Source: Own work
Author: Victoria Edwards
Permission: Public Domain

Figure 1.24
Description: English: The Ark of God Carried into the Temple
Date: between 1412 and 1416 Source: (1945) Les très riches heures du Duc de Berry: Musée Condé à Chantilly, France: Les Éditions Nomis, pp. Folio
Author: Pol, Hermann and Jannequin de Limbourg (1370s–1416); Jean Colombe (c. 1440–93)
Permission: Public Domain

Figure 1.25
Description: English: Fruit on display at La Boqueria market in Barcelona.
Date: 5 July 2005
Source: Own work
Author: Dungodung
Permission: Public Domain

Figure 1.26
Artist: Carl Heinrich Bloch (1834–1890)
Title: The Sermon on the Mount
Medium: oil on canvas
Source/Photographer: Unknown
Permission: Public Domain

Figure 1.27
Description: English: Destruction of Korah Dathan and Abiram, illustration from the 1890 Holman Bible
Date: 1890
Source: http://thebiblerevival.com/clipart/1890holmanbible/bw/destructionofkorahdathanand-abiram.jpg Author: publishers of the 1890 Holman Bible
Permission: Public Domain

Figure 1.28
Moses Views the Land of Israel (woodcut by Julius Schnorr von Carolsfeld from the 1860 *Bible in Pictures*)
Description: English: Woodcut for "Die Bibel in Bildern", 1860.

Date: 1851-1860
Source: Die Bibel in Bildern
Author: Julius Schnorr von Carolsfeld (1794–1872)
Permission: Public Domain

Figure 1.29
Artist: Anthony van Dyck (1599–1641)
Title: Allegorical personification of charity as a mother with three infants
Date: between 1627 and 1628 Medium: oil on oak Dimensions: 148.2 × 107.5 cm (58.3 × 42.3 in)
Current location: National Gallery Room 29
Source/Photographer: http://www.nationalgallery.org.uk/paintings/anthony-van-dyck-charity
Licensing: Public Domain

Figure 1.30
Description: A wall mirror, reflecting a vase.
Date: 21 July 2003
Source: English Wikipedia (http://en.wikipedia.org/wiki/Image:Mirror.jpeg)
Author: Cgs
Permission: Public Domain

Figure 1.31
Date: 1728
Source: http://www.mythfolklore.net/lahaye/027/LaHaye1728
Figures027GenXXV32-33EsauSellsBirthright.jpg Author: illustrators of the 1728
Figures de la Bible, Gerard Hoet (1648-1733) and others, published by P. de Hondt in The Hague
in 1728
Licensing: Public Domain

**Copyright Licenses For: Chapter #2 Why Jesus said Only Five out of Ten Virgins Will Be
Raptured Part 2**

Figure 2.1
Description: English: Stained glass at St John the Baptist's Anglican Church [1], Ashfield,
New South Wales. Illustrates Jesus' description of himself "I am the Good Shepherd" (from the
Gospel of John, chapter 10, verse 11).
The memorial window is also captioned: "To the Glory of God and in Loving Memory of William Wright. Died 6th November, 1932. Aged 70 Yrs."
Source: A derivative work of File:StJohnsAshfield StainedGlass GoodShepherd.jpg Author:
Stained glass: Alfred Handel, d. 1946[2], photo:Toby Hudson
Permission: Public Domain

Figure 2.2
Raphael (1483–1520)
V&A—(1515).jpg Raphael, Christ's Charge to Peter
Permission: Public Domain because of age

Figure 2.3
Art: William-Adolphe Bouguereau (1825-1905) –
Title: Charity (1878)
Permission: Public Domain

Figure 2.4
Description: The New Jerusalem (Tapestry of the Apocalypse)
Date: 23 May 2006
Source: own work (14th century)
Author: Kimon Berlin, user: Gribeco
Licensing: Public Domain:

Figure 2.5:
Description: The Last Judgement. The Louvre.
Date: Not known, but the work was engraved in 1615. It was probably painted in the last decades of the Valois dynasty (1560–89), since Cousin's work, most of which has not survived, was praised during that time (see Blunt, p. 100).
Source: Blunt, Anthony. Art and Architecture in France: 1500–1700. New Haven (CT): Yale University Press, [1957] 1999 edition. ISBN 0300077483. Page 99.
Author: Jean Cousin the Younger, also called Jehan Cousin Le Jeune (lived c. 1522–1595).
Permission: Public Domain

Figure 2.6:
Description: Image of an etching by artist William Strutt in 1896. Isaiah 11:6,7: The wolf will live with the lamb, the leopard will lie down with the goat, the calf and the lion and the yearling together; and a little child will lead them. The cow will feed with the bear, their young will lie down together, and the lion will eat straw like the ox.
Date: 1896 Source: cropped version of http://www.mlode.com/~thehills/webpage/peace.htm
Author: William Strutt
Permission: Public Domain

Figure 2.7
Artist: Pieter van der Heyden (fl. 1551–1572)
Title: The Blind Leading the Blind
Date: circa 1561 Medium: engraving Current location: New York Public Library Source/Photographer: Web Gallery of Art: Image Info about artwork
Permission: Public Domain

Figure 2.8
Artist: Raphael (1483–1520)
Title: Transfiguration
Date: 1518-1520
Source/Photographer: Downloaded from Artist Hideout
Permission: Public Domain

Figure 2.9
Title; The Incredulity of Saint Thomas by Caravaggio.
Category: Artistic portrayals of Jesus
Description: 13 April 2005 (original upload date)
Transferred from en.wikipedia; transferred to Commons by User:Tm using CommonsHelper.
Source: Original uploader was Dante Alighieri at en.wikipedia
Permission: Public Domain-US

Figure 2.10
Description: English: Illustration of the Parable of the Unjust Judge from the New Testament
Gospel of Luke (Luke 18:1-9) by John Everett Millais for The Parables of Our Lord (1863)
Date: 1863 Source: http://myweb.tiscali.co.uk/speel/pici/millais3.jpg
Author: John Everett Millais (1829–1896)
Permission: Public Domain

Figure 2.11
Description: Saint Michael and the fall of angels—painting by Johann Georg Unruhe (1793).
Date 6 June 2009
Source Own work
Author Wolfgang Sauber
Licensing: Public Domain

Figure 2.12
Catholic parish church of de: Mary cleaning (Steinheim) in de: Steinheim an der Donau, ceiling
fresco of 1776 by Matthäus Günther, representation of the Archangel Michael in the battle
against Lucifer
Date: 1 October 2010 Source: Own work
Author: G. Freihalter
Permission: Public Domain

Figure 2.13
Artist: Französischer Meister um 1675
Title: German: the construction of the Ark of Noah Date: circa 1675
Medium: color on canvas
Dimensions: 158,5 × 109 cm:
Current location: : Budapest
Source/Photographer: The Yorck Project: 10.000 Meisterwerke der Malerei. DVD-ROM, 2002.
ISBN 3936122202. «German: painting episode» the four seasons ", scene: winter».«German:
painting episode» the four seasons ", scene: winter».«German: painting episode» the four sea-
sons", scene: winter». Distributed by DIRECTMEDIA Publishing GmbH.
Permission: Public Domain

Figure 2.14
Artist: Nicolas Poussin (1594–1665)
Title: French: Winter or the flood

Date: 1660-1664
Current location: Louvre Museum, 2nd floor, room 16 Paris Notes http://www.cineclubdecaen.
com/peinture/peintres/poussin/hiver.htm paintings
Permission: Public Domain

Figure 2.15:
Artist: Joachim Patinir (circa 1480-1524) Title: Landscape with the destruction of Sodom and
Gomorrah.
Date: circa 1520 (1495-1524)
Medium: oil on panel
Dimensions: 23 × 29.5 cm (9.1 × 11.6 in)
Current location: (Inventory)Museum Boijmans Van Beuningen : Extern
Accession number: 2312 (OK)
Object history: by 1934: Franz Koenigs (1881-1941), Haarlem
from 1935 until 19 April 1940: lent to the Museum Boijmans Van Beuningen, Rotterdam, by
Franz Koenigs, Haarlem[1]
2 April 1940: ownership transferred to Lisser & Rosenkranz (bank), Amsterdam, by Franz Koe-
nigs, Haarlem
10 June 1940: acquired by A. Miedl (art dealer), Amsterdam
10 June 1940: acquired by W.A. Hofer, Berlin
10 June 1940: acquired by Hermann Göring (1893-1946)
Unknown date: transferred to Stichting Nederlands Kunstbezit, The Hague, inv. NK2670
Unknown date: ownership transferred to Dienst voor 's Rijks Verspreide Kunstvoorwerpen, The
Hague, inv. NK2670
1948: lent to the Museum Boijmans Van Beuningen, Rotterdam, inv. 2312 (OK), by Dienst
voor's Rijks Verspreide Kunstvoorwerpen, The Hague, inv. NK2670 References: Museum Boij-
mans Van Beuningen collection online.
Herkomst Gezocht
RKDimages, Art-work number 28662. Source/Photographer: collectie.boijmans.nl : Home :
Info: Pic
Permission: Public Domain

Figure 2.16
Title: Balaam and his Ass
Date: 1626
Artist: Rembrandt (1606–1669) Medium: oil on oak panel Dimensions: Height: 63 cm (24.8 in).
Width: 46.5 cm (18.3 in).
Current location: Musée Cognacq-Jay Object history by 1641: Alfonso López, Paris (?)
Date unknown: acquired by Simon Maris, Amsterdam
by 1905: Jacob Goudstikker (art dealer), Amsterdam
by 1907: Ridder Gustav Heschek von Mühlheim, Prague
Date unknown: acquired by F. Kleinberger, New York
by 1918: Ferdinand Hermann, New York
Date unknown: acquired by Ernest Cognacq, Paris
1928: ceded to the city of Paris by Ernest Cognacq

1928 (?): lent to the Musée Cognacq-Jay, Paris, by the city of Paris (?) Notes Signature and date bottom center: RH 1626
References: RKDimages, Art-work number 46370, as Bileam en zijn ezelin (Numeri 22:22-35).
Source/Photographer: www.allartpainting.com
Web Gallery of Art: Home page Image Info about artwork
Permission: Public Domain

Figure 2.17
Artist: Léon Comerre (1850–1916) Description:
English: The Flood
Current location: Musée des Beaux-Arts de Nantes
Source / Photographer: Musée des beaux arts de Nantes
Permission: Public Domain

Figure 2.18
Artist: John Martin (1789–1854) Title: English: The Great Day of His Wrath
Date: 1853
Medium: oil on canvas
Dimensions: 197 × 303 cm (77.6 × 119.3 in)
Current location: Tate Britain
London, UK:
Source/Photographer: http://www.artrenewal.org/asp/database/image.asp?id=24776 Other versions: originally uploaded in December 2007 to the English language Wikipedia by AAA765 (log).
Permission: Public Domain

Figure 2.19
Description: English: Image of what Earth may look like 5-7 billion years from now, when the Sun swells and becomes a Red Giant.
Date: 2008-02-27 (log)
Source: en:File:Red_Giant_Earth.jpg
Original text: self-made.
Author: Fsgregs (talk)
Permission: Public Domain

Figure 2.20
Artist: John Martin John Martin (1789–1854)
Title: The Last Judgment
Date: 1853
Dimensions: 1968 x 3258 mm
Current location: Tate Gallery (Tate Britain) : London Accession number: T01927
Notes: www.tate.org.uk—The Last Judgment Source/Photographer: http://www.muian.com/muian05/05Martin09.jpg
Permission: Public Domain
Figure 2.21
Description Last Judgment and the Wise and Foolish Virgins

Date 1450s
Source Web Gallery of Art: Image Info about artwork
Author unknown Flemish master
Permission: Public Domain

Copyright for Chapter #3 Fruit of Faith Part I

Figure 3.1
Current: Art location
Manchester Gallery
Resurrection of the Widow's son from Nain, altar panel by Cranach the Younger, c. 1569, in the Stadtkirche Wittenberg
Permission: Public Domain :

Figure 3.2
Resurrection at Nain Franciscan Chapel 2009.jpg
English: Picture of the altar in the chapel at Nain, Israel. XIX cent.
Data: 17 czerwca 2011 Źródło: "Developing" of the photo image:Niin 198.jpg (Ori~)
Author: Abraham Sobkowski OFM
Permission: Public Domain

Figure 3.3
Description: Christ cleansing a leper by Jean-Marie Melchior Doze, 1864. Sour Original uploader was History2007 at en.wikipedia. Later version(s) were uploaded by Aavindraa at en.wikipedia.
Permission: Public Domain-US; Public Domain-ART

Figure 3.4
Jan van Eyck painting "Ghent Altarpiece", finished 1432.
Detail: adoration of the lamb
Permission: Public Domain

Figure 3.5
Description: Ficus carica
Date: 27 August 2005 Source: Own work
Author: Eric Hunt
Permission: Public Domain

Figure 3.6
Description: The Sacrifice of the Old Covenant
Date: 1626
Source: http://skepticsannotatedbible.com/1kg/8.html
Author: Peter Paul Rubens (1577–1640)
Permission Public Domain

Figure 3.7
Description: English: The Holy of Holies, as illustrated in The History of the Church of God from the Creation to the Present Day
Part I—Bible History, by Rev. B. J. Spalding, copyright 1883 by The Catholic Publication Society Co. Illustrator unknown.
Date: 13 August 2006 (original upload date)
Source: Transferred from en.wikipedia; transferred to Commons by User:Darkwind using CommonsHelper.
Author: Original uploader was Mobussell at en.wikipedia
Permission: Public Domain-US

Figure 3.8
Artist: Master of the Gathering of the Manna (fl. circa 1470)
Title: The Gathering of the Manna
Date: Ca. 1460-1470
Medium: oil on panel
Dimensions: 66.6 × 50.7 cm
Current location: Charterhouse Museum in Douai :
Douai Notes: Probably formed part of a larger altarpiece. The master was named after this painting
Source/Photographer: from ISBN 978-90-6918-225-4, p. 215.
Permission: Public Domain

Figure 3.9
Sefer Torah at old Glockengasse Synagogue (reconstruction), Cologne
Description: English: Torah inside of the former Glockengasse Synagogue in Cologne
Date: December 2007
Source: eigenes Foto (Zeughaus)
Author: Horsch, Willy
Permission: Public Domain

Figure 3.10
Artist: José de Ribera (1591–1652)
Title:. Moses and the Ten Commandments
Date: 1638
Medium: oil on canvas
Dimensions: 168 × 97 cm (66.1 × 38.2 in)
Current location: Museo di San Martino, Naples Source/Photographer: YorckProject
Permission: Public Domain

Figure 3.11
Description English: Aaron's Rod Budding
Date 1728(1728)
Source http://www.mythfolklore.net/lahaye/068/LaHaye1728
Figures068NumXVII8-10AaronsRodBuds.jpg

427

Author illustrators of the 1728
Figures de la Bible, Gerard Hoet (1648-1733), and others, published by P. de Hondt in The Hague in 1728
Permission: Public Domain

Figure 3.12
Artist: El Greco (1541–1614) Title: The Agony in the Garden
Date: circa 1590 Medium: oil on canvas
Dimensions: Height: 104 cm (40.9 in). Width: 117 cm (46.1 in).
Current location: Toledo Museum of Art Source / Photographer: Web Gallery of Art: Image Info about artwork
Permission: Public Domain

Figure 3.13
Description: English: The Ark of God Carried into the Temple
Date: between 1412 and 1416 Source: (1945) Les très riches heures du Duc de Berry: Musée Condé à Chantilly, France: Les Éditions Nomis, pp. Folio 29r The page of the original manuscript can be viewed here.
Author: Pol, Hermann and Jannequin de Limbourg (1370s–1416); Jean Colombe (c. 1440–93)
Permission: Public Domain

Figure 3.14
Artist: Ary Scheffer (1795–1858) Description: English: The Temptation of Christ, 1854
Date: 1854 Current location: Walker Art Gallery Source / Photographer
Permission: Public Domain-Art

Figure 3.15
Artist: Caravaggio (1573–1610)
Title: supper at Emmaus
Date: 1601
Current location: National Gallery
Source/Photographer: Own work
Permission: Public Domain

Figure 3.16
Artist: Alessandro Magnasco (1667–1749)
Title: English: The Raising of Lazarus.
Dutch: the resurrection of Lazarus.
Date: 1715-1740
Current location: Rijksmuseum Amsterdam :
Provenance / Herkomst:
May 1948: lent to the Rijksmuseum Amsterdam
Source/Photographer: www.rijksmuseum.nl
Permission: Public Domain

Figure 3.17
Artist: Anonymous.
Title: Eastern Orthodox icon of Jesus Christ as the True Vine.
Date: English: 16th century.
Current location: English: Byzantine and Christian Museum, Athens, Greece.
Source/Photographer: http://lib.pstgu.ru/icons/index.php?option=com_content&view=category&layout=blog&id=2&Itemid=4.
Permission: Public Domain

Figure 3.18
Description: English: The barren fig tree. French School.
Date: 05.02.2010
Source: H1. Bowyer Bible Print 4911. in An illustrated commentary on the Gospel of Mark. Section F to H. by Phillip Medhurstpdf.pdf. https://docs.google.com/folder/d/0B2YLMqqfd6EeNGRlYWU5ZDUtYWU0Ny00OGFiLTk5NzAtM2E3YTI0MzgyMTMz/edit?pli=1&hl=en&docId=0B2YLMqqfd6EeZGRlOTM1MzAtYjU4OC00ODNkLThmMDEtY2QxNDYxNGNhZmI5
Author: Phillip De Vere
Permission: Public Domain

Figure 3.19
Description: English: The erection of the Tabernacle and the sacred vessels, as in Exodus 40:17-19
Date: 1728 Source: http://www.wcg.org/images/b2/_0303160501_038.jpg
Author: illustrators of the 1728
Figures de la Bible, Gerard Hoet (1648–1733) and others, published by P. de Hondt in The Hague in 1728
Permission: Public Domain

Figure 3.20
Description: English: Aaron's rod that Budded, as in Numbers 17:8, illustration from the 1890 Holman Bible
Date: 1890 Source: http://thebiblerevival.com/clipart/1890holmanbible/bw/aaronsrodthatbudded.jpg
Author: Publishers of the 1890 Holman Bible
Permission: Public Domain

Figure 3.21
Description: English: **Aaron's rod Budded and Blossomed**, Woodcut for "The Bible in pictures", 1860.
Date: 1851-1860
Source: The Bible in pictures
Author: Julius Schnorr von Carolsfeld (1794–1872)
Permission: Public Domain

Figure 3.22
Description: English: Aaron's Sons, Nadab and Abihu, Destroyed by Fire; Leviticus 10:2; 1625-30 engraving by Matthäus Merian Date: 1625-30
Source: http://. halden.net/rolf/merian/m044.jpg Author: home Matthäus Merian the Elder (1593–1650)
Permission: Public Domain

Figure 3.23
Artist: William Holman Hunt (1827–1910)
Title: The Scapegoat Date: 1854–1855
Medium: oil on canvas
Dimensions: 33.7 x 45.9 cm
Manchester, England, United Kingdom
Permission: Public Domain

Figure 3.24
Artist: Caravaggio (1573–1610) Title: English: The Taking of Christ
Current location: National Gallery of Ireland Polski: Pojmanie Chrystusa Dulin
Date: circa 1602 Medium: oil on canvas
Source/Photographer: Scan
Permission: Public Domain

Figure 3.25
Artist: Gerard Douffet (1594–1660/1661)
Title: English: Taking of Christ with the Malchus episode
Date: circa 1620 Medium: oil on canvas
Dimensions: Height: 147 cm (57.9 in). Width: 194 cm (76.4 in).
Current location: Museum of Fine Arts, Boston Source / Photographer: Web Gallery of Art: Image Info about artwork
Permission: Public Domain

Figure 3.26
Artist: Dirck van Baburen (circa 1594/1595–1624)
Description: English: Taking of Christ
Date: circa 1616-1617
Medium: oil on canvas
Dimensions: 125 x 95 cm
Current location: Fondazione di Studi di Storia dell'Arte Roberto Longhi, Florence
Source/Photographer: Web
Permission: Public Domain

Figure 3.27
Artist Mihály Munkácsy (1844–1900)
Description Hungarian painter

Date of birth/death 20 February 1844(1844-02-20) 1 May 1900(1900-05-01)
Location of birth/death Munkács Endenich
Work location Austria-Hungary, France, Germany
Authority control VIAF: 29801564 I LCCN: n50031986 I GND: 118735268 I WorldCat I WP-Person
Title Christ in front of Pilate
Date 1881(1881)
Medium oil on canvas
Dimensions 417 × 636 cm (164.2 × 250.4 in)
Object history Déri Museum, Debrecen (loan till 2007, now in Canada).
Source/Photographer This file is lacking source information.
Permission: Public Domain

Figure 3.28
Description: English: The Flagellation of Christ by Anton Raphael Mengs, originally one of four in a cycle on the Passion of Christ as supraportas for the bedroom of King Carlos III, now in the Palacio Real, Madrid. Oil on canvas, 185 x 185 cm.
Date: ca. 1780
Source: Steffi Roettgen, Anton Raphael Mengs 1728-1779, vol. 2: Leben und wirken (Munich: Hirmer, 2003), plate 31.:
Scan: James Steakley Author: Anton Raphael Mengs (1728–1779)
Permission: Public Domain

Figure 3.29
Description: Peter Paul Rubens, Flagellation of Christ
Antwerp, Church of St. Paul. Date: 28 April 2008 Source:
http://www.aiwaz.net/uploads/gallery/flagellation-of-christ-3728.jpg
Author: Peter Paul Rubens
Permission: GFDL

Figure 3.30
Flagellate Jesus, author desconhecido. Século XVII
Description
Author desconhecido. século XVII. Museu de Arte Sacra de Pernambuco, Brasil.
Date: 2005 Source: taken by Ricardo André Frantz
Author: Ricardo André Frantz (User:Tetraktys)
Permission: Public Domain

Figure 3.31
Artist: Caravaggio (1573–1610)
German title: Christ crowned with thorns of Christ
Date: 1602/1604
Medium: oil on canvas
Author desconhecido. Século XVII
Museu de Arte Sacra de Pernambuco, Brazil.

Current location: Deutsch: Kunsthistorisches Museum, Gemäldegalerie : Deutsch: Wien
Notes: Deutsch: Inv.-Nr. GG_307 Provenienz: Rom, Smlg. Marchese Vincenzo Giustiniani (inv. 1638, II, n.3); um 1809 in Rom von Baron Ludwig von Lebzeltern für die Kaiserliche Galerie erworben; am 16. April 1816 in Wien eingetroffen; 1816 in der Galerie
Source/Photographer:
Permission: Public Domain

Figure 3.32
Description: Gustave Doré, Christ leaving the courtroom, oil on canvas, Museum of modern art of Strasbourg
Date: 1867-72
Source: Own work (photo or scan: Ji-Elle) Author: Gustave Doré (1832–1883)   Permission: Public Domain

Figure 3.33
Artist: Titian (1490–1576) Title: Christ Carrying the Cross
Date: circa 1565 Medium: oil on canvas
Dimensions: Height: 98 cm (38.6 in). Width: 116 cm (45.7 in).
Current location: (Inventory)Prado Museum Source/Photographer: Web Gallery of Art: Image Info about artwork
Permission: Public Domain

Figure 3.34
Artist Peter Paul Rubens (1577–1640)
Alternative names Rubens, Pierre Paul Rubens, Pieter Paul Rubens, Sir Peter Paul Rubens
Description Southern Netherlandish painter, sculptor, draughtsman and printmaker
Title Christ on the Cross between the Two Thieves
Date between 1619(1619) and 1620(1620)
Medium oil on panel
Dimensions Height: 429 cm (168.9 in). Width: 311 cm (122.4 in).
Current location Royal Museum of Fine Arts, Antwerp
Source/Photographer Web Gallery of Art: Image Info about artwork
Permission: Public Domain

Figure 3.35
Description:
Artist: Rogier van der Weyden (1399/1400-1464)
Title: Deposition of Christ
Date: English: before 1443
Dimensions: Deutsch: 220 × 262 cm
Current location: Madrid
Source / Photographer: Locutus Borg
Permission: Public Domain

Figure 3.36
Description: English: Titian, the Burial of Christ, 1559,
oil on canvas, 136 x 174,5 cm, Prado museum (Madrid, Spain)
Date: 1559 Source: http://www.museodelprado.es/imagen/alta_resolucion/P00440.jpg Author:
Titian (1490–1576) Permission: Public Domain

Figure 3.37
Artist Tintoretto (1518–1594)
Alternative names Il Tintoretto, Il Furioso, Jacopo Robusti, Birth name: Jacopo Comin
Description Italian painter
Date of birth/death 29 September 1518(1518-09-29) 31 May 1594(1594-05-31)
Location of birth/death Venice Venice
Work period from 1539(1539) until 1594(1594)
Work location Venice
Title English: The Descent into Hell
Date 1568(1568)
Medium oil on canvas
Dimensions Height: 342 cm (134.6 in). Width: 373 cm (146.9 in).
Current location San Cassiano, Venice
Source/Photographer Web Gallery of Art: Image Info about artwork
Permission: Public Domain

Figure 3.38
Description: French: Cathedral Saint-Paul de Liège; the Chair, by Guillaume Geefs, of neo-
Gothic style, dating from the middle of the 19th century. Detail: Lucifer, on the back of the Chair.
Date: 24 August 2009 Source: Own work
Author: Vassil
Permission: Public Domain

Figure 3.39
Artist: Rembrandt (1606–1669)
Title: The Ascension.
Date: 1636 Medium: oil on canvas
Dimensions: 93 × 68.7 cm (36.6 × 27 in)
Current location: Alte Pinakothek : Munich Accession number: 398
Notes: Part of Rembrandt's Passion Cycle for Frederick Henry, Prince of Orange
Signed and dated bottom, centre right: Remb[...]dt f [.]636
Provenance: Unknown date: commissioned by Frederick Henry, Prince of Orange (1584-1647),
The Hague
by 20 March 1668: Amalie zu Solms-Braunfels (1602-1675)
by 1716: Johann Wilhelm, Kurfürst von der Pfalz (1658-1716), Düsseldorf
1716: inherited by Karl III. Philipp von der Pfalz, Düsseldorf
1742: inherited by Karl Theodor, Kurfürst von der Pfalz und Bayern, Düsseldorf
1799: inherited by Maximilian I Joseph of Bavaria (1756-1825), Düsseldorf

1806: acquired by Alte Pinakothek, Munich Source/Photographer: www.uni-leipzig.de : Home : Info : Pic
Permission: Public Domain

Figure 3.40
Artist: William Holman Hunt (1827–1910)
Title: English: The Scapegoat
Date: 1854
Location: Lady Lever Art Gallery : Current location
Port Sunlight, Merseyside, England, United Kingdom:
Source/Photographer: : Козёл отпущения
Permission: Public Domain

Copyright for: The Fruit of Faith Part 2 Chapter 4

Figure 4.1
Artist: [show]Pieter de Grebber (circa 1600–1652/1653)
Title: God Inviting Christ to Sit on the Throne at His Right Hand
Date: 1645 Medium: : oil on canvas
Dimensions: Height: 115 cm (45.3 in). Width: 133 cm (52.4 in).
Current location: [show]Museum Catharijneconvent Source/Photographer: Web Gallery of Art: Image Info about artwork Permission: Public Domain

Figure 4.2
Description: Satan presiding at the Infernal Council. Victoria and Albert Museum, London, UK.
Date: 1824
Source: The Bridgeman Art Library (images.bridgeman.co.uk)
Author: John Martin
John Martin (1789–1854)
Permission: Public Domain

Figure 4.3
Description: English: Unknown painter 18th century, probably Spanish, representing St John the Evangelist, the Virgin and Saint Maria Magdalena with the dead Christ. Museu de Aveiro, Portugal.
Date: 25 March 2012 Source: Own work
Author: Alvesgaspar
Permission: Public Domain

Figure 4.4
Description: English: Photograph of "The Last Judgement" by Viktor Vasnetsov 1904.
Oil on canvas 690*700. Located in the Crystal Museum, St. George's Cathedral, Gus Khrustalny, Vladimir Region, Russia.
Artist: Viktor Vasnetsov (1848–1926)
Date: [2010-03-06]

Figure 4.5
Title: God as Architect/Builder/Geometer/Craftsman
From: The Frontispiece of Bible Moralisee
Style: Gothic
Date: mid-13th C.
Location: France
Codex Vindobonensis 2554 (French, ca. 1250), in the Österreichische Nationalbibliothek.
Modified from: http://www.mlahanas.de/Greeks/JesusGreek.htm
Famously used as the first color illustration to Benoit B. Madelbrot's The Fractal Geometry of Nature...

Figure 4.6
Artist William-Adolphe Bouguereau (1825–1905)
Description French painter
Title: The First Mourning
Date 1888
Medium oil on canvas
Dimensions 79 7/8 × 99 1/8 inches (203 × 252 cm)
Current location National Museum of Fine Arts in Buenos Aires
Location Buenos Aires (Argentina)
Established 1895
Website www.mnba.org.ar
Buenos Aires, Argentina
Source/Photographer Art Renewal Center Museum, image 1743.

Figure 4.7
Description: English: God took Enoch, as in Genesis 5:24: "And Enoch walked with God: and he was not; for God took him."
Date: 1728 Source: http://www.mythfolklore.net/lahaye/006/LaHaye1728
Figures006GenV24GodTookEnoch.jpg Author: illustrators of the 1728
Figures de la Bible, Gerard Hoet (1648–1733) and others,
published by P. de Hondt in The Hague in 1728

Figure 4.8
Description: English: The Earth was corrupt before God and filled with violence (right plate); as in Genesis 6:5: "And God saw that the wickedness of man was great in the earth, and that every imagination of the thoughts of his heart was only evil continually."; illustration from the 1728 Figures de la Bible; illustrated by Gerard Hoet (1648–1733) and others, and published by P. de

Hondt in The Hague; image courtesy Bizzell Bible Collection, University of Oklahoma Libraries
Date: 1728 Source: http://www.mythfolklore.net/lahaye/008/LaHaye1728
Figures008GenVI11GodSawCorruptionRight.jpg Author: illustrators of the 1728
Figures de la Bible, Gerard Hoet (1648–1733) and others, published by P. de Hondt in The
Hague in 1728
Permission: Public Domain

Figure 4.9
Artist: József Molnár (1821–1899)
Title: Abraham's Journey from Ur to Canaan
Date: 1850 Medium: oil on canvas
Dimensions: Height: 112 cm (44.1 in). Width: 130 cm (51.2 in).
Current location: Hungarian National Gallery
Permission: Public Domain

Figure 4.10
Artist: Rembrandt (1606–1669)
Title: Sacrifice of Isaac.
Date: 1635 Medium: oil on canvas
Dimensions: 193.5 × 132.8 cm (76.2 × 52.3 in)
Current location: Hermitage: Saint Petersburg Accession number 727
Notes: Signature and date bottom left: Rembrandt f. 1635
Provenance: by 1736: Sir Robert Walpole, London/Houghton Hall, Norfolk
by 1779: George Walpole, 3rd Earl of Orford (1730-1791), Houghton Hall, Norfolk
1779: purchased by Catherine II of Russia (1729-1796), Saint Petersburg, from George Walpole,
3rd Earl of Orford, Houghton Hall, Norfolk
Source/Photographer: Internet
Permission: Public Domain

Figure 4.11
Description: Isaac blesses his son Jacob
Date: 1728 Source: http://www.mythfolklore.net/lahaye/029/LaHaye1728
Figures029GenXXVII22-29IsaacBlessesJacob.jpg Author: illustrators of the 1728
Figures de la Bible, Gerard Hoet (1648-1733) and others, published by P. de Hondt in The Hague
in 1728
Permission: Public Domain

Figure 4.12
Artist: Lawrence Alma-Tadema (1836–1912)
Title: The finding of Moses
Date: 1904 Medium: oil on canvas
Dimensions: 137.5 × 213.4 cm (54.1 × 84 in)
Current location: Private collection Source/Photographer
Permission: Public Domain

Figure 4.13
Description: English: Moses Trampling on Pharaoh's Crown, as in Josephus' Antiquities 2:232-36, by Enrico Tempestini, pen and brown ink, black chalk; brown, grey and pink washes; 390 x 503 mm, dated 1846
Date: 1846
Source: http://www.mattiajona.com/schede/tempestini.html#Anchor121247
Author: Enrico Tempestini
Permission: Public Domain

Figure 4.14
Description: English: The Death of the Firstborn.
Date: 1897
Dimensions: 205 × 272 cm (80.7 × 107.1 in) Source: http://associate.com/photos/Bible-Pictures--1897-W-A-Foster/page-0063-1.jpg Author: Illustrators of the 1897 Bible Pictures and What They Teach Us by Charles Foster; after Lawrence Alma-Tadema
Permission: Public Domain

Figure 4.15
Artist: Frederick Arthur Bridgman
Frederick Arthur Bridgman (1847–1928) Description: English: Pharaoh's army engulfed by the Red Sea, oil on canvas, by Frederick Arthur Bridgman
Date: 1900 Source/Photographer http://www.artrenewal.org/images/artists/b/Bridgman_Frederick_Arthur/large/Bridgman_Frederick_Arthur_Pharaoh%20s_Army_Eng`ulfed_By_The_Red_Sea.jpg
Permission: Public Domain

Figure 4.16
Description: Gideon (around 1550), oil on wood
by Martin van Heemskerck, Museum of fine arts in Strasbourg. Originally, an array of the Virgin (lost) was placed between the two panels.Date: ca. 1550
Source: This file has been extracted from another image: File:M.v.H. M.d.B.A. Strasbourg—Gideon.jpg.
Author: Maarten van Heemskerck (1498–1574)
Permission: Public Domain

Figure 4.17
Artist Guercino (1591–1666)
Authority control VIAF: 49248688
Description Italian painter, draughtsman and fresco painter
Title English: Samson Captured by the Philistines.
Date 1619
Current location Metropolitan Museum of Art, New York City, USA

Accession number Metropolitan Museum of Art (Accession Number 1984.459.2)
Notes [1]

Source/Photographer [2]
Permission: PD

Figure 4.18
Artist Italian anonymous
Title David thanking God after the death of Goliath
Date c. 1700-1750
Current location Museum of Fine Arts of Lyon

Native name Musée des Beaux-Arts
Location Lyon, France
Coordinates 45° 46' 0.65" N, 4° 50' 1.7" E
Established 1801
Website www.mba-lyon.fr

Paintings department
Accession number A 89
Credit line Sent by the French State, 1803
Notes Courtesy of Musée des beaux-arts de Lyon
Source/Photographer Rama
Own work
Permission: PD

Figure 4.19
Artist: Briton Rivière (1840–1920)
Description: Daniel's Answer to the King
Date: 1890
Current location: Manchester City Art Gallery
Source/Photographer: http://www.intaglio-fine-art.com/proddetail.php?prod=G122
Permission: Public Domain

Figure 4.20
Title: Shadrach, Meshach, and Abednego in the Fiery Furnace
French artist Gustave Doré (1832-1883)
Source: Now in the Public Domain (i.e. Free to Copy)
Posted in: www.creationism.org/images/
Permission: Public Domain

Figure 4.21
Description: Joshua Commanding the Sun to Stand Still upon Gibeon
Date: 1816
Source: http://www.wikigallery.org/wiki/painting_260429/John-Martin/Joshua-Commanding-
the-Sun-to-Stand-Still-upon-Gibeon-1816
Author: John Martin
Permission: Public Domain

Figure 4.22
Description: English: Elijah Resuscitating the Son of the Widow of Zarephath
Date: 1777-1862
Source: http://www.bridgemanartondemand.com/art/144259/Elijah_Resuscitating_the_Son_of_
the_Widow_of_Sarepta
Author: Louis Hersent
Permission: Public Domain

Figure 4.23
Artist: Henryk Siemiradzki (1843–1902)
Title: English: Nero's Torches (Christian Candlesticks).
Date: 1876
Medium: oil on canvas
Current location: National Museum, Kraków
Notes: Gallery of 19th-Century Polish Art at Sukiennice
Source/Photographer www.abcgallery.com
Permission : Public Domain-Art

Figure 4.24
Artist: Jean-Léon Gérôme (1824–1904)
Title: English: The Christian Martyrs' Last Prayer
Date: 1883 Medium: oil on canvas
Source/Photographer: http://www.artrenewal.org/asp/database/image.asp?id=97andhires=1
Other versions: : File:Jean-Léon_Gérôme_-_The_Christian_Martyrs'_Last_Prayer_-_Wal-
ters_37113.jpg
Permission: Public Domain

Figure 4.25
Artist: Rembrandt (1606–1669)
Title: Belsazar's Feast
Date: circa 1635
Permission: Public Domain

Figure 4.26
Exorcising a boy possessed by a demon from very rich hours of Duc de Berry, 15th century. Les
Très Riches Heures du duc de Berry, Folio 166r—The Exorcism the Musée Condé, Chantilly.
Permission: Public Domain

Figure 4.27
Artist: Rembrandt (1606–1669)
Title: The Storm on the Sea of Galilee.
Alternate title(s):
Christ in the Storm on the Lake of Galilee (Matthew 8:23-25). Date: 1633 Medium: oil on canvas
Dimensions: 160 × 128 cm (63 × 50.4 in)

Current location: [show]Isabella Stewart Gardner Museum Object history: 1898: purchased by Isabella Stewart Gardner (1840-1924) from Colnaghi through Berenson

Unknown date: ownership transferred to Isabella Stewart Gardner Museum, Inventory number P21S24, Boston

18 March 1990: stolen from Isabella Stewart Gardner Museum, Boston Inscriptions: Signed and dated bottom right on the rudder: Rembrandt. f. // 1633

Source/Photographer http://www.gardnermuseum.org/collection/artwork/2nd_floor/dutch_room/christ_in_the_storm_on_the_sea_of_galilee?filter=artist

Other versions : Version from 10.000 Meisterwerke der Malerei.

Permission: Public Domain

Figure 4.28

Artist: Très Riches Heures du Duc de Berry

Description: Jesus exorcising the Canaanite Woman's daughter from 15th century

Permission: Public Domain

Figure 4.29

Artist: Paolo Veronese (1528–1588)

English: Raising of the Daughter of Jairus

Date: circa 1546 Medium: English: Oil on paper mounted on canvas

Dimensions: Height: 42 cm (16.5 in). Width: 37 cm (14.6 in).

Current location: (Inventory) Louvre Museum Accession number: : Inventory number INV. 141

Source/Photographer: Web Gallery of Art: Image Info about artwork

Joconde database: entry 000PE027359

Permission: Public Domain

Figure 4.30

Artist: Paolo Veronese (1528–1588)

Title: The Woman with the issue of Blood

Date: 1570

English: c. 1570

Medium: oil on canvas

Current location: Kunsthistorisches Museum

Source/Photographer: The Yorck Project: 10.000 Meisterwerke der Malerei. DVD-ROM, 2002. ISBN 3936122202.

Distributed by DIRECTMEDIA Publishing GmbH.

Permission: Public Domain

Figure 4.31

Description:

Christ Heals a Man Paralyzed by the Gout. Mark 2:4. Engraving by Bernhard Rode, 1780

Date: engraving: 1780; photo: 2009.01.18

Source: Eigene Fotografie (own photography)

Author: Bernhard Rode (1725–1797) file: James Steakley

Permission: Public Domain

Figure 4.32
Title English: Saint Peter Attempting to Walk on Water
Artist: François Boucher (1703–1770)
Date: 1766
Medium: oil on canvas
Dimensions: 235 × 170 cm (92.5 × 66.9 in)
Current location: Cathédrale Saint-Louis : Versailles (commune)
Source/Photographer: Unknown
Permission: Public Domain

Figure 4.33
Description: English: Fine Art Giclée Reproduction Carl Heinrich Bloch, 1883
Title: Christ Healing the Sick at the Pool of Bethesda
Date: 1883 Source: http://cfac.byu.edu/fileadmin/moa/user_files/00TRANSFER/Shop_at_MOA/
images/christhealingthesick.jpg Author: Carl Heinrich Bloch (1834–1890)
Permission: Public Domain

Figure 4.34
Artist: Angelica Kauffman (1741–1807)
English: Christ and the Samaritan woman at the well
Date: 1796 Medium:
English: Oil on canvas
Dimensions: 123,5 x 158,5 cm
Current location: Neue Pinakothek
Source/Photographer: Upload 1: repro from art book
Upload 2: Own Work, photo taken by Cybershot800i.
Permission: Public Domain

Figure 4.35
Artist: Fra Angelico (1395–1455)
German title: cycle of frescoes in the Dominican monastery of San Marco in Florence, scene:
crucifixion with the Lanzenstich of Captain of Longinus
Date: 1437-1446
Medium: Fresco
Current location: Florence
Source/Photographer: The Yorck Project: 10.000 Meisterwerke der Malerei. DVD-ROM, 2002.
ISBN 3936122202.
Distributed by DIRECTMEDIA Publishing GmbH.
Permission: Public Domain

Figure 4.36
Description: Seventy Apostles
Date
Source: http://chattablogs.com/aionioszoe/archives/
Author: Ikonopisatelj

Permission: Public Domain

Figure 4.37
Artist: Joan de Joanes (1523–1579)
Title: Jesus the Eucharist
Date German: 3rd quarter of 16th century
Medium: Deutsch: Lindenholz
Dimensions: Deutsch: 101 × 63 cm
Current location: Budapest
Source/Photographer: The Yorck Project: 10.000 Meisterwerke der Malerei. DVD-ROM, 2002.
ISBN 3936122202.
Distributed by DIRECTMEDIA Publishing GmbH.
Permission: Public Domain:

Figure 4.38
Description: English: The Angel of Death and the First Passover
Date: 1897 Source: http://associate.com/photos/Bible-Pictures--1897-W-A-Foster/page-0062-1.jpg
Author: Illustrators of the 1897 Bible Pictures and What They Teach Us by Charles Foster
Permission: Public Domain

Figure 4.39
Artist: David Roberts (1796–1864)
German title: the exodus of the Israelites from Egypt English: The Israelites Leaving Egypt
Date: 1830 (1828?)
Medium: : oil on canvas
Dimensions: 119 × 212 cm
Current location: Birmingham Museum and Art Gallery Source/Photographer: Use net
Permission: Public Domain

Figure 4.40
Artist: Jan van Eyck
Title: "Ghent Altarpiece", finished 1432.
Detail: adoration of the lamb
Permission: Public Domain

Figure 4.41
Artist Follower of Jan van Scorel (1495–1552)
Title the baptism of Christ in the Jordan River
Date circa 1550
Medium oil on panel
Dimensions 80.6 × 95.9 cm (31.7 × 37.8 in)
Current location Indianapolis Museum of Art
Location Indianapolis, Indiana
Permission: PD

Figure 4.42
Author: Bernardo Strozzi
Description: English: Jesus feeding a crowd with 5 loaves of bread and two fish
Date: early 1600's
Source: http://www.1st-art-gallery.com/Bernardo-Strozzi/The-Miracle-Of-The-Loaves-And-Fishes.html
Permission: Public Domain

Figure 4.43
Artist Ludolf Bakhuizen (1631–1708)
Title Christ in the Storm on the Sea of Galilee
Date 1695
Medium oil on canvas
Current location Indianapolis Museum of Art
Native name Indianapolis Museum of Art
Location Indianapolis, Indiana
Website www.imamuseum.org
Carolyn & William C. Griffith Gallery
Source/Photographer [1]
Permission: PD

Figure 4.44
Description: English: Jesus healing the sick by Gustave Dore, 19th century Source: http://www.morethings.com/god_and_country/jesus/healing-jesus-240.jpg
Date: 24 October 2009 (original upload date)
Source: Transferred from en.wikipedia; transferred to Commons by User:Cezarika1 using CommonsHelper.
Author: Original uploader was History2007 at en.wikipedia
Permission: Public Domain-US; Public Domain-ART.

Copyright for: Chapter #5 The Keys to The King of Heaven

Figure 5.1
Artist: Peter Paul Rubens (1577–1640)
Description: English: Saint Peter as Pope—here shown with the pallium and the en: Keys to Heaven
Medium: Painting
Source/Photographer: Originally from en.wikipedia;
Permission: Public Domain

Figure 5.2 The Pearl of Great Price
French: Parable of the hidden treasure, 1630 (?). Rembrandt and Gerard Dou. Museum of fine arts in Budapest. Collection Esterházy, 1871. N ° 342 inv
Date: 17th century
Medium: oil on poplar

Dimensions: 60.5 x 44 cm
Current location: Kunsthistorisches Museum, Gemäldegalerie
Notes: Deutsch: Inv.-Nr. GG_130 Provenienz: Slg. Leopold Wilhelm
Source/Photographer: [1]
Domenico Feti (1588–1623)
Permission: Public Domain

Figure 5.3
Artist: Pietro Perugino (1448-1523)
Title: delivery of the keys of St. Peter. Date: 1480-1482
Medium: Fresco
Dimensions: ca. 335 × 550 cm
Current location: Sistine Chapel Notes: Client: Pope Sixtus IV., cycle of frescoes created in cooperation with the painters Domenico Ghirlandaio, Cosimo Rosselli and Sandro Botticelli Botticelli,
Source/Photographer: See below.
Permission: Public Domain

Figure 5.4
Description: English: Detail from Saint Peter,
Painted by Grão Vasco for the See of Viseu (1535-1542); now in the Grão Vasco Museum, Viseu.
Date: 1506 Source: See of Viseu
Author: Vasco Fernandes aka Grão Vasco
Permission: Public Domain-Art

Figure 5.5
Description: English: Abbey of Rodengo Saiano, San Nicola church, Alessandro Bonvicino, called il Moretto, Jesus giving to St. Peter the keys and giving to St. Paul the Doctrine's Book, ca. 1540
Artist German: Workshop Fetti, Domenico
Date November 2008(2008-11)
Source Own work
Author Laurom
Permission is granted to copy, distribute and/or modify this document under the terms of the GNU Free Documentation License, Version 1.2 or any later version published by the Free Software Foundation; with no Invariant Sections, no Front-Cover Texts, and no Back-Cover Texts. A copy of the license is included in the section entitled GNU Free Documentation License.

Figure 5.6
Published by Jeff Miztah Rogers
There has long been a writer trapped in this brain and body. I now consent to let it go free, I am not responsible for the damage it may do or the good that may come of it, I merely let it go free as it should be.
Jeff Miztah Rogers, Yahoo! Contributor Network
Nov 13, 2011 "Share your voice on Yahoo! websites"

Copyright License For: Chapter #6 The Garden of Whatever Your Name Is

Figure 6.1
Artist: William Blake (1757–1827) Title: English: Elohim Creating Adam
Date: 1795 Medium: Deutsch: Farbstich mit Feder, aquarelliert
Dimensions: 43 × 53,5 cm
Current location: Tate Gallery
London Source/Photographer: The Yorck Project: 10.000 Meisterwerke der Malerei. DVD-ROM, 2002. ISBN 3936122202.
Distributed by DIRECTMEDIA Publishing GmbH.
Permission: Public Domain

Figure 6.2
Artist: Jan Breughel (II) (1601–1678)
Title: Creation of Adam in the Paradise
Date: 17th century
Medium: oil on copper Dimensions: 69.9 × 87.5 cm (27.5 × 34.4 in)
Current location: Stedelijk-Museum Louven Source/Photographer: http://www.hampel-auctions.com/
Permission: Public Domain

Figure 6.3
Description: English: Genesis : Creation of Eve; marble relief on the left pier of the façade of the cathedral; Orvieto, Italy
Date: 30 April 2008 Source: Own work (Own photo)
Author: Georges Jansoone (JoJan)
Permission: Public Domain

Figure 6.4
Artist: Jacob Savery (1565/1567–1603)
Description: The Garden of Eden
Date: 1601 Medium: Painting
Source/Photographer: Artnet.com
Permission: Public Domain

Figure 6.5
Artist Erastus Salisbury Field (1805–1900)
Description American painter
Date of birth/death 19 May 1805(1805-05-19) 28 June 1900(1900-06-28)
Location of birth/death Leverett, Massachusetts Sunderland
Work location New York City; Sunderland
Authority control VIAF: 3869534 | GND: 143444484
Title English: The Garden of Eden
Date circa 1860(1860)
Medium oil on canvas
Dimensions 88.26 × 116.52 cm (34.7 × 45.9 in)
Current location Museum of Fine Arts, Boston
Native name Museum of Fine Arts, Boston
Location Boston, Massachusetts
Source/Photographer [1]
Permission: Public Domain

Figure 6.6
Artist: Tintoretto (1518–1594)
Title: English: The Temptation of Adam
Date: between 1551 and 1552
Medium: oil on canvas
Dimensions: Height: 150 cm (59.1 in). Width: 220 cm (86.6 in).
Current location: Academy of Venice 32 Hall of Bassano and Tintoretto
Notes: www.wga.hu Source/Photographer: Web Gallery of Art: Image Info about artwork
Permission: Public Domain

Figure 6.7
Description: Paradise tree and Maria in the Apocalypse
: Choir ceiling fresco in the beautiful mountain church of Ellwangen (Jagst):
Artist: Melchior Steidl
Date 10 June 2007(2007-06-10)
Source Own work
Author Sigurd Betschinger
Permission: Public Domain
Permission is granted to copy, distribute and/or modify this document under the terms of the GNU Free Documentation License, Version 1.2 or any later version published by the Free Software Foundation; with no Invariant Sections, no Front-Cover Texts, and no Back-Cover Texts. A copy of the license is included in the section entitled GNU Free Documentation License.

Figure 6.8
Artist: Benjamin West (1738–1820)
Description: English: The Expulsion of Adam and Eve from Paradise
Date: 1791 Medium: oil on canvas
Dimensions: overall: 186.8 x 278.1 cm (73 9/16 x 109 1/2 in.)

Current location: National Gallery of Art Source / Photographer: [1]
Permission: Public Domain

Figure 6.9
Description: English: Genesis: Expulsion from Paradise; marble bas-relief
by Lorenzo Maitani on the left pier of the façade of the cathedral. Orvieto, Italy
Date: 30 April 2008 Source: Own work (Own photo)
Author: Georges Jansoone (JoJan)
Permission: Public Domain

Figure 6.10
File:Cole Thomas Expulsion from the Garden of Eden 1828.jpg
Artist: Thomas Cole (1801–1848)
Title : Expulsion from the Garden of Eden
Date: 1828 Medium: oil on canvas
Dimensions: 100.96 × 138.43 cm (39.7 × 54.5 in)
Current location: Museum of Fine Arts, Boston Object history:
The artist Dr. David Hosack, New York
Dr. J. Kearny Rodgers, New York, 1848
James Lenox, New York, 1849
Lenox Library, New York, 1870
Lenox Foundation, New York Public Library, 1895
with Parke-Bernet Galleries, April 14-16, 1943, no. 533
with Arnold Seligmann, Rey, & Co., New York, 1943
to Maxim Karolik, Newport, R.I., 1943
to MFA, 1947, gift of Martha C. (Mrs. Maxim) Karolik.
Source / Photographer: Museum of Fine Arts, Boston
Permission: Public Domain

Figure 6.11
Description: English: An icon depicting the Sower. In Sts. Konstantine and Helen Orthodox
Church, Cluj, Romania.
Author: Sulfababy of en.wiki
Permission: Public Domain

Figure 6.12
Description: Image of the Sower Parable
Date: 1874 Source: WCG
Author: Alexander Bida
Permission: Public Domain

Figure 6.13
Description: Picture of the lamp on a stand and the parable of the growing seed, from the New
Testaments
Date: 1695

Source: http://www.pitts.emory.edu/woodcuts/1695Bibl/00006350.jpg
Author: Johann Christoph Weigel
Permission: Public Domain

Figure 6.14
Description: English: Christ True Vine
Date: before 20 c.
Source: from ruwiki
Author: Anonymous
Permission: Public Domain

Figure 6.15
Artist: Thomas Cole (1801–1848)
Title: The Garden of Eden
Date: 1828 Medium: Painting
Object history: Unknown
Source/Photographer: Unknown
Permission: Public Domain

Figure 6.16
Deutsch: Mihály Zichy: "Lucifer"
Source: http://www.whiterosesgarden.com/Nature_of_Evil/fallen_angels/FAngels_S/images/
MIHALY_ZICHY_LUCIFER.JPG
Permission: Public Domain

Figure 6.17
Artist: Peter Paul Rubens (1577–1640)
Title: Woman of apocalypse
Date: Seventeenth-century
Medium: Painting
Credit line: http://www.getty.edu/art/gettyguide/artObjectDetails?artobj=881
Source / Photographer: This file is lacking source information.
Permission: Public Domain

Figure 6.18
Description: Fall of Lucifer oil painting by Peter Paul Rubens, early 17th century
Alte Pinakothek, Munich
Date: 4 June 2006 (first version); 4 June 2006 (last version)
Source: Transferred from de.wikipedia; transferred to Commons by User:EvaK using CommonsHelper
Original uploader was Dr. Meierhofer at de.wikipedia Author: Peter Paul Rubens (1577–1640)
Permission: Public Domain

Figure 6.19
Description: the fall of the rebel angels, Charles Le Brun, after 1680, oil on canvas, Museum of fine arts in Dijon, France.
Date: Après 1680
Source: Work of the Museum of fine arts in Dijon Source: Work of the Museum of fine arts in Dijon
Author: Charles Le Brun (1619–1690)
Permission: Public Domain

Figure 6.20
Artist: Sebastiano Ricci (1659-1734)
Title: fall of the rebel Angels
Date: Deutsch: um 1720
English: c. 1720
Medium: oil on canvas:
Dimensions: Deutsch: 78,1 × 64,8 cm
Current location: Dulwich College Picture Gallery : London
Source / Photographer: The Yorck Project: 10.000 Meisterwerke der Malerei. DVD-ROM, 2002. ISBN 3936122202
Distributed by DIRECTMEDIA Publishing GmbH.
Permission: Public Domain

Figure 6.21
Artist: William Blake (1757–1827)
Title: German: the great Red Dragon and the woman clothed with the Sun
Date: 1805-1810
Medium: Deutsch: Aquarell
Dimensions: 40 × 32,5 cm
Current location: National Gallery of Art Washington (D.C.)
Source / Photographer: The York Project: 10.000 Meisterwerke der Malerei. DVD-ROM, 2002. ISBN 3936122202. Distributed by DIRECTMEDIA Publishing GmbH.
Permission: Public Domain

Figure 6.22
Artist: Unknown (French school)
Title: hours of the Constable Anne de Montmorency
Woman of the Apocalypse.Date: 1549 16th century
Dimensions: 21 × 14 cm (8.3 × 5.5 in)
Current location: Musée Condé
Permission: Public Domain

Figure 6.23
Description: St Michael the archangel, dressed somewhat like a Roman soldier, about to slay the devil (in the form of a dragon) with a fiery sword.
 He has a shield with the Latin phrase QUIS UT DEUS? "Who is like unto God?", which is a literal translation of the Hebrew name Mi-Ka-'El מי־כאל . .
Date 17 July 2007(2007-07-17)
Source selbst
Author Michael Jaletzke
Permission: PD

Figure 6.24
Artist: Anonymous, attributed to Athanasius
Title: English: Blessed Be the Host of the King of Heaven...
Medium: tempera on wood
Dimensions: Height: 143.5 cm (56.5 in). Width: 395.5 cm (155.7 in).
Current location: Tretyakov Gallery, Moscow : Room 61
Source / Photographer: Google Art Project: Home—pic Maximum resolution.
Permission: Public Domain

Figure 6.25
Description: English: Page 284v: The Vision of the Seven Candlesticks, Revelation 1:12-20
Date: 1530-1532
Source: CGM Source: German: Ottheinrich-Bibel, Bayerische Staatsbibliothek, CGM 8010: Matthias Gerung (1500–1570)
Permission: Public Domain

Copyright License for: Chapter #7 "The Power and Force of One"

Figure 7.1
Artist William Holman Hunt (1827–1910)
Description British painter
Date of birth/death 2 April 1827(1827-04-02) 7 September 1910(1910-09-07)
Location of birth/death London Kensington
Work location London, Palästina, Florence
Title The Finding of the Saviour in the Temple
Date 1860(1860)
Medium oil on canvas
Current location Birmingham Museum and Art Gallery
Location Birmingham England
Source/Photographer [1]
Permission: Public Domain

Figure 7.2
Artist: Pietro da Cortona
Title: Stoning of Saint Stephen (1660)
Permission: Public Domain

Figure 7.3
Artist: Vassil
Description: The conversion of Saint Paul (1690s), pair Luca Giordano (1634-1705 Naples Naples).
Date: 30 January 2008 Source/Photographer: Own work
Permission: Public Domain

Figure 7.4
Artist: Hans Speckaert (circa 1540–circa 1577)
Title: English: Conversion of St Paul on the Road to Damascus
Date: between 1570 and 1577
Medium: oil on canvas
Dimensions: Height: 147 cm (57.9 in). Width: 196 cm (77.2 in).
Current location: (Inventory)Louvre Museum
Source/Photographer: Web Gallery of Art: Image Info about artwork
Permission: Public Domain

Figure 7.5
Description: A splendid canvas (c.1631) by Pietro da Cortona in the Capuchin church of S. Maria della Concezione. I like the boy with the tea set to the right.
Date: 16 August 2005, 15:39
Title: Ananias restoring the sight of Paul
Author: Anthony M. from Rome, Italy
Permission: Public Domain

Figure 7.6
Description: English: The Tabernacle in the Wilderness; illustration from the 1890 Holman Bible
Date: 1890 Source: http://thebiblerevival.com/clipart/1890holmanbible/color/thetabernaclein-thewilderness.jpg
Author: illustrators of the 1890 Holman Bible
Permission: Public Domain

Figure 7.7
Description: The Holy of Holies; illustration from the 1890 Holman Bible
Date: 1890 Source: http://thebiblerevival.com/clipart/1890holmanbible/color/theholyofholies.jpg
Author: illustrators of the 1890 Holman Bible
Permission: Public Domain

Figure 7.8
Artist: Jan van Eyck
Description: painting "Ghent Altarpiece", finished 1432.
Detail: adoration of the lamb
Permission: Public Domain

Figure 7.9
Description: English: The Israelites eat the Passover, as in Exodus 12:1-8, 27
Date: 1728 Source: http://www.mythfolklore.net/lahaye/050/LaHaye1728
Figures050ExodXII1-27Passover.jpg Author: illustrators of the 1728
Figures de la Bible, Gerard Hoet (1648–1733) and others, published by P. de Hondt in The
Hague in 1728 summary
Permission: Public Domain

Figure 7.10
Artist: [show]Joan de Joanes (1523–1579)
Title: English: The Last Supper
Date: English: 3rd quarter of 16th century
Medium: English: Wood
Dimensions: English: 116 × 191 cm
Current location: English: Museo del Prado
English: Madrid
Source/Photographer: The Yorck Project: 10.000 Meisterwerke der Malerei. DVD-ROM, 2002.
ISBN 3936122202. Distributed by DIRECTMEDIA Publishing GmbH.
Permission: Public Domain

Figure 7.11
Description: English: The Shekinah Glory Enter the Tabernacle; illustration from The Bible and
Its Story Taught by One Thousand Picture Lessons.
Edited: by Charles F. Horne and Julius A. Bewer. 1908.
Date: 1908 Source: http://www.wcg.org/images/b2/_0303160501_039.jpg
Author: illustrator for The Bible and Its Story Taught by One Thousand Picture Lessons, vol. 2.
Permission: Public Domain

Copyright for Chapter # 8 : Why The Foolish Virgins had no Oil in their Lamp

Figure 8.1:
Artist: Nikolas Kornilievich Bodarevsky (1850–1921)
Title: English: Trial of the Apostle Paul
Date: 1875 Medium: oil on canvas
Dimensions: 135 × 226 cm (53.1 × 89 in)
Current location: English: Regional Art Museum, Uzhgorod, Ukraine
Source/Photographer: [1]
Permission: Public Domain

Figure 8.2
Artist: William Holman Hunt
William Holman Hunt (1827–1910) Title: The Light of the World
Date: between 1853 and 1854 Medium: oil on canvas on wood
Dimensions: Height: 125 cm (49.2 in). Width: 60 cm (23.6 in).
Current location: Keble College, Oxford
Oxford, United Kingdom Source/Photographer: Web Gallery of Art: Home page Image Info
about artwork
Permission: Public Domain

Figure 8.3
Artist: Rembrandt (1606–1669) Title: The Woman taken in Adultery.
Date: 1644 Medium: oil on oak panel Dimensions: Height: 83.8 cm (33 in). Width: 65.4 cm (25.7 in).
Current location: National Gallery London Accession number: NG45
Notes: Signature bottom right: 1644
Provenance:
1824: purchased by National Gallery, London Source/Photographer: •: www.allartpainting.com
Web Gallery of Art: Image Info about artwork
Permission: Public Domain

Figure 8.4
Artist: Paul Perret after Pieter Brueghel the Elder
German title: Christ and the woman taken in adultery
Date: post 1564/65
Medium: Engraving
Dimensions: 26,7 × 34,2 cm
Current location: Bibliotéque Albert Ier, Brussels, Belgium
Source/Photographer: University of Leipzig—Faculty of theology—Institute for religious educa-
tion—religious pictures and art design in teaching http://www.uni-leipzig.de/ru/bilder/umwelt.
jes/bruege02.jpg (http://www.uni-leipzig.de/ru/bilder/umwelt.jes/brueget2.htm)
File: Bruege02.jpg
Permission: Public Domain:

Figure 8.5
Description: English: Christ as the True Light (Christus vera lux). Woodcut, 8.4 × 27.7 cm, Kun-
stmuseum Basel.
Date: c. 1526, published 1527
Source: Stephanie Buck, Hans Holbein, Cologne: Könemann, 1999, ISBN 3829025831
Author: Hans Holbein the Younger (1498–1543)
Permission: Public Domain

Figure 8.6
Description: English: Moses Pointing to a Great Snake. Caption: "Moses is standing up and pointing to a great snake, or serpent. The serpent is made of brass. It is fastened to the top of a pole. Moses is telling the people to look at it. For some live serpents have come among the people and are biting them. The serpents are poisonous.
Date   1897
Source http://associate.com/photos/Bible-Pictures--1897-W-A-Foster/page-0079-1.jpg
Author Illustrators of the 1897 Bible Pictures and What They Teach Us by Charles Foster
 Permission: PD

Figure 8.7
Artist: Gustave Dore
Date: 1883
Title: "Joshusa and The Children of Israel Crossing the Jordan"
Source: Dore_joshua_crossing.jpg (535 × 411 pixels, file size: 93 KB, MIME type: image/jpeg)
Permission: Public Domain

Figure 8.8
Artist: [show]John Martin (1789–1854)
Title: Fallen angels in Hell
Date: circa 1841
Medium: oil on canvas
Dimensions: 61 × 76 cm
Current location: Tate Britain London
Accession number: N05435
Notes: Landscape art
Source/Photographer: The Yorck Project: 10.000 Meisterwerke der Malerei. DVD-ROM, 2002. ISBN 3936122202
Distributed by DIRECTMEDIA Publishing GmbH.
Permission: Public Domain (Reusing this file) [1]

Figure 8.9
Artist: Albrecht Dürer (1471–1528)
Title: Lot Fleeing with his Daughters from Sodom
Date: circa 1498 Medium: oil and tempera on panel Dimensions: Height: 52 cm (20.5 in). Width: 41 cm (16.1 in).
Current location: National Gallery of Art Source/Photographer: Web Gallery of Art: Home page
Image Info about artwork Permission: Public Domain

Figure 8.10
Description English: The Death of Moses, illustration from the 1890 Holman Bible
Date 1890
Source http://thebiblerevival.com/clipart/1890holmanbible/bw/thedeathofmoses.jpg
Author illustrators of the 1890 Holman Bible
Permission: Public Domain

Figure 8.11
Description: English: Pen and watercolour of William Blake's A Vision of the Last Judgment, 1808.
Date: 1808 Source: Plate 109 in Bentley, G. E. The Stranger from Paradise. New Haven: Yale University Press, 2003.
Author: William Blake (1757–1827)
Permission: Public Domain

Figure 8.12
Description: Church of St. Brendan the Navigator, Bantry, County Cork, Ireland
Detail of the third window of the north wall with stained glass depicting Jesus: I am the light of the world (John 8:12).
Date: 9 September 2009 Source: Own work
Author: Andreas F. Borchert
Reference: 2009/4970
Permission: Public Domain

Copyright For Chapter #9: The Parable of the Foolish and Wise Virgins

Figure 9.1
Description: Depiction of the Parable of the Ten Virgins. Photograph of stained glass window at Scots' Church, Melbourne
Date: 28 October 2007
Source: Own work
Author: St. Anselm
Permission: Public Domain

Figure 9.2
Description: English: Parable of the lost sheep, An etching by Jan Luyken illustrating Matthew 18:12 in the Bowyer Bible, Bolton, England.
Date: 10 August 2009
Source: Photo by Harry Kossuth
Author: Phillip Medhurst
Permission: Public Domain

Figure 9.3
Description: English: Cellar painting in Peace church in Schweidnitz (an Apocalyptic scene)
Author: 12/08/2008
Permission is granted to copy, distribute and/or modify this document under the terms of the GNU Free Documentation License, Version 1.2 or any later version published by the Free Software Foundation; with no Invariant Sections, no Front-Cover Texts, and no Back-Cover Texts. A copy of the license is included in the section entitled GNU Free Documentation License.

Figure 9.4
Description: English: Antichrist, beast, image of the beast, 666
Date: 2 January 2010 Source: Own work
Author: Johnreve
Permission: Public Domain

Figure 9.5
Description: English: The most famous depiction of the 1833 meteor storm actually produced in 1889 for the Adventist book Bible Readings for the Home Circle—the engraving is by Adolf Vollmy based upon an original painting by the Swiss artist Karl Jauslin, that is in turn based on a first-person account of the 1833 storm by a minister, Joseph Harvey Waggoner on his way from Florida to New Orleans.
Date: April 1888 (artwork); 1833 (event depicted)
Source: Via http://star.arm.ac.uk/leonid/Meteor-Shower.jpg
Author: Adolf Vollmy.
Permission: Public Domain-US
(Original text : published before 1923 and also through Library of Congress)
Other versions : The Leonids: King of the Meteor Showers
The 1833 Leonid Meteor Shower: A Frightening Flurry
Leonid viewing info
About the Leonids
The world's most famous meteor shower picture

Figure 9.6
Description: Page 290: Angels Holding the Four Winds / The Sealing of the 144,000, Revelation 7:1-8
Date: Deutsch: um 1530-1532
Source German: Ottheinrich Bible, Bavarian State Library, Cgm 8010
Author: Matthias Gerung (1500–1570)
Permission: Public Domain

Figure 9.7
Description: English: The Earth was corrupt before God and filled with violence (right plate); as in Genesis 6:5:
"And God saw that the wickedness of man was great in the earth, and that every imagination of the thoughts of his heart was only evil continually."; illustration from the 1728 Figures de la Bible; illustrated by Gerard Hoet (1648–1733) and others, and published by P. de Hondt in The Hague; image courtesy Bizzell Bible Collection, University of Oklahoma Libraries
Date: 1728 Source: http://www.mythfolklore.net/lahaye/008/LaHaye1728 Figures008GenVI11GodSawCorruptionRight.jpg Author: illustrators of the 1728 Figures de la Bible, Gerard Hoet (1648–1733) and others, published by P. de Hondt in The Hague in 1728
Permission: Public Domain

Figure 9.8
Artist John Martin (1789–1854)
Description English painter
Title: The Eve of the Deluge
Location Berkshire
Established 1070s
Date 1840
Current location Royal Collection, Windsor Castle
Website www.royalcollection.org.uk
Source/Photographer Web Gallery of Art
Permission: Public Domain

Figure 9.9
Description English: "The Deluge", Frontispiece to Doré's illustrated edition of the Bible.
Based on the story of Noah's Ark, this shows humans and a tiger doomed by the flood futilely attempting to save their children and cubs.
Date The first cdition was 1866. This edition is probably from about that time - may well be a first edition - but in any case is certainly not later than 1900 or so.
Source The Holy Bible: Containing the Old and New Testiments, According to the Authorised Version.With Illusrations by Gustave Doré. (Cassell / Company, Limited: London, Paris & Melbourne)
Author Gustave Doré (1832-1883) The "Pannemaker" in the lower right refers to Adolphe François Pannemaker (1822-1900) one of Doré's assistants in turning his art into a full-fledged engraving, and a reasonably notable engraver in his own right.
Other versions a detail of this image is available:
Permission: Public Domain

Figure 9.10
Description: English: The Rapture: One in the Field, An etching by Jan Luyken illustrating Matthew 24:40 in the Bowyer Bible, Bolton, England.
Date: 6 August 2009
Source: Photo by Harry Kossuth
Author: Phillip Medhurst
Permission: Public Domain
Copyleft: This work of art is free; you can redistribute it and/or modify it according to terms of the Free Art License. You will find a specimen of this license on the Copy left Attitude site as well as on other sites.

Figure 9.11 Description English: The Rapture: One at the Mill, An etching by Jan Luyken illustrating Matthew 24:41 in the Bowyer Bible, Bolton, England.
Date 6 August 2009(2009-08-06)
Source Photo by Harry Kossuth
Author Phillip Medhurst
Copyleft: This work of art is free; you can redistribute it and/or modify it according to terms of the Free Art License. You will find a specimen of this license on the Copy left Attitude site as well as on other sites.

Figure 9.12
Description: English: The Faithful and Wise Servant An etching by Jan Luyken illustrating Luke 13:41- 48 in the Bowyer Bible, Bolton, England.
Date: 6 August 2009 Source: Photo by Harry Kossuth
Author: Phillip Medhurst
Copyleft: This work of art is free; you can redistribute it and/or modify it according to terms of the Free Art License. You will find a specimen of this license on the Copyleft Attitude site as well as on other sites

Figure 9.13
Description: English: The Rapture: One in the Bed An etching by Jan Luyken illustrating Luke 17:34 in the Bowyer Bible, Bolton, England.
Date: 6 August 2009 Source: Photo by Harry Kossuth
Author: Phillip Medhurst
Copyleft: This work of art is free; you can redistribute it and/or modify it according to terms of the Free Art License. You will find a specimen of this license on the Copyleft Attitude site as well as on other sites

Figure 9.14
Artist Fra Angelico (1395–1455)
Alternative names Beato Angelico, (Fra) Giovanni da Fiesole, Guido di Pietro Trosini
Description Italian painter and monk
Date of birth/death 1387(1387) or 1395(1395) 18 February 1455(1455-02-18)
Title English: Triptych: The Last Judgment
Date circa 1450(1450)
Current location Gemäldegalerie
Source/Photographer Web Gallery of Art: Image Info about artwork
Permission: Public Domain

Figure 9.15
Artist: Hieronymus Francken (II) (1578–1623)
Title: Parable of the Wise and Foolish Virgins
Date: circa 1616 Medium: oil on canvas
Dimensions: 111 x 172 cm
Current location: Hermitage Museum Notes:
[1] Source/Photographer: Web Gallery of Art: Image Info about artwork
Permission: Public Domain
This Picture also appears on the Front Cover

Figure 9.16
Artist: Friedrich Wilhelm Schadow (1788–1862)
Description: English: The Parable of the Wise and Foolish Virgins
Date: 1838–1842
Permission: Public Domain

Figure 9.17
Description: Title - English: Last Judgement, Triptych
Artist: Hans Memling (circa 1433–1494)
Date 1466-1473
Medium- oil on panel
English: Oil on canvas
Current location: Polski: Gdánsk
Source/Photographer: www.aiwaz.net
Permission: PD

Figure 9.18
Artist: Fra Angelico (1395–1455)
Title: The Separation of the Sheep and the Goats
Date: 1432-1435
Medium: Deutsch: Tempera auf Holz
Dimensions: 105 × 210 cm (41.3 × 82.7 in)
Current location: English: Florence
Notes: It represents the Last Judgment, executed by Jesus. In the right side, it represents the condemned (to Hell) and, in the left side, it represents the saved ones and the saints. In the center, the opened tombs symbolizes the resurrection of the dead.
Source/Photographer: The Yorck Project: 10.000 Meisterwerke der Malerei. DVD-ROM, 2002. ISBN 3936122202. Distributed by DIRECTMEDIA Publishing GmbH.
Permission: Public Domain

Figure 9.19
Artist: Sebastian Vrancx (1573–1647)
Description: English: The Blind Leading the Blind
Date: 17th century
Medium: oil on canvas
Source/Photographer: http://www.oceansbridge.com/oil-paintings/product/74310/theblindleadingtheblind
Permission: Public Domain

Figure 9.20
Description: The works of mercy, oil on wood, 64 x 88.5 cm links below means "p. Brueghel", right below called "Ma? h-29 (79?)"
Date: 17th century
Source http://www.hampel-auctions.com/
author German: Dutch painters in the district by Pieter Brueghel the younger (1564-1637), probably involving Cornelis Mahu (1613-1689)
Permission: Public Domain

Figure 9.21
Description: Last Judgment and the Wise and Foolish Virgins
Date: 1450s
Source: Web Gallery of Art: Image Info about artwork Author: unknown Flemish master
Permission: Public Domain

Figure 9.22
Description: The Bar and the Splinter
Date circa 1700
Dutch print from the Mortar Bible, published by Pieter Mortier circa 1700
Source Dutch Bible Society
Author Dutch: possible b. Picart, Jan Luyken or g. Hoet
Permission: Public Domain

Figure 9.23
Description: The image to the broad and the narrow way Charlotte Reihlen (idea) / Paul Beck-mann (model), as it is sold in 2008 by John-Verlag as a poster. Bible by the Bible 1984. In the original existing eye of Providence was in this version out retouched. Date: original: 1866 / this version: late 20th or early 21st century
Source: http://www.luziusschneider.com/php/bsweg/Deutsch/bswegd.php Author: Charlotte Rei-hlen (idea); Paul Beckmann (version)
file) is in the public domain because its copyright has expired.
This applies to Australia, the European Union and those countries with a copyright term of life of the author plus 70 years.
This image (or other media The origins of the image go back to Charlotte Reihlen (1805-1868), the co-founder of the Diakonissenanstalt Stuttgart. Bible Luther 1984

Figure 9.24
Description: English: Bell Rock Lighthouse
Date: NA
Source: Alan Stevenson: Biographical Sketch of the Late Robert Stevenson: Civil Engineer. W. Blackwood, 1861. Online: Google Books Author: illustration by "Miss Stevenson"
Licensing: PD

Copy Right License for Chapter 10: The Heavenly Wedding Do Not Miss It

Figure 10.1
An 1880 Baxter process illustration of Revelation 22:17 by Joseph Martin Kronheim.
: : This image was selected as picture of the day on the English Wikipedia for April 8, 2012.
Description: Dansk: Joseph Marin Kronheims farveillustration (efter George Baxters metode) fra 1880 af Johannes ' Åbenbaring 22: 17, fra The Sunday at Home: A Family Magazine for Sab-bath Reading udgivet af Religious Tract Society.English: Kronheim's Baxter process illustration of Revelation 22:17 (King James' Version), from page 366 of the 1880 omnibus printing of The Sunday at Home. Scanned at 800 dpi. The greyish border around the flowers is a metallic silver ink, however, shininess cannot be reproduced in an electronic medium.

Date: 1880
Source: The Sunday at Home: A Family Magazine for Sabbath Reading, 1880 [collected volume], London, Religious Tract Society, Paternoster Row, 164 Picadilly.
Author: •: Joseph Martin Kronheim (1810-1896)
Permission: Public Domain

Figure 10.2
Description: English: The Man without a Wedding Garment, An etching by Jan Luyken illustrating Matthew 22:11-14 in the Bowyer Bible, Bolton, England.
Date: 6 August 2009 Source: Photo by Harry Kossuth
Author: Phillip Medhurst
Permission: Public Domain

Fig 10.3
Description: English: The Invitation to a Great Banquet, An etching by Jan Luyken illustrating Luke 14:16-24 in the Bowyer Bible, Bolton, England.
Date: 6 August 2009
Source: Photo by Harry Kossuth
Author: Phillip Medhurst
Permission: Public Domain

Figure 10.4
Description: English: The Marriage Feast by John Everett Millais, from "Illustrations to 'The parables of our Lord'", engraved by the Dalziel Brothers, 1864.
Date: 1864 Source: http://www.tate.org.uk/servlet/ViewWork?cgroupid=999999961&workid=9491&searchid=4861&tabview=image
Author: John Everett Millais (1829–1896)
Permission: Public Domain

Figure 10.5
Artist: Jan Wijnants (1632–1684)
Title: Parable of the Good Samaritan
Date: 1670 Medium: oil on canvas
Dimensions: 127 × 137 cm (50 × 53.9 in)
Current location: [show]Hermitage Museum Source/Photographer: Unknown
Permission: Public Domain

Figure 10.6
Description: English: Illustration to Book of Revelation
Date: 1893 Source: Revelation of St .John Book printed in 1893 year
Author: Unknown
Permission: Public Domain

Figure 10.7
Artist: Limbourg brothers
Title: English: Saint John on Patmos
French Description: Saint Jean on an island, an eagle at his side, surmounted by Christ and 24 old men, a town in the background image
Date: between 1411 and 1416
Medium: tempera on vellum
Dimensions: Height: 29 cm (11.4 in). Width: 21 cm (8.3 in).
Current location: Musée Condé Accession number : Ms.65, f.17
Permission: Public Domain

Figure 10.8
Description: English: Page 287r: John's Vision of Heaven, Revelation 4:1-11, 5:1-14
Date: 1530-1532
Author: Matthias Gerung (1500–1570)
Permission: Author died more than 70 years ago—public domain

Figure 10.9
Description: Русский: Воины Апокалипсиса
English: Four Horsemen of Apocalypse, by Viktor Vasnetsov. Painted in 1887.
Date: 1887 Source: http://lj.rossia.org/users/john_petrov/166993.html Author: Viktor Vasnetsov (1848–1926)
Permission: Public Domain

Figure 10.10
Description: English: Death on a Pale Horse is a version of the traditional subject, Four Horsemen of Revelation.
Date: 1796 Source: Detroit Institute of Arts: http://www.dia.org/object-info/79abe09c-81f9-4bad-92a6-e2189d62fac5.aspx Author: Benjamin West
Permission: Public Domain

Figure 10.11
Description: English: Page 290: Angels Holding the Four Winds / The Sealing of the 144,000, Revelation 7:1-8
Date: 1530-1532
Source: English: Ottheinrich Bible, Bavarian State Library, Cgm 8010
Author: Matthias Gerung (1500–1570) Permission: : public domain

Figure 10.12
Description: The Opening of the Seventh Seal and the First Four Sounding Trumpets, Revelation 8:1-13
Date: Deutsch: um 1530-1532
Source: Deutsch: Ottheinrich-Bibel, Bayerische Staatsbibliothek, Cgm 8010
Author: Matthias Gerung (1500–1570) Permission: public domain

Figure 10.13
Description: English: Page 292: The Fifth and Sixth Trumpets, Revelation 9:1-12
Date: Deutsch: um 1530-1532
Source: Deutsch: Ottheinrich-Bibel, Bayerische Staatsbibliothek, Cgm 8010
Author: Matthias Gerung (1500–1570) Description: German painter: Date of birth/death: 1500-1570
Location of birth/death: Nördlingen / Lauingen:
Work location: Lauingen:
Permission: Public Domain

Figure 10.14
Description: German: Sheet 293r: John devouring the book, Rev 10, 1-11
Date German: to source 1530-1532, German: Ottheinrich-Bibel, Bayerische Staatsbibliothek, CGM 8010
Author: Matthias Gerung (1500–1570) Permission: Public Domain

Figure 10.15
Description
German: the measurement of the temple and the testimony of the two prophets, Rev. 11, 1-14
Date: 1530-1532
Source: German: Ottheinrich-Bibel, Bayerische Staatsbibliothek, CGM 8010
Author: Matthias Gerung (1500–1570) Permission: Public Domain

Figure 10.16
Artist: Tobias Verhaecht (1561–1631)
Description: English: Landscape with St John the Evangelist at Patmos
Date 1598
Source/Photographer
Permission: Public Domain

Figure 10.17
Artist: Albrecht Dürer (1471–1528)
Title: English: The Revelation of St John: 12. The Sea Monster and the Beast with the Lamb's Horn
Date: between 1497 and 1498 Medium: woodcut Dimensions: Height: 39 cm (15.4 in). Width: 28 cm (11 in).
Current location: [show]Staatliche Kunsthalle Karlsruhe Source/Photographer:
Web Gallery of Art: Image Info about artwork
Permission: Public Domain

Figure 10.18
Media file This is a file from the Wikimedia Commons. Information from its description page there is shown below.
Commons is a freely licensed repository. You can help.
Title: The Beast

Artist: William Blake (1757–1827)
Permission: Public Domain

Figure 10.19
Description: Page 298: The Giving of the Seven Bowls of Wrath / The First Six Plagues, Revelation 16:1-16
Date: Deutsch: um 1530-1532
Source: Deutsch: Ottheinrich-Bibel, Bayerische Staatsbibliothek, Cgm 8010
Author: Matthias Gerung (1500–1570) Permission: Public Domain

Figure 10.20
Description: Page 299: The Giving of the Seventh Bowl of Wrath, Revelation 16:17-21
Date: Deutsch: um 1530-1532
Source: Deutsch: Ottheinrich-Bibel, Bayerische Staatsbibliothek, Cgm 8010
Author: Matthias Gerung (1500–1570)
Permission: Public Domain

Figure 10.21
Description: Colored version of the Whore of Babylon illustration from Martin Luther's 1534 translation of the Bible.
Date: Published in 1534.
Source: Skydreams: http://skydreams.com.au/whore-of-babylon-live-videos/ Author: Workshop of Lucas Cranach.
Permission: Public Domain
This file has been identified as being free of known restrictions under copyright law, including all related and neighboring rights. Other versions Smaller version with less saturated colors, Smaller version, same colors

Figure 10.22
Description: German: sheet 302v: the fall of Babylon, revelation 18, 9-24; Rev 19: 11-21
English: Page 302v: The Fall of Babylon, Revelation 18:9-24, 19:11-21
Date: Deutsch: um 1530-1532
Source German: Ottheinrich-Bibel, Bayerische Staatsbibliothek, CGM 8010
Author: Matthias Gerung (1500–1570)
Permission: Public Domain

Figure 10.23
Description: English: Woodcut for "The Bride of Christ", 1860.
Source: Die Bibel in Bildern
Author: Julius Schnorr von Carolsfeld (1794–1872)
Permission: Public Domain

Figure 10.24
Description: English: Page 303v: The Heavenly Jerusalem / The Bound Devil, Revelation 20:1-3 and 21:9-27

Date: 1530-1532:
Source: Deutsch: Ottheinrich-Bibel, Bayerische Staatsbibliothek, Cgm 8010
Author: Matthias Gerung (1500–1570)
Permission: public domain

Figure 10.25
Artist: English: John Martin
Description: English: Pandemonium—a print.
Date: English: Approx. 1825
Current location: (Inventory)Louvre Museum
Source/Photographer: English: Louvre, Paris, France
Permission: Public Domain

Figure 10.26
Title: The New Jerusalem
Artist: Gustave Doré 1832–1883
Date engraving—1865
Permission: Public Domain
Now in the Public Domain (i.e., Free to Copy)
Posted in: www.creationism.org/images/

Lightning Source UK Ltd.
Milton Keynes UK
UKOW02f0727190314

228407UK00006B/93/P